Caribbean
Afoot!

Caribbean Afoot!

M. Timothy O'Keefe

A Walking & Hiking Guide to
Twenty Nine of the Most Popular Islands

Menasha Ridge Press
Birmingham, Alabama

Disclaimer
Storms and hurricanes can change walking and hiking conditions in the Caribbean overnight. The information contained in this book should be current for years to come. At the same time, neither the author nor the publisher assumes responsibility or liability for any errors or omissions that may have occurred. If you spot any, please let us know; and please keep us informed of any changes you may encounter on your hikes. Your suggestions for subsequent editions are also sought.

Library of Congress Catologing-in-Publication Data
O'Keefe, M. Timothy
    Caribbean afoot! : a walking & hiking guide to 29 of the most popular islands/M. Timothy O'Keefe
        p. cm.
    ISBN 0-89732-110-3
    1. Hiking—Caribbean Area—Guidebooks. 2. Caribbean Area—Guidebooks. I. Title.
    GV199.44.C27054   1993
    917.29'0452—dc20
                                                    93-29250
                                                       CIP

Menasha Ridge Press
3169 Cahaba Heights Road
Birmingham, Alabama 35243

Dedication

This book is dedicated to Karl Wickstrom and the late Bill Hallstrom of *Florida Sportsman Magazine*. Time may have sent us on different paths, but without you both my own journey might never have begun.

 Contents

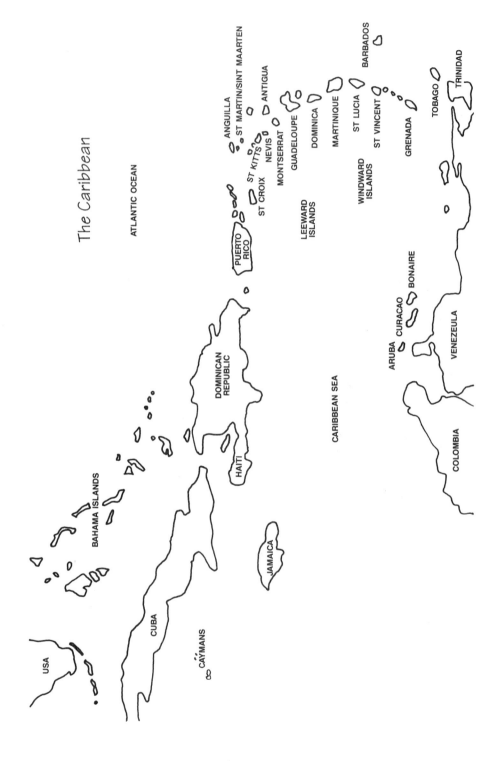

The Caribbean

# List of Maps

 # Acknowledgments

This book would not exist without the help of many people in both the U.S. and Caribbean. Marcella Martinez of the Caribbean Tourism Organization, along with her capable staff members Mary and Mark, were responsible for helping make many of the travel arrangements—and then attempting to ensure that everything went as planned (it didn't, but we came close, didn't we?).

American Airlines and LIAT flew me where I wanted to go and, incredibly, were on time (if not earlier).

I am particularly fortunate to have two good friends who aided tremendously: Lee Elliott applied her artistic talents to the map making. She was even crazy enough to tackle the first edit and, like me, was amazed and slightly terrified to watch the project take on a life of its own. Thanks, Sis! Charlanne Fields was responsible for the detail in the Guadeloupe and Martinique chapters—she translated many of the island hiking guides, which were available only in French. Thanks, Charlanne, for sticking with it after it turned out to be a far more prodigious task than either of us imagined.

On the islands themselves:

Dominica: Superintendent David Williams of the National Parks & Forestry Division; Ken Dill of Ken's Hinterland Tours; and Henry Shillingford.

Grenada: Denis Henry of Henry's Tours and guide Telfor Bedeau.

Guadeloupe: Berry Gerard of the Forest Station at Matouba.

Jamaica: Peter Bentley of SENSE Adventures.

Martinique: Jose Nosel of the National Parks and the Azimut guide service.

Nevis: Elmeader Prentiss and Sylvester Pemberton.

Puerto Rico: Forestry technician Roberto Rijos of the Caribbean National Forest.

St. Kitts: Greg Pereira of Greg's Tours.

St. Lucia: Guide Martial Simon and the staff of Anse Chastanet.

Tobago: Forester William Trim and Game Warden Newton George.

Trinidad: Guide Tony Poyer and the Asa Wright Nature Center.

U.S. Virgin Islands: Supervising park ranger Schuler Brown of the National Park Service.

My heartfelt appreciation to the people at Menasha Ridge Press: Leslie Cummins, my editor; Mike Jones, Associate Publisher; and Bob Sehlinger, the publisher, who first listened to the proposal for the book over the phone when he didn't know me from Adam. Thank you all for letting me do this book my way.

 Preface

Old West Indian Proverb:
Crab walks too much, he looses his claw.
He does not walk, he does not get fat.

Translation:
While it may be risky to go adventuring,
it is also unproductive and unrewarding
to be too cautious and stay at home.

The information in this book is based both on first-hand experience and local contact with each island's most knowledgeable experts. This is not an armchair guide written by someone who never left his office. But because most of the descriptions are subjective, it's possible you might hate a hike that I enjoyed. Or you might like one that didn't particularly impress me. I have tried to tell why I liked or disliked a particular city or trail (or island) so you will be aware of the basis and bias of my opinions.

Bear in mind that conditions change dramatically according to the season and weather. A pleasant walk I took during a dry period may be a hellish nightmare in the rainy season when hiking trails are slick and slippery. The same considerations apply to the city walks, which will also be affected by the company you keep and whether you get along with the locals. No walk is ever exactly the same twice.

Storm damage can change the face of an island, often permanently. Trails once popular become impassable. Furthermore, clearing trails will be the last item on the agenda for a society struggling to restore electrical power, re-open roads and restore life to normalcy. The plain fact is that many islands are too poor to be able to take efficient and prompt action. I would advise waiting six to twelve months before visiting any island severely damaged by a hurricane or tropical storm—especially if hiking and walking are your main objectives.

You'll note that time, length, and difficulty information is compiled for most of the hikes and walks. In some instances, length will be omitted because the distances are unknown, even to locals. The time estimates supplied are for an average walker stopping to smell the flowers or watch the birds. If anything, the given walking times are more likely to be over-estimated than underestimated.

The reverse is true of the difficulty level of each hike or walk; consider these ratings the absolute minimum. Although weather conditions can dramatically increase a hike's difficulty, nothing, except perhaps the installation of escalators, is likely to make any of the walks easier.

Here is how the difficulty scale applies:

1: Easy, with level walking or with very little climbing. Anyone capable of ambulatory movement should be able to finish the described walk in the length of time given.
2: Some ascents and descents, but nothing you shouldn't anticipate on a walk in almost any forest.
3: Expect to sweat (or perspire, if you prefer). Stamina and good balance are essential to enjoy this kind of hike, as are appropriate shoes designed for serious walking and climbing. Anyone in average physical condition should find these trails just a good stretch of the legs.
4: Time to get serious about the amount of exertion you're willing to expend. A fair amount of stamina is required because of the distance or the terrain. Probably muddy and slippery and/or steep in many parts, and may require some scrambling. Probably only those in good physical condition will enjoy this hike.
5: A gut buster. Requires extreme, sustained effort. Do not attempt a hike of this level unless you are in excellent physical condition. Expect this to be demanding, challenging, possibly even dangerous in spots...depending on conditions. Any hike rated a 5+ is bound to demand all of your attention and skill. Being part mountain goat is a definite asset.

Level 3-5 hikers should:
- Wear good, non-skid walking shoes. The quality of your footwear has a lot to do with how much walking—as opposed to stumbling, falling and sliding—you do.
- Use backpacks so your hands will be free to clutch and grab tree roots, vines or other vital flora.
- Carry food and water to sustain energy.
- Not be hung over or using drugs of any type—including alcohol.
- Always go prepared for rain above 1,800 feet.

# Best of the Best: The Top Ten Hikes

The walks and hikes covered by this guide are so diverse it is difficult to choose a Top Ten. These are the ones that stand out because they were unusual, not necessarily because they were tough. The first one listed, however, could be used in an Ironman competition.

1) **Dominica: Valley of Desolation and Boiling Lake Hike.** A seven-hour, round-trip marathon up and down the mountains of Dominica to what seems like a prehistoric setting.

2) **Guadeloupe: La Soufriere Volcano Hike.** An easy climb to the summit of an active volcano whose last major eruption was in 1976.

3) **Jamaica: Blue Mountain Peak Climb.** Leave your bed at 2 a.m. and walk seven miles and 3,500 feet up to the peak of Blue Mountain (7,402 feet high) in time to catch the sunrise (assuming it's not raining or cloudy).

4) **Tobago: Little Tobago.** A pleasant, easy walk on the small cay of Little Tobago, a sea bird sanctuary.

5) **Trinidad: Asa Wright Nature Preserve.** Pleasant pathways cut through this huge, open-sky aviary. More hummingbirds at close range than you ever thought possible.

6) **U.S. Virgin Islands: St. John. The entire island.** Two-thirds of it is a national park criss-crossed with twenty different hiking trails, most quite short.

7) **Virgin Gorda: The Baths.** As much a tourist attraction as Walt Disney World but understandably so.

8) **Puerto Rico: El Yunque.** For sheer spectacle, variety and accessibility, the Caribbean National Forest is difficult to top.

9) **Grenada: Mt. Qua Qua Hike.** A walk through tropical rainforest with excellent panoramic views on one of the Caribbean's lushest and friendliest islands.

10) **St. Kitts: Bloody River.** A brief walk to a canyon containing about 100 petroglyph rubbings made by the Carib Indians.

Summary: This brief list of Top Ten hikes should give you an idea of the tremendous variety that awaits in the Caribbean. Experiences that would fill more than one lifetime are waiting.

 Introduction

Old West Indian Proverb:
See me is one, come live with me is the other.

Translation:
Don't be taken in by first appearances.

The Caribbean is made up of a variety of cultures, some as different from each other as they are from our own. How these people look at life—and at tourists—needs to be discussed in candid detail if you want to do more than take a bus ride through the countryside. While I do not claim to be an expert on the Caribbean mind or culture, I can tell you what I have observed during three decades of travel in the region.

So, How Do You Say Caribbean?

The islanders say "Car-i-BEE-an," and this is also the preferred pronunciation in the dictionary. A second option is "Car-RIB-ee-an." Common sense would seem to indicate there is only one proper pronunciation, but consider this remarkable statement from the novel "Caribbean" about why author James A. Michener and others embrace the second choice:

"A wag explained, 'The hoi polloi use the first, but intellectual snobs prefer the second.' And so do I."

My own philosophy differs. According to the dictionary, the term "hoi polloi" is a contemptuous term used to refer to the common people, the masses; in other words, the islanders themselves. I travel to the Caribbean to be *with* the locals, to interact with them and have fun.

Almost all of the Caribbean hiking guides are locals, black islanders, and you will be spending six to eight hours a day walking and talking together. Hiking through the countryside, you will be exposed to far more of the West Indian culture than the average visitor. If you find the idea of being *with* islanders uncomfortable and would rather simply be *around* them, plan to hike alone, or go somewhere besides the Caribbean.

Cruise ship passengers have the chance to walk more islands than resort vacationers.

1. What Walking & Hiking in the Caribbean are All About

The Heat

Many people imagine walking/hiking in the Caribbean as a stroll through a hothouse or steam room, with every stitch of clothing sticking to them. How enjoyable can that be?

Actually, the Caribbean has a tremendous range of temperatures. At sea level in the lowland jungle, the middle of the day is just as blistering and miserable as you may imagine it to be. Fortunately, the Caribbean's best hiking is in the mountains and cool rain forest. Much Caribbean hiking is above the 1,000-foot mark, more often at the 2,000 to 3,000-foot level, sometimes going as high as 7,000 feet. The temperatures are much lower at this altitude, regardless of what the thermometer says at the seashore. With the constant tradewinds, you may have more trouble staying warm than keeping cool if you go underdressed.

In Puerto Rico's Caribbean National Forest (El Yunque), the rangers have developed the following temperature chart:

Sea level: 80°
500-1,800 feet: 75°
1,800-2,400 feet: 70°
2,400-3,000 feet: 65°
3,000-3,500 feet: 60°

Note that it drops about five degrees for each 500-600 feet.

In Jamaica's Blue Mountains, the guides estimate a three-degree drop for every 1,000 feet of altitude, quite a different reckoning.

Whose figures are correct? And why such disparity? Both temperature estimates may indeed be right. Then again, because hiking in the Caribbean is still in the formative stage, this may be one of many instances of contradictory and conflicting information.

Who is precisely correct is not important. The essential point is this: it can get downright chilly in the Caribbean. A windbreaker is a good idea anywhere above 2,000 feet, particularly in winter months. It can also get cold at relatively low altitudes if it rains, which it often does, especially between June and October. In exposed places, the tradewinds can reach twenty-two mph. So the problem often isn't the heat, but figuring out how to stay warm.

The Bugs

I had lots of surprises hiking around the Caribbean, but the biggest revelation was the scarcity of biting insects. I went prepared with repellent and even a repellent-treated mesh jacket. I get bitten more often at home than I ever did in the islands.

Mosquitoes: Generally not found at higher altitudes. Found frequently in the lowlands and the beaches, depending on the season. On St. Lucia I was told the reason mosquitoes are rarely a problem is the lack of standing, stagnant water in which they can breed. The only things in the rain forest that hold water for more than a few seconds are some of the plants. Mosquitoes are much more apt to be a problem in your hotel room or campsite than while hiking.

No-see-ums: Also called midges and sand flies, they are so tiny that they are invisible—but what there is of them must be all teeth. Usually found on beaches around sunrise and sunset. In Spanish, they are known as "mi-mis" (pronounced "me-mees" as in "a case of the screaming me-mees!"). Long pants and shoes/socks are the best protection.

Ants: These are found all over the place in many rain forests but usually don't bite, except for the appropriately named fire ant. If you're allergic to ant bites, carry medication.

Repellent: Avon's Skin So Soft is not only effective, it doesn't have the industrial chemical odor of most strong commercial repellents. Pour the Skin So Soft into an aerosol sprayer and liberally spray your ankles and waist to repel ticks and mites. Also spray your clothes. Otherwise, rely on chemical preparations with Deet. Avoid sweet-smelling soaps, perfumes and colognes, which attract insects better than they do the opposite sex.

Bites: Baking soda solutions help relieve itching. Papaya, the main ingredient in Adolph's Meat Tenderizer, is a native of the Caribbean. It's a good pain killer for nonpoisonous stings: the papaya enzyme breaks down the insect venom. Antihistamine tablets also help reduce swelling and itching; antihistamine in cream form may cause skin allergies. Cortisone cream helps stop itching rashes. One way to reduce bites: always wear socks.

Vitamin Supplements: Ever notice how some people get eaten alive by insects while others just stand around and watch? Body chemistry appears to contribute to this. Vitamin B supplements and odorless garlic capsules seem to work as natural insect repellents for some people.

The People

I find Caribbean islanders to be very friendly and fun-loving people. Many of them are very poor and not well educated, but they have something far more important than wealth, technological advances or book learning. They have discovered—or retained—what life is all about: to have fun, whatever you're doing.

Most West Indians have a natural joy in their manner and their style of living. It is the relaxed, laid-back, "No-problem-don't-worry-be-happy" approach of so many islanders, particularly in the countryside, that I think of them all as "The Joy People." Watch how much the locals laugh, talk, joke and interact with each other. On many islands strangers are readily embraced and treated the same way. On others, it takes time for locals to drop their reserve. Islanders are generally quite shy and this can be mistaken for an unfriendly or indifferent attitude.

Still, you'll always find a few who perfectly fit the negative stereotype of any people. You may meet some who won't hide their dislike for outsiders. But how the situation resolves itself can be largely up to you.

Speaking Protocol: One of the greatest cultural misunderstandings between tourists and locals is who should speak to whom first. Islanders normally are polite people and expect to be treated with courtesy. They like to be spoken to when you pass them, even if it's just a nod. They expect visitors to initiate any conversation or the passing "hello." Considering that many visitors come from big cities where they are afraid to make eye contact, this type of old-fashioned politeness is a foreign way of behavior.

You may walk to a hotel desk and find that no one pays any attention to you. As the paying guest, you feel frustrated because you're being ignored. In your country, the customer always receives preferential treatment. Before long, you get so irritated that the first words that pop out of your mouth tend to be less friendly than they could be. The desk clerk responds in the same less-than-friendly way you greeted him/her. Words and conduct on both sides may escalate from there.

From the West Indian point of view, the visitor has been rude by not acknowledging the desk clerk and then starting the conversation in a hostile manner. Hotels are training their staffs in the quirks of tourists—

that strangers visiting the Caribbean expect islanders to speak first—but it will be decades before that trait is fully instilled.

The easiest approach on any island is to always speak first, as politely as you would converse with a colleague at work, and say it with a smile. It's almost always returned.

I had this who-should-speak-first pattern explained to me in Antigua. Once I discovered the proper protocol, I was amazed at how much friendlier everyone all over the Caribbean suddenly became. They hadn't changed—I had.

Poverty: The chance of encountering someone who is hostile because of your skin color, whatever it may be, is remote in the British West Indies. If there is a problem, it's probably based on something else: poverty, which breeds envy. The unemployment rate on some islands is as high as 25%. There are no jobs, except perhaps seasonal sugar cane cutting and banana picking.

Tourists on vacation have clothes, spending money and a lavish resort lifestyle most islanders can only dream of. After watching plane- and boat-loads of tourists for many years, some islanders feel resentful. A few have taken to panhandling, begging for a share, though in the West Indian culture such conduct is considered impolite.

Some islanders try to sell you carvings or shells—things you have no need for. It is the best their circumstances allow them to produce. And if you refuse, they may resent it. You are their only source of livelihood.

So, instead of another T-shirt, why not buy a shell or a necklace? Consider it a way of avoiding other peddlers: show the next salesperson what you have already bought, and they'll usually leave you alone. As much as they would like you to buy from them, whether it's spoken or not, there is an acknowledgment that you've already helped a brother.

Helping one another is what island life is all about. Unemployment may be high, but usually no one starves or has to sleep in the streets. Family and friends take care of their own.

A healthy tourist economy is one of the most important economic bases an island can have. Some island governments are making their people aware of this; that tourists in their mysterious and sometimes irritating ways are good for everyone's economic health. On the island of Bonaire in the Netherlands Antilles, the importance of making visitors welcome is a part of the school curriculum.

Photographing People

Photographing people in the Caribbean can be tricky. The guiding principle is to ask first. Islanders don't dress in colorful costumes and speak quaintly to impress tourists; this is their lifestyle.

Islanders usually react according to how tourists treat them.

If you're not carrying a camera, or if you have it slung over your shoulder so it's not about to be used, people are generally friendly and open. With your camera in your hand, these same people may be reserved or hostile.

Some islanders don't like to be photographed unless they are dressed in their finest. Others have been hassled so often by tourists they resent posing. I asked a woman at the fish market in Grenada if I could photograph her. She turned her back to me and said "I no monkey!" I was welcome to take pictures of her fish.

For a few islanders, having their photograph taken is considered a dangerous thing. While Christianity is the avowed religion of most islands, what we call "voodoo" is still practiced. The most dangerous thing a believer in the dark arts can imagine is someone capturing their likeness. The photograph can then be used in spells to cause sickness and misfortune.

Some islanders expect to be paid for having their picture taken. They've seen their photos show up in magazines, so they know pictures must be worth something.

If you are dealing with someone who operates a roadside stand or other business, you could be amazed at the cooperation you may receive if you purchase an item first, even if it is as trivial as a soft drink. That way it becomes a give-and-take situation with both parties gaining something.

The best thing to do is always ask permission, and when a person declines to be photographed, respect their wishes.

Caribbean Time

You enter a strange time dimension when you land on a Caribbean island. It's not that time stands still, or that it runs backwards. Things just don't happen as quickly or as precisely as you may be accustomed to. This characteristic varies enough from island to island that each seems to have its own unique set of clocks.

It can be frustrating, no doubt about it. After rushing to put things in order at work, dashing to shop and pack, and hurrying to the airport, many visitors arrive in the Caribbean in warp drive. Some quickly get upset when islanders don't share the same sense of time pressure. Others become infuriated that locals won't respond as promptly and as efficiently to every request as employees or service personnel do back home.

There are two ways to deal with the situation—a situation none of us is going to change. Either adapt to it, or fight it. Yes, your visit is on a time budget. You want to fit in as much as you can—but you also want to enjoy every activity as much as possible. It's the old "quantity time vs. quality time" issue. The setting has just changed.

One way to decompress quickly from Western-style living is to do nothing the day of your arrival except have something to drink and eat, look around a little, and go to sleep early. You should wake up in a more relaxed mood the next morning. If you arrive tired and stay tired—the hiking itself is a vigorous activity—your vacation may turn into nothing but an ordeal. Find out what the time flow is and go with it. Do things usually start ten minutes late? Or is the average closer to thirty minutes? Or maybe—and this does happen at well-managed properties—real time is the norm.

The amazing thing is that if you don't try and fight the system, everything eventually gets done. Perhaps not in the way you expect, but it eventually happens. Visitors to Jamaica, after their first few days of getting acclimated to the usual delays, quickly adopt the phrase "No problem, mon," as part of their standard vocabulary.

Explains Peter Bentley, one of the Caribbean's leading hiking guides and president of the Jamaica Alternative Tourism, Camping and Hiking Association: "Here's how we work. Push, you don't get much. Take it easier, get much more." And have a happier time, too.

Some visitors never do adapt to the concept of Caribbean time. They usually don't go back. There is a difference, however, between poor, sloppy service and doing things at a different tempo. Definitely complain about poor, sloppy service.

Staying Healthy in the Tropics

Colds & Allergies: It is possible to catch a cold in the tropics. It is more likely, however, that you will have an allergic reaction to a plant you may have never encountered before. With hundreds of species of trees, flowers and orchids, something is always in bloom, always dropping pollen. Bring non-drowsy antihistamines to stop the sniffles and tear-streamy eyes during the day. At night, don't worry about something that may knock you out. Take whatever works best and get some sleep.

High Humidity & Dehydration: You will lose a lot of liquid walking around, and not replacing it will make you feel lousy. It takes about two weeks to adjust to the Caribbean's high humidity, but you can keep your energy level up several ways:

1) Air conditioning: if you're accustomed to it at home, sleep with it on at night. You will feel far more rested than if you sleep with a ceiling fan and a natural breeze; you're making a lot of high energy demands on your body during the day, so pamper it at night.

2) Salt: while generally something to avoid, you need to increase your intake in the tropics to conserve body fluid.

3) Potassium/rehydration salt supplements: Before you try these, eat

several bananas every morning. If you still feel drained and can't kick into gear, try them in moderation. I always take potassium supplements before a particularly long hike.

Intestinal Problems: Inflammation is usually the result of a bacterial infection or consuming strange food and drink (beware those rum punches). Always carry your own water while hiking and avoid drinking from streams or falls, no matter how clear and clean they look or how much the locals reassure you. In some remote regions, tap water may be unsafe during the rainy season. Diarrhea and dehydration are the most serious problems: drink plenty of fluids (avoid alcohol and milk, which seem to prolong bouts of diarrhea). A bland diet of tea and toast seems to help some people. Although diarrhea usually clears up on its own after a couple of days, medication can control attacks almost immediately. Use loperamide (brand name, Imodium) and atropine (Lomotil).

If you have fever and severe abdominal cramps, pass blood in your stool and feel weak, you may have been unlucky enough to contract either amebic or bacillary dysentery. If in doubt, see a doctor immediately and definitely see a physician once you return home to minimize possible long-term health effects.

Bilharzia: (Also called schistosomiasis.) This parasite is common in lakes or slow-moving streams infested with snails. It can enter the body through an open cut or by drinking the water. This disease has been around a long time, as the mummies of ancient Egyptian pharaohs have revealed. Bilharzia can be fatal. Islands where this is a problem are: Martinique, Guadeloupe and St. Lucia.

Hookworms: Besides comfort, this is a good reason for always wearing shoes: hookworms are picked up by walking barefoot.

Prickly Heat: When the humidity is high, it's easy to develop a rash. Avoid it by powdering yourself in the morning and evening with talcum powder or powder containing zinc, such as Gold Bond. Never hike in tight jeans or clothes that bind.

Sun: The sun is far more intense near the equator than anywhere else in the world. Gradual exposure to the sun—only twenty-thirty minutes the first day, maximum—is mandatory to avoid that painful Larry-The-Lobster look. The sun is at its strongest between ten a.m. and three p.m. Wear sun block (SPF20 and higher) and drink lots of non-alcoholic liquid to keep from becoming dehydrated.

Marijuana Farming: Never, ever, go where you suspect it's growing, much less sample the crop. It could get you killed. In many remote mountain areas, marijuana (ganja) farming is an important way of life. If you are on your own, without the company of a local guide, you could be mistaken for a thief or police spy. Most marijuana farmers are armed. In certain places, they set booby traps to blow away the unwary and the unwanted. Never assume an island is yours to roam about freely, particularly Jamaica and Trinidad. Marked trails like those described here are generally safe. Hiring a local guide is your best insurance policy. Your guide will know who and where to stay away from.

Finding a Doctor: The likelihood of requiring medical attention is remote. To be prepared in case of an accident, know before you go: contact the International Association for Medical Assistance to Travelers, 745 5th Avenue, New York, NY 10022; or Intermedic, 777 3rd Avenue, New York 10017. They have the names and locations of well-trained English-speaking physicians all over the world. Remember to check your insurance to see if your policy covers overseas travel; otherwise, consider temporary medical/accident insurance. Carry your insurance card.

Basic Supplies:

❑ polarized sunglasses
❑ waterproof sunblock
❑ insect repellent including coils to burn in your room/tent
❑ Band-aids® for blisters
❑ water-sterilizing tablets or portable water purifier
❑ dusting powder for groin & feet
❑ anti-diarrhea medicine
❑ anti-constipation medicine (we all react differently)
❑ aspirin
❑ antacid tablets
❑ ankle support device in case of sprain
❑ commercial rehydrating salts
❑ travel sickness medicine, if so prone
❑ antihistamines
❑ first aid cream
❑ first aid kit with tweezers

Things to Avoid

AIDS: It is increasing, but nowhere near the levels of the U.S. The primary means of transmission is through heterosexual contact. Condoms are not plentiful. Women as well as men who intend to seek a new sexual partner should carry their own condoms. Warning: A lot of rum combined with a lot of sun and a lot of hiking in an exotic locale, capped off with a relaxed moonlit swim/walk on the beach, can produce surprising libido stimulation.

Malaria: It is currently found only in Haiti and the Dominican Republic, neither a subject of this book, and in Trinidad. Anti-malaria treatment, available under a doctor's care, begins well before departure and must continue afterwards. Most tourists are content with insect repellent and suffer none the worse for it.

Scorpions: Found in drier regions, they have a nasty habit of crawling into hiking boots at night and making their presence known the next morning. They are easier to avoid than to treat. Shake out your boots or keep them wrapped in a plastic bag (though the resulting smell may be worse than the bite). Scorpion stings hurt, but are rarely lethal. Treatment: heavy, sustained cursing during the first few minutes seems to alleviate tension and divert attention from the wound. Pounding the offending scorpion to a bloody pulp with your boot is extremely satisfying. If you have a scorpion sting kit, use it. See a doctor if conditions don't improve.

Centipedes: Remember "Dr. No," the first James Bond movie set in Jamaica, and the graphic scene where Bond found himself in bed with a tarantula crawling up the length of his body? A spider was used in the movie for dramatic visual effect and instant audience identification. However, in the Fleming novel (written in Jamaica, as were all the Bond books), 007 was confronted with something far deadlier: a centipede. Fortunately, poisonous centipedes are scarce and you are not likely to encounter one. If you do, don't pick it up out of curiosity to examine it, as some tourists have done. Happily, fatal bites are rare.

Snakes: Let's hear it for the mongoose! This weasel-like animal was introduced into the Caribbean by Europeans to eliminate rodents and vipers, and the animal is credited with killing off the poisonous snakes in most of the Caribbean. His deeds may be over-rated—as some scientists have pointed out there are still poisonous snakes on some islands which have mongoose. Still, the mongoose is the Caribbean's St. Patrick, and—as such—is above mere scientific debunking.

Only a few Caribbean islands have poisonous snakes: Aruba has a small, rarely seen rattlesnake. Martinique, Trinidad and St. Lucia are home to the deadly fer-de-lance, most often found in dry coastal areas. It supposedly is easy to frighten away the fer-de-lance if it knows you're coming. Rather than walking while wearing bear bells—which may work better on these skittish snakes than on cranky grizzly bears—some people use walking sticks to poke ahead in the thick, dry bush. Or they like to walk third or fourth in the hiking line. The bite of the fer-de-lance can be fatal if not properly treated, but attacks are rare. Locals know where the snakes hide; follow their warnings. Besides the fer-de-lance, Trinidad also has several other poisonous species. Again, attacks are rare. Carry a commercial snake bite kit if it will make you feel better. Hospitals stock snakebite serum but they will need to know what kind of snake bit you.

Sun: Mentioned previously, it's worth emphasizing again. Who wants to hike when their skin is the color of a Santa Claus suit and they're afraid it will crinkle with every step? The sun is the greatest danger you will encounter. It may be necessary to wear sunblock even on your lips. Be particularly careful to cover ears, jaws and the lower part of your neck. Sunglasses are essential: bright sun reflected off the ocean is as much as 10,000 times brighter than is comfortable to the eye.

Sunstroke/Sun Poisoning: OK, so you didn't listen. Symptoms of oncoming sunstroke are dizziness, vertigo, fever, blisters, headache, nausea, sudden lack of sweat and delusions. Get out of the heat immediately. Take a cool bath or shower. Drink fruit juices or Gatorade, if available, to replace lost electrolytes. If improvement is not immediate, see a doctor.

Fish Poisoning/Ciguatera: A deadly toxin found primarily in reef fishes, such as snapper, very large grouper, and barracuda, symptoms include tingling, itching or numbness of the fingertips and lips, stomach cramps, nausea and vomiting. In severe cases, seek medical help immediately. It can be fatal. Freshness of the fish or its handling has nothing to do with whether or not the fish is tainted. It's a toxin that gets carried up the food chain; you get it from something you ate, which also ate something, which also ate something...

Stick to ocean-roaming fish such as tuna, wahoo, mahi-mahi (dolphin fish, not Flipper) and you should not have a problem. I once dined with eight people, and we all ate from the same fish. One person got a mild case of ciguatera (lip tingling). Why him and not the rest of us? Some scientists theorize it may also be a matter of individual susceptibility.

Razor Grass: Just as sharp as its name implies, this grass causes cuts that take a long time to heal. Usually found in rain forest areas, it's sharp enough to cut through light-weight clothing. Ask someone to point it out to you before you make its acquaintance.

Manchineel Tree (also called the Manzanillo Tree): Look for and avoid this tall tree in the lowlands, particularly around coastal regions. It produces a small green crab-apple fruit that is very poisonous, sometimes fatal, known on some islands as "the apple of death." Apparently a lot of early Spanish explorers ate these things on landfall, only to die of severe throat constrictions. According to conventional wisdom, when it rains, the mere run-off from the manchineel tree's leaves and branches can cause a rash and the sap itself may blister you. Some people have far more severe skin reactions than others. Gel from an aloe plant will work wonders in healing the rash. Quite often these trees are marked with a warning sign in heavily trafficked areas. Have someone point out a specimen.

Oleander: Another very poisonous plant. Have one shown to you.

Poinsettias: If you have never eaten the leaf of one at home during the Christmas season, there's no reason you would want to sample one on vacation, except that we tourists sometimes do bizarre things. These plants are poisonous.

Clothes to Wear and Tear

Unlike hiking in a lot of exotic places that require special clothing of almost an expeditionary nature, Caribbean wear is relatively simple and inexpensive.

Shoes: These are the most important element. While many people will simply wear an old pair of sneakers, if you're going to do some serious hiking, you need to be serious about your footwear. A lot of trails are rocky and unstable; high-top hiking boots offer more ankle support. They should be comfortable when wet, because your feet will be muddy most of the time. More importantly, they should have non-skid soles. You will encounter lots of mud, but the real problems are the rain-slicked and moss-covered rocks. Flip-flops are a disaster in the making. Some local guides can hike the rain forest in bare feet, but that doesn't mean you should try. Not only have they been walking on this slippery and tricky terrain since their very first steps, but their feet have calluses as thick as horse hooves. Try and go native and you may have to be carried out. Use one pair of shoes for everyday walking, another specifically for hiking. The hiking pair will be too dirty and damp to wear for anything else.

Slacks/Shorts: Loose, quick-drying running shorts are all you need on some islands. On others, because of razor grass or high altitude temperatures, you will need full-length slacks. Take both and consult your guide before setting out; each trail is different. An ideal compromise is the "Kenya convertibles" sold by Cabelas and other outfitters. These cotton pants are essentially shorts that have legs you can zip on and off, according to conditions.

Socks: Always wear them. They help prevent scratches and insect bites. They also make walking a lot more comfortable. Be prepared to throw them away at the end of a trip. Some of the mud, especially in Dominica, is impossible to get out.

Shirts: Those with collars offer more protection against the sun. Long sleeves help prevent sunburn and can always be rolled up (or down) according to temperature.

Hat: Baseball caps help protect your nose but little else. Wide-brimmed hats protect your ears (which can burn surprisingly easily) and your neck against the sun. They also keep the rain off your face.

Windbreaker: Buy lightweight nylon which can be easily stuffed in a pack. You will need it for protection against rain and chilly winds.

Umbrella: The small, collapsible kind that will fit in a day sack is best. When walking through open, exposed areas in direct sunlight for mile after mile, nothing offers better protection or keeps you cooler than an umbrella. It also keeps the rain off your face or out of your contact lenses. Buy a light-colored one.

Plastic Garbage Bags: Use these for wrapping clothes and cameras on rainy days. They are also good for transporting your damp and filthy hiking shoes home in your suitcase. Makes a great instant poncho, too.

Sunglasses: Sunglasses are vital. The best are polarized and provide complete protection against UV rays, which have the potential to cause permanent eye damage.

Clothing Care: Plan on washing clothes in a sink at the end of every afternoon and letting them dry overnight. This way, you can get by with only three changes of hiking wear, regardless of how long you stay. Shampoo works almost as well as liquid soap.

Cameras: By all means, carry one, though it will be a lot of trouble if you don't prepare. On some of the more strenuous ascents you need both hands free as you scramble up a hill or hug the side of a mountain trail. Be sure you can put the camera well out of the way, in your knapsack or a special padded hip holster designed for this purpose. If you're crossing difficult terrain and the camera is dangling around your neck, it could divert you, throw you off balance or crash against something. Be prepared to waterproof it instantly in case of rain. You will also need a flash because of the low light of the rain and cloud forests, unless you are using incredibly fast film. Also, you will want flash to bring out the color and detail on many of the plants.

Here's a checklist of items:
- Day sack
- Hip camera holster or waterproof plastic bags to protect camera
- Spare batteries for camera and flash
- Wide-brimmed hat
- Loose cotton clothing
- Non-skid hiking boots
- Two water bottles, one for day sack, another to be worn on your belt
- Windbreaker
- Sweater
- Small collapsible umbrella
- Flashlight with spare batteries
- Snacks
- Gray duct tape (always good for something on every trip)

Hiking Guides

With this guidebook you will be able to make most of the walks and hikes on your own, but I'd suggest using a local guide whenever you first visit an island. Tropical forests are so diverse and every island so different that local knowledge is mandatory to appreciate fully everything you're

It's safe to wade streams on most—but not all—islands. Local guides can show you where it's safe to hike. Climbing Dunn's River Falls in Jamaica is a very popular short hike.

seeing. A written guide can't begin to provide the history, folklore and botanical knowledge that a personal guide can. Besides, a personal guide will know precisely where to take you to see rare St. Lucia parrots or something else you would never find on your own. Guide companies are listed in the general information section for each island. Prices for guides are usually very reasonable, from $30-$75 per person per day depending on food and transport provided.

Camping

Camping in the Caribbean can be a problem. It is forbidden by law on many islands. Those laws are enforced, often at customs: your camping gear could be confiscated and held until your departure. Part of the reason for this restriction is to make certain that only a certain type of visitor (one with money) is permitted on the island. With a greater emphasis on promoting ecotourism and hikes into the bush, this attitude will probably change. Check with the individual tourist bureaus listed in each chapter for the latest additions/changes.

Prices

The cost of a Caribbean trip is strongly influenced by the time of year you travel. Traditionally, hotel prices double or triple every December 15 and come down from their astronomical levels on April 15. Weather in the Caribbean is certainly good during winter, but visitors pay premium prices to flee the cold back home. If you have plenty of money, you may be willing to pay exorbitant prices to travel in the winter, but Caribbean weather is good year-round.

If, however, you are most concerned about spending your funds on activities rather than hotel accommodations, consider traveling April through May, a period which typically offers prime hiking conditions with clear skies and sun. The weather may be as good as February or March but prices are far lower.

The only island that has really tried to accommodate budget tourists more interested in activities than amenities is Jamaica, which supports the Alternative Tourism Association. Please see the Jamaica chapter for more information.

Weather

Summer humidity is higher and it's warmer then, so you are paying less to sweat more. However, if you're not interested in photography, cloudy weather provides what is actually the most comfortable hiking. Don't avoid the Caribbean just because it's the rainy season. Elderly islanders no longer try to predict with the same accuracy they once did what the weather will be at a particular time of year. They say the patterns are changing too much. So it may rain during the sunny season, and vice-versa. You have no guarantees.

Sahara Sands: A strange phenomenon that occurs annually from about mid-May to mid-June. Sands blown over from the Sahara desert in Africa create hazy conditions in the Caribbean, so you lose those incredible long-distance vistas from the mountain tops. If you have dust allergies, you might want to learn more about the Sahara sands and whether they might impact you.

Hurricanes: The season begins in June, with the greatest activity typically in August, September and October. September is often the most active month, a time some islands almost shut down because tourism is so dead. If you and a hurricane are headed toward the same island destination, change your path. Cancel or postpone.

# 2. Historical Overview

Old West Indian Saying:
Where horse is tied, is there he eats grass.

Translation:
You must make the best of wherever you find yourself.

The islands of the Caribbean may be scattered, but their stories are basically the same, with only slight variations. Here, the historical perspective of the entire region is presented in condensed form rather than being detailed for every island.

The Indians

The first settlers were an unknown race of Stone Age people who lived in the Caribbean about 4,000 years ago. Apparently without permanent settlements, they were hunter-gatherers. They left behind no pottery, only stone tools which the Arawaks found useful 1,000 years later when they moved into the islands. The Arawaks called this unknown race Ciboney, after the Arawak word "ciba" for stone. Modern archaeologists still have no idea where the Ciboney wandered in from or off to, but they were gone from the Caribbean long before the Arawaks arrived.

Paddling their big dugout canoes from South America, the Arawaks spread out into the Caribbean from the Orinoco region of Venezuela between 1,000 to 2,000 years ago. Thus the Arawaks had already discovered the Caribbean more than a thousand years before Columbus. Their prior claim was ignored. The Spanish quickly and completely obliterated the Arawaks.

The significant impact of the Arawaks on the modern world is not generally appreciated. They are credited with introducing Europeans not only to the hammock and its wonderfully restful properties, but also to tobacco and syphilis.

For at least a millennium, the Arawaks, a peaceful race, lived a Caribbean idyll similar to the South Seas Islanders of the Pacific. They wore almost no clothing, hunted and fished as they needed, and grew crops such as yams and cassava, which was ground to make bread. The Arawak concept of beauty was an interesting one. The ultimate turn-on was a pointed head, so babies had their heads pressed between slats of wood to enhance their beauty. Not surprisingly, the Arawaks lived in conical-shaped shelters, made of thatch rather than pressed wood.

They liked to while away a day by dancing and playing games similar to volleyball and badminton. Often they partied while under the influence of maize alcohol and a powdery drug ingested up their nostrils. Reportedly, the early Spanish were scared silly when they first saw Arawaks puffing on firebrands of tobacco, one of the earliest versions of cigarettes.

Possessions apparently meant little to the individual Arawak unless someone tried to steal them. Theft was considered a major crime, and the culprit would be slowly skewered to death with a pole.

When the early Spanish explorers showed up, the Arawaks were more than happy to share what they owned. Columbus himself noted the Arawaks were generous, gentle and honest. The Arawaks should have skewered *him*.

Within 50 years of the discovery of the New World, the Arawaks as a race were destroyed, forced by the Spanish into slavery to work their gold mines. Though peaceful, the freedom-loving Arawaks were not the most cooperative of slaves. The Indians had a strong belief in an afterlife, in a place they called "Coyaba" where one feasted and danced all day long without the interference of hurricanes, sickness or the Spanish. Many Arawaks committed suicide rather than submit to a life of servitude.

The Carib Indians, immortalized today through both the name of the Caribbean region and island-brewed Carib beer, were not such pushovers. The Caribs, who had come from the Orinoco region only 200 years before Columbus, were extremely fierce fighters. They were in the process of expanding throughout the Caribbean, killing off the Arawaks as they went, when Columbus arrived.

If the European and Carib sides had been evenly matched in weaponry and manpower, I would have bet on the Caribs. They were known for the speed with which they could fire arrow after arrow at a target. It's said they could split a coin at a hundred yards. The huge fort on the island of St. Vincent is noted for the direction its cannons point—inland. The British soldiers hiding inside were far more afraid of being attacked from land by the Caribs than by any European warships.

The Caribs enjoyed dressing up, painting their skin red and wearing parrot feathers and necklaces made from the teeth of their victims; the

Caribs were also cannibals. At least that is the accepted theory, though there is some dispute.

When the Caribs went to war, they rarely harmed women but took them as property. The male captives were served for dinner, after their legs and backs were split open and stuffed with herbs and pimento, then flame-broiled on a spit. The Caribs were not indiscriminate in their tastes. It's said they found the Spanish too stringy and preferred the French above all others for their tastiness. Next in preference were the English and Dutch. Christianity made little impact on the Caribs, never much concerned with any kind of religion anyway. They consented to be baptized for the gifts that went along with the ceremony.

Try as they might, the Europeans never could exterminate the Caribs. Almost, but not quite. They used the Caribs as slaves, though not always successfully. The Indians would kill themselves by jumping off of cliffs or eating dirt until they died. A Carib reservation, some 3,000 strong, still exists on the island of Dominica. The last person known to have spoken true Carib died in the early 1900s.

Columbus and the Spanish

Wrong-way Columbus, never fully realizing where he was or what he was accomplishing, fortunately lived in the 1400s and was not aboard the first lunar-bound Apollo rocket. On the other hand, we would have gotten to Mars decades earlier.

Columbus landed in the New World either in the Turks & Caicos chain (probably the correct theory), or on the island of San Salvador in the Bahamas, where several markers honor his landing. According to historical artifacts uncovered on the North American continent, Columbus was not the first European to discover the New World, yet no one has been anxious to change all those encyclopedias. Myth seems harder to change than fact, except in Portugal where students are taught that Portuguese sailors found the western lands about a dozen years earlier and returned with tales that motivated Columbus.

Even after four voyages to the New World, Columbus was still convinced he was somewhere in Asia or India, which is why he called the natives "Indians." This, of course, made no sense to the natives, who called themselves "the people."

Columbus, who was born in Genoa, Italy, sailed under the Spanish flag for the Spanish monarchs, Ferdinand and Isabella. Even though he had no idea where he was, Columbus was considered a skilled navigator. Following the tradewinds on a westerly course across the Atlantic, he and his three ships made landfall October 12, 1492. He returned to Spain triumphant in 1493, convinced he had discovered Japan.

He returned (1493-1494), to found the first settlement on the island of Hispaniola, this time bringing seventeen ships and hundreds of volunteers. His third voyage (1498-1500) ended in disgrace. Columbus was made governor of Santo Domingo, but the people there rebelled against his harsh authority and he was returned to Spain in chains in 1500. He was allowed to make a fourth voyage (1502-1504) if he promised to stay away from Santo Domingo, which he did. He explored the coast of Central America and was later shipwrecked in Jamaica.

By this time, it's clear how Columbus was regarded by those who knew him and worked under him. Two of Columbus's co-survivors paddled to Santo Domingo but couldn't hire anyone to come and rescue the former governor. The Santo Domingans preferred to let Columbus rot in Jamaica for a year before he was rescued. Columbus returned to Spain and died in 1506 at the age of fifty. His daughter-in-law had his remains interred in Santo Domingo in 1544. There is a dispute as to whether his body was or was not removed after the Haitian invasion of 1796 and whether it was taken to the nearest Spanish soil, Cuba.

But presumably it was, because remains identified as Columbus's were sent to Seville a century later. Columbus (or whoever) was supposed to be returned to Santo Domingo with much pomp and circumstance for the 500th anniversary of the discovery of the New World. Somehow, all this confusion about the location of Columbus's remains seems bizarrely appropriate, since he never knew where he was while alive.

Dividing Up the New World

Columbus not only sailed under the Spanish flag, he acted as an ambassador of God, and the Catholic Church in particular, in his discoveries. Consequently, the Pope was allowed to carve up the New World: anything 100 leagues west of the Azores was Spanish territory and trespassers would be shot on sight. As this division had overlooked the tip of Brazil, the Portuguese were allowed to settle there. The rest of the Caribbean became contested territory, as other European countries became aware of the gold being plundered from the Indians.

The British were especially interested, sending privateers under contract to the government to steal what they could. These included such well-known historical figures as Francis Drake and Walter Raleigh (who later had a cigarette named after him). The French also sent freelancers, some more interested in pillaging Spanish settlements than in exploring for their own gold; these raiders were generally known as pirates.

The true buccaneers of the Spanish Main originated on Hispaniola. These pirates sold cured beef to passing ships. They became known as "buccaneers" because the oven they used for smoking meat was called a "boucan." They gradually grew in number and spread out through the islands, looking for Spanish ships to attack. Then they would return to ports in St. Thomas and Jamaica to sell their spoils.

Although the Spanish claimed the Caribbean, they did not attempt to settle there except for Hispaniola, Puerto Rico and Cuba. They found far more profit in extracting gold from the Indians on the mainland of South America.

Through default, the Spanish left many islands to the British, French and Dutch, allowing them to fight out claims among themselves. Many islanders today speak a blend of both English and French, a patois carryover from the continuous political turmoil.

Sugar and Slavery

Sugar cane and the enormous wealth it generated is what made the island colonies worth fighting for. Originally brought from the Canary Islands, sugar was first grown in this hemisphere in Brazil, then Barbados.

For maximum profit, sugar cane required the islands be stripped of all native vegetation—literally to be scalped—except in the highlands where the cane wouldn't grow well. The islands were deforested so dramatically to grow sugar cane, it's said that Dominica—rugged and mountainous and inhospitable to farming—is the only island Columbus would still recognize.

To prosper, the plantations needed cheap labor, lots of it. It's recorded that even the smallest sugar plantation needed as many as 250 slaves.

The slaves, mostly taken as prisoners of war or in night raids by other black Africans, endured a cruel, six to twelve-week-long ocean voyage to the West Indies. An average of 12% of the "cargo" died. Slaves were chained and forced to stand in the holds like telephone poles, without enough space to sit. Some died of disease; others preferred to jump overboard and drown in their chains.

Before long, the slaves dominated the Caribbean, far outnumbering the white planters. To maintain control, planter discipline was strict and violent. Any uprisings were quickly put down.

In 1804, a full-scale rebellion in Haiti led that country to declare its independence. In 1833, the British outlawed slavery in all of its colonies. In 1834, the Dominican Republic (which shares the island of Hispaniola with Haiti) declared its independence. In 1848, the French colonies and the Danish West Indies banned slavery. In 1886, slavery ended in Spanish-owned Cuba.

Unfortunately, freedom did not automatically bring economic independence, or even a hint of the former prosperity of earlier times. Former slaves, now independent West Indians, found the era of colonialism even more poverty-ridden. Most of the West Indies went into a severe economic decline.

World War I brought an increase in the price of sugar and encouraged the islands to diversify into other crops, such as bananas, spices, cocoa and coffee. Tourism became popular after World War II.

By the end of the 20th century, most of the British West Indies chose independence, though the Cayman Islands decided to remain British. Guadeloupe, Martinique and St. Martin, pretending to be an extension of Europe, saw their most prosperous future as French outposts in the Caribbean.

Since the end of the great plantation days, the tropical vegetation of the Caribbean has slowly reclaimed the land. The original growth is gone in most places, replaced by secondary growth, a mix of native trees and exotic (imported) plants such as bamboo. Altered, perhaps, but not necessarily any worse. The argument could well be made that the forests have never been more beautiful or colorful due to the variety supplied by the imports.

Indeed, it is almost impossible to distinguish between what is "imported" and what is "native" to the Caribbean anymore. Sugar cane, bananas, coffee and cocoa—all important economic staples—are not native species.

Thanks to tourism, the tropical vegetation is better protected now than ever before. New parks and gardens are planned on many islands. Much more needs to be done, and quickly, to limit agricultural development in some pristine areas. Yet it is happening, perhaps more on Caribbean time than real time.

Caribbean Flora and Fauna: How It Evolved

Except Trinidad, which is considered an extension of South America, all Caribbean islands are classified as oceanic islands formed by fiery volcanic upheavals and other cataclysmic events. As a result, they start out bare.

Some plants, such as the mangrove, have seeds able to float the ocean currents for months, make landfall and still sprout. For other species, "rafting" may be a more common method: one in which a seed or animal hitches a ride on a floating platform, something as small as a leaf, and rides to an island.

Hurricanes in the Caribbean have made rafting a relatively easy and regular phenomenon, uprooting whole trees (if not sections of forests) to send scores of hitchhikers (snakes, lizards, frogs) floating out to sea. Storms, with their prevailing air currents have also helped distribute birds and insects, which have been known to stay aloft for days. This is how the common cattle egret is believed to have come over from Africa.

Mangroves, which form the shoreline of many islands, are important nurseries for fish, crab and other marine life.

Where Are All the Animals?

Supporting the rafting theory of plant and animal dispersal is the scarcity of mammals and amphibians, who need fresh water to survive. The most common Caribbean mammals are rodents and bats. Amphibians are equally scarce. Only about three dozen species of frogs and toads are found in the Caribbean.

The appearance of man since the days of the Ciboneys 4,000 years ago has, of course, affected the flora and fauna. The Arawaks brought with them the first dogs, which did not bark and which the greedy Spanish quickly consumed to extinction. Native iguanas, sea turtles, manatees and many colorful birds were also over-hunted. At the same time, cows, pigs and chickens were introduced. So was the mongoose, which did such a good job hunting snakes that it now preys on chickens.

Types of Tropical Forest

Except for major urban areas, most Caribbean walking is done in forest. Since the plants offer the primary scenery, a basic outline of the forest zones is essential to know. The different zones are determined primarily by altitude and rainfall.

All of the islands fall in the tropical zone, but West Indian vegetation is technically classified as neo-tropical, meaning it grows in the New World tropical zone.

Two lines of latitude—the Tropic of Cancer in the north and the Tropic of Capricorn in the south—determine the earth's tropical boundaries. Tropical temperatures stay fairly constant regardless of season. It's often hotter in New York City in the summer than the Caribbean, where it rarely gets above ninety degrees.

The amount of daylight also stays constant over the year, featuring twelve-hour days/twelve-hour nights year-round. Rainfall, however, can vary dramatically from season to season. It's not the amount of rain an area receives—but whether it falls consistently and in quantity throughout all twelve months—that determines whether the vegetation is that of a true rain forest or of a humid green/dry forest. It's possible to have both humid and arid regions on the same island, depending on how high the mountains are and the direction of the wind. The rule of thumb: the higher you go, the wetter it gets. It is the cloud-covered mountains, not the tropical palm-lined shores, that receive the greatest rainfall.

The windward sides of the islands tend to be the wettest. On these coasts, from the lowlands to about 3,300 feet, are the famed evergreen tropical rain forest. A tropical rain forest has a tree canopy extending as high as 130-150 feet. The rich tree crowns of the rain forest absorb most of the light so the ground is almost in perpetual shade. The jungle, therefore, is in the thick canopy above, not on the ground.

Rain forests are where you find Tarzan-sized vines hanging from trees and colorful, flowershop-quality bromeliads and orchids. Ferns are incredibly dense and rich: 500 species of fern grow on Jamaica alone. Moss and lichen flourish profusely, making rock-hopping a tricky maneuver. The Caribbean Rain Forest (El Yunque) of Puerto Rico is a classic example of evergreen tropical rain forest.

Between 3,300-6,500 feet the vegetation changes and is classified as mountain rain forest. From 6,500-13,000 feet, it is called montane cloud forest, or elfin woodland. In both the mountain and montane zones, the trees grow broader and farther apart. Due to the cold and wind, they also grow more slowly than in the lower rain forest. At altitude, epiphytes (mosses, lichens and orchids) still appear in great numbers, but many of the lowland creeping plants disappear. The highest level, the cloud forest, is so named because it is always covered in clouds, mist and haze. It is frequently called elfin woodland; the combination of twisted and stunted vegetation, moss, dense foggy atmosphere, clouds and the eternal eastern tradewinds combine to create a sinister, mysterious atmosphere...just the kind the elves of German literature were said to inhabit.

One kind of lowland jungle is the thick mangrove forest. With an almost impenetrable, interlocking root system, mangroves thrive on the sheltered shorelines of many islands. The different mangrove species, red, white, black and button mangroves, provide a nursery for many species of crab, shrimp and fish. They also seem to house great quantities of mosquitoes. Mangrove leaves are thick and evergreen, and the trees vary tremendously in height from only several feet tall to twenty or more.

On islands where there are alternate wet and dry seasons, such as the Virgin Islands, the trees shed their leaves during the dry season to resemble a winter scene. But when the water turns back on, everything is green again. This alternating pattern of grimness and greenness, which makes up a great deal of the Caribbean, is referred to as dry and green humid forests.

In the driest regions where little rain falls during the year, scrub vegetation thrives. The arid islands of Aruba, Bonaire and Curaçao fit this category perfectly. The cactus in these dry regions come in many different varieties and shapes. Agaves, spiny opuntias and thorny shrubs are earmarks of this kind of rugged, tough terrain. Hiking in such regions calls for extra water and very good shoes, since the spines of some cactus can penetrate shoe soles.

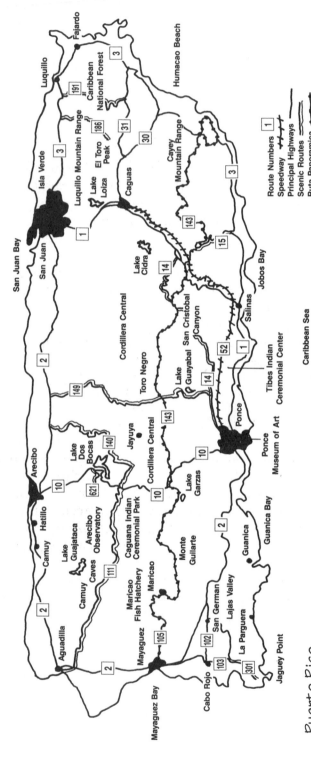

Puerto Rico

 # 3. Puerto Rico

Puerto Rican saying:
A shrimp that falls asleep will be taken by the current.

Translation:
If you're slow, you'll blow it.

Puerto Rico, the "Shining Star of the Caribbean," is a thousand miles southeast of Miami. Thanks to American Airline's huge San Juan hub, with direct or connecting service from more than a hundred cities, it's easier to fly to Puerto Rico than to many parts of the U.S. This accessibility means that 80% of Puerto Rico's tourists are from the United States. Consequently, English is spoken almost as widely as Spanish.

One hundred ten miles long by thirty-five miles wide, Puerto Rico is a land of great geographical contrasts. It is roughly 75% mountainous. All lakes on the island are artificial, man-made early in the 20th century for water supply and energy production. The north coast is wetter and greener than the southern tip, where cactus are common. In the northwest, caves, sinkholes and haystack hills characterize the karst terrain. In the central mountain range, the altitude reaches an impressive 4,389 feet at Cerro la Punta.

Puerto Rico is a commonwealth of the United States. By law, the U.S. and Puerto Rican flags must always fly side by side. The U.S. dollar is the standard currency, though locals may sometimes refer to it as "pesos."

Travel Tips

Area: 110 miles long, 35 miles wide; 3,515 square miles
Language: Spanish; English is secondary.
Population: 3,277,000, principally in the San Juan area.
Time Zone: One hour ahead of Eastern Standard Time, the same during Daylight Savings Time.

Rainy Season: The most frequent rain occurs August through October, though the climate varies across the island.

Getting There: American Airlines offers connections from more than one hundred U.S. cities, plus daily flights from London-Heathrow to Miami with immediate connections to San Juan. Delta and USAir also fly into San Juan from the U.S. British Airways flies in from Gatwick once a week.

Getting Around: By far the easiest and least expensive way to travel is to rent a car. *One that does not have offices at the airport is Target, which has been known to negotiate rates (US $28 a day for a small car, not including insurance which is a steep US $12.50 per day);809/783-6592 or 782-6381.* Get a road map because signs are scarce in many places. Texaco gas stations offer a good map for US $1.50.

Where to Stay: In the countryside, the best places to stay are the Paradores, a chain of inns located in some of the most historic and scenic places: such as an old coffee plantation, or somewhere by the sea. Although most have swimming pools, the Paradores are simpler and much less expensive than the big resorts. Prices range from US $40-US $70 per night. They can be booked directly from the U.S. by calling 800/443-0266 or in San Juan at 809/721-2884 during normal Puerto Rico business hours. The Paradores are operated by the Puerto Rico Tourism Company, charged with promoting the island.

Camping: Primitive camping is available in El Yunque in several areas. At present, there is no charge but a permit is necessary. Permits may be obtained at the Catalina Field Office, the Rio Piedras Office or at the Sierra Palm Interpretive Service Center at km 11.6 on Route 191, open from 9 a.m. to 5:30 p.m. year-round. For further information, write El Yunque Ranger District, P.O. Box B, Palmer, PR 00721; 809/887-2875. In addition—and this is rare for the Caribbean—camping is permitted on some of the public beaches. Contact the Recreation and Sports Department at 809/722-1551 or 721-2800, ext. 225. Beaches may be closed because of recent storm damage.

Taxes & Tips: The standard tax is 7% on hotel rooms, 9% if your hotel has a casino. Tipping of 10-15% is standard for restaurants and may automatically be added to your bill.

Dining: Puerto Rico has more restaurants than you can ever hope to sample in this lifetime. Highly recommended for their value and variety are the *mesones gastronomiques*, a network of thirty-five restaurants set up by the Puerto Rico Tourism Company throughout the island. Like the Paradores, they cater to those traveling to out-of-the-way places. These restaurants serve local cuisine for as low as US $7. It is as cheap to dine in the smaller restaurants as it is to pack picnics, because most supermarket food is imported.

If you become thirsty traveling around the island, look for the hand-lettered signs, "Refrescos del pays." You'll find enterprising locals selling ice-cold fruit juices out of the backs of their trucks or cars. For a true Caribbean specialty, ask for "coco frio"—chilled coconuts with the tops hacked off so you can drink the sweet water. These come with and without straws. If the sugarcane is being harvested—and you want a real sugar rush like you've probably never had before—try the "guarapo de cana," fresh sugar cane juice served over ice. It tastes nothing like the refined stuff that comes in bags and boxes.

Documents: U.S. citizens need a birth certificate or voter's registration card and photo ID. Citizens of other countries need a U.S. visa or a U.S. visa waiver.

Currency: The US Dollar is the standard rate of exchange. Credit cards are accepted in larger cities, but be prepared to pay cash in the countryside. Keep lots of small bills handy for drinks, snacks, etc. Banks are open weekdays from 8:30 a.m. to 2:30 p.m. and on Saturdays from 9:45 a.m. until noon.

Electrical Current: 110 volts/60 cycles

Safety/Health Warnings: San Juan is a large urban area with all the usual crime problems that implies. Unaccompanied women should be especially careful in the Condado area. Cars should be kept locked and valuable possessions left in hotel safes. Avoid swimming in rivers since bilharzia could be present. There is a common flu-like illness called "la monga," which is not serious and disappears after a few days.

Hiking/Walking Services: At present, neither the Puerto Rico Tourism Company nor I could identify any companies that specialize in countryside hikes, with one major exception. To find out about the annual fourteen-day hike from one end of the island to the other (a distance of 165 miles or 238.3 km) contact Fondo de Mejoramiento, P.O. Box 364746, San Juan, PR 00936-4746; 809/759-8366.

Snakes and Other Venomous Creatures: Puerto Rico has four kinds of snakes but none are venomous.

For More Information: The Puerto Rico Tourism Company sounds like a conglomerate but that is the government's office of tourism. In the U.S., write 575 Fifth Ave., 23rd Floor, New York, NY 10017; 800/223-6530 or 212/599-6262. In Canada, 11 Yorkville Ave., Suite 1003, Toronto, Ontario M4W 1L3; 416/925-5587. In the UK, P.O. Box 15, Coulsdon, Surrey CR3 2UZ; 0800/898920. There are also branch offices at the international airport and in most towns. Be sure to pick up a copy of "Que Pasa," which lists all the major hotels, attractions, etc.

🦀 Walking Tour of Old San Juan

The crown jewel of Puerto Rico is Old San Juan, a seven-block area once enclosed by a city wall and guarded by one of the hemisphere's mightiest fortresses. Founded in the early 1500s as a military stronghold, Old San Juan had transformed into a picturesque residential and commercial district by the 19th century. Today, this thriving community rising above narrow streets looks like a movie set, with pastel-colored buildings flanked by wrought-iron, filigreed balconies. Old San Juan takes at least a full day to thoroughly explore.

Because traffic is often heavily congested and parking spaces almost impossible to find, the best way to explore Old San Juan is on foot. Start at the island's main landmark, the fortress San Felipe del Morro:

1) El Morro Fortress: Begun in 1540, the great fort rises six stories or 140 feet above the pounding sea. El Morro underwent many modifications until 1783, when it became the formidable structure standing today. Although impenetrable when attacked by sea (Sir Francis Drake failed in 1595), it was taken by the Earl of Cumberland in 1598 who came over land. He held the fortress only temporarily, evacuating when the bottom fell out in a dysentery epidemic.

2) San Juan Cemetery: Adjacent to El Morro and visible from its ramparts, the Cemetery is the burial place of many prominent Puerto Ricans. It is an impressive display of elaborate tombstones surrounding a circular neoclassic chapel which was dedicated to St. Mary Magdalene in 1863. Near one of the poorer sections of the city, it is considered safe to visit only in groups. A view from a hill or El Morro is just as appealing.

3) City Wall: The cemetery is flanked by a section of the massive city wall that completely surrounded Old San Juan in the 1630s. The wall consisted of two separate forty-foot-high, parallel limestone-block walls with the space in between filled with sand. To discourage attackers, the exterior face was slanted, varying from twenty feet wide at the base, to only twelve feet at the top. "Garitas," tiny rounded sentry posts that have become the symbol of Puerto Rico, line the top.

4) San Juan Museum of Art and History: On Norzagaray, corner of McArthur. Built in 1855 as a marketplace, it was used in the early 20th century for government offices before being turned into a cultural center in 1979. It has been undergoing extensive repair.

5) Plaza de San Jose: Flanked by some of the most impressive and important buildings in San Juan, the plaza itself seems bland until you realize the statue of Ponce de Leon, presiding over the plaza square, is made of captured British cannon, seized after the unsuccessful attack of Sir Ralph Abercromby in 1797.

6) Pablo Casals Museum: On Plaza de San Jose, the museum is

The El Morro Fortress is one of the great battlements of the Western Hemisphere. The lighthouse marks the entrance to the old city.

dedicated to the cellist who came to Puerto Rico to live in 1957. The unimposing building contains manuscripts, photographs and a library of videotapes of Festival Casals concerts that may be played on request. Open Tuesday-Saturday 9:30 a.m. to 5:30 p.m., Sunday 1 p.m. to 5 p.m.; 809/723-9185.

7) **San Jose Church:** Dominating the Plaza de San Jose and dating back to 1532, this is the second-oldest church in the Western Hemisphere. It has

a remarkable series of vaulted Gothic ceilings. The figure of Christ on the Cross on the left side of the church is believed to date from the mid 16th-century. Open Monday-Saturday 8:30 a.m. to 4 p.m.. Mass at noon Sunday; 809/725-7501.

8) Casa Blanca: Built in 1521 as the home for Governor Ponce de Leon, in gratitude for his achievements. However, he did not occupy it. He was killed in Cuba before he could move in. Then, Casa Blanca was destroyed by a hurricane. However, by 1523 his family was able to move in and make Casa Blanca the de Leon ancestral home for the next 250 years. Today, Casa Blanca is a museum of island life, depicting the early colonial days. Open daily 9 a.m. to noon and 1 p.m. to 4 p.m.; 809/724-4102.

9) Plazuela de la Rogativa: This statue of a bishop followed by three women holding torches refers to the 1797 British siege of Old San Juan. As legend goes, the British had second thoughts about attacking at night because they saw many torches moving along the wall. The British believed San Juan was being reinforced. Instead, it was a religious procession (rogativa) of women carrying torches and singing as they followed their bishop.

10) La Fortaleza: Overlooking San Juan Bay from the top of the city walls, this governor's mansion was initially built as a fortress in 1532 against the fierce Carib Indians. The oldest executive mansion still in use in the Western Hemisphere, it is open to guided tours Monday-Friday 9 a.m. to 4 p.m. Tours in English on the hour, in Spanish on the half hour. It is a working government office, so proper attire is required; 809/721-7000, ext. 2211.

11) San Juan Gate: The large wooden gate at the base of La Fortaleza was part of the city's extensive defense system. Upon arrival here, important dignitaries were escorted to San Juan Cathedral to celebrate a mass in thanks for a successful voyage.

12) San Juan Cathedral: Begun in 1521 as a thatch-roofed structure, this magnificent Spanish colonial church is topped with three red and white cupolas. It is a rare and authentic example of medieval architecture in the Americas. The body of Ponce de Leon was moved from San Jose Church to a marble tomb here in 1913. Restoration of the entire church was completed in 1977.

13) La Princesa Jail: Dating to 1837, this distinctive gray and white building is now the home of the Puerto Rico Tourism Company. It probably never looked this good when used as a lock-up.

14) Plaza de Armas: In the heart of the old city, this was the military parade ground, now an open piazza with fountains. The Alcaldia (City Hall) with two layers of arches is a copy of the City Hall in Madrid.

15) Main Shopping District: Conveniently located near the cruise

Old San Juan

ATLANTIC OCEAN

Fort
El Morro

To El Morro

SAN JUAN BAY

Fort San Cristobal

Avenida Munoz Rivera

Avenida Ponce de Leon

Paseo de la Covadonga

Calle Comercio

Calle Marina

Tourism Pier 3

Catano
Ferry
Terminal

Tourism Pier 1

Calle O'Donnel

Calle Norzagaray

Calle Sol

Calle Luna

Calle San Francisco

Calle Fortaleza

Calle Tetuan

Parking
Building

Calle Tanca

Post
Office

Calle Recinto Sur

Tourist
Information
Center

Calle San Justo

Calle Luna

Calle Sol

Calle Cruz

Calle San Jose

Calle San Sebastian

Calle Cristo

Calle Fortaleza

Calle Tetuan

Paseo de la Princesa

La Puntilla

Calle Cristo

Caleta San Francisco

Calle San Juan

Caleta las Monjas

Calle Recinto Oeste

Calle Norzagaray

1. El Morro
2. San Juan Cemetery
3. City Wall · · · · · · · ·
4. San Juan Museum
of Art & History
5. Plaza de San Jose
6. Pablo Casals Museum
7. San Jose Church
8. Casa Blanca
9. Plazuela de la Rogativa
10. La Fortaleza
11. San Juan Gate
12. San Juan Cathedral
13. La Princesa Jail
14. Main Shopping Area
15. Plaza de Colon
16. Tapia Theater
17. El Castillo de San Cristobal
18. The Casino
19. The Capitol

ship docks, these streets are where most of the major shops await your credit card.

16) Plaza Colon: Named in honor of Christopher Columbus on the 400th anniversary of his discovery of Puerto Rico, bronze tablets at the foot of the Columbus statue record events of the explorer's life. The plaza was restored not long ago to further dramatize the statue. Some nice open-air cafes border the north side.

17) Tapia Theater: Where theater, dance and other cultural activities are held. Construction on this theater began in 1832 and continued until the last quarter of the 19th century. It was financed by taxes on bread and imported liquor and by subscription.

18) El Castillo de San Cristobal: Another huge fort, rising 150 feet above the sea and covering twenty-seven acres, San Cristobal is located just above the Plaza Colon. It was built in 1771 to defend the city from inland attacks after successful invaders like the Earl of Cumberland made such a mess back in 1598. A rather belated response to the problem, San Cristobal is considered a strategic masterpiece. Attackers could storm the main fortress only after taking five structures connected by tunnels and a dry moat. Operated by the National Park Service, hours are from 9 a.m. to 6 p.m.; 809/729-6536.

19) The Casino: Looking like a French mansion of the Louis XIV style and now used by the State Department, in 1917 the building was opened as an aristocratic social club. The Casino's proper name is the Manuel Pavla Fernandez Government Reception Center. Open Monday-Friday, 8 a.m. to 4 p.m.; 809/724-5985.

20) The Capitol: Just to the east of the old city, this white-pillared building is the seat of the Puerto Rican legislature. Elaborate dome friezes depict island history. Open Monday-Friday, 8:30 a.m. to 5 p.m.; call 809/721-7305 to arrange a guided tour by appointment.

The Caribbean National Forest (El Yunque)

Some of the Caribbean's lushest terrain, Puerto Rico's prime woodlands are protected through a system of forest reserves, many established by the Spanish government as far back as 1876. These are among the oldest forest reserves in the Western Hemisphere.

The most popular and most-visited place outside of San Juan is the 28,000-acre Caribbean National Forest, forty km southeast and a forty-five minute drive from San Juan. Better known simply as El Yunque, the nickname comes from the good Indian spirit Yuquiyu who ruled from the mighty forest peaks to protect the Taino Indians, the island's original inhabitants. El Yunque is both the smallest and the only tropical forest in

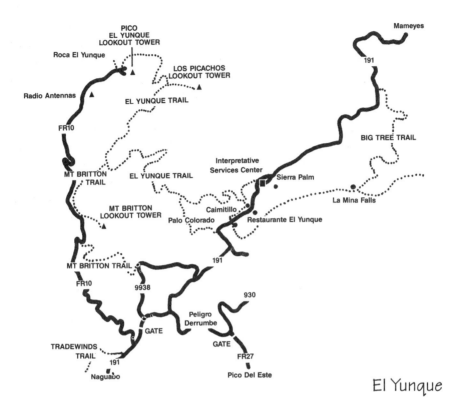

El Yunque

the U.S. National Forest System. In its highest and most inaccessible altitudes, the virgin forest remains much as it was 500 years ago. This is rare, because over the centuries Puerto Rico has been subject to such intensive agricultural development that only 1% of the land is considered virgin.

The higher peaks annually receive as much as 240 inches, while lower slopes are deluged with 200 inches of precipitation each year. The Forest Service has figured that all this rain amounts to almost 100 billion gallons of water every twelve months. Understandably, there is a serious erosion and trail maintenance problem in El Yunque.

Severely damaged by Hurricane Hugo, El Yunque is recovering faster than most experts predicted. Hugo toppled some trees and stripped all vegetation of its leaves so that the landscape resembled the dead of winter. Not only is the forest returning to normal, new panoramic vistas have opened which were previously blocked by a dense mantle of thick green vegetation. Eventually, these lookout points will be obscured by the new growth regenerating quickly in this warm, moist climate.

You won't have much problem walking the different trails; most are surfaced with asphalt or concrete. In fact, you may be disappointed at how hard-surfaced the forest pathways are. There are two reasons for this. One is to combat erosion. Some sections of forest sidewalk have to be repaired and replaced almost every year because of the torrential runoffs. The second reason for the hard-surfaced paths is wonderfully unique, even for the Caribbean. As one Puerto Rican tourism official explained to me, "We don't like to walk. We are a 'car' people and we like to drive everywhere. The idea of walking through the forest on dirt paths where you might get your shoes dirty does not truly appeal to a lot of us."

And so a mini-road system (the width of a typical bicycle path) travels through the El Yunque wilderness to make the forest as accessible and as alluring as the Puerto Rican culture will allow. With this kind of cultural perspective, it should be no surprise that at present there isn't a single company specializing in hiking or wilderness guide service.

Animals

El Yunque's best known and most vocal inhabitants are its millions of tiny tree frogs. Known as coquis because of their "co-kee" call, they sing loudest when it rains. Despite how often that occurs, the frogs seem to become deliriously happy with each new sprinkle. If you want to hear the coquis sing, expect to get wet; you probably will, anyway, at some point during the day. The coquis of El Yunque are only about an inch in length and vary in color from gray-brown to green-yellow.

Although the coqui name applies to all thirteen species of tree frogs in El Yunque, only two, the Forest and Common Coqui actually produce the famous "co-kee" sound. Each of the other species has its own distinct call; some sound like "bob white" quail.

The Puerto Rican parrot can also be heard squawking, but won't be seen often. In 1968, the wild parrot population in El Yunque was estimated at only twenty-seven birds, barely a surviving population. Currently making a comeback, their numbers are still small. You can identify the parrots, largely green in color, by the brilliant blue of their wings, visible when in flight. Twelve inches in size, they have a vivid red forehead which you're most likely to see only at close range. Although the Puerto Rican parrot is the most famous, fifty other bird species are found in the Caribbean National Forest.

You may see a fair number of lizards and crabs, but snakes are rare. None of them are poisonous. The largest is the Puerto Rican boa (harmless to adults) which grows to a length of more than seven feet.

The Forests

The Rain (Tabonuco) Forest: More than 240 different species of trees, epiphytes, giant ferns, mosses and vines populate El Yunque; twenty-six of these are found nowhere else in the world. The most visually spectacular sections are not up high but on the slopes below 2,000 feet, the section considered true rain forest (also called the tabonuco forest).

Ironically, all this diversity causes some visitors to leave El Yunque frustrated and disappointed. As forestry technician Robert Rijos explained, "You can go to Sequoia National Forest and walk for miles and see the same tree and basically the same setting. The uniqueness in El Yunque is its diversity, that so many different species can share the same habitat. But the scenery may seem to lack any organization — it looks more like a jungle than a forest. Some people leave disappointed, unimpressed, because they came expecting to see only one or two different kinds of trees. Instead, they find all this."

Instead of disappointment, many first-time visitors probably feel overwhelmed. If you don't have a guide or a guidebook to explain what you are viewing, El Yunque is not only dazzling, it is incomprehensible. Advance reading is mandatory unless you have a personal guide. Get all the information available at the Sierra Palm interpretive center before exploring. Otherwise, everything may blur into a maze of meaningless, moist, emerald objects.

Palo Colorado Forest: This forest type ranges from 1,9870-2,950 feet in valleys and mountains. The palo colorado (Cyrilla racemiflora), a crooked, reddish-colored tree, dominates this zone. This is the region where the endangered Puerto Rican parrot nests, using openings in the palo colorado trunk made by other animals.

Sierra Palm Forest: The sierra palm forest is found at the highest points in the mountains of Luquilla and in ravines over 968 feet above sea level. This is the most open of the four forest systems. Compared to the tremendous diversity of the rain forest, the palm forest is unique, a kind of monoculture consisting only of the sierra palm (Presstoea montana). Sierra palms have white flower spikes and erect prop roots. Its fruit is the main food source for the rare Puerto Rican parrot.

The Dwarf (Elfin) Forest: Of El Yunque's four distinct forest zones, the smallest (only 3%) is the stunted and twisted vegetation of the dwarf forest. It grows only on the highest peaks and mountain ridges. Although referred to as dwarf forest in Puerto Rico, this same zone is also known on other islands as "elfin woodland" or "cloud forest."

The weather is often harsh, and evolution has created a vascular flora that is almost 40% endemic to Puerto Rico, found nowhere else in the world. As in most dwarf forests, animals are scarce. Amphibians include mainly tree frogs like the common coqui, the burrow coqui, the tree-hole coqui and the warty coqui. Reptiles are limited to anoles, including the Puerto Rican giant anole. Only fourteen different bird species have ever been sighted in the dwarf forest. The Elfin Woods Warbler was unknown to science until its discovery here in 1971.

El Yunque Fast Facts

Getting There: Reach El Yunque from San Juan by Route 3, connecting with Route 191, which leads directly into and through the forest.

Safety Warning: Keep cars locked. Do not carry valuables. Women should not hike alone. Some residents consider this a high crime area.

Rain: The most concentrated rains fall in June, August, September and October. July tends to be drier, but no guarantees. Summer and early fall are when one tropical wave after another brings humidity and rain to the forest.

Temperature & Clothing: El Yunque is much cooler than the coastal areas. The Forest Service gauges the temperature range according to altitude.

If it is 80-85° on the beaches, it may be:
> 75° @ 500-1800 ft.
> 70° @ 1,800-2,400 ft.
> 65° @ 2,400-3,000 ft.
> 60° @ 3,000 ft.

Since it does get remarkably cool at higher elevations, bring a water-proof jacket with hood and a sweater for the wind. Good hiking shoes are essential; none of the trails should be attempted barefooted.

Hiking Trails of El Yunque

Unless otherwise indicated, all trails begin on Route 191, which winds through much of the forest. Distances in Puerto Rico are measured in both miles and kilometers: 1 km equals .6 of a mile.

 **1. Big Tree Trail**

Length: Less than 1 mile. **Time:** 25 minutes each way. **Difficulty:** 1-2.

Beginning at kilometer mark 10.4, Big Tree Trail is probably El Yunque's most popular walk. It is the best walk through the tabonuco or true rain forest, offering more diversity in one small area than perhaps anywhere else. You can try counting and distinguishing the 160 different tree species here, not counting ferns and vines (good luck!). This short walk also goes to La Mina falls.

One distinctive species of the rain forest is the candle tree. The smooth gray bark oozes a pungent white resin (smells similar to pine pitch) that can be used to start fires. Even more remarkable is the laurel sabino which grows nowhere else in the world except in the Caribbean National Forest. The laurel sabino is draped with a dense community of vines and airplants that use the tree for support. They do not cause it any harm.

With luck, you may see some of El Yunque's eight different lizard species, most of whom live in the rain forest zone. Each type has adapted to its particular niche so that none compete. For instance, some species live on the ground, others in trees; one in the sun, another in the shade...a good example of peaceful coexistence.

Don't expect to see the usual, forest-type creatures in this or any other rain forest. They would need to float to survive here.

2. La Mina (The Mine) Trail

Length: about 1 mile to the mine beyond La Mina Falls **Time:** 1 hour each way. **Difficulty:** 2.

An extension of The Big Tree Trail opened in 1992, it picks up at La Mina Falls. It leads through the rain forest to another waterfall three to four times as large. It also goes to a mine where the Spanish discovered and took a considerable amount of gold. Visitors may enter the mine tunnel, a seven to eight foot-wide opening, high enough to stand. The tunnel extends forty feet back, then is cut off by a landslide.

3.-4.-5. El Yunque/Bano de Oro/ Mt. Britton Trails

Length: 4.7 km to El Yunque Peak and 3.3 km to Mt. Britton. **Time:** 2-1/2 to 3 hours, round trip to El Yunque Peak. **Difficulty:** 2, some mild ascending. Note: At the higher levels the asphalt trail turns to gravel.

Beginning at the Palo Colorado Visitor Center, this asphalt trail eventually leads to El Yunque Peak, 3,496 feet high. It also connects with several other trails and branches to the Caimitillo picnic area. All the trails separate and leave from the main El Yunque Trail; a sign clearly marks each turnoff, so it's almost impossible to get lost.

At the beginning is the Palo Colorado Stream. You can detour left up to the old concrete swimming pool at the end of the 1/2-mile long Baño de Oro Trail.

Back on the main El Yunque Trail, after just a few hundred yards, another branch leaves to the right. It leads to the Caimitillo Picnic Area and the short walking trail there. The trail to follow (unless you're hungry for a picnic) goes left. This is the main El Yunque Trail and the one from which all the other major trails eventually branch off.

Palo colorado, or red trees, dominate this lower level. You'll also see giant ferns, bamboo, moss and large vines. In the wild, the parrots use palo colorado trees for nesting, so watch for parrot's nests, one of the few opportunities to see the rare Puerto Rican parrot. You're most likely to spot one near dawn or dusk. In this vicinity, you'll see artificial woodpecker nests: man-made wooden boxes.

In several places you'll begin to appreciate the massive problem of erosion the Forest Service personnel face here because of the tremendous runoff. In some spots, the asphalt trail is actually eight inches below ground level. That's how much the surrounding land has slowly built up. When rain pours down the pathway, it flows like a stream. The Forest Service employs about ten people to continually cut back and dig out the trails. In addition, another fifteen elderly people help with the maintenance, serving as senior citizen volunteers.

On the trail, you'll pass beautiful beds of pink-blossomed impatiens. They grow wild here and bloom all year. This trail leads to both the sierra palm forest and the dwarf forest, where the contorted trees are completely enshrouded by mosses, bromeliads and leafy liverworts. To give you an idea of how wet this region is, the trunk epiphytes here hold so much moisture that the animals living in these pools are found elsewhere in the forest only in ponds and streams.

You can't help but note the unusual shape of the Mt. Britton observation tower. Resembling a castle turret, you almost expect to see Robin Hood or the Sheriff of Nottingham. Actually, this is one of the Conservation Corps projects dating back to the 1930s. There's a similar observation tower on Route 191—both offer a fine overview.

 6. Los Picachos Trail

Length: 3.5 miles. **Time:** 1-1/2 hours each way. **Difficulty:** 3.

This is the longest route to El Yunque Peak. Initially, you'll see the many redwood-type trees called palo colorado, which grow seventy to seventy-five feet tall. One palo colorado in the forest has a girth of seventeen feet; it's believed to be at least 2,000 years old. This approach to El Yunque Peak uses many switchbacks. Once you're at the top, you'll find some steep steps cut into a rock. They take about five minutes to climb. There, on the highest part of the pyramid-shaped peak, you should be able to see much of the coast.

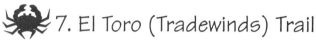 7. El Toro (Tradewinds) Trail

Length: Approx. 6 miles one-way. **Time:** 4 hours, round trip. **Difficulty:** 2-3.

This is El Yunque's longest and probably most difficult walk. You will pass through all four different forest systems to reach Pico El Toro at 3,523 feet, the highest point in the forest. This is the only maintained trail without gravel or hard surface. The soil is too unstable. In the rainy season, this route can be quite muddy. The marked path begins on Route 191 just beyond the El Yunque trail. It comes out on Route 185, where you might be able to arrange for a ride back.

The State Forest Reserves

In addition to El Yunque, Puerto Rico has a variety of state forest preserves, each quite different. Also called commonwealth forest reserves, they are coordinated by the Natural Resources Department, P.O. Box 5887, San Juan, PR 00906; 809/722-1726. The normal office hours are from 8 a.m. to 4:30 p.m.

Pinones Forest

Directly east of and very close to San Juan, Pinones Forest contains Puerto Rico's largest mangrove forest as well as a rich variety of animal species which have adapted to living in an ever-increasing urban environment. Because it is so close to San Juan, Pinones Forest is heavily visited, used for snorkeling, fishing and skiing as well as nature walks. Several small restaurants are located in the vicinity. Take Route 187 from Isla Verde to Boca de Cangrejos to Pinones Road. For a guided tour of selected regions of this forest, contact La Lanmcha Paseadora; 809/791-0755.

The mangroves, which make up 70% of the forest, include all four species: red, white, black and button. Pinones is home to about forty-six species of birds, including various seagulls and pelicans. This reserve is one of the few remaining regions in Puerto Rico where gulls still nest regularly. Lakes Torrecilla and Pinones contain thirty-eight different species of fish. Ghost crabs and lizards live in the sand dunes.

Guanica Forest

West of the town of Ponce and the site where American troops first landed in Puerto Rico in 1898, this dry forest is one of the most important of the state reserves. Guanica Forest houses the largest number of bird species found anywhere on the island: at least 40 of the 111 resident species (including fourteen endemic and nine endangered), as well as numerous migratory visitors, can be located here.

Because it has been altered so little by human development, Guanica has the distinction of being the best preserved subtropical forest anywhere in the world. It contains a great diversity of organisms and specimens unique to this one spot, including 700 tree and plant species. Like El Yunque, it has been recognized by UNESCO as an International Biosphere Reserve.

Guanica Forest is located on the southeast coast a short distance from the town of Guanica. Route 334 goes into the heart of the forest, while route 333 goes along the southern coastal edge. Camping is permitted. Ranger stations are found along both roads.

The Bay of Guanica is one of the sunniest (temps can reach to 100°), driest regions of Puerto Rico with annual rainfall of only thirty inches. It is rocky and hilly, except on the western part. In addition to trails, the forest is explored by walking the dirt roads which are closed to traffic.

Of the 246 trees and bushes that grow in Guanica, about 48 are endangered species and 16 are endemic to this region only. Deciduous trees comprise as much as 61% of the forest, evergreens another 18.6%.

Guajataca Forest Reserve

Located between Arecibo and Aquadilla and bisected by Route 446, Guajataca is situated in what's known as karst country. This is characterized by haystack-shaped hills and crater sinkholes, terrain that resembles an upside down egg carton. This is the kind of classic, mystical Chinese landscape found around Guilin that Oriental artists have painted for centuries.

Karst is the result of millions of years of rain pounding on and dissolving the porous limestone base. The rain water flows along cracks underground, widening and deepening the cracks until they become underground caverns or stream channels. If water eats away enough ground close to the surface, the soil collapses, creating a sinkhole—one of the main features of karst country.

Guajataca Forest has twenty-five miles of well-maintained hiking trails for exploring this unusual countryside. Ask at the ranger station for a map. One trail leads to an observation tower, another goes around a large depression framed by the haystack hills. Like most karst terrain, there is little ground water here. More than a dozen man-made reservoirs make up the reserve.

The Rio Abajo Forest Reserve

South of the Arecibo river valley on Route 621, off Route 10 near Utuado, this forest is part of a management program that has produced plantations of balsa, teak and mahogany, all native species, as well as imports such as bamboo and Australian pines. You'll also find a wide variety of natural formations: caves, lakes and more spectacular views of karst country.

Hiking is possible on some of the old lumber roads and foot paths. A mantle of vegetation conceals many of the terrain's karst features. Consequently, some people do not find the typical karst characteristics as starkly apparent as at other sites.

Carite Forest Reserve

This 6,000-acre forest is easily accessible off the Ponce Expressway near Cayey. Bordering a lake with the same name, the Carite Reserve has a camping area shaded by eucalyptus and royal palms, a marked contrast to the sierra palms, which seem to outnumber all other species. This is another excellent birdwatching reserve: almost fifty varieties, including the Puerto Rican bullfinch and Puerto Rican tanager, both endemic species, and hummingbirds.

The main hiking trail, less than a mile in length, leads from the Charco Azul picnic site. It first passes a natural swimming hole about ten yards across: the Charco Azul, which is remarkably blue. The path crisscrosses a stream which you must ford repeatedly. Eventually you climb to Cerroa la Santa, the reserve's highest peak, at 2,730 feet.

Mt. Gilarte

Just off the Panoramic Route and near several coffee plantations, this 3,600-acre forest reserve offers what may be the most scenic hike in the Cordillera Central. Camping is also available but, as usual, check with the ranger first for permission. Also ask the ranger to point out the beginning of the hike to Mt. Guilarte, which is near the intersections of Routes 131 and 518. The trailhead is unmarked. It's usually a slick, steep, forty-minute climb to the peak that passes through rain forest, sierra palms and beautiful beds of pink impatiens, similar to El Yunque. Once at the summit, you have no radio or TV towers to violate the view, as occurs at the tops of El Yunque and Cerro de Punta.

Maricao Forest Reserve

On the western slopes of the Cordillera Central near Mayaguez, the Maricao Forest Reserve hosts many bird species, particularly hawks, year-round. This is one of the best places for camping: two campsites and an attractive complex of cabins with swimming pool. Nearby is the Parador Hacienda Juanita, one of the chain of country inns operated by the Puerto Rico Tourism Company.

Maricao is home to more diverse tree species than any other reserve: 278 in all, of which 37 are endemic to this particular reserve and another 133 are native only to Puerto Rico. Bird life is almost as prolific, with 44 species that include the Puerto Rican lizard-cuckoo, the Puerto Rican woodpecker, the sharp-shinned hawk and even the rare elfin woods warbler.

Although the vegetation is more like that of karst country than the rain forest, this region receives a lot of rain. However, the soil is of submarine volcanic origin, best suited to supporting dry-weather vegetation. The unusual soil condition also accounts for the tremendous plant diversity.

The walking/sightseeing here can be exceptional, if the weather cooperates. The sign leading to Casa de Piedra, a stone mountain house, goes to a campsite with a fine view of the west coast. A stone observation tower at the reserve's highest peak, the 2,625-foot high Las Teta de Cerro Gordo, provides an excellent panorama of three coasts and distant Mona Island, fifty miles out to sea.

Toro Negro Forest Reserve

Straddling the Cordillera Central, this 7,000-acre reserve includes Puerto Rico's highest peak (4,390-foot high Cerro de Punta) and highest lake (bamboo-fringed Guineo Reservoir). When not cloud covered and rainy, the views of the Atlantic and Caribbean coasts can be stunning. Unfortunately, you have to ignore the communications antennas sharing the top with you to appreciate it all. This is a region known for its unkind weather: the lowest temperature ever recorded on the island was here: 40° F.

Route 143 and Route 149 effectively divide Toro Negro into its eastern and western sections. Off Route 143 on the north side is a short but extremely steep road of several hundred yards that leads to the highest peak in Puerto Rico, the 4,390-foot Cerro de Punta. Although the road is paved, you may want to make the twenty-minute walk up.

If you really want to struggle to rise to the mountain top, you can make a three-hour hike from Parador Hacienda Gripinas (809/828-1717) in the town of Jayuya, off Route 527. You'll be going up the hillsides of old coffee plantations, following paved road, tire track paths and eroded trails.

Aquirre Forest Reserve

Descending from the highlands to the south coast near Salinas, the reserve is adjacent to the Jobos Bay National Marine Estuarine Sanctuary. Camping is permitted if you decide to stay overnight to view the unique plant and marine life.

Out On the Island

To Puerto Ricans, the term "out on the island" (en la isla) means anywhere beyond the San Juan metropolitan area. Certainly El Yunque and the state forests qualify for such a designation, and so do these other places also worth exploring on foot:

Around Ponce

The Ponce Expressway, a modern highway running north to south, links San Juan with Puerto Rico's second largest city, Ponce (pronounced "Pon-tse"). The heart of Ponce is the old plaza central, Plaza las Delicias ("Plaza of Delights"). On one side, benches, pruned India-laurel fig trees and statues surround the Cathedral of Our Lady of Guadeloupe, a 17th-century Spanish creole church topped with rounded silver towers.

The Casa Armstrong Poventud, a restored early 20th century neoclassic mansion, faces the plaza and now serves as both a city museum and tourist information center. Ponce's most famous sight is its fire station, the Parque de Bombas, a red and black building built in 1883 for an architectural fair.

All the streets leading into the Plaza are under restoration, including installation of replicas of the original gas lamps. Isabel Street is an example of how it will look. On Las Americas Avenue, across from Catholic University, is the Ponce Museum of Art containing more than 1,000 paintings (painters include Rubens and Gainsborough) and 400 sculptures. It is the best European art collection in the Caribbean. The building itself is something of an artwork, designed by Edward Durrell Stone, architect of New York's Modern Museum of Art. Open weekdays only 10 a.m. to noon and 1 p.m. to 4 p.m.; 809/840-0505.

On weekends a ferry leaves the Ponce pier for a one-hour boat ride to Caja de Muertos, the only regularly scheduled guided walks on any of the offshore islands. It's mostly arid vegetation such as aloe and century plants and scrub forest. The one-mile long island is rocky and the walking tough with little sun protection anywhere. Go prepared.

A ten-minute drive on Route 503 from Ponce brings you to a recreated Taino Indian village and a museum at the Tibes Indian Ceremonial Center

(809/844-5575 or 840-2255, open 9 a.m. to 4:30 p.m. except Monday). An Amerindian site discovered in 1974, it is the oldest burial ground yet uncovered in the Antilles. An audio-visual program in English describes the discoveries, which included 187 skeletons of the Igneri culture (300 A.D.) A museum houses axe-heads, ceramic pots and ceremonial idols. Seven ceremonial ball courts and two dance grounds date from 700 A.D. One may also be a pre-Columbian astronomical observatory. Stone points on one of the dance courts (which happens to be shaped like a rising sun) are said to line up with the sun during equinoxes and solstices.

La Parguera Phosphorescent Bay

About forty-five minutes west of Ponce, near the Guanica Forest Reserve, is the sleepy fishing village of La Parguera. Phosphorescent Bay glows with the millions of microscopic organisms known as dinoflagellates that sparkle when disturbed. This phenomenon occurs only in the tropics, typically in mangrove-protected bays like this one. The best time to watch the ocean light up is a moonless night. Boats can be rented or you can take the nightly one-hour boat trip that begins at 7:30 p.m. and continues until there is no more demand. This is the best of the many different phosphorescent bays on the Puerto Rican mainland. (The best of all, however, is probably on the offshore island of Vieques.) You can stay here overnight at Parador Villa Parguera; 809/899-3975. If this parador is full, check on the several others in the vicinity. This is one time you might hope for rain. Then, the whole bay will light up, spectacularly glowing green, pink and blue as the raindrops stir the water.

San German

The second oldest town in Puerto Rico, San German retains its distinctive colonial flavor with closely-spaced old white homes, narrow balconies and old-fashioned gas street lamps. You'll find two main plazas, each dominated by an architecturally important church. Off Calle Doctor Veve is the Porta Coeli Church, primarily a religious art museum, which was built in 1606, a rare example of Spanish medieval architecture still surviving in the Caribbean. More ornate and at the other end of the plaza is the newer (19th century) San German de Auxerre Church. You might want to stay in the heart of San German in a converted 200-year-old family mansion. It is now the thirty-four-room Parador Oasis with its own pool, restaurant and weekend entertainment; 809/721-2884 or 892-1175.

Rio Camuy Cave Park

One of Puerto Rico's best-kept secrets is its extensive cave system, considered some of the most important in the Western Hemisphere. The Rio

Camuy is the world's third-largest subterranean river. Yet it and the caves are relatively unknown because most visitors never venture into the countryside to discover them.

More than 220 caves have been discovered so far in Puerto Rico's karst country. Some are great, huge systems of passageways; others are only small openings in the earth. The biggest, best and most easily accessible system is The Rio Camuy Cave Park, near Lares on Route 129. Operated by the Administracion de Terrenos (809/893-3100) and open Wednesday to Sunday from 8 a.m. to 4 p.m., the extensive system of passageways has been mapped for seven miles, though all of it is not open to the public. The current capacity is 1,500 visitors per day.

After taking a bilingual tram tour down the mouth of a vegetation-filled sinkhole to the mouth of Clara Cave, you are guided past huge stalactites and stalagmites and into caves as much as 200 feet high (you can fit a twenty-story building into this particular chamber). A side trip is also available to the 650-foot-wide Tres Pueblos sinkhole which overlooks the Rio Camuy 400 feet below, seething through during flood periods.

If this park is closed, the smaller and privately run Cueva de Camuy is nearby.

Humacao Wildlife Reserve

Located in the southeast section of Puerto Rico, you reach this humid and subtropical reserve via Route 3 at km 74.3 in the area of Santa Teresa. Including wetlands and lowlands, this estuarine system (mix of fresh and salt water) is ranked as one of the most productive in the world because of its rich commercial fish population. It receives eighty-eight inches of rain annually, mostly from May to December.

Camping is permitted at El Morrillo, though the facilities are primitive. A permit is needed from the refuge office. It may be obtained only during normal hours (7:30 a.m. to 3:30 p.m.) so officials can orient you to the facilities; phone 809/852-6088.

About ninety species of both resident and migratory species live in the Humacao preserve, including ducks and gulls. The beach is a vital nesting place for two sea turtle species.

Caguanda Indian Ceremonial Park

These 800-year-old stone playing fields located eight miles west of Utuado were built by the Tainos for ballgames and religious ceremonies. Covering thirteen acres, it is a landscaped and shaded site with native trees including royal palms and guava. Each of the ball courts was named for a different Taino chief, and several are bordered with stone monoliths, some decorated with petroglyphs. The Institute of Puerto Rican Culture operates the small museum open daily 8:30 a.m. to 4:30 p.m.; 809/894-7325. Free admission.

Around Mayaguez

This industrialized port city is Puerto Rico's third largest. The traditional plaza contains a stone walk, benches, bronze figures and a statue of Columbus. The Tropical Agricultural Research Station attached to the University of Puerto Rico grows plants from all over the world. Cinnamon, citrus and clove (smell the leaves!) are but some of the items neatly set out. On Route 65 north of the town, the Research Station is open weekdays from 7:30 a.m. to 4:30 p.m.; 809/834-2435. No charge.

The Panoramic Route

This country road connects Mayaguez in the west with the town of Yabucoa in the southwest via Puerto Rico's mountainous backbone, the Cordillera Central. The vistas are spectacular. Although this network of roads extends for only 165 miles, it takes at least two-three days by car to cover this territory in a leisurely manner. One of the finest sights is the San Cristobal Canyon, a river ravine as much as 500 feet deep that is filled with tropical plants. However, there is a much better way to enjoy the Panoramic Route and see the real Puerto Rico:

The Annual Panoramic Hike: Walk the Entire Length of Puerto Rico in Fourteen Days. Every spring the Fondo de Mejoramiento sponsors a fourteen-day hike the full length of Puerto Rico, from Yabucoa in the southeast to Mayaguez in the west. Most people see the Panoramic Route only from behind a car windshield, staying on edge because of the series of spine-tingling, hair-pin turns and the confusing lack of signs. Instead, relax and walk it—all 165 miles/238.3 km of it.

The panoramic hike explores a different Puerto Rico every day. The richness of the country is evident as you walk through a knotted, twisting network of more than forty roads that extend the full length of the Cordillera Central. The route includes not only tropical beauty but some strenuous climbing as well; these are some of the steepest parts of the island.

This two-week hike is unique not only in all the Caribbean but anywhere, in that you can hike as many or as few days as you like: for just one day or all fourteen. If it turns out not to your liking—or if it's better than you imagined—you can adjust your plans accordingly. The number of hikers varies from day to day, from 200 or so on a weekend to a few dozen during the week. All the hiking is done on the roadside of the twisted, winding Panoramic Route, none in the woods.

Normally, the interior would not be the safest place for individual hikers, but the annual hiking group is accompanied by a police escort, a civil defense wagon to supply water and a "broom bus" to pick up those who lag too far behind. The broom bus is easily identifiable—by a broom sticking out the front. Should first aid be needed, it is available in one of the small mountain towns.

The hike includes forests and farmland (coffee, bananas, citrus, vegetables). Four of the state forest reserves also cross the route. Expense is minimal, determined by each individual hiker. For the first several nights, hikers are close enough to return to San Juan in the evening; or you can stay in small hotels in the back country. The countryside hotels run about $30-$40 per person for a double and include breakfast. Lunch and dinner are an individual expense. The cost to participate on the hike itself: $5 per day or $50 for all fourteen days, one of the best bargains anywhere.

Besides lodging, the only other cost is transportation. If you're going back and forth to San Juan, that could run as much as $25 per day per person on the special bus run exclusively for the hikers. If you have your own car and overnight in the mountains, there is a $3 per day charge to bus you back to your car left at the last end point.

Everyone starts the hike at the same time, and a day's walking covers an average of 17 km. The sponsors stress that this is a recreational walk, not a competitive one; no one is in any rush to get there first. You'll find all types of people, mostly locals, from retired persons to those who took the day off from work just to make this walk.

On most trails you will find small cafes typical of the back country of Puerto Rico, where you can get something to eat or take out food. Or bring your own provisions, if you wish. Trash bags are provided.

The hike is usually held from the end of March through the beginning of April. For complete information, contact Fondo de Mejoramiento, Apdo. 4746, Correo Central, San Juan, PR, 00936; 809/759-8366. There is no better way to see Puerto Rico or meet its people.

Offshore Islands

Culebra

Located only seventeen miles off the east coast of Puerto Rico, Culebra is seven miles long and three and a half miles wide, covering an area of about 7,700 acres. It has some gorgeous white sand beaches. The population of about 2,000 took on the entire U.S. Navy to retain their island. For forty years, the U.S. Navy used Culebra as a gunnery range day and night. Getting sick and tired of the noise (and probably grouchy from lack of sleep) the Culebrans finally protested by holding picnics in the target areas and exploding a few fireworks of their own (petrol bombs). In 1975, when the Navy stopped making all its racket, Culebra again became a sleepy fishing village where not much happens. However, there is some excellent wildlife viewing here, both above and below the waterline.

The most popular regions are Flamenco, Tamarindo, Resaca and Larga beaches. Culebra also has a phosphorescent bay, and coral gardens border much of its shoreline, ideal for snorkeling. You can camp at Flamenco Beach, with its own picnic and sanitary facilities. Camping is US $4. A portable refrigerator (this is tropical luxury!) is US $2. You need a camping permit from the Conservation and Development Authority of Culebra; phone 809/742-3880 or 742-3525.

Culebra also has several small hotels including the La Hamace, one of the paradors; 809/742-3516. You can buy all your foodstuffs on island. Regular ferry service is provided from Fajardo for only about US $5. The trip takes about two hours. It's also possible to ferry a vehicle over for about $35 but that requires a three-week advance reservation. Air service from San Juan is about $40 roundtrip on Flamenco Airways; 809/725-7707 or 724-7110. Transportation (except on foot) is limited.

You'll find a tremendous variety of bird and marine life. The Culebra National Wildlife Refuge includes four land tracts on the island and twenty-three offshore islands. Known for its large nesting seabird population that includes terns and boobies, the refuge was established in 1909 by President Theodore Roosevelt. Besides four-foot-long iguanas, you'll find about 372 plant varieties, thirty-three of which are rare and three which are endemic to this island. Perhaps the most interesting aspect of Culebra is the sea turtle nesting. Four species come here to nest on the beaches at night between April and July. You can get a guide or go on your own. Finding a sea turtle laying eggs is a very hit-or-miss proposition; you may have to stay up all night.

Vieques

Pronounced "Byekess," Vieques is seven miles off the coast and twenty miles southeast from Fajardo, the closest ferry. Vieques has some of Puerto Rico's best beaches. It is twenty-five miles long by five miles wide and two-thirds of the island still belongs to the U.S. Navy which practices here (the 1983 Grenada invasion was dress-rehearsed on these beaches). When not playing war games, the Navy does open the beaches to the public. Mosquito Bay is a phosphorescent bay considered more spectacular than Parguera on the mainland. Don't come looking for the liquid flames: you have to create them yourself by paddling around in the water and stirring up the creatures responsible for the amazing phenomenon. If possible, use a mask to absorb the full splendor of the green and gold fires.

You can stay at the Parador Casa del Francis (809/741-3751) or Parador Villa Esperanza (809/741-8675).

Mona

Shaped like an oval sapphire (but a huge one, twenty-five miles long), Mona is fifty miles offshore and completely deserted. The only way to reach it is by plane or by boat from Mayaguez. The Mona Passage is often rough, so choose your boat from Mayaguez carefully. The island is administered by the Department of Natural Resources (809/722-1726 for the mainland office) as a reserve. They can tell you about the camping area at Playa Sardinera on the west coast and the few cabins they have to rent. You must bring all supplies, including water. With cliffs that tower 200 feet high topped with dry forest, inland caves containing stalactites and stalagmites and four-foot-long iguanas, this island offers the romance of the unexplored. However, the Taino Indians visited here, as did pirates, and for a time the caves were mined for bat guano. Domestic animals also were once raised here. Their feral descendants, including wild hogs, roam free.

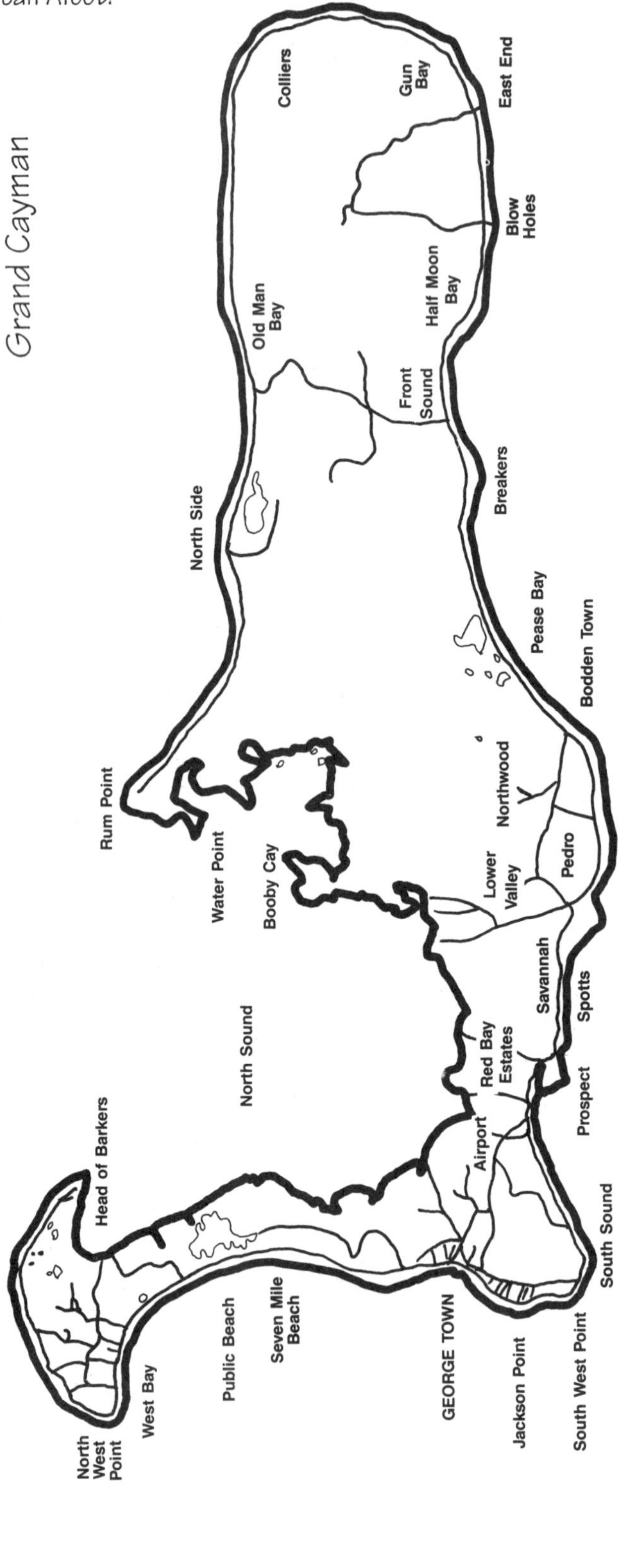

Grand Cayman

North West Point

West Bay

Head of Barkers

Public Beach

North Sound

Seven Mile Beach

Water Point

Rum Point

Booby Cay

North Side

Old Man Bay

Colliers

GEORGE TOWN

Airport

Red Bay Estates

Lower Valley

Front Sound

Gun Bay

East End

Jackson Point

Savannah

Northwood

Blow Holes

South West Point

Prospect

Spotts

Pedro

Half Moon Bay

South Sound

Bodden Town

Pease Bay

Breakers

# 4. Cayman Islands

Old Caribbean Proverb:
Beg water can't boil cow skin.

Translation:
One cannot live off the proceeds of charity.

Grand Cayman, Little Cayman and Cayman Brac form the tiny Cayman Islands chain located 500 miles south of Miami and west of Cuba. In terms of size, they are little more than specks in the ocean. All three islands are actually the jutting peaks of a huge undersea mountain. Not surprisingly, all three are very popular diving destinations.

The largest and most commercially developed is Grand Cayman, which houses ninety-four percent of the Cayman population. It also has one of the Caribbean's best self-guided town walking tours, beautiful Seven-Mile Beach, plus a few rather unusual attractions—watching marine turtles breed or literally going to Hell, at a small patch of bizarrely shaped rock.

Grand Cayman is one of the most prosperous islands in the Caribbean. A melting pot of British colonists, Canadians, Americans and Caribbean islanders, it is ranked as one of the world's three major international banking centers, on par with Switzerland and Liechtenstein. It has a staggering total of 500 registered banks and 300 insurance companies. But they are discreetly hidden; they don't stick out on every corner like 7-Elevens.

What is very obvious is the wealth these financial institutions have brought to the island. Like many places, Grand Cayman has been experiencing a condominium boom. Shopping malls are popping up all over, and the island now boasts more restaurants per capita than any other Caribbean island. George Town, Cayman's main city and the country's capital, is a clean, pleasant community that many find reminiscent of Florida's Sanibel Island.

Like the number of banks, scuba diving operations are a very disproportionate part of the economy. More than twenty dive outlets serve the island; for many years, scuba divers were the only tourists. The diving is so good that Grand Cayman is often referred to as the Super Bowl of Scuba

Grand Cayman's biggest celebration occurs every October during "Pirate's Week," a festival recalling buccaneer days. Locals dress in festive pirate costumes (tourists are encouraged to do so as well) and, in general, everyone tries to see how much grog they can drink.

Little Cayman is at the opposite extreme. With fewer than fifty permanent residents, Little Cayman is like Grand Cayman was many decades ago. Little Cayman's airport is still nothing but a grass airstrip, and only a handful of guest houses—no hotels—have been built to provide guest accommodations.

Little Cayman's nearby neighbor of Cayman Brac is in a transitional stage between Grand and Little Cayman. Still mostly rural, tourist development so far has been limited to three small hotels on one tip, which are often filled with anglers, divers and nature lovers ready to explore the largely unspoiled island.

Considering the diversity of the three islands, it's unfortunate that most visitors never get beyond Grand Cayman to Little Cayman or the Brac. But it's quite understandable since Grand Cayman has the best airline connections, the biggest hotels and the best beaches.

Regardless of the island you visit, you'll find the Caymanians to be genuinely likable people who also like us. That makes it especially easy to relax and see the sights.

Travel Tips

Area: Grand Cayman, located 180 miles northwest of Jamaica and 480 miles south of Miami, is twenty-two miles long, four miles wide. Cayman Brac, situated 89 miles northeast of Grand Cayman, is twelve miles long and slightly more than one mile wide. Little Cayman, five miles west of Cayman Brac, is ten miles long and just over a mile wide.

Language: English, the King's kind, spoken better than many Americans.

Population: 28,000

Time Zone: Eastern Standard.

Getting There: Grand Cayman is only 480 miles south of Florida, an easy hour's flight from Miami, the major U.S. gateway. Direct flights are also available from some of the larger cities, including Tampa, Atlanta, New York and Houston. U.S.-based American Airlines flies daily from Miami and Dallas. Northwest flies daily from Miami. The national airline, Cayman Airways, offers the most extensive schedule, flying from Miami,

Tampa, Orlando, Houston, Atlanta and New York. Cayman Airways also offers the only inter-island service from Grand Cayman to Cayman Brac or Little Cayman.

Getting Around: Motor scooters are popular and rental cars are easily available. Several companies offer island tours via motorcoach. Driving is on the left.

Where to Stay: Grand Cayman can be a very expensive island and has sometimes been referred to by shocked tourists as "Grand-a-Day Cayman." However, the hotels are some of the Caribbean's most varied. They can be broken down into four main categories:

Luxury Hotels: The Hyatt Grand Cayman is clearly the island's most upscale (and expensive) lodging but well worth the money for those able to afford it. The five-story Radisson is another good option.

Condominiums and villas: This is a popular family choice because the kitchen facilities can save considerable money. These are also a favorite for people who want privacy or don't want to go out for every meal. There are two clearinghouses for these properties: Reef House Ltd., Box 1540; 809/949-7093 and Cayman Rent-A-Villa, Box 68; 809/947-4144.

Smaller Hotels/Guest Houses: These are among the least expensive choices, realizing at the same time that nothing in Grand Cayman is cheap. Choices include the forty room Beach Club (809/949-8100), the eighteen room Ambassador's Inn (809/949-7577) and Irma Eldemire's Guest House (809/949-5387).

Camping is not permitted anywhere.

Taxes & Tips: Government room tax of 6% and a 15% service charge is usually added automatically to all bills, so don't tip twice.

Documents: A birth certificate and photo ID will suffice for U.S. and Canadian citizens. All others require passports.

Currency: Cayman has its own dollar but everyone takes US currency. The US dollar is worth only 80 cents CI. That exchange rate is another factor that makes Cayman so expensive.

Electrical Current: Even though this is a former British colony, most of the buildings are of such recent vintage that they have standard 110 volt, 60 cycle.

Safety/Health Warnings: Because so much of the area is lowlands and close to mangroves, carry insect repellent any time you're in the bush. Beware the Maidenplum, a bush which looks like the North American sumac. It can cause painful skin blisters if the sap gets on you.

Hiking/Walking Services: Except for the usual bus tours around the island, there are none. And there really isn't any need for any, either, since it's so easy to find your way anywhere alone.

Snakes and Other Venomous Creatures: None.

For More Information: Contact the Cayman Department of Tourism, 250 Catalonia Ave., Suite 604, Coral Gables, FL 33143; (305) 444-6551. In Canada, Earl Smith Travel Consultants, 234 Eglinton Avenue East, Suite 306, Toronto, Ontario M4P IK5; 416/485-1550. In the UK, Trevor House, 100 Brompton Road, London SW3 1EX; 071/581-9418 or fax 071/584-4463.

1. Walking Tour of George Town

Time: about 1-1/2 hours. **Length:** about 2 miles. **Difficulty:** 1

Grand Cayman's original capital was not George Town but a place called Bodden Town. At the time, George Town was known as The Hogstyes, apparently a reference not to the citizenry but to edible animals kept penned at the site. Cruise ships land at what is still called Hogstye Bay.

1) Cruise Ship Landing: Where tenders usually unload cruise ship passengers.

2) Port Authority Building

3) Elmslie Memorial Church: This building, named for the first Presbyterian missionary to serve in Cayman, was constructed in 1920-22 but is on the site of a church built in 1846. Until modern times, the tolling of the church bell signified a death on the island. The old grave markers, moved from one side to allow building of the carpark, date back to the 1800s.

This church was the first concrete structure ever made in Cayman. The builder, a Captain Rayal, was obviously more familiar with building ships than churches. He bought the molds to make the concrete blocks, but no one on the island knew how to properly mix the concrete. He wrote to the Portland Cement Company for instructions, then went to Jamaica to learn how to work with cement. The church's timber ceiling, largely salvaged from a shipwreck, is said to be Captain Rayal's unique signature: timbers that resemble the upturned hulls of the schooners he built.

The pews were fashioned by another shipbuilder who imported the mahogany from Belize. They cost five English pounds each and members were asked to pay for them. Parishioners did, thereby obtaining informal family pews.

4) War Memorial: Located in the churchyard, this is a memorial to Caymanian sailors lost at sea in WWII. Although not subject to conscription, 200 Caymanians served in the British Merchant Navy and hundreds more served in the Royal Navy to defend Britain itself. In addition, 800 joined the Trinidad Royal Navy Volunteer Reserve; roll call must have

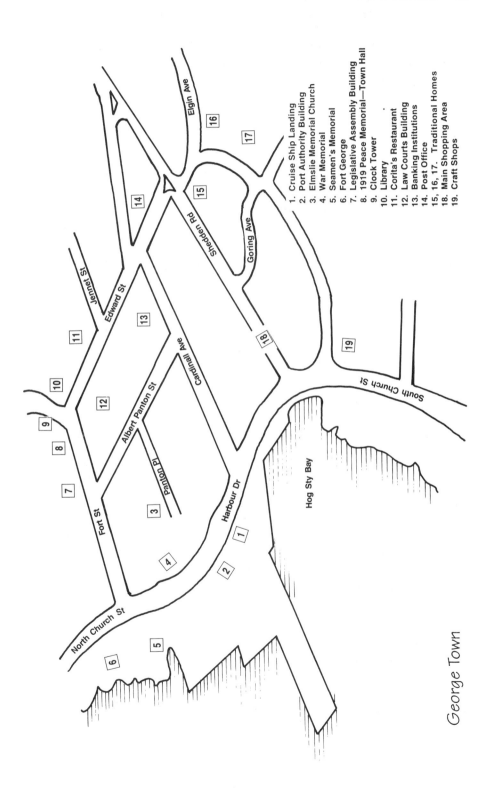

1. Cruise Ship Landing
2. Port Authority Building
3. Elmslie Memorial Church
4. War Memorial
5. Seamen's Memorial
6. Fort George
7. Legislative Assembly Building
8. 1919 Peace Memorial—Town Hall
9. Clock Tower
10. Library
11. Corita's Restaurant
12. Law Courts Building
13. Banking Institutions
14. Post Office
15, 16, 17. Traditional Homes
18. Main Shopping Area
19. Craft Shops

George Town

been confusing—forty of these volunteers were named Ebanks, one of the island's most prolific families.

5) Seaman's Memorial: Also the George Town Harbour navigational light, the names of the 153 Caymanians known to have been lost at sea are inscribed on tablets around the base. The light is powered by solar cells. The beacon's eternal message, as stated at the dedication, is "Come home safely, as we would have liked you to do."

6) Fort George Ruins: Built by islanders around 1790 to defend against attack from neighboring Cuba, Fort George commands the harbor entrance. It has had nothing but bad luck. One local tale about the fort says that when invaders landed, the Caymanians discovered to their horror they were out of cannon balls. They loaded the cannon with nails and fired, which caused the invaders to flee.

The fort was demolished in 1972 following a war between the Port Authority and a developer who used a backhoe to push down the walls. A few outraged residents placed themselves between the remaining walls and the heavy equipment. The fort was deeded to the protection of the National Trust in 1987.

Subsequent archeological excavation revealed that treasure hunters had already dug to at least seven feet below the road level. The site was so disturbed it was impossible to find the foundations on the southern side. The outline today is based on old drawings and photographs. The oval-shaped fort was made of coral rock and wall thickness varied from five feet on the sea side to two feet landward.

7) Legislative Assembly Building: Looking like a misplaced Mayan pyramid, the design was the first-place winner of an international architectural competition. The controversial structure, built in 1971-72, was the first poured concrete building in the Caymans. Even fifty years after Elmslie Memorial was built, the locals hadn't quite gotten the hang of mixing concrete, so it had to be poured pail-by-pail by bucket brigade. It is fitting that the cornerstone was laid in 1971 by the same Captain Rayal who traveled to Jamaica in the early 1920s to study the marvel of concrete blocks.

When the assembly is in session, visitors (no bathing suits) are allowed to watch the proceedings from the Visitors' Gallery. The first floor is decorated with old photos of George Town.

8) 1919 Peace Memorial-Town Hall: Located next to the assembly building, the Town Hall was Captain Rayal's second civic structure, built in 1923, immediately after Elmslie Church. For many years this was the hub of Caymanian life since the building served also as the Court House and Assembly Room as well. That the 1919 memorial commemorating WWI was called a Peace Memorial instead of a War Memorial discloses a key aspect of the Caymanian nature.

9) Clock Tower: Built in 1937 for a princely sum of £140, it commemorates the reign of King George V, grandfather of Queen Elizabeth II.

10) Public Library: More of Captain Rayal's handiwork, the library dates from 1939. The distinctive ceiling is decorated with the shields of Britain's most distinguished places of higher learning. The area behind the library was a U.S. Navy base in WWII.

11) Corita's Restaurant: Grand Cayman's first lawyer (an English-trained Jamaican) had his office here. The old building was also a storehouse for a huge quantity of rice salvaged from a ship wreck in George Town Harbour. Caymanians dined on that rice for years afterward.

12) Law Courts: Designed and built by the same individual who built the Mayan-looking Legislative Assembly Building. Wigged barristers still argue before elaborately robed judges, as in England. Tourists are permitted to observe from the back of the courtrooms, located on the second floor.

13) Financial District: Edward Street, once a residential section, is an important part of the Cayman financial district. Look at the listings at the building entrances and you'll see the names of banks from around the world that are registered here.

14) Post Office: Considered Captain Rayal's second-best edifice after the Elmslie Church. Built in 1939, its wooden doors curve to follow the curved building facade. The vaulted ceiling may be Rayal's best timber work of all.

Stamp collectors will want to pay special attention to the post office. Grand Cayman long has been known as a philatelist's center because of the island's beautiful and exotic stamps. The Philatelic Bureau usually has many on hand as First Day Covers.

15)-16)-17) Traditional Cabin-Style Houses: Built of woven strips of wood spread with a plaster of lime made from coral rocks. The houses are on raised posts known as ironwood because of its hardness and longevity; ironwood posts are good for at least a century. The kitchen or "cook room" is separated from the house to keep the house cool, and because the cooking was done in a sand-filled, wooden box which would occasionally catch on fire. Better not to take the whole house with it.

18) Main Shopping Area: This is where most of the larger clothing, perfume and jewelry stores are located. Besides black coral torn from the coral reefs (a destructive practice, so boycott all coral products), the jewelry stores specialize in a mineral known as Caymanite. It is comprised of metals and fossils created millions of years ago. It is found only in the Cayman islands, and scientists cannot explain such uniqueness. Caymanite is made into rings, pendants and sculptures.

19) Craft Shops: Several small shops here are known for their handicrafts, including black coral jewelry.

2. Going to Hell

Time: 15-20 minutes. **Difficulty:** 1, as long as you don't lose your footing on the rocks.

Hell is a small formation of jagged ironshore that some say resembles the fires of hell (although how they know for certain has not been determined). Ironshore, which looks very much like volcanic rock, is limestone estimated to be 1-1/2-million years old. Initially a white color, the black surface is a coating of algae which secrete acid and create the unusual shapes.

Hell even has its own post office, a souvenir stand rivaling any T-shirt emporium, as people send home postcards with the Hell postmark. Ironshore is also a characteristic of the coastline south of George Town, hardly an enticing area for sunbathers, but there is an appropriate tradeoff: the area is noted for its fine snorkeling and aquatic life.

3. Beach Walks

Time: 3-4 hours to circuit Seven Mile Beach, 45-60 minutes for most others. **Difficulty:** 1.

Seven Mile Beach, which is actually five and one-half miles long, is the main water-sports center featuring sailboats and jet skis. It is one of the few people-packed Caribbean beaches where peddlers are rare. Sunbathers are allowed to doze, readers are permitted to read, and people watchers are allowed to stare without any confrontations with bead and coral salesmen.

Less-crowded but equally fine beaches are found at West Bay, Cayman Kai and Rum Point. You'll need a car to reach any of them if you're staying at Seven Mile Beach.

The east-end coastline from the Tortuga Club to Spotter's Bay is virtually undeveloped, a walk that includes both beaches and ironshore.

4. Turtle Farm

Time: 30-45 minutes. **Difficulty:** 1.

Like a freak show at the fair, there is something irresistible and voyeuristic about watching turtles mate at the Cayman Turtle Farm, the world's only farm devoted to raising endangered green turtles.

Ten thousand marine turtles, ranging from newborns to mature

Seven Mile Beach may be crowded, but West Bay contains beautifully deserted beaches.

adults, live at the Turtle Farm, which furnishes all of the island's fresh turtle steaks. The farm demonstrates how the turtles are reared and bred. Turtling was an important livelihood for islanders for many years; a peg-legged turtle is the island's symbol. Although the Turtle Farm releases many thousands of creatures into the wild each year, none of its products can be imported into the U.S. due to a ban on turtle products. Several thousand mature greens never make it beyond the restaurant kitchens, appearing as turtle burgers and turtle steak on menus. Don't hesitate to try them because, on Grand Cayman, the turtles were pen-raised for this purpose. It does not deplete the species.

 5. Botswain Bay

Time: 45-60 minutes. **Difficulty:** 1.

A walk of about one mile will take you past an old cemetery and old school house. The rocky ironshore along the coast to Spanish Bay Road provides dramatic views of big waves rolling in during winter storms. There is no offshore reef to blunt the powerful waves before they reach shore.

6. Dike Roads

Time: 1 hour. **Difficulty:** 1.

Actually mosquito canals, these mangrove areas offer good birdwatching, including the chance to see parrots. Bring the insect repellent!

7. Cayman Brac

Time: 2-3 hours for the complete hike. **Difficulty:** 2-3.

Eighty-nine miles northeast of Grand Cayman and a world away are Little Cayman and Cayman Brac, which so far have been spared the boom in tourism. The word "brac" is Gaelic for bluff, and the one that tops out at 130 feet makes up virtually one end of Cayman Brac.

From the end of the ascent path, it's a two-mile walk to the lighthouse along a rocky path that requires sure footing and plenty of liquids, because it gets hot up there. Little Cayman Brac is the large rock off the island's northeast tip, an excellent place for birdwatching, featuring peregrine falcons and long-tailed tropical birds that nest in the bluff in spring.

The bluff walk is the most famous hike in the Caymans, and the only true one. The bluff trail at Spot Bay takes a rugged farmer's path to the top, passing caves and interesting photo stops on the way. At the top, you overlook the village of Spots Bay and have a magnificent view of the Atlantic.

If you want to avoid the rocky path to the lighthouse, take the tarmac Bluff Road. The south coast road, which ends in a cul-de-sac, offers a rugged walk along the ironshore or the chance to climb up to more caves. Sea birds are common here.

The services of a local guide can be arranged through any of the hotels. Hiring a guide is a wise idea since locals are familiar with the parrot nesting areas, often on private land. Never open fences, even when passing through land that may appear long unused.

8. Little Cayman

Time: 3-4 hours for an island walk. **Difficulty:** 1.

Little Cayman, only nine miles long and a single mile wide, is the kind of deserted island some vacationers dream of running away to. Actor Burgess Meredith had the perfect getaway home here before the permanent

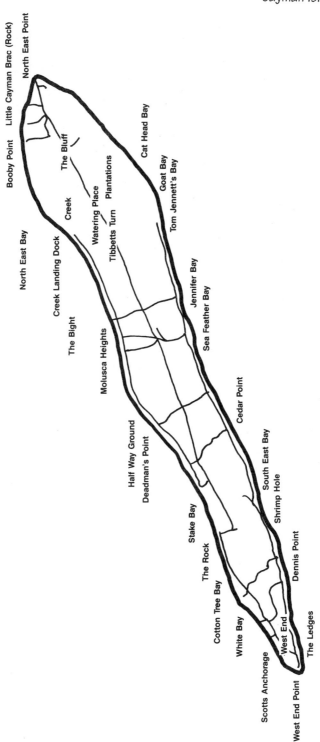

North East Point

Little Cayman Brac (Rock)

Booby Point

The Bluff

Cat Head Bay

Creek

Watering Place

Plantations

Goat Bay

Tom Jennett's Bay

North East Bay

Creek Landing Dock

Tibbetts Turn

The Bight

Jennifer Bay

Molusca Heights

Sea Feather Bay

Cedar Point

Half Way Ground

Deadman's Point

South East Bay

Shrimp Hole

Stake Bay

The Rock

Dennis Point

Cotton Tree Bay

White Bay

West End

The Ledges

Scotts Anchorage

West End Point

Cayman Brac

Walks on the beach are the Cayman's most popular form of hiking.

population swelled to twenty-five and three guest houses were built. Most visitors are scuba divers or hard-core anglers who enjoy some of the finest bonefishing and tarpon angling anywhere.

For walkers, Little Cayman offers excellent birdwatching around the inland ponds and groves. Wild iguana can be seen in the bush.

Owen Island is a small offshore island in South Hole Sound which can be reached only by small boat. It is an excellent spot for a picnic while stalking bonefish on the shallow flats which surround the island.

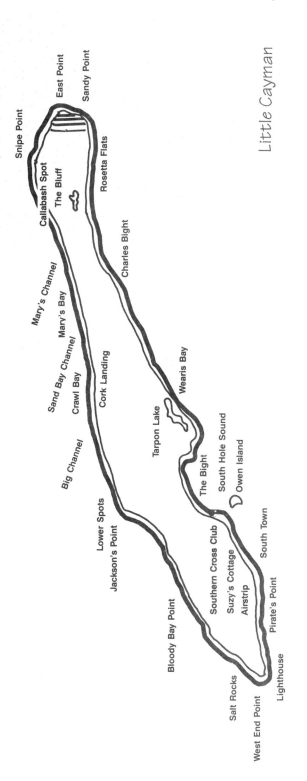

Little Cayman

East Point
Sandy Point
Snipe Point
Callabash Spot
The Bluff
Rosetta Flats
Charles Bight
Mary's Channel
Mary's Bay
Sand Bay Channel
Crawl Bay
Cork Landing
Wearis Bay
Big Channel
Tarpon Lake
The Bight
South Hole Sound
Owen Island
Lower Spots
Jackson's Point
Southern Cross Club
Suzy's Cottage
Airstrip
South Town
Bloody Bay Point
Pirate's Point
Salt Rocks
Lighthouse
West End Point

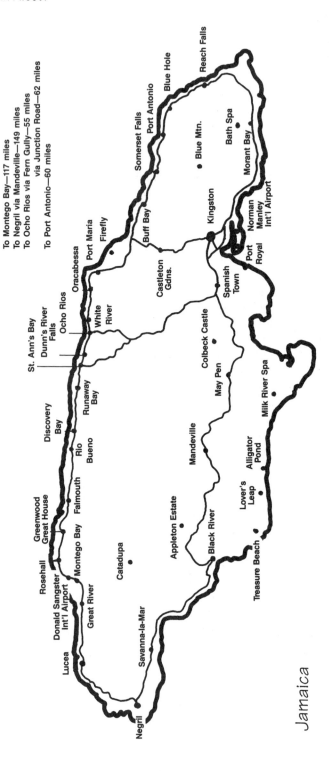

FROM KINGSTON
To Mandeville—61 miles
To Montego Bay—117 miles
To Negril via Mandeville—149 miles
To Ocho Rios via Fern Gully—55 miles
via Junction Road—62 miles
To Port Antonio—60 miles

Jamaica

# 5. Jamaica

Jamaican proverb:
Bottle without cap belong to cockroach.

Translation:
Unprotected possessions could become anyone's property.

I must admit at the outset that I am prejudiced when it comes to Jamaica. I like the people and the country. A lot.

I consider the ascent up Blue Mountain Peak one the Caribbean's best hikes. Blue Mountain is the tenth tallest peak in the Caribbean, a Matterhorn among islands that rarely project above 5,000 feet.

The Arawaks, Jamaica's earliest known inhabitants, named their land well: Xaymaca, "land of woods and streams." They left out the mountains, however. Jamaica is about 80% hilly and 40 to 50% is forested. It has more geographic variety than any other island: desert, high mountains, beaches...almost everything but snow (though it may get below freezing on Blue Mountain Peak in winter). Jamaica offers some of everything.

Yet some people feel uneasy about visiting Jamaica. They don't want to witness the poverty for which the island is so well known. So they stay away. No doubt about it, Jamaica is a very poor country. The small shacks some people call home are disturbing to see. Yet if one is genuinely concerned about a country's economy, the thing to do is visit it and spend money. That creates jobs and keeps people employed.

Then there is the matter of drugs and crime. The major tourist areas, like towns everywhere, do have parts that shouldn't be visited after dark. As most hotels have their own security staff, room break-ins are more rare than crime on the street.

How safe is it to walk/hike around Jamaica? Probably as safe as anywhere else if you show reasonable care. As one who was almost killed here in 1977 when I blundered into a drug pickup, I do not say this lightly. I was in the wrong place at the wrong time and no one knew what to do with me: to live or let die. I still get uneasy around machetes.

Ten years passed before I went back to Jamaica. I was in no hurry to test the hospitality. Now I go there at least once a year. I feel safe and welcome—but whenever I go off into the bush, it's with a reliable Jamaican.

Don't be foolish enough to hire a "guide" who approaches you. You may get shaken down instead of shown the sights. Would you entrust your safety to the first stranger who approached you in London, New York or Miami and offered to show you around, especially take you off the beaten path?

Although a minority of the Jamaican population, Rastafarians are the obvious standout. Their dreadlocks, almost like a lion's mane, are a symbol of their faith, which in essence is a peaceful protest against their oppression, particularly by whites. Basically a non-violent movement, members believe in the divinity of Haile Selassie I, the last Emperor of Ethiopia, who also bore the name Ras Tafari. Rastas, as they call themselves, base their belief on one quotation of Haile Selassie's in particular: "Until the philosophy that considers any one race superior to another is finally and absolutely challenged and discarded, till there are no longer first-class and second-class human beings, the dream of a lasting peace will remain an illusion."

Rastas believe they are a people in exile, that one day their God "Jah" will lead them back to Ethiopia, their promised land, also called Zion. Jamaican hero Marcus Garvey, who predicted Selassie would become emperor, is considered the religion's major prophet. Garvey, who is recognized internationally as an early leader in creating black awareness and unity, suggested the formation of a black homeland in Africa as early as 1916. When Haile Selassie was named Emperor of Ethiopia in 1930, that was divine sign enough to create the Rasta religion. Poor Jamaicans had already given up on whites and Christianity.

Genuine Rastas do not eat meat but are vegetarians. Ganja is their sacred herb. They see the world, which they call Babylon, destroying itself because of its inequality and materialism and they attempt to stay self-sufficient—apart from it. Ironically, there are men who go around looking like Rastas because it impresses tourists and makes it easier to sell drugs and wood carvings.

The protest music of the Rasta religion, and the most important development in Caribbean music since the steel band, is called Reggae. Unlike calypso, which sings about yellow birds and other idyllic things, reggae is an honest, often harsh look at the world through the eyes of the blacks. Anything but sentimental, reggae is primarily message music about poverty, social injustice and worshipping Jah. Bob Marley (the museum to him in Kingston is holy ground to reggae lovers) is credited with developing the form, as a prophet singing the praises of Jah. However, as with every music form, there is good reggae and there is junk. It is not all just "sacred music." If possible, listen to tapes before buying any. Some reggae is awfully repetitious.

Be prepared for the open sale of drugs almost everywhere, particularly the local herb, ganja (marijuana). Pot is one of Jamaica's major cash crops; in the countryside, it is consumed the way Americans drink beer. Expect to be offered a sociable smoke and decide in advance how you want to handle it. If you don't care to take a few spliffs, that's agreeable with the locals. They never push it on you, only offer.

Particularly annoying, however, are the persistent drug sellers who seem to pop up everywhere around places like Negril. Just saying "no" or "not interested" usually won't discourage them. Instead, say something like "I don't smoke." Once you make it clear you're not in the market, not just haggling over price, your friendly pusher will give up. Remember, some sellers are on a different level of consciousness and not totally tuned into this world.

The great contradiction: Jamaican courts hand down harsh penalties for drug use. An estimated fifty foreign tourists may be in Jamaican jails at any one time for breaking the drug laws. No one in his wildest, most drug-drenched dreams should ever consider taking any out of the country when he leaves.

Jamaica, more than most islands, is a rose with very obvious thorns. The best description of how Jamaica works comes from Peter Bentley, hiking expert and president of the Jamaica Alternative Tourism, Camping and Hiking Association (JATCHA):

"Push, you don't get much. Take it easier, get much more. When we speak, expect to be baffled! Our patois sounds like a foreign language. Sometimes it might sound like you are being scolded, but we love you. We argue hard, but at the same time we will happily share a rum or a smoke with you. We can be mighty inquisitive, or extremely shy. We are a poor country. Hustling is almost a way of life, a necessity—meet the hustler with humor and compassion, and continue with your mission.

"We like to be acknowledged even if it is only slightly raising the index finger as a greeting or saying one word, "Irie" (pronounced 'Eye-ree' and meaning everything's going wonderful or just great—a greeting also to describe a person or the day or 'Good Morning' or 'Good Night,' i.e., meaning 'Good Evening.')"

Yes, it is disconcerting the first time a Jamaican greets you in the evening and his first words are "Good Night." No, he's not leaving or dismissing you. After all, it is night. Why should you be content with a "Good Evening" when evening is the briefest part of nightfall? The

Jamaican perspective—and it is the same for several other islands, as well—is a very logical one. We don't classify our morning greetings with such precision, differentiating between "Good Sunrise" or "Good Daylight." Perspective...Jamaica will probably change it for you in many ways.

Travel Tips

Area: 142 miles long, 52 miles wide.

Language: English and a Jamaican patois

Population: 2,500,000 centered near Kingston, Montego Bay, Ocho Rios and Negril.

Time Zone: Eastern Standard Time all year.

Rainy Season: Different regions receive dramatically different amounts of rainfall. For instance, the capital city of Kingston gets about thirty-five inches per year. Jack's Hill, the first of the Blue Mountains, receives about seventy-five. Farther up in the Blue Mountains at sites called Hollywell and the Fairy Glades Trail, the annual rainfall is 125 inches. On the highest peaks, we're talking 150-200 inches plus. The wettest place is in the John Crow Mountains, named after the local vultures. This region receives an estimated 400 inches of rain a year. Understandably, not many people hike there.

The rainy season also varies from region to region. For Central and Western Jamaica it is summertime; for Eastern Jamaica, October-November and a small rainy season in May-June. It can rain along the north coast in high season, when all the hotel prices have doubled. Vacations can literally get washed out for a week. For hiking, it really doesn't make much difference. Clouds provide the coolest, most enjoyable walking conditions. Be prepared for rain and it won't make as much difference as you might think.

Climate Warning: Jamaica may be considered a tropical island, but most organized hiking is done at altitude in the Blue Mountains near Kingston. Here, there is a temperature drop of three degrees Fahrenheit for every 1,000 feet. On Blue Mountain Peak on a clear morning after a winter cold front, it can even drop below freezing.

Getting There: Jamaica is served by American, BWIA, Air Jamaica, and Northwest. American, flying through Miami, serves Montego Bay and Kingston (closest point to the Blue Mountains hiking). Northwest flies into Montego Bay from Tampa, Florida. Air Jamaica flies daily from Miami and several times weekly direct from Orlando. Trans Jamaica runs regular shuttles, early and late, between Montego Bay and Kingston.

Regardless of airline, it is essential to be at the Montego Bay airport at least two hours ahead of your return departure. All flights depart at the same time in the afternoon, and it often takes an hour to go through immigration and security, not counting the check-in line.

Getting Around: You're hotel can often arrange very reasonable transfers from the Kingston airport. Taxis are everywhere and unless you plan to do a lot of touring on your own, they're the cheapest form of transportation. Rentals cars are expensive, averaging US $400 per week plus tax and insurance; that's about double anywhere else in the Caribbean. In general, Jamaicans tend to drive like the devil is after them—and closing fast.

With Port Antonio only 133 miles east of Montego Bay and Negril only fifty-two miles to the east, it sounds plausible to dash from one end of the island to the other trying different sites in a single day. I can't emphasize enough: the seemingly short distances are deceptive. The winding narrow roads make for slow traffic. It is, for instance, about three hours from Negril to Ocho Rios. Almost another three to Port Antonio. Take the island commuter airline, Trans-Jamaica, and leave the long-distance piloting to them.

Where to Stay: The best hiking is in the Kingston area, in the Blue Mountains, although the most famous resorts are in Negril, Montego Bay and Ocho Rios. However, only fifteen minutes outside Kingston at 2,000 feet elevation on Jack's Hill is the Maya Lodge and Hiking Center, a fifteen-acre property offering rustic cabins and tent sites. Owner Peter Bentley, also president of the Jamaica Alternative Tourism, Camping and Hiking Association, is able to make overnight accommodations in guest houses and small hotels in all parts of the island, including Kingston.

Peter has been in business since 1981 to accommodate guests more interested in spending their money to experience Jamaica rather than in renting an extravagant room and sleeping in it. As Peter explains, "When we started in 1981, we termed our program alternative tourism because there was nothing else like it in the Caribbean. Now it's known everywhere as 'ecotourism.' We specialize in letting visitors see, feel, experience and understand the real Jamaica. We design our tours to be environmentally sensitive and consciously integrated into the cultural life of the communities we visit."

The guide service arm of Maya, known as SENSE Adventures, is Jamaica's pioneer in adventure travel, detailed in the Hiking Guide/Services section that follows.

Staying at Maya Lodge, in the foothills of the Blue Mountains, is an experience in itself. With facilities for up to fifty people, it has fifteen bare tent sites that accommodate two to four people each. Four cottage/cabins sleep up to two (bed mattress on the floor) and are illuminated with a kerosene lamp. Three rooms are available in the lodge itself. No individual toilet or bath facilities at the tent sites or in the cabins, but they are available in the main lodge building. A single communal shower is shared by both sexes.

The mood at Maya is totally casual. Guests mingle freely with the guides in the kitchen to talk about the day, the upcoming hike, whatever. The dress code is not only relaxed but at times optional, particularly for Peter, who will arrange clothing-optional snorkeling trips to several islands off Port Royal.

Maya has a small cafe that handles six people at one seating. The food is traditional Jamaican, and the different guides take turns every night preparing their specialty. You'll sense the competition between them, which is all to your benefit. You may choose to cook your own food at one of the campsites.

Rates are incredibly reasonable. Cabins are US $25 per day, tent sites are US $10. General guides are US $25 per day, up to $100 for specialists in ornithology or entomology. Standard hiking packages with meals, lodging and guide service average about US $60 per day. All accounts must be settled in US$ or J$ or traveler's checks; no credit cards.

Contact Peter Bentley, P.O. Box 216, Kingston 7, Jamaica; 809/927-2097. Mail takes seven to twelve days to reach Jamaica. The best time to talk to Peter himself, assuming he's not away on an overnight hike, is between 7:30-8 p.m.

If you want to be in walking distance of Maya Lodge but in more luxurious and even better scenic surroundings, try Ivor Guest House, an old 19th-century villa with just three guest rooms and full dining room service. Ivor overlooks the city of Kingston, a spectacular sight at night. Cost is about US $65 for a double; another bargain. Call 809/927-1460.

In other parts of the island, you might consider the more expensive all-inclusive resorts which, in Jamaica, live up to their name. One flat fee paid in advance covers rooms, meals, roundtrip airport transfers, all sports activities and all drinks (beer, wine—everything).

In addition, the Jamaican Forestry Department offers cabins and dormitories in the Blue Mountains, but permits must be paid for and picked up in advance at the Kingston office. You cannot simply show up at the site and pay. JATCHA can make the reservations and have the permits waiting for you. No linens, blankets or kitchen utensils are at any of the forest camps.

Hollywell offers several cabins with fireplace, small kitchen and full bathroom. Clydesdale is an old coffee plantation/pine nursery at 3,700 feet with a bunk bed dormitory that can sleep thirty or more. Amenities include flush toilets, showers and a fire pit for cooking.

On the hike up Blue Mountain Peak, most people overnight at the privately-owned Whitfield Hall Hostel, which may also permit you to tent camp; 809/927-0986. About one to one-and-a-half hours beyond Whitfield Hall is the Portland Gap forestry hut at 5,200 feet. The hut is rustic (you sleep on the floor) and has running water and an outhouse. Tent space is available. Given a choice between Whitfield Hall, which does supply linens, etc., and the forest hut, there is no contest. Atop Blue Mountain Peak itself is a rough, graffiti-covered forest hut often used on weekends by partying groups from Kingston. Water may not be available, and it gets quite cold at the peak from December through February. Tent camping is permitted.

Taxes & Tips: There is a government consumption tax of 10% on all hotel rooms. Tipping is 10-15% although a service charge of this amount is usually added to all bills.

Dining: The Jamaican version of fast food, jerk is a terribly misleading name for the best barbecue you will ever eat in the islands. It is a process of slow-cooking highly seasoned meat over green pimento wood (allspice). Jerk pork is the classic but jerk chicken is equally tasty. Every small village has jerk stands, many of them using old oil drums that have been transformed into a huge cooker. Jerk food often tastes best when accompanied by the good local beer, Red Stripe. Ask for Red Stripe cold; some Jamaicans like to drink it at room temperature.

Documents: For U.S. and Canadian citizens, a notarized birth certificate or voter's registration card with some sort of photo ID will suffice. All others require passports.

Currency: Jamaican dollars can be purchased in the Montego Bay airport at a currency exchange bureau even before you go through customs. Keep the exchange slip if you intend to convert back before leaving the country. There is a bank in the departure lounge but it often has long lines. Prices are usually posted in Jamaican dollars but check to make sure. The Jamaican dollar is fluctuating considerably.

Electrical Current: In most places it's 110/50 cycle instead of 60-cycle. Some of the older hotels still run on 220 but have converters on request.

Safety/Health Warning: Be careful where you walk after dark, particularly around downtown Kingston. Crime, mainly pick-pocketing, is an increasing problem. Despite the occasional glaring publicity, however, Jamaica's crime rate is lower than most North American cities. Don't leave valuables unattended anywhere; use hotel safes. Police use surprise roadblocks to catch those carrying drugs. Use the obvious care you would traveling anywhere and you should be fine; don't get caught off guard by too relaxed an attitude.

Shopping: Many of the same crafts are available all over the country. Negril has the highest prices, followed by Montego Bay, Ocho Rios.

Kingston is by far the cheapest because it sees fewest tourists. Items in Kingston may sell for half of their Negril price. Prices are fairly standard in each region, but haggle with the street vendors. They expect it. Of course, a few have been known to throw a voodoo curse on a customer who's really upset them. But what's a little superstition compared to cold hard cash? Right? Right? Are you sure you won't pay that extra US $1 for that Rasta cap after all?

Blue Mountain Coffee: Potent and strong and considered some of the world's finest. There are many opportunities to purchase it but the best buys are in the Blue Mountains. Buy from the farmers themselves and remember that the best comes from the higher altitudes.

Getting Your Hair Braided: Mostly women but even a few men will have their hair braided at the beginning of their Jamaica jaunt, the style Bo Derek immortalized in the old film "10," with Dudley Moore. The problem is you won't be able to keep the braids forever. Untangling it back to normal is said to be a painful, time-consuming process. Having your hair braided has been compared to getting drunk and waking up with a tattoo: it just seemed like the thing to do at the time. Costs from US $25 up. Haggle.

Hiking/Walking Services: Compared to many islands where the maximum hike may be six miles or less, hiking on Jamaica is more adventurous. The leading guide service is SENSE Adventures, based at the Maya Lodge at Jack's Hill, Kingston. From the Maya Lodge you can make four, five or up to nine-day hikes into the bush, doing what's called "hut-to-hut hiking," overnighting in camps run by the forest department or staying in private guest houses.

Other trails (locally called "tracks") starting at Maya: three hours to the top of Jack's Hill (2,050 feet) or Peter's Rock (2,900 feet); return the same route. It's seven hours either to Mount Horeb (5,000 feet) via Hollywell or Mount Roseana (4,100 feet), also circular hikes. A tough walk is the eleven-hour trek and return to the Chinchona Botanical Gardens (5,200 feet). There are about thirty different SENSE Adventures to choose from, including canoeing, horseback riding and snorkeling in addition to hiking.

Contact Peter Bentley's SENSE Adventures at Box 216, Kingston 7, Jamaica; 809/927-2097. You will be sent brochures, descriptions of hikes and other activities along with a questionnaire. The questionnaire and a US $15 service charge should then be returned to Peter. Reservations—an entire vacation program—can be worked out by Peter and SENSE. Why the service charge? Peter explains: "When we started from scratch in 1981, no one else had fully (or even partially) scouted our trails, let alone our rivers. We hope you understand the need to cover the costs of servicing you."

Hiking in Jamaica is still in its pioneering stage. Therefore, SENSE

Adventures' contract contains a clause warning that you may not get to where you're supposed to because you can never predict what will happen. A landslide may block the road or trails so that you spend a couple of extra days in the mountains. The hike up Blue Mountain Peak has a 99 percent success rate, but no guarantees.

One of the most memorable parts of my Blue Mountain Peak hike was where things went wrong. An unnamed agency (not Peter's) was supposed to send a car to Mavis Bank to pick up me and my guide to take us back to Kingston, well over an hour away. The car never showed. The local bus to Kingston was broken and there was no telling when a replacement would be sent. There were forty of us waiting for the bus back to Kingston that night.

Rescue came in the form of a driver with a high-sided flatbed truck, probably used for hauling bricks or garbage. He would take us to Kingston, for a price. Buckey, my SENSE Adventures guide, was able to get us aboard where we were jammed together like telephone poles.

As the truck pulled away, we all began to realize just how drunk the driver was. I grasped the side of the truck nearest the trees, continually ducking palms and other branches as we sped down the Blue Mountains.

As he barreled down the mountain with a great grinding and shifting of heavy gears, the driver began stopping at every little rum shop to replenish his empty bottle. All of us in the truck would yell at the shop not to sell him any. Thankfully (or I might not be writing this) all the owners responded to our pleas. The driver would return to the truck, cursing and grumbling, threaten to make us all get off his truck, then lurch off again.

Although the truck's great horn blared at every curve, we didn't always slow down. Many times I wondered if we would successfully navigate the next corner. Was my Caribbean hiking odyssey going to end suddenly in the back of a truck with all these laughing and yelling Jamaicans? Before long, I found myself yelling and laughing along with them. This situation was out of my control. Either I would or I wouldn't make it. What a roller coaster ride! My fingers cramped for thirty minutes after we got off the truck in Kingston.

When I first met Peter, I wondered about the name of his company, why it wasn't called something more traditional like "Sense of Adventure" instead of SENSE Adventure. By the end of my trip, I knew why. Every sense I possessed had been challenged and tested, particularly later that same night when Peter, several locals, and I climbed the water tank overlooking Kingston somewhere around midnight. What an unforgettable view...and climb down.

There is a saying: "The Jamaica you find depends on the company you meet."

Snakes and Other Venomous Creatures: None.

For More Information: For hotels, sports information, virtually any-thing, from the U.S. call the Jamaica Tourist Board toll free at 800/JAMAICA. From Canada, 1110 Sherbrooke St. West, Montreal Quebec H3A 1G9; 514/849-6386. From the UK, 111 Gloucester Place, London W1H, 3PH; 071/224-0505.

Hikes in the Blue Mountains

The Blue Mountain and John Crow National Park: funded by the Jamaican government and the United States Agency for International Development, it has a budget of US $3 million. The World Wildlife Fund and the Nature Conservancy have also contributed to the effort to create what will be Jamaica's first national park: about 70,000 acres of the Blue Mountains as well as the John Crow mountains.

An estimated 3% of the country's forests are lost annually for charcoal making, vegetable growing and ganja farming. In the Blue Mountains, you will pass many small farms where squatters have moved in and started raising vegetables. Their produce is certainly needed to help feed the Kingston area, but at the same time they are doing irreparable damage. Much of the forest that remains includes many introduced species, par-ticularly from Australia.

Eventually there will be a an extensive trail system through the region. Talked about for many years, it is slowly becoming reality. Scores of existing trails already criss-cross the mountains, but almost all are bushed-over and need clearing. The proposed Grand Trail of the Blue Mountains would run along the Grand Ridge, with various access points and sleeping huts along the way (Jamaica's version of the famed Milford Track in New Zealand).

1. Blue Mountain Peak Hike

Time: 3-5 hours the first afternoon, climbing 7 miles to Whitfield Hall Hotel where you overnight. **Length:** 21 miles, including the distance from the town of Mavis Bank to the peak and back down to Whitfield Hall Hostel. **Difficulty:** 3-5 depending on the part of the track.

Without doubt, this is one of the Caribbean's Top Five hikes. I rank it #3. If you make no other walk in Jamaica, the hike to the top of Blue Mountain Peak is the one to plan for. What makes it unique is that you leave Whitfield Hall at 2 a.m. to climb seven miles in the dark to the highest point in

A ranger in the new Blue Mountain park.

Jamaica. After enjoying the sunrise, you make the return for a hearty breakfast at Whitfield Hall.

Although some people cut out the first segment, the full hike begins in the town of Mavis Bank, situated at about 2500 feet. You immediately descend to 1500 feet to cross the Clyde and Green rivers. This initial descent is well-shaded. The toughest part of the entire hike probably occurs after Green River where you must climb in the open to the community of Penlyne Castle and then onto the Whitfield Hall Hostel. The afternoon hike is at the warmest part of the day, completely exposed, and if there's no wind and or cloud cover, you can work up quite a sweat getting to Penlyne Castle. Under such conditions, an umbrella is a good idea to keep the sun off.

Whitfield Hall Hostel, made mostly of cedar, is a 200-year-old coffee plantation home surrounded by eucalyptus trees. It sleeps thirty people in bunk and double beds and offers a full bathroom, including a shower. A huge fireplace cuts the chill in the large communal dining area. Kitchen facilities are available, but you must bring your own food. Cost is US $6 per night. If you're hiking on your own, make advance reservations to ensure a place to sleep: 809/927-0986.

Vinny Edwards, the caretaker since 1966, checks the sky at ten o'clock every evening to predict whether the peak will be cloudy or clear the next morning. From experience, his forecast is usually accurate. He can also make you a deal on Blue Mountain coffee if you haven't purchased any yet. After dark, ask Vinny to show you the guest comment book by kerosene lamp, the only illumination available. From the guest comments, foreigners seem to enjoy the walk more than Jamaicans.

The second day of the climb is the highest and steepest, and definitely the most intriguing. Before setting out, eat something and gulp some strong Blue Mountain coffee; you'll need the energy quickly. Good flashlights are essential because there are some sharp dropoffs and you don't want to put your foot in the wrong place. Even Jamaicans have wandered astray in the dark, not finding their way back for several days.

During the nighttime ascent, you'll have a wonderful, unpolluted view of the stars, and the coastal town of Kingston, which looks as brightly lit as Los Angeles. The first hour is the hardest, climbing a stretch called Jacob's Ladder which you blunder into almost immediately, while you're still partially asleep.

Through a series of switchbacks you continue the climb. You know you're close when you reach "Lazy Man's Peak," a steep slope where the trail appears to turn inland. The sight of the track disappearing farther uphill is enough to convince many to stop here and declare it the finish line. However, it's only another five-seven minutes from Lazy Man's to the actual top. From this point, the psychological torture is worse than the physical, because it just doesn't look like you're anywhere near the peak. Did the guide just tell you this to lure you on a few more miles? Then you turn a corner—and there is one of the sweetest sights on earth. The true peak, the place to sit down and truly say "I've done it!" Even though children can make this walk, it still is a good feeling of accomplishment.

Coming down, you use the same trail which looks very different in the daylight. Some hikers have sworn that if they had seen in advance the route they had to climb, they would never have attempted it, fearing the track too difficult. You can be back down the mountain and at Whitfield Hall between 9 a.m. and 11 a.m., depending on how long you tarry at the top.

2. Old Vinegar Hill Trail

Time: 2-3 days to do it enjoyably. **Length:** about 25 miles one-way. **Difficulty:** 3.

This hike in particular is a beauty, because it takes you right through the wilderness area along an historic route going back to the 1600s, when people would go by mule or donkey or horse or on foot. The north side of the mountain is good for growing yams and root crops, while the south is better for cultivating spices, herbs and vegetables. Once the only regular trading route between Port Antonio on the North Coast and Kingston, the trail is little used now.

It begins at Maya Lodge, at Juba Springs on Jack's Hill. It goes up to Hollywell, along an especially striking stretch called the Fairy Glades Trail, through Silver Hill Gap and over Morris Gap at about 5,700 feet, on the Grand Ridge of the Blue Mountains. Old Vinegar Hill is the only trail that does go over the Grand Ridge. On the north side is genuine wilderness. The montane forest here is truly special, even more so than the Fairy Glades because it's pristine, mature montane forest, some of Jamaica's last. It surpasses the vegetation on Blue Mountain Peak because it is so untouched; maybe a handful of people a month, local farmers, go along this route.

Then you go through Vinegar Hill at about 3,000 feet and come down to about 2,000 feet where you can be picked up and taken to Crystal Springs, about a half-hour drive. Crystal Spring is a 200-acre property with cottages not quite as rustic as Maya's. Each has its own bathroom and kitchen and good camping facilities. Cost is $30 per person per night in a cottage, $10 for tent camping. Owner Pauline Stewart has the largest orchid collection in Jamaica, about 25,000 plants, and her property is located right beside the Spanish River.

3. Maya Lodge Circle Hike

Time: 6-9 hours roundtrip. **Length:** 12 miles total. **Difficulty:** 3.

Begin at the Maya Lodge doorstep and do a circle with a pickup at Gordon Town to make it a little easier.

Passing through coffee plantations and montane forest, you come back down along waterfalls, a river valley and through a couple of villages. Steepest part is the Fairy Glades Trail, which requires a couple of scrambles.

4. Jack's Hill Area

Time: numerous hikes from 1 to 5 or 6 hours at elevations between 1000 and 3000 feet. **Difficulty:** 2-3-4.

At these lower levels, you hike along streams, waterfalls and rivers, features lacking at higher altitudes. Day hikes include Guava Ridge, Content Gap and Gordon Town. At Jack's Hill, a park on the north side will link with the botanical gardens on the south side to provide a green area immediately north of Kingston.

5. Newcastle/Fairy Glades Trail

Time: 2-1/2 hours to hike over Mt. Horeb, which will bring you onto a road; another 30 minutes to take it back to Newcastle. **Difficulty:** 2-3.

The Fairy Glades Trail, which can either be hiked separately or is used as a connecting link with other tracks, is one of the prettiest spots in all the Blue Mountains. Hundreds of varieties of ferns, including huge tree ferns, and orchids grow in this misty, humid place. Taken all the way to Newcastle, the walk passes through several different forest systems, including montane and elfin woodland. Not a particularly difficult trail, it may require a few scrambles at the outset. Depart from the Old Stables Inn (160 years old) in Newcastle.

Also starting from the Old Stables Inn are several other excellent hikes: Woodcutter's Gap, Fern Gap and 5,000-foot-high St. Catherine's Peak, named for Catherine Long who climbed it in 1760, the first woman known to have scaled it.

Newcastle, still used today by Jamaican troops, was established by the British in 1841 because troops manning the lowland forts were dying of yellow fever in alarming numbers. Buttercups, which grew in great

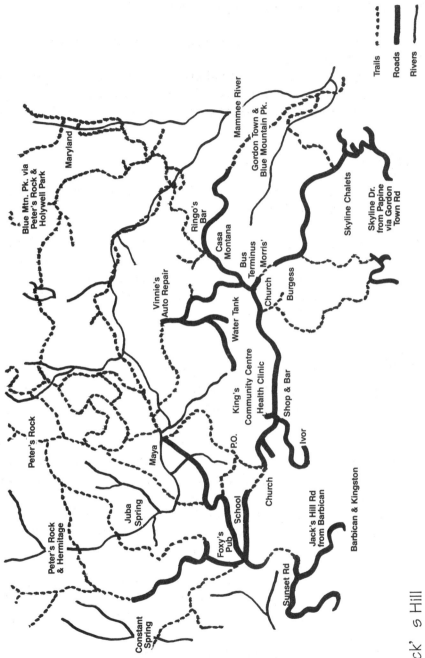

Jack's Hill

numbers following the rains, were blamed for exuding some sort of effluvium that caused the deadly sickness. By putting troops high in the forest, they would be too far away from the buttercup fields to be affected. It was much later before someone made the connection between yellow fever and the hearty, thriving mosquito population that—along with the buttercups—mushroomed with the rains.

Black slaves were much less susceptible to yellow fever than their British owners. Slaves named the buttercups after the white people (or "backras"), calling them "kill-backras." The saying also developed that "If backra wants to live long, he must ask nayga leave" because it appeared the less sickly negroes knew the secret to good health and long life.

6. Port Royal-Blue Mountains Hike

Time: about 1/2-day. **Length:** the route can be varied to last from 3-7 miles. **Difficulty:** 2.

A standard SENSE Adventures offering, you first climb up Mt. Rosanna (4,100 feet), past the prime minister's private residence, then come back down through Guava Ridge and Content Gap, stopping at a coffee farm where you can have a well-laid-out lunch. On the return near Gordon Town you'll see some beautiful waterfalls. Then it's offshore for some snorkeling around the cays off Kingston (small deserted islands sheltered by a small barrier reef untouched by pollution from Kingston Harbour). The cays are said to have some of the best fish you'll see while snorkeling anywhere in Jamaica. Finally, if time permits, a tour around Port Royal.

7. Hellshire Hills

Time: from 1-3 days. **Difficulty:** 3-4.

Dry tropical forest that gets only thirty to forty inches of rain, located very close to Kingston. The tree canopy here is a low fifty feet. Lots of cactus and what is known as macca bush, with prickles and thorns. There you will find the seven to eight-foot-long, endemic Jamaican iguanas which until recently were thought to be extinct. It turns out they may even be thriving. Also wild horses, donkey and hogs in the western Hellshires. This is not easy hiking because the vegetation doesn't coat the rocks as thoroughly, so everything is brownish. Rain makes the exposed limestone rock very sharp. The Hellshires are a very different type of wilderness area which would take a couple of days to completely hike through. Most people are content to go in and come back out the same day. Only one trail actually goes through the Hellshires, the other goes along the coast. It's so dry that not many people even try to use it for ganja farming.

8. John Crow Mountains

Time: up to 2 weeks to penetrate, though this is rarely attempted. **Difficulty:** 4-5.

The wettest part of the island is the John Crow Mountains, which absorb the full brunt of the moisture-laden air coming off the Caribbean. This region reportedly receives as much as 400 inches of rain annually.

The John Crows are considered almost inaccessible because of the great amount of rainfall, which plays havoc with the limestone terrain. As on Blue Mountain Peak, your feet may break through the thin crust. It is also steep in places and the rain forest is impassable following a downpour.

There are no trails going through the John Crows, only along the edge and a short way into it. It would be an extensive undertaking, requiring cutting the trails as you go.

9. Bath Fountain to Millbank Trail

Time: 6 hours. **Length:** 14 miles, one way. **Difficulty:** 5.

This hike through the John Crows starts at the Bath Fountain mineral springs north of Morant Bay and ends up twenty miles south of Port Antonio, at Millbank, in Portland. It passes through some of Jamaica's last true, virgin rain forest where the only residents are birds and butterflies. Part of this trail requires fording streams that may be as much as waist deep.

10. Crossing the Cockpit Country

Time: 2 days or about 14 hours of steady walking time. **Length:** 2 trails about 8 miles each way. **Difficulty:** a rugged 5.

Ants and mosquitoes can be a bother. Be careful of your footing, not to break through the limestone crust or slip on the leaves. So, unless you're a seasoned pro, I strongly recommend joining a SENSE Adventure tour. It's easy to get hurt in the Cockpits.

The Cockpit Country has tough hiking terrain similar to the John Crow

Mountains, but this at least is open for exploration. The Cockpit Country is a high plateau southeast of Montego Bay in the remote center of the island. It is surrounded by mountains and limestone hills shaped like cones, known technically as karst formations. It's still impassable except on foot; not even four-wheel-drive vehicles attempt the Cockpits.

Cockpit terrain is characterized by lots of caves and ravines and thick, thorny vegetation, very different from the high altitude montane forest of the Blue Mountains. It is also typical lowland rain forest with a forest canopy of 80-100 feet. Broadleaf, mahogany, silk cotton and mahoe trees all grow here. You may see hawks, parrots and red-crested woodpeckers in the trees. Avoid a green plant with serrated leaves called a "scratchbush;" it will leave you itching for days. This is a good area for long pants.

It takes about a day to cross the Cockpit Country. You need to camp overnight or have someone to pick you up at the other end. Camping is usually the easier option. This can be quite warm walking, very humid with jungly rain forest, so take lots of water. A bromeliad called "wine pine" contains as much as a pint of water if you run short. Most comfortable walking is in the winter months, the driest part of the year for a region which receives 100-150 inches of rain. Mist often rolls in early and late.

There are two trails, each about eight miles in length, that cross the Cockpits between 750 and 1500 feet. The peaks extend to about 3,000 feet at the highest, so it can get cool. You should take a guide because the tracks are not regularly used and they can be quite overgrown, requiring some machete work. Progress is about one mile per hour because of all the up and down walking—no possibility of going straight as the crow flies. Trails go from Quickstep to Deeside and from Troy to Crown's Land and onto Windsor Cave.

The Cockpit Country residents are descendants of the Maroons, slaves freed by the departing Spanish. The Maroons also had to fight the occupying British to keep from becoming their property. The cut-off remoteness of the Cockpit region suited the Maroons for hiding, as it suits their heirs' reclusive lifestyle still today.

11. Montego Bay Great Houses: Rose Hall & Greenwood

Time: 1 hour each. **Difficulty:** 1.

For a change of pace take a couple of nice easy walks on the grounds of two restored plantation houses, Rose Hall and Greenwood. Both are east of Montego Bay on the road to Ocho Rios. In the 1700s, Rose Hall may have been the finest great house in the West Indies. Rose Hall has one of Jamaica's best legends, about its second mistress, Annie Palmer, who murdered three husbands and a plantation overseer. Open 9:30 a.m. to 6 p.m.

Domestic conditions were less volatile at the lesser known Greenwood Great House, which is actually a better visit for an idea of what life was like on one of the old sugar plantations. A highlight of the tour is the rare book library with copies going back as far as 1697. Open 9 a.m. to 6 p.m.

# 12. Montego Bay River Valley Hike

Time: a half to full day. **Length:** most hikes in the Montego Bay district are 6-9 miles long. **Difficulty:** 2-3.

Surprisingly, this is a virtually unknown region seldom seen by tourists. However, guided walks are expected to become a major attraction here in the years to come. The river valley has some excellent hiking but it's difficult to know where the trails start. The trails are unmarked and only the local people know of them for their own use. You definitely need a guide to set off on the proper foot. You're walking at an altitude of between 500 and 1000 feet, so it's low level hiking among streams and rivers with interesting views but no forest. The trail system is excellent, link adding to link so you can cover quite a distance. In fact you can walk all over Jamaica that way; it's a matter of knowing where the link-up trails are.

13. Black River Gorge

Time: full or half-day hikes. **Length:** about 2-1/2 miles.
Difficulty: 3-4, depending on conditions.

A very special area where you'll see twenty-nine waterfalls in just two-and-a-half miles. Picturesque, but you won't see any giant cascades; the tallest falls is about forty feet, the smallest around ten. Going into and coming out of the gorge is quite steep. It also can be very slippery.

# 14. Negril

Time: half to a full day. **Difficulty:** 1-2.

No true hiking to speak of, only walking along the five-and-a-half mile beach (not seven miles as the brochures say) and then the paved road that runs along the cliffside. Lots of interesting guest houses and hotels, large and small, so this is more of a resort walk than a genuine beach walk. However, you'll probably be hustled and hassled like nowhere else in Jamaica, offered everything under the sun, including sex, ganja and even cocaine, which is imported.

Fronting the western-most tip of Jamaica, you'd expect Negril to witness many spectacular sunsets and it does. Rick's Cafe is the favorite overlook, a tamer Caribbean version of Key West's famous sunset celebration. The music is loud, the beer is cold and the women worth watching (veteran travelers agree that Jamaica is home to some of the world's most beautiful women).

In terms of walking and hiking, Negril is worth about an afternoon for walking the beach and seaside craggy cliffs, and watching the sunset. Then it's time to move on, unless you are ready for resort-town living.

15. Bob Marley's Grave

Time: varies personally. **Difficulty:** 1.

Bob Marley, the high priest of reggae, is buried near his birthplace, in the tiny village of Nine Miles, south of Runaway Bay between Philadelphia and Alexandria. It's a small place and not on all maps. The stained glass windows of the small chapel containing the crypt are in the rasta colors of gold, green and red. Ganja sometimes grows in the church garden. Marley's birthday is April 6; on that night his fans gather to play his music, usually until dawn.

16. Ocho Rios

Personally, I find Ocho Rios the most scenic part of Jamaica. The name, incidentally, apparently does not derive from the Spanish term "eight rivers" as is popularly supposed but instead is a corruption of the word "chorreras," a Spanish term which describes the many streams and rivers that plunge down the limestone rocks.

17. Dunn's River Falls Ascent

Time: 1 hour. **Difficulty:** 2-3.

Just two miles from Ocho Rios toward Montego Bay is the most famous cascade in Jamaica, if not the entire Caribbean: Dunn's River Falls. This very scenic spot is used more than any other place to advertise and symbolize Jamaica. Dunn's River Falls is 650 beautiful feet of waterfalls, which can be climbed either with the assistance of a paid river guide (hanging out everywhere, don't worry about finding one) or on your own.

One advantage of a guide is that he can carry your camera and take pictures of you while you splash in the pools and stand under the falls. Some river guides walk with so many cameras draped around them they look like they're covering the arrival of the queen. Either way, you will pay an admission fee to enter the lushly landscaped park. The rocks are slick, and some routes definitely work better than others. Watch where the guides go.

Considering that this is cold mountain water, it's most comfortably climbed when the sun and temperatures are at their highest, in the middle of the day. In afternoon, the main falls are fairly shaded. However, this also tends to be the least crowded period, a good time to walk up the rocks and enjoy the solitude. Open 8 a.m. to 5 p.m..

18. Shaw Park Gardens

Time: 1 hour. **Difficulty:** 1.

Shaw Park sits on a hillside overlooking Ocho Rios and is usually filled with the blooms of bougainvillaea and hibiscus. It also has streams and lily ponds, another easy scenic walk. Open 9 a.m. to 5 p.m.

19. Fern Gully

Time: 1 hour each way. **Difficulty:** 2.

Jamaica has more than 500 species of ferns, and you can see at least 300 of them in this dark, shaded gorge almost three miles in length. Until an earthquake in 1907, the gorge was one of the eight flowing rivers of the Ocho Rios area. The river disappeared during the earthquake and the river bed was turned into a paved road. The dense fern growth appears to have been growing in place since the beginning of time, despite such a recent start. Often crowded with auto traffic, there is talk of closing it to vehicles and turning it into a park. You will find several places to turn off and look around. The gully is on the road connecting Ocho Rios and Kingston that passes through Spanish Town.

The White River at Ocho Rios.

# 20. Orcabessa Area

Time: 30-45 minutes each site. **Difficulty:** 1.

Writers Ian Fleming and Noel Coward wouldn't seem to have much in common, but they both did much of their writing on estates near Orcabessa, about twenty miles from Ocho Rios on the way to Port Antonio. Both had excellent taste in wonderfully scenic real estate; Fleming's home is beachfront and Coward's is mountaintop.

Stop at the Texaco station in Orcabessa for directions to Fleming's "Goldeneye," where he wrote all thirteen of the James Bond novels. Goldeneye is not always open to the public, but if you are fortunate enough to be able to stroll the grounds you'll be able to see the modest white, blue-shuttered house whose interior has been totally remodeled. The house sits on a high cliff above the private bay below. A stairway to the right leads down to the beach where Fleming snorkeled many mornings just before pitting Bond against the world's worst villains.

Noel Coward's estate "Firefly" is well marked and sits 1,000 feet above the coast. The view from the top, now a government-sponsored museum dedicated to the English author, is magnificent. The land originally belonged to the pirate Henry Morgan. Coward lived here from the 1950s until his death in 1973. The estate has four acres of grounds and gardens to walk at the top of the hill, but you don't have to make the climb up unless you want to. You can drive to the parking lot. Fireflies are supposed to gather regularly atop the hill at night, supplying the inspiration for the name. Open 10 a.m. to 5 p.m.

 21. Port Antonio

Time: 2-3 hours. **Difficulty:** 1-2.

Beyond Ocho Rios is Port Antonio, 133 miles east of Montego Bay. The birthplace of Jamaican tourism, Port Antonio is usually ignored in favor of other resort areas. It attracted such cruise ship passengers as Rudyard Kipling, William Randolph Hearst, Clara Bow and J.P. Morgan. Actor Errol Flynn loved Port Antonio so much he moved there. The sixty-eight-acre Navy Island, once owned by the actor, can be reached by ferry. It has two beaches (one nudist) and a pricey restaurant. Boston Bay, Fairy Hill Beach, San San Beach, Frenchman's Cave and Blue Lagoon all have beautiful, small beaches. Nonsuch Cave and Somerset Falls are other potential stops. Most people come to raft the Rio Grande River rather than walk Port Antonio, which has many beautiful old buildings.

# 6. U.S. Virgin Islands

Old West Indian Proverb:
Ingratitude is Worse than Witchcraft

The U.S. Virgin Islands were discovered by Columbus on his second voyage in 1493. His choice of names has long puzzled historians. While sailing among the lushly fertile, gently rounded, warm and welcoming islets after a long, hard voyage, Columbus apparently was reminded of St. Ursula. According to legend, Ursula herself undertook a long voyage of her own, accompanied by 11,000 virgins. Tragically, they were all raped and killed.

All well and good, but historians—who have obviously never spent prolonged, celibate periods at sea—cannot figure out why Columbus didn't name the new land St. Ursula. It would go nicely with the other saintly names, John, Thomas and Croix. Perhaps it was the virgins Columbus fixated on. Columbus singled out one voluptuous landmass—obviously a favorite—as his "Fat Virgin"(Virgin Gorda in the British Virgin Islands.)

Columbus apparently found the islands more compelling than did later visitors. The British and Dutch came and saw and split. The French took control in 1650, laying out townsites, plantations and forts, but left by the end of that century.

By 1733, the Danes controlled the islands, with the intent of turning sugar into gold, and lots of it. St. Croix, the largest and flattest island, was a natural for sugar cultivation and became the leading sugar cane producer by 1750. Slaves were imported to work the fields in 1763. Sugar brought St. Thomas and St. Croix great wealth, and planters commissioned the elaborate, substantial buildings you see standing today. Few other islands can boast such attractive and durable structures.

With the fall of the sugar economy, the Danish West Indies became a financial drain instead of a valuable asset. The United States became interested in buying St. Thomas and St. John in 1867, shortly after the Civil War. Denmark was agreeable but the U.S. Congress was not. The U.S. made an offer for all three islands in 1902 but that attempt also failed.

In World War I, the U.S. feared that Germany might capture the area and turn St. Thomas into a submarine base. The Danes accepted an offer of US $25 million in 1917. It was an expensive sale for its time; $300 per acre. (Alaska was a much better initial deal for the U.S., costing about two cents an acre. However, today a single acre of U.S. Virgin Island beachfront may go for well over a quarter million dollars, while there is waterfront real estate in Alaska no one wants to touch.) Through this purchase, the U.S. Virgin Islands became the first territory under the U.S. flag actually discovered by Columbus.

After experiencing what is probably the Caribbean's best duty-free area, the gentle hikes of St. John are a good way to introduce novice walkers to the fun and adventure of hiking in the tropics. St. John offers magnificent views and trails. Where hiking is total pleasure, never an ordeal.

Travel Tips

Area: St. Thomas, 32 square miles. St. John, 28 square miles. St. Croix, 84 square miles. Approx. 75 cays and rocks form the entire U.S. Virgin Island chain, which lies 40 miles east of Puerto Rico.

Language: English

Population: St. Thomas 45,000; St. John, 2,500; St. Croix, 50,000.

Time Zone: Atlantic Standard Time, one hour ahead of Eastern Standard Time.

Rainy Season: Forty inches per year, mostly from June to October.

Getting There: For years, St. Thomas was notorious for having one of the worst airport facilities and one of the most dangerous runways in the entire Caribbean. That situation has changed dramatically with the opening of its new multi-million-dollar airport.

American Airlines has direct flights from many parts of the U.S. to St. Thomas and St. Croix; St. John does not have an airport. Delta flies to San Juan, where you can connect with other major carriers.

On the basis of personal experience, I recommend flying one of the major airlines into St. Thomas or St. Croix directly or—if you must go through San Juan—fly only American Airlines. The small island commuters from San Juan are notoriously unreliable operations. They often leave late and your chances of finding your luggage at your destination are not good. Having flown several, I can't say enough bad things about them.

Getting Around: Taxis and rental cars are available everywhere. In exploring St. Thomas, it's a good idea to take a taxi tour first to get a feel for the island. Road signs are almost nonexistent and traveling on your own can get confusing. St. John, on the other hand, is quite easy to explore. Because things are so spread out on St. Croix, a rental car is the only way to move around; taxi fares will eat you alive. If you drive, drive on the left. You're on American soil, but these American territories have used the "English" side of the road since they were under Danish rule.

Where to Stay: The U.S. Virgin Islands have more hotels per square inch of land than anywhere else in the Caribbean. The best hiking is on St. John. Both St. Thomas and St. Croix have interesting city tours and picturesque countryside. St. John, alone, has everything you come to the Virgin Islands for.

For an interesting St. Thomas stay, try Blackbeard's Castle, a five story, sixteen-room, tower-shaped inn overlooking Charlotte Amalie. Built in 1678 by a local resident, it's doubtful Blackbeard (who did anchor here occasionally) ever slept in it.

If hiking/walking is only one reason for your visit, it would make sense to stay on St. Thomas for some shopping, take the ferry over to St. John for the hiking, then move on to St. Croix for the historic sites. The most interesting way to hop between St. Thomas and St. Croix is by seaplane, locally called the "goose." The seaplane base on St. Thomas is at Charlotte Amalie, at Christiansted in St. Croix.

Taxes & Tips: A government tax of 7.5% is added to all hotel bills. In addition, some resorts add a 15% service charge, plus another US $5 per night as an energy surcharge. For taxis and restaurants, tips of 10-15% are expected.

Documents: A passport is necessary for all except U.S. citizens, who can get by with either a voter's card or birth certificate. Although the U.S. Virgin Islands are an unincorporated territory and all residents are citizens of the U.S., everyone—regardless of nationality—has to clear customs upon departure. Keep that in mind when budgeting time for your return to the airport. When several flights are departing at the same time, customs can get very backed up.

Shopping: U.S. citizens are allowed to bring back $1,200 worth of merchandise duty free, $400 more than any other Caribbean island allows. An unlimited number of gifts (excluding perfume, liquor or tobacco) may also be mailed back to the U.S. as long as the value is less than $100 per parcel. Goods cost as much as 60% less than Stateside. Shops normally are closed on Sundays unless a cruise ship is in port. Cruise ships tend to pile up on Wednesdays, when as many as four or five vessels may be in port. That's when the streets of St. Thomas really seem narrow.

Electrical Current: Same as for most of North America, 110 volts, 60 cycle.

Dress Code: Swim suits are fine for the beach but are prohibited in downtown Charlotte Amalie. They're also frowned on in St. Croix.

Currency: The US dollar is standard. Credit cards are accepted almost everywhere. Banking hours are 9 a.m. to 2:30 p.m. Monday through Friday and 3:30 p.m. to 5 p.m. Friday afternoon.

Getting Married: A fair number of couples get married in the U.S. Virgin Islands every year. Write for a marriage license application to: Territorial Court of the Virgin Islands, Box 70, St. Thomas, USVI 00801; 809/774-7325. There's an eight-day waiting period following the return receipt of the notarized application in St. Thomas.

For More Information: U.S. Virgin Islands Division of Tourism, 1270 Avenue of the Americas, New York, NY 10020; 212/582-4520. In the UK, 2 Cinnamon Row, Plantation Wharf, York Place, London SW11 3TW; 071/924-3171.

Health/Safety Warning: You may suffer harm if you don't watch where you go after dark, especially in Charlotte Amalie on St. Thomas, which has a crime rate that would make any American city proud. Never leave anything unattended anywhere, especially on the beaches. Prowling land sharks are far more bothersome than the ones cruising offshore.

Snakes and Other Venomous Creatures: No poisonous snakes—hats off to the mongoose! You may be fortunate enough to see a three-to four-foot-long marine iguana meandering along one of the beaches. Though fierce and prehistoric looking, marine iguanas are totally harmless.

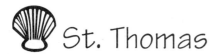# St. Thomas

Although St. Croix is the largest of the group, St. Thomas is the capital and the most developed island. The harbor area is like any large American city with its attendant traffic; but up in the hills a more tranquil pace prevails. You will find cattle grazing emerald fields in a countryside that reminds many travelers of France. In fact, just outside the busy downtown is a place called Frenchtown.

St. Thomas has eight beaches, most of them ideal for short walks and snorkeling. Heart-shaped Magens Bay was named one of the world's ten most beautiful beaches by *National Geographic*. I'll take St. John's Trunk Bay or Cinnamon Bay over Magens Bay anytime. If you prefer development on a small scale, you may agree.

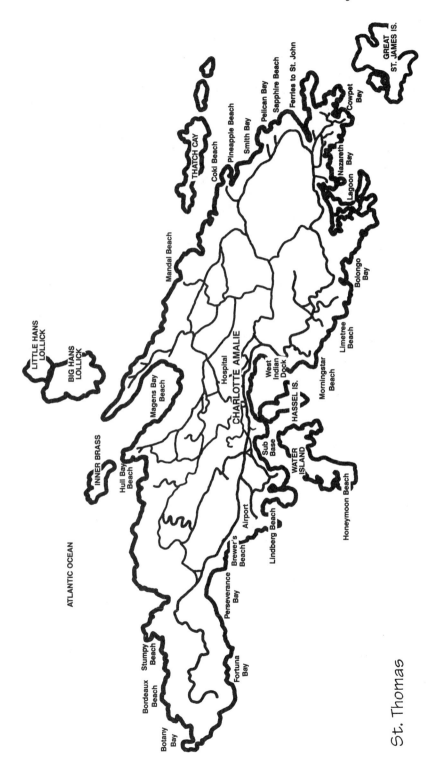

St. Thomas

Walking Tour of Charlotte Amalie
Time: 2-3 hours. **Difficulty:** 1

At some point, you should enjoy an overview of Charlotte Amalie from the mountains or the water. Only then will you appreciate the dazzling checkerboard roofs of silver and red. Motor traffic is congested because the streets, built by the Danes for horse and carriage, are too narrow for automobiles. Walking is the easiest and most pleasant way to tour Charlotte Amalie.

The majority of the midtown buildings are of thick masonry, originally old warehouses, built to replace burned-out wooden structures. Living by candlelight may appear romantic to us, but in the 1600s and 1700s it was extremely dangerous. The dried, weathered buildings were piles of kindling, waiting for a flame. Most of the old warehouses have been safely remodeled into colorful stores bursting with duty-free goods from all over the world.

Charlotte Amalie's original name was Tap Hus, Danish for "rum shop," in honor of its most popular product. St. Thomas has always been appreciated by people who like a good time, and never more appreciated than by pirates who used it as an "R&R" stop, right under the nose of the Danish authorities. The Danes were canny enough not to drive off their best customers, as long as they behaved while in port. Honest pirates who paid their bills were always welcome.

In fact, it was through the pirates and the plunder they offloaded in St. Thomas that the harbor city became a great port. The Danes declared it a free port in 1724, and nothing has changed: You can still find a "steal" compared to the price-plus-tax elsewhere. In 1730, Tap Hus was renamed Charlotte Amalie, after the wife of Danish King Christian V.

1) Blackbeard's Castle: Originally Fort Skytsborg, now part of a small hotel. This five-story tower supposedly is the "oldest extant historical structure in the Virgin Islands." Pirates, including the infamous Blackbeard, reputedly used it for a lookout tower.

If the stories about Blackbeard are to be believed, he was as much a freak show as a swashbuckler. He's said to have gone into battle after these preparations: braiding his long black beard, tying the tails of it around his ears and putting lighted candles in his hair. Another version has him wearing lighted fuses. Now, that would have been an interesting sight, indeed: the sputtering ends looking like snakes gone wild. This is the way I prefer to picture Blackbeard, as a demonic Medusa and not as a rum-belching Christmas tree.

2) 99 Steps: Dating to the 1700s, these steps from Government Hill to Lille Tarne Gade (Danish for "Little Tower Street") were a shortcut up the

The first voyagers to St. Thomas were pirates who turned their city called Tap Hus, Danish for "rum shop," into a duty free port. Tap Hus, now renamed Charlotte Amalie, is still one of the Caribbean's greatest duty free ports.

hill. If you climb them, count and see how many you come up with; there are more than 99 of the low steps. Many such staircases were built to get up and down the steep hills.

3) Hotel 1829: On Kongen's Gade, this 19th-century, Spanish-style building with its narrow passages, dark bar and picturesque open court-yard holds one of the island's better restaurants. You are welcome to simply look around.

4) Government House: On Government Hill on Kongen's Gade, Government House is the residence of the governor of the U.S. Virgin Islands. Visitors are allowed on the first two floors of the three-story building. The floors are of wood and the walls are decorated with paintings and murals by Camille Pissarro, the impressionist who was born here and whose house you visit on this tour.

5) Grand Hotel: Built in the 19th century, it now houses offices and gift shops. It opened in 1840 as a hotel and coffee house. The Greek Revival building had a third story, but lost it to hurricane damage around 1896.

6) Emancipation Park: Containing a gazebo and a replica of Philadelphia's Liberty Bell, the park commemorates the freeing of the slaves in 1848. Official ceremonies are still held here occasionally. Grab a bench, relax and watch the local children at play.

7) Frederick Lutheran Church: At the head of the street leading to Fort Christian, the building was erected in 1793, replacing earlier structures lost

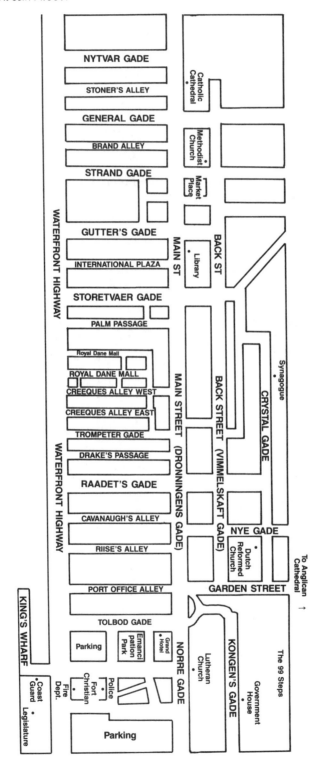

Charlotte Amalie

to fire. It's the second-oldest Lutheran church in the Western Hemisphere. Refurbished in 1826, this was the official church of the Danish West Indies.

8) Fort Christian: The dark red walls of this fort were begun in 1672, as soon as the Danes arrived. That first colony was so small that everyone could fit inside the fort. It was completed in 1687; the bell tower was added in the 19th century. The fort has served as a jail, governor's residence, courthouse and church. A museum of local history is located in the dungeons. Along with Blackbeard's Tower, it claims to be the oldest standing structure in the U.S. Virgin Islands.

9) Legislative Building: This lime-green building with beautiful flower gardens is where the Virgin Islands Senate meets. The building, dating from 1874, was built as barracks for Danish troops.

10) Homeport: This small town is the main yachting marina and dock for cruise ships. When the Danes sold their islands to the U.S. in 1917, they held onto this small strip of land, which has turned into something of a gold mine.

11) Synagogue: On Crystal Gade. Rebuilt several times, this is the second-oldest Jewish temple in the Western Hemisphere. The oldest is in Curacao. The sand on the temple floor is a reference to the Exodus from Egypt.

12) Pissarro Building: Located on Main Street between Storetvaer and Trompeter Gades, this is where impressionist painter Camille Pissarro was born. He lived upstairs in what is now a perfume shop. A plaque commemorating his birth is around the block on Back Street. There is no museum here; the best exhibition of his paintings is at Government House (see above).

13) Market Square: On Strand Gade, fruits and vegetables from all over the island are sold from open-air stalls here. The roof now sheltering the stalls was purchased from a European railway company in the early 1900s.

14) Main Duty Free Shopping Districts: This couldn't be easier: All the stores lining both Main and Back Streets are duty free. In case you can only find Danish street signs, Main Street is Dronnigens Gade; Back Street is Vimmelskaft Gade. For 300 years, these streets have featured some of the world's greatest shopping. Arguably, they could be the birthplace of the strip mall. Remember, the State-side duty-free allowance is higher for the U.S. Virgin Islands that for most other islands.

15) Havensight Mall: Another intense shopping spot, recently built near the West India Dock so cruise ship passengers wouldn't have to go into town. Featuring three lines of air-conditioned boutiques, the prices are the same as in Charlotte Amalie, but this high-tech mall lacks that downtown ambiance (that of a feeding frenzy).

16) Hassel Island: Part of the Virgin Islands National Park system and located just in front of Charlotte Amalie, this island has plenty of old ruins to explore, from military sites of the 1700s to an old marine yard. Go by water ferry.

 Water Island Hike

Time: 2-3 hours. **Difficulty:** 2-3, depending on heat.

At 491-acres, Water Island is the fourth largest of the U.S. Virgin Islands. It can be reached from the Crown Bay Dock on the west side of the city. Following its earliest incarnation as Fort Segarra in WWII it underwent an amazing metamorphosis to become an exclusive resort. It is such a unique tale that it inspired Herman Wouk's *Don't Stop the Carnival*, a classic novel describing the pitfalls and heartaches of Caribbean hotel ownership. Once you read this book, you'll better understand why things so often go wrong at tropical resorts.

After WWII, Army troops pulled out of Water Island and the Chemical Warfare Division laid claim to it for experiments with poison gas. The program was discontinued in 1950, and the Army retained ownership of the island but did nothing more with it.

In 1951, retired New York stockbroker Walter H. Phillips and his wife visited Water Island in search of a likely homesite. Although the land was deserted and desolate without a single resident, Phillips decided the island had resort potential. He enlisted the help of local officials who wanted to see the island developed, and a bill was passed through Congress that transferred ownership of Water Island from the Army to the Interior Department.

Phillips then leased the entire island—without charge—from the government for a period of forty years in return for developing it. In essence, Water Island became a separate principality: it was exempt from all taxes, and it was up to Phillips to supply all roads, garbage collection and other services.

Because many people dream of running away to a Caribbean island to start a resort of their own, Phillips' Water Isle Hotel attracted considerable media attention. Not only did novelist Herman Wouk draw upon Phillips' problems as a hotel owner for *Don't Stop the Carnival*, *The Saturday Evening Post* (1956) and *Life* Magazine (1962) also highlighted his saga.

What made Phillips so notable was—despite shortages of building materials and good help—he was making his fantasy work. Of course, the fact that he was building on the foundations of an old Army outpost also helped him become a standout. In addition to constructing the hotel, Phillips was also leasing individual land plots for $2,500, and many of his leaseholders were converting old gun turrets, concrete latrines and soldiers' barracks into small homes and apartments. It made terrific copy.

Phillips' hotel is now closed, but private residents still come and go. In fact, they are the ones who normally provide the ferry service for visitors, for a fee.

Even today Water Island is still the kind of place to which people would gladly run away. Construction was slow and orderly, partly because that was Phillips' original plan, partly because some people were reluctant to make a big commitment to a property which could vanish anytime after the lease from the U.S. government expires.

Hiking the island, you must stroll the 1,000-foot long Honeymoon Beach built by Walter Phillips in the 1950s. Originally a strip of sand only fifty feet long and ten feet wide, it was created after moving more than 200 truckloads of rock and brush, breaking the beach stone with a bulldozer, and dredging away the seaweed and building up the sand. It is considered one of the safest swimming beaches in the Virgin Islands and a favorite anchorage for sailboats.

The island's rugged terrain has several roads criss-crossing it. There are still a few remains of old Fort Segarra to see; perhaps a small botanical garden with coral and shell collections, and the tiny, almost miniature combination post office/library that was once unique in the U.S. because of its small size. Iguanas and hummingbirds are also commonly spotted on Water Island treks.

 St. John

It's just a fifteen-minute ferry ride from Red Hook on St. Thomas to St. John, an island as big as St. Thomas but without its big city ways. Most of St. John is a national park, and consequently, both the land and waters surrounding it are well protected. Cruz Bay, the main town, is a tiny backwater village compared to thriving Charlotte Amalie. For those who like to feel they're in the uncrowded Caribbean, St. John is the place to be.

Like St. Thomas, St. John has some spectacular beaches. The best-known is at Trunk Bay, whose underwater snorkeling trail with its red, white and blue markers isn't nearly as well known (or crowded) as the Buck Island Trail at St. Croix.

St. John remains green and natural—a stark contrast to intensely developed St. Croix and St. Thomas—thanks to developer Laurence

Rockefeller. In 1956, Rockefeller and his Jackson Hole Preserve Corporation donated two-thirds of St. John to the U.S. National Park system, which has allowed approximately 10,000 acres of landscape to evolve naturally into second-generation forest including sea grape, kapok trees, cactus and century plants.

The Park Service has opened the forest to visitors with twenty different walking/hiking trails, among the easiest and most scenic paths in the Caribbean. Some paths are actually old donkey-cart trails, in use as late as the 1940s.

It's hard to believe that today's quiet, laid-back St. John was like other prosperous islands in the 1700s; most of the hillsides were clean-cut and terraced to grow the sweet green gold—sugar cane. St. John is the site of one of the most successful slave rebellions, when African workers took control of the island for nine months in 1733. The Danes, who owned St. John at the time, were unable to quell the revolt alone and had to call in both British and French forces to finally subdue the slaves. Rather than return to servitude, many Africans committed suicide by jumping off the Mary's Point cliffs.

Because most of St. John is only slightly above sea level, it is one of the Caribbean's few major hiking islands where you'll be concerned about mosquitoes, mostly early and late in the day, or during rainy periods. It's also drenchingly hot much of the time because of the low altitude, so water bottles are essential. You won't find much in the way of supplies outside of Cruz Bay.

There is no bus service, so your best bet is to rent a car or jeep at about $50 per day. Cabs are too expensive to keep one waiting while you explore. Most of the major car rental agencies have offices right at the Cruz Bay ferry dock. Shop several for the best price. Important reminder: even though St. John is in the U.S. Virgin Islands, you drive on the left, a carryover from the days of the Danes.

The Park Service information center is just left of the ferry dock in Cruz Bay; after disembarking, follow the road to the left for five to ten minutes. You can't miss the building on the left, almost directly across from Mongoose Junction, a small mall that is Cruz Bay's main shopping district.

Where to Stay: Choices are few, compared to St. Thomas or St. Croix. The massive Hyatt Virgin Grand is the island's most expensive and luxurious hotel. The Caneel Bay Hotel, which Rockefeller started, looks better from the outside than the inside. Much less expensive are two small inns in Cruz Bay itself, Raintree Inn (809/776-7449) and Cruz Inn (809/776- 7688).

Camping: Both campgrounds on St. John are very popular, so reservations need to be made well in advance. Tenting at the Cinnamon Bay

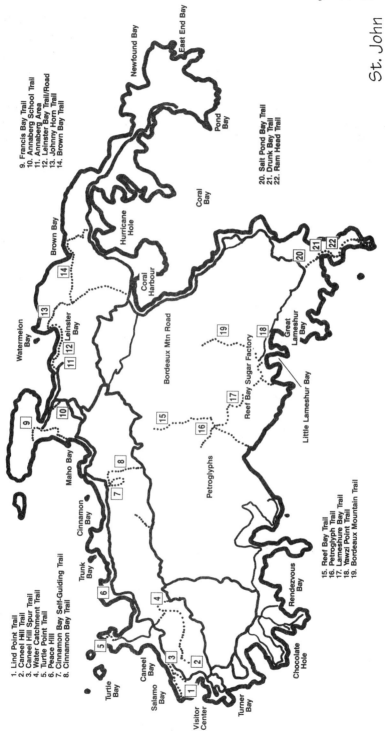

St. John

1. Lind Point Trail
2. Caneel Hill Trail
3. Caneel Hill Spur Trail
4. Water Catchment Trail
5. Turtle Point Trail
6. Peace Hill
7. Cinnamon Bay Self-Guiding Trail
8. Cinnamon Bay Trail

9. Francis Bay Trail
10. Annaberg School Trail
11. Annaberg Area
12. Leinster Bay Trail/Road
13. Johnny Horn Trail
14. Brown Bay Trail

15. Reef Bay Trail
16. Petroglyph Trail
17. Lameshure Bay Trail
18. Yawzi Point Trail
19. Bordeaux Mountain Trail

20. Salt Pond Bay Trail
21. Drunk Bay Trail
22. Ram Head Trail

Newfound Bay
East End Bay
Pond Bay
Coral Bay
Hurricane Hole
Brown Bay
Coral Harbour
Watermelon Bay
Leinster Bay
Bordeaux Mtn Road
Great Lameshur Bay
Little Lameshur Bay
Reef Bay Sugar Factory
Maho Bay
Petroglyphs
Cinnamon Bay
Trunk Bay
Rendezvous Bay
Turtle Bay
Caneel Bay
Salamo Bay
Visitor Center
Turner Bay
Chocolate Hole

Campground in the national park is one of the Caribbean's great bargains. It costs only about US $12 per night for a bare site, but there are only about a dozen of them. Forty ready-pitched tents and forty one-room cottages rent for US $40-US $50 per night for two people in summer, US $60-US $75 in winter. Tents and cottages come with 2-burner propane stove, charcoal grill, ice chest and eating utensils. Contact Cinnamon Bay Campgrounds, 501 Camino Real, Boca Raton, FL 33432;800/223-7637.

Maho Bay Campground is slightly larger, with 113 tent cottages that sleep one to four persons. These fully furnished units, $50 per couple in summer, $75 in winter, are mostly concealed in hillside vegetation. Contact Maho Bay Campground, 17-A East 73rd Street, New York, NY 10021; 800/392-9004.

Hiking/Walking Services: Guided walks are conducted several times weekly by National Park Service guides, who are very familiar with the island's history and resident wildlife, including the wild donkeys, mangrove cuckoos, gallinules and pelicans. A walking schedule is posted at the interpretive center. This is an excellent place to stock up on books describing the native vegetation if you decide to take self-guided hikes, which is what most people do.

Hiking Trails

The precise distance of these trails has been measured by the Park Service, a rare service in the Caribbean, where walks/hikes are normally measured only by time.

North Shore Trails:

 ## 1. Lind Point Trail

Time: 45 minutes to 1 hour. Length: 1.1 miles. Difficulty: 1.

The easiest-to-reach trail in the park, it begins less than a half mile from the Cruz Bay ferryboat landing and combines the two things people seek in St. John: a hike and a beach.

The trail starts behind the **National Park Visitor Center** at Cruz Bay. It leads to tiny Salomon Beach, which is only a hundred yards long. Salomon is one of the two beaches on the island where people sunbathe nude, though technically it's illegal.

From the parking lot, the trail ascends .3 miles to a scenic view at Lind

Point Battery Overlook (elevation, a dizzying 160 feet). To reach Salomon Beach, take the left spur .2 miles northeast of Lind Point, passing through mostly dry forest and cactus scrub. If you continue on another .2 miles and turn right, you'll connect with the North Shore Rd. and the Caneel Hill Trail.

 ## 2. Caneel Hill Trail

Time: 2 hours. **Length:** 2.4 miles. **Difficulty:** 2.

One of the few loop trails on St. John, the Caneel Hill Trail begins .8 miles from Cruz Bay and is most easily reached by walking the North Shore Road. It's on the right, just past the guard rail, and well marked. This hike, mostly a steep ascent, brings you to an overlook tower on Caneel Hill after .9 miles, finally reaching Margaret Hill at 1.4 miles. It then descends steeply back to the North Shore Road and comes out near the entrance to the Caneel Bay Resort.

 ## 3. Caneel Hill Spur Trail

Time: 10 minutes. **Length:** .3 mile. **Difficulty:** 1.

Here's a chance to use the beach enjoyed by those staying at the exclusive Caneel Bay Resort.

Located on the left side of the North Shore Road near the entrance to the Caneel Bay Resort—almost directly across from where the Caneel Hill Trail descends—this trail is easy to spot because it starts next to the big brown Virgin Islands National Park sign. Take this short trail and cool off in the water at Caneel Bay after completing the Caneel Hill Walk. All beaches in the Virgin Islands are public beaches, so everyone has the right to swim and sun on the sand. However, you won't be allowed to use resort amenities such as beach chairs or be allowed to enter the resort grounds themselves.

4. Water Catchment Trail

Time: 30 minutes. **Length:** 1 mile. **Difficulty:** 2

This forest-canopied road runs between Centerline Road and the Northshore Road. At one point, it also joins the Caneel Hill Trail.

 5. Turtle Point Trail

Time: 30 minutes. **Length:** .6 mile. **Difficulty:** 1-2.

This trail, which begins at the north end of Caneel Bay Plantation, requires that you register at the front desk first.

6. Peace Hill

Time: 5 minutes, one way. **Length:** .1 mile. **Difficulty:** 1.

This is a scenic overlook of Hawksbill Bay, but the main attractions are the old sugar mill tower and the Christ of the Caribbean statue.

The trail starts next to the parking lot on the hill at the end of Hawksbill Bay, 2.8 miles from Cruz Bay. Look for the lot about a hundred yards past a huge boulder on the left shoulder of the road. There is no sign indicating that this is Peace Hill or what is to be seen. The Christ statue looks like a huge, modeling clay figure sculpted by an elementary school class. It was donated to the Virgin Islands National Park in 1975, and placed adjacent to a sugar mill tower. Overall, this spot offers a superb photo opportunity of the ruins, water and surrounding hillsides. It's a popular stop for bus/ cab tours.

7. Cinnamon Bay Self-Guiding Trail

Time: 30-45 minutes. **Length:** .5 miles. **Difficulty:** 1.

One of the park's most popular trails, this loop tours the ruins of an old Cinnamon Bay sugar plantation.

The trail begins on the right, just a few yards past the Cinnamon Bay campground. The ruins are visible from the road. Park in the campground parking lot. This is a shaded walk with appropriate signs explaining the parts of the old factory and identifying many of the trees. At the horse mill, horses once turned the rollers to crush the cane. The huge copper pots held boiling cane juice. The trail also goes past a number of old Danish graves.

 8. Cinnamon Bay Trail

Time: 1 hour, one way. **Length:** 1.1 miles. **Difficulty:** 2.

This is another popular trail, but unlike the neighboring self-guided path with virtually the same name, this is a true hike.

The trail begins just to the left of the Cinnamon Bay plantation ruins about 100 yards beyond the campground. The moderately steep ascent follows an old Danish plantation road through a moist shady forest. It comes out on the Centerline Road, requiring a return descent. While there, you can walk another .9 miles east on Center Line Road to reach the Reef Bay trailhead, the park's most popular trail.

However, since the roundtrip Reef Bay hike is 4.4 miles, most people don't combine the two. If you do climb Cinnamon Bay Trail, walk to the Reef Bay trail, make the Reef Bay hike and return to your vehicle on North Shore Rd., you will have traveled a total of 8.4 miles, which would take about half of a day.

9. Francis Bay Trail

Time: 15 minutes. **Length:** .3 miles. **Difficulty:** 1.

This is a good place to view bird life, particularly during winter months.

Located at the west end of the paved Mary Creek Road, the path goes through dry scrub forest and past the ruins of the Francis Bay Estate House. Before ending at the beach, it also takes you past a mangrove forest and a brackish pond, which is where you're apt to see most the birds.

10. Annaberg School Trail

Time: 15 minutes. **Length:** .2 miles. **Difficulty:** 1.

This leads to one of the oldest public school houses in the Caribbean.

The trail is on the left just before the road Y's to Annaberg and Francis Bay. The school house is just a shell of the building and not really worth visiting unless you have a real affinity for ruins.

11. Annaberg Area

Time: 30 minutes. **Length:** .25 mile. **Difficulty:** 1.

These are the finest sugar plantation ruins on St. John and should not be missed.

The buildings are just off the paved road to the right of the Leinster Bay Trail. The road dead-ends in a parking lot. Technically, this isn't a hike but a walking tour of the old plantation, where you'll also enjoy a terrific view of Tortola and Jost Van Dyke in the British Virgin Islands.

The 18th-century Annaberg estate exhibits its windmill tower and slave quarters made of stone, ballast brick and coral, although nothing is fully restored or in working order. Great vats once turned the sugar cane into molasses and are still present on the site.

12.-13.-14. Leinster Bay/Johnny Horn/ Brown Bay Trails

Three trails that lead off from one another into very different habitats. Many of today's hiking trails and paths follow roadways that once connected the thriving Danish plantations.

Leinster Bay Trail
Time: 30 minutes. **Length:** .8 mile. **Difficulty:** 1.

You can drive most of the .8 mile Leinster Bay Trail, an old Danish road skirting the water's edge, which leads to Watermelon Bay. You'll find cobblestone remnants along this old route which ends at the ruins of the Leinster Bay Estate.

Follow the old road west from the Annaberg picnic area to Watermelon Bay. The road borders the shoreline, a popular boat anchorage and swimming area. This is a good spot for snorkeling, and marine turtles come ashore on summer nights to bury their eggs on the beach. If you walk the seashore of Leinster Bay, you may hear the laughter of a psychopathic maniac: it's the cry of the duck-like bird known as a coot and apparently the source of the term, "crazy as a coot."

Johnny Horn Trail
Time: 2 hours, one way. **Length:** 1.8 miles. **Difficulty:** 2.

This trail begins at the end of Leinster Bay. It ascends to an upland dry forest and scrub, following the ridges southward to Emmanus Moravian Church, on a paved road. The trail is seldom used.

Brown Bay Trail
Time: 2 hours, one way. **Length:** 1.6 miles. **Difficulty:** 2-3.

This spur turns off to the east .7 miles from the beginning of the Johnny Horn Trail, and is not maintained. It descends through a hot, dry valley, borders Brown Bay for a time and then ascends to overlook Hurricane Hole. It comes out on East End Road 1.2 miles east of the Emmanus Moravian Church.

South Shore Trails

Most of these trails begin somewhere along Centerline Road. Road signs also refer to Centerline Road as Route 10.

 ## 15. Reef Bay Trail

Length: 2.2 miles. **Time:** 2 hours, each way. **Difficulty:** 2, descending; 3, ascending. Carry insect repellent and water.

This is the best hike in the park, since it is so representative of the island's vegetation. Longer than most, it is also the most popular since this is the trail on which the Forest Service provides scheduled tours: the trail descends nicely all the way from the Centerline Road to Reef Bay. On these outings, a boat picks you up at Reef Bay and brings you back to Cruz Bay so you don't have to make the return ascent. You also have the chance to see Indian petroglyphs.

The trail begins 4.9 miles east of Cruz Bay on Centerline Road. A stone barrier on the side of the road marks the beginning. Descend a flight of stone steps to reach the sign marking the trailhead. Most of the vegetation here is second- and third-growth, since most of the trees were cut down during plantation days to clear cane fields and to make charcoal. However, the high, steep valley at the beginning was never completely cut, so you can get a sense of what the original subtropical forest was like. This upper stretch gets more rainfall, so parts of the path can be quite slippery.

The Reef Bay Trail is a microcosm of the entire island. Among the species you'll pass at the outset are the bay rum tree, whose oil-laden leaves were used to make bay rum cologne which was popular from the 1890s to the 1940s, and the West Indian locust, source of wood used for shipbuilding, fence posts and furniture. The locust tree has seeds with a strong-smelling yellow pulp that originally gave it the name of "stinkin toe." Actually, this pulp is quite edible and sweet tasting. The kapok (silkwood) tree's seed pods contain a fluffy cotton-like fiber that planters once used to stuff mattresses.

You'll pass several drainage gullies but watch for the pockets of shale;

they can be icy-slick even when dry. These drainage gutters, centuries old, are what keep the trail in such good condition. The Danes built the stone gutters to carry water across—not down—the road, preventing washouts, despite the steep terrain. At one time, when more of it was paved with volcanic rock, the path could easily withstand heavy loads of sugar-filled hogsheads carried here in ox carts.

Note how several of the trees are bound with strangler figs, so named because the fig may overrun and kill the host tree. The latex of the bark and fruit of the strangler fig were once used for caulking boats. Its broad green leaves have served as writing paper and playing cards.

Wild donkeys, wild hogs, huge termite mounds and beautiful golden orb spiders may be seen along the trail. In the fall you may witness a hermit crab migration when the crabs go to sea to reproduce and find new, larger shells.

Thirty minutes along the trail, you'll reach the Jossie Gut Sugar Estate. The ruins include a circular sugar cane grinding platform from the 18th century. The sugar boiling room and several other parts of the factory still stand. The walls are a mosaic of stone, coral and red and yellow brick. Mortar was made from a mixture of lime from seashells, sand, and sweet molasses from the sugar cane. The entire exterior once was covered with a reddish plaster, so it must have been quite a sight.

You'll see a thorny lime tree, imported from Southeast Asia and cultivated as an export crop on St. John. Sailors ate the limes to prevent scurvy (vitamin C deficiency) on long voyages. Other good uses for lime juice you may not have known: the juice helps dissolve sea urchin spines, should you step on one. It also helps heal sand fly bites.

About forty-five minutes down the trail is the Par Force Village, the foundations of a plantation workers' village. Although sugar cane was no longer cultivated after 1916, some workers tried to stay on by raising cattle and farming. They finally abandoned the land in the 1940s. Old bottles, pots and glass shards are displayed on the foundation to be admired, not taken. Walk just five minutes more and you reach the right turnoff for the Petroglyph Trail, (see below).

After examining the plantation and farming ruins, you'll enter a much drier forest as you near the beach. Eventually you'll reach a small picnic area and pit toilets near the Reef Bay sugar mill ruins. The plantation, one of four on this route, produced brown sugar and molasses from the 1860s until 1916.

16. Petroglyph Trail

Time: 15 minutes, round trip. **Length:** .2 miles. **Difficulty:** 1.

This trail starts 1.5 miles, or about fifty minutes, from the beginning of the Reef Bay Trail on Centerline Road. The beginning is marked and much of the path borders an old stone wall.

After a five-minute walk, the path leads to a small freshwater pool. In the rainy season, you can enjoy a waterfall. Crayfish and shrimp live in the pool, but they may be difficult to see because of the algae cover. Because this is a rare supply of fresh water, you'll hear lots of birds; and near dark, lots of insects humming overhead.

The petroglyphs are difficult to see; they are only faint impressions in the rock at the pool waterline. They vary quite a bit in shape, style and location and it's likely that each new group of inhabitants left their own graffiti. Most of the drawings, some of which are attributed to the Arawak Indians, are located at the far right end of the pool. However, at the opposite corner is an obvious crucifix which is of much more recent origin. This watering spot is an interesting cultural crossroad of those who have lived on St. John.

17. Lameshure Bay Trail

Time: 1-1/4 hours, round trip. **Length:** 1.5 miles. **Difficulty:** 1.

This trail connects Lameshure Bay with the Reef Bay Trail.

This hike takes you through open dry forest. About 1.2 miles from the Reef Bay junction a spur of .3 miles leads off to a small salt pond and Europe Bay, which is mostly coral rubble beach.

18. Yawzi Point Trail

Time: 20 minutes. **Length:** .3 mile. **Difficulty:** 1.

This very short trail is named for the outcasts—those infected with yaws, the West Indian version of leprosy—who were forced to live in isolation on this narrow peninsula. Yaws, which is confined almost exclusively to the warm moist tropics, causes eruptions on the skin and is highly contagious, transmitted either by flies or by direct contact with an open sore. Once considered a tropical form of syphilis, yaws can appear on any part of the body. Sexual contact is the least likely way it is spread. It is easily treated today. Consider what it must have been like to be exiled to this region of thorny scrub vegetation and isolated coves.

19. Bordeaux Mountain Trail

Time: 1-1/2 hours, round trip. **Length:** 1.2 miles. **Difficulty:** 3

Don't be fooled by the shady beginning, atop Bordeaux Mountain. This steep, hot, open trail descends 1,000 feet to Lameshure Bay. It begins on the Bordeaux Mountain Road; Centerline Road is 1.7 miles northwest of the trail junction with Bordeaux Road.

20.-21.-22. Salt Pond Bay/Drunk Bay/ Ram Head Trails

These three trails are connected and continuous. The trailhead for all three is the parking area 3.9 miles south of the town of Coral Bay.

Salt Pond:
Time: 15 minutes, round trip. **Length:** .2 miles. **Difficulty:** 2.

This graded trail, which is hot and open, descends through cactus scrub to Salt Pond Beach, where the swimming and snorkeling is particularly good. There is a picnic area and a chemical toilet. In May and June you may see locals harvesting salt from Salt Pond.

Drunk Bay:
Time: 20 minutes, round trip. **Length:** .3 miles. **Difficulty:** 1.

From the south end of Salt Pond Bay Beach and turn east to follow the Drunk Bay Trail. The vegetation is stunted and windswept near the rocky bay, where swimming is dangerous.

Ram Head:
Time: 1 hour, round trip. **Length:** 1 mile. **Difficulty:** 1-2.

This rocky, exposed trail also starts at the southern end of the Salt Pond Bay Beach and leads to a blue cobblestone beach. Your destination is 200 feet above the Caribbean, reached through a series of switchbacks leading to a magnificent overview. Be careful near the cliff edge.

 St. Croix

The largest of the U.S. Virgins, St. Croix (pronounced "St. Croy") covers a total of 82.2 square miles, four times the size of St. John. Its name is the French version of the name Columbus gave it: Santa Cruz. The Danes bought the island from the French in 1733, after establishing themselves on St. Thomas.

St. Croix was pre-eminent among the U.S Virgin Islands, particularly during the days of sugar cane. Just how important sugar was to the local economy is still clearly evident: the island is dotted with the ruins and restorations of more than 100 old sugar mills and great houses. After the slaves were emancipated, labor costs made growing cane unprofitable. Owners of the big sugar plantations began abandoning their estates, the island's population dwindled as the economy went into a severe slump.

St. Croix is separated into two distinct regions marked by the cities of Christiansted and Frederiksted. Both cities are characteristically Danish, adapting 18th-century European styles to the West Indies. Strict building codes kept the towns from becoming shoddily-built tinderboxes; therefore unlike some of the more ramshackle British-ruled outposts, these cities were never leveled by fire. By law, the first floor had to be constructed of brick and stone, so yellow brick was shipped as ballast from Denmark for this purpose. Wood could be used only in the second floor, normally the living quarters. The first floor contained the shops and retail stores. It was common to build long galleries across the front on the second floor and support them with stone arches, leaving the sidewalks well shaded from the sun.

The Danes offered tax concessions to anyone who would come to raise sugar cane or cotton, and many British, Dutch and Portuguese took up the offer. By 1800, 375 different estates were growing sugar cane, cotton, tobacco and indigo. Soon the English controlled the economy by producing most of the sugar cane and rum, and English became the everyday language on this Danish island. Many of the old estate names still used today—Good Hope, Judith's Fancy—are in English, not Danish.

St. Croix

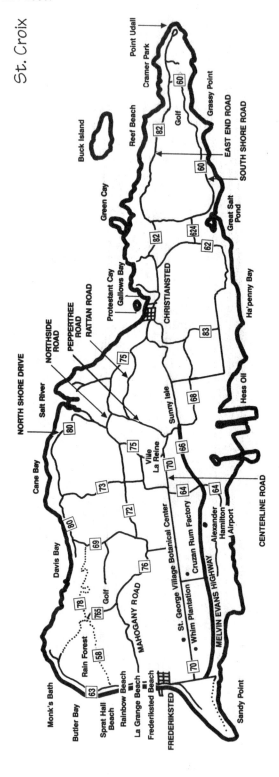

Walking Tour of Christiansted

Most of the hotels and shopping are located in Christiansted, considered one of the Caribbean's loveliest ports. Featuring a lingering Danish influence, several blocks along the waterfront are part of a twenty-seven-acre Christiansted National Historic District, including six historic buildings operated by the U.S. National Park Service. With its colonial buildings and open air restaurants, Christiansted is a joy to explore on foot. It takes less than two hours to do it thoroughly.

1) Fort Christiansvaern: This is the most outstanding building when viewed from the harbor, a bright yellow color the Danes seemed to favor. Begun in 1733 with yellow ballast-brick, the fort was partially destroyed by a hurricane and then rebuilt in 1837. It saw its last use by the military in 1878, then became a police station and courthouse. Fort Christiansvaern, the best preserved of the five Danish forts through the U.S. Virgin Islands, is restored to its 1830s incarnation and contains an exhibit of local military history. Dungeons, ramparts and old cannons are but a few of its features.

2) Protestant Cay: The small island-hotel at the harbor entrance is typically called the Hotel on the Cay. Its original name comes from the era of French ownership, when only Catholics could be buried on the big island. Protestants were buried on this tiny spit of land. After the French left St. Croix in 1696, pirates turned it into a favorite meeting point.

3) Old Danish Customs House: This is where the Danish captains would report to pay their customs fees. Part of the first floor was built in 1751, but most of the building was constructed between 1828-1830.

4) Visitor's Bureau: Built in 1856 as the Old Scalehouse, this was the site of the huge scale that weighed all merchandise being imported into Christiansted. It was also where exports were inspected and where troops attached to the Customs Service were garrisoned. The scale is still present.

5) Old Danish West India and Guinea Company Warehouse: This building is located across Company Street from the Visitor's Bureau. It is the home of the company that purchased St. Croix from France and turned it into a sugar cane factory. The building's history dates back to 1749 when it first housed provisions, offices and personnel. Slave auctions were held in the courtyard. After 1833, the Danish military used it as a depot and later a telegraph office. It is now the post office.

6) The Steeple Building: Built as a Lutheran Church by the Danes in 1753, the steeple was added in 1794. After 1831, the Danish government turned the church into a military bakery, then a hospital and then a school. This prominent landmark is now a National Park Museum with archaeological, black history and architectural exhibits.

7) Government House: Located on King Street beyond The Steeple Building, Government House is considered one of the finest examples of

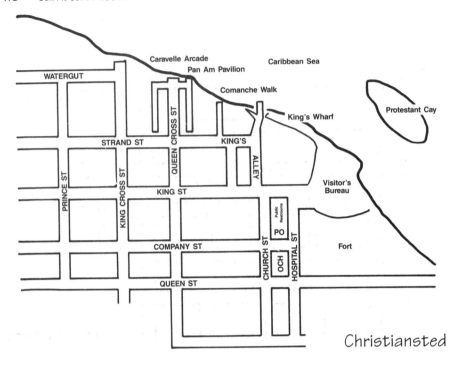

Christiansted

Danish architecture remaining in the islands. It was built in 1747 as a home for a wealthy Danish merchant. The Danish government purchased the house in 1771 and connected it to another house at the corner of Queen Cross Street to become the seat of the island government. The building still houses government offices and a court. Its most striking feature is its elegant 18th-century staircase.

8) **Apothecary Hall:** Located on Company Street, this was an 18th-century pharmacy and a private residence. It has been carved up into offices, a restaurant and boutiques.

9) **The Market Place:** Another half-block beyond Apothecary Hall on Company Street, the market is not as colorful or as interesting as the markets on other islands. Since 1735, this has been the place to buy fresh, locally-grown vegetables and fruits.

10) **King Street/King's Alley:** A prime waterfront shopping area housed in what were once old trading houses, this section features boutiques and open air restaurants. It is an enjoyable place to window shop.

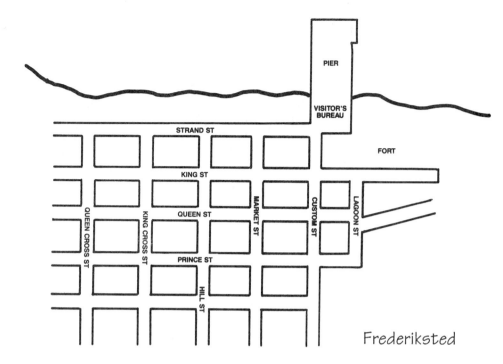

Frederiksted

Frederiksted

Frederiksted is located at the western tip of St. Croix, a forty-five-minute drive from Christiansted. Since its founding in 1751, it has been St. Croix's main deepwater harbor; all cruise ships dock here. Visitors are then transported by bus to Christiansted and other points of interest.

If you are arriving by cruise ship, my advice is take the first taxi out of town and leave Frederiksted for last. The fort is really the only thing worth seeing.

1) Fort Frederik: Where the Governor General in 1848 announced the emancipation of all Danish-owned slaves; for this reason, the town today is still sometimes called "Freedom City" by locals. The Fort, begun in 1752, is where the flag of the thirteen rebelling U.S. colonies was first saluted by a foreign flag, in 1776. The fort is now a museum, restored to the way it looked in 1820.

2) Shops: Recently opened near the wharf to take advantage of the cruise ship traffic.

3) Market Place: On Queen Street, this can be a lively bartering place for fresh fruit and vegetables.

4) The Old Pier, Now Underwater: Hikers/divers please take note: this is one of the finest night dives anywhere in the Caribbean and can be arranged through Cruzan Divers in Frederiksted (809/772-3701).

Elsewhere on/around St. Croix

The Rain Forest

Despite the name, this is not true rain forest; it doesn't receive nearly enough precipitation. However, the vegetation is definitely more luxuriant than other places on the island and the tree canopy towers a hundred feet overhead with orchids and ferns, just as you would expect to find in a genuine rain forest. It's cooler here, making it an exceptionally nice place to walk.

Mahogany Road (Hwy. 76) leads through a major section of the forest. Look for the sign to the right, leading to St. Croix's Leap, a good place to purchase mahogany handicrafts made by local artisans. There are also several dirt roads entering the dense forest from the top of West End Road. These roads are best traveled by foot or four-wheel-drive vehicle. You'll also find a number of footpaths in this area.

The Great Salt Pond

Going west on Route 60, the road follows the profile of Great Salt Pond— a shallow, saltwater pond fringed with mangroves. This area is a protected nature preserve and is home to egrets, white-crowned pigeons, herons and yellowlegs.

Ham's Bay/Scenic Road West

Follow paved Rt. 63 until the hard surface ends at concrete pillars marking the Scenic Road West. To reach Ham's Bay, walk east along the beach to Ham's Bluff and the lighthouse there, a thirty-minute walk. Some excellent views and shell-finding opportunities.

The Scenic Road West is a dirt road best traveled on foot or with a four-wheel-drive vehicle. This is a very isolated stretch, so provision yourself well: it takes five hours to walk one-way, and it's occasionally strenuous terrain. After thirty minutes, you'll reach a path to the left, leading to an overlook at Hamm's Bluff. Continuing on the Scenic Road West, you'll ascend a ridgeline covered with kapok, mahogany trees and long trailing vines. Stay left at the next intersection, and walk four miles to a superb view of Davis Bay to the north, Blue Mountain to the east and the rolling fairways of the Fountain Valley Golf Club off to the south. Another one and one-half miles will put you at the end of the Scenic Road West and place you on paved Rt. 69. This is perhaps the best panoramic view on the entire island.

St. George Village Botanical Garden

Located just off Centerline Road, three and one-half miles east of Frederiksted in Estate St. George, you can walk through sixteen acres of gardens, considered one of the finest botanical collections in the Caribbean. In addition, you'll find the ruins and restorations of a 19th-century Danish sugar plantation workers' village. A map takes you on a self-guided tour through sites identified as the Rain Forest, Laura's Garden, the Cactus Garden, the original sugar factory, a cemetery and the largest Arawak Indian settlement on St. Croix. For information on fees and hours, call 809/772-3874.

Whim Estate House

The Whim Estate, just west of Frederiksted, is the finest surviving plantation great house of the approximately 300 built in the 1700s. The oval-shaped, high-ceilinged plantation has been carefully restored and is furnished with period antiques. Architecturally unique, it has a small moat around the base, used not for defense but to help cool the air. Besides the restored cook house, mills and a gift shop, the Whim Estate has the island's most photogenic windmill, complete with giant white blades, something you rarely see on any of the islands. Open daily, the estate charges an admission fee.

Point Udall

The easternmost point of the United States, Point Udall is a dry, fairly barren area worth visiting only because of its unique geographic location. Take the East End Road (Rt. 66) to its second junction with Rt. 66 and turn left (east) if you're coming from Christiansted. Park at Cramer Beach Park and walk for an hour to reach Point Udall, or drive along the same dirt road leading right to it. Get out and find the trail to Isaac Bay, a secluded area where the seas can be foaming and turbulent.

Buck Island

Buck Island Reef National Monument, two miles north of St. Croix, is the most-visited and best-known snorkeling/diving site anywhere in the Virgins. Under the protection of the U.S. National Park Service since 1962, it uses underwater markers in the shape of grave headstones to mark the famed underwater trail, which is suffering from both its popularity and the effects of hurricanes. The protected zone underwater covers about 700 acres.

However, you can also hike on 180-acre Buck Island itself. Once a major grazing location for goats, Buck Island was stripped of its trees to create pasture. Now free of domestic animals and humans, the land is

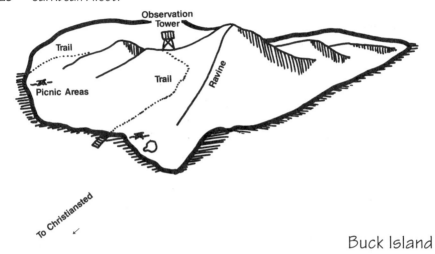

Buck Island

returning to a more natural state. There is a trail going into the interior to the top of the island, more than ample activity for a half-day's walk.

Bring water, since this is a dry place, particularly the eastern and southern sections where vegetation is mostly cactus and low thorny bushes. Trees are found in some moist areas, on the western slopes and in ravines.

Walks on Buck Island become more popular all the time. The Park Service has installed two picnic areas, and the forty-five-minute hike to the 300-foot high summit has an observation tower for even better views of Buck Island and St. Croix. This trail is rocky, so wear shoes. A combination snorkel/hike excursion from St. Croix will take almost a full day. Boat transport can be arranged through, among others, Mile Marker Charters on King's Wharf in Christiansted; 809/773-2285.

7. British Virgin Islands

Sixty miles east of Puerto Rico lie the British Virgin Islands, a place abounding with so many colorful stories it's difficult to separate fact from fable. For instance, it was on Dead Man's Chest Island (one of fifty islands, rocks and cays that comprise the British Virgins) that Blackbeard marooned fifteen of his buccaneers with only a bottle of rum and a cutlass. It's not known how many survived, but we still commemorate their ordeal with "Yo-Ho-Ho and a Bottle of Rum."

This is also the land of Long John Silver and *Treasure Island*. Robert Louis Stevenson visited the British Virgin Islands shortly before writing his classic, though what he called Treasure Island is actually known as Norman Island, named for the pirate whose treasure is believed still buried there.

The British Virgin Islands, adjacent to the U.S. Virgin Islands, are an extremely picturesque group. Most are mountainous and—during the early summer rainy season—lushly green. When it's dry, the landscape turns deep brown and more arid, yet palms, mangoes, cactus, loblolly, frangipani, hibiscus and bougainvillea all manage to thrive here. Temperatures are almost perfect: 77°-85° in winter, 80°-90° in summer, with temperatures dropping about ten degrees each evening.

Traditionally, the British Virgin Islands are a water-oriented community, with little in the way of night life or other social opportunities. All after-dark activities, other than night dives, are confined to the hotels or the private boats.

Travel Tips

Area: 59 square miles of land mass

Language: English

Population: 12,579 of which 2,300 live in the capital city of Road Town, Tortola.

Time Zone: Atlantic Standard Time. One hour ahead of Eastern Standard Time.

Rainy Season: Forty inches per year, mostly from June to October.

Getting There: American Eagle flies several times daily from San Juan to Beef Island, just a few minutes' drive from Road Town in Tortola. Eastern Metro and Air BVI also fly to Beef Island.

If necessary, you can fly to St. Thomas, then reach the main island of Tortola by inter-island ferry, seaplane or regular flight on a puddle jumper. Ferryboats from Tortola make daily trips to Virgin Gorda, the only other major island in the British Virgin Island chain. Peter Island, a privately owned resort, has its own ferry.

Getting Around: Rental cars are readily available, about $35 per day. Another of those irritating, tax-gouging temporary driver's permits: US $10 available from the rental agency.

Where to Stay: Most hotels are clustered on Tortola and Virgin Gorda. To visit as many landfalls as possible, you may wish to charter a sailboat with crew, or captain your own boat (but you must have the necessary experience). Approximately 1,000 sailboat rentals are available from several different companies. Most boats carry four to six persons.

Camping is forbidden except in three designated areas, and the prohibition is strictly enforced. Due to its strong sailing tradition, the British Virgin Islands have managed to convince tourists to do their camping on the water, anchored on an expensive charter sailboat, instead of staying in a cheap canvas/nylon shelter on land. The strict no-camping enforcement helps keep the beaches clean for everyone.

Brewer's Bay Campground on Tortola offers prepared sites that include a 10'x14' floored tent with beds, linen, stove and all cooking implements. It offers a few open spots for people who bring their own tents. Contact Brewer's Bay Campground, Box 185, Road Town, Tortola; 809/494-3463.

On Jost Van Dyke, Tula's N&N Campground has both prepared and bare sites: Box 1364, St. Thomas, USVI; 809/774-0774. In Anegada, the Anegada Beach Campground; 809/495-8038.

Taxes & Tips: 7% hotel tax and 10% service charge.

Documents: U.S. and Canadian citizens need an authenticated birth certificate or voter's registration card. Passports are required of everyone else.

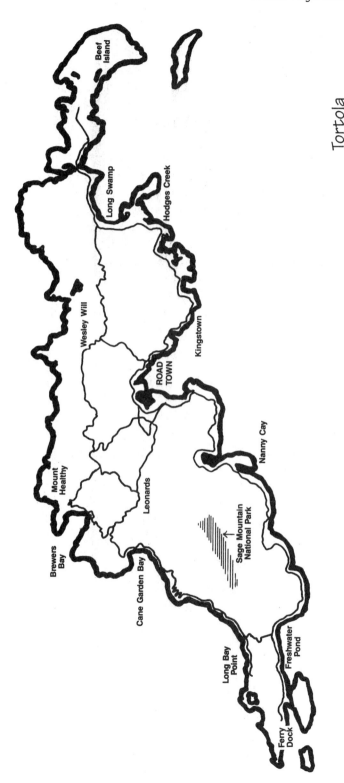

Tortola

Beef Island

Long Swamp

Hodges Creek

Wesley Will

Kingstown

ROAD TOWN

Mount Healthy

Leonards

Nanny Cay

Brewers Bay

Sage Mountain National Park

Cane Garden Bay

Long Bay Point

Freshwater Pond

Ferry Dock

Every landfall in the BVIs has a potential beachwalk. However, you can reach most islands only by private boat.

Currency: The U.S. dollar is the official currency. Major credit cards are accepted in many places, but not personal checks. Banks are open 9 a.m. to 2:30 p.m. weekdays, from 4:30 p.m. to 6 p.m. on Friday.

Electrical Current: Deferring to its largely American clientele, the electrical current is 110 volts, 60 cycles instead of the usual 220 volts.

Hiking/Walking Services: Not really needed in the British Virgin Islands because everything is so well-marked. Should you like a local guide to explain the history and flora, contact The National Park Trust, Administration Bldg., Road Town, Tortola, BVI; 809/494-3904. They do not offer tours but will be able to recommend someone.

Snakes and Other Venomous Creatures: None.

For More Information: In the U.S., contact the British Virgin Islands Tourist Board at either 370 Lexington Ave., Suite 511, New York, NY 10017; or 1686 Union St., San Francisco, CA 94123. Toll-free nationwide except Calif. (800) 922-4876. In Canada, British Virgin Island Information Office, 801 York Mill Road, Suite 201 Don Mills, Ontario M3B 1X7; 416/443-1859. In the UK, Suite 338, Great Eastern Hotel, London EC2M 7QN; 071-283-4130. Be sure to ask for *The Welcome Tourist Guide.*

Beach Walks

Time: extremely variable. **Difficulty:** 1.

Tortola Beach Walks

On the north coast is Brewer's Bay, the location of one of the three campgrounds in the British Virgin Islands. This is an exceptional walk. Long Bay is a full mile of white sand beach with relatively little commercial development as yet. Cane Garden Bay has the best beach in all of the British Virgin Islands: one and one-half miles of white sand, but largely developed. Cane Garden Village is home of the small Calwood Rum Distillery, after 200 years, the oldest—in fact the only—one still bottling in the British Virgins.

Tortola's Apple Bay is worth visiting the night of the full moon when a wild party is thrown at Bomba's Shack. Bomba's monthly mind-blower is staggering...as in, barely walking. It's an important local ritual to observe even if you don't participate. Bomba's is a real shack, too; you must see it by daylight to appreciate its true shackiness. Picturesque is only skin deep, but shacky goes to the bone.

Peter Island

This private resort island has its own ferry service several times daily. The beaches and roads are easy to follow from the marina landing. You can see most of the island in three to four hours.

Anegada

Jost Van Dyke and Anegada offer good hiking possibilities. Little-known Anegada is the second largest of the British Virgin Islands, a mass of fifteen square miles with a maximum elevation thirty feet above sea level. No volcanic upstart like other impetuous land masses we could name, Anegada is a large coral midden that grew gradually from the ocean floor. The north coast offers twenty miles of white sand beaches, one of the longest unbroken beach walks in the Caribbean. But without any shade or water, you need to come to Anegada properly prepared.

 Walking Tour of Road Town

Time: 1-2 hours. **Difficulty:** 1.

If you don't stop to look at sailboats or shop, you can easily walk from one end to the other of Tortola's capital city in less than thirty minutes. To see Road Town at its liveliest (and even at its peak, that's not saying much),

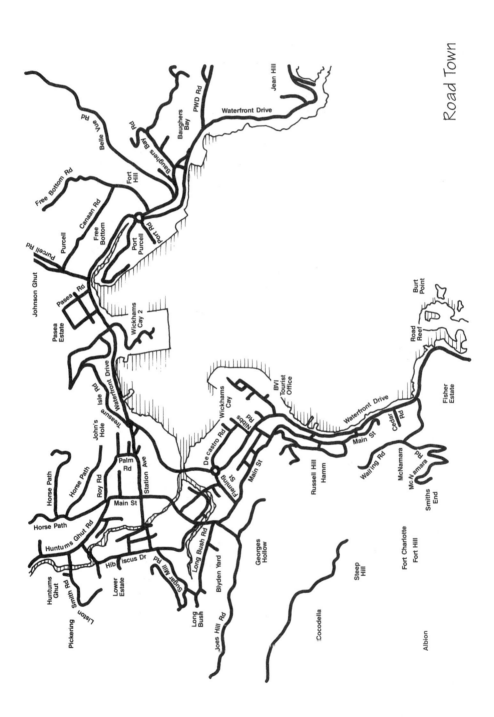

Road Town

avoid a Sunday visit when all the stores will be locked up tight...unless a cruise ship happens to be in.

1) The Moorings: This is where you get nautical. The Moorings is the main charter dock of the British Virgin Islands, the place to arrange day sails or boat rentals.

2) Botanic Gardens: Located on Main Street several blocks inland, this often overlooked site is one of the prettiest spots on Tortola. It is only four acres, but the botanical display features colorful tropical flowers and herbs, a palm garden, fern house, bamboo and grass exhibits as well as a pond and waterfall.

3) Main Street: *The* shopping street of tiny Road Town, it is located one block off Waterfront Drive. None of the shops are large or fancy but almost all are interesting. You can buy spices, honey, spiced rums, Cuban cigars, model sailboats and hand-painted fabrics.

4) Pusser's Company Store and Pub: Located on Waterfront Drive, The Company Store is a nautical version of Banana Republic, with a complete and well-done fashion line. Pusser's Rum not only tastes good, it's a good gift. The pub lunches are superb; try the shepherd's pie. This all may seem pretty touristy, but a lot of locals hang out here.

5) Ferry Dock: For the ferryboats to Virgin Gorda or the U.S Virgin Islands. Located diagonally across from Pusser's.

6) Bougainvillea Clinic for Aesthetic Plastic Surgery: Two violet-colored buildings with white shutters overlook Road Harbour from the hillside. People come here from all over the world to get their faces lifted and their tummies tucked.

 Tortola

It's not often you can hike an entire national park in a leisurely two hours, but that is part of the charm of the ninety-two-acre Sage Mountain National Park on Tortola. Consisting of three short trails, the park has relatively few visitors even though it offers one of the most scenic views in all the islands. Most visitors come to Tortola to sail, dive and drink rum, though not necessarily in that order. Rum is one of the cheapest things you can buy in the British Virgin Islands.

No signs point the way to Sage Mountain from Road Town, but the park is easy to find. Drive up Joe's Hill Road to the top of the hill, turn right and keep climbing until the next intersection. A small (very small) arrow sign points left to Sage Mountain. Follow the road to its end. Part of the road is quite steep and unpaved, a challenge in rainy weather, but don't give up. You'll know you've arrived when you see a small round dirt

Sage Mountain Park Trail

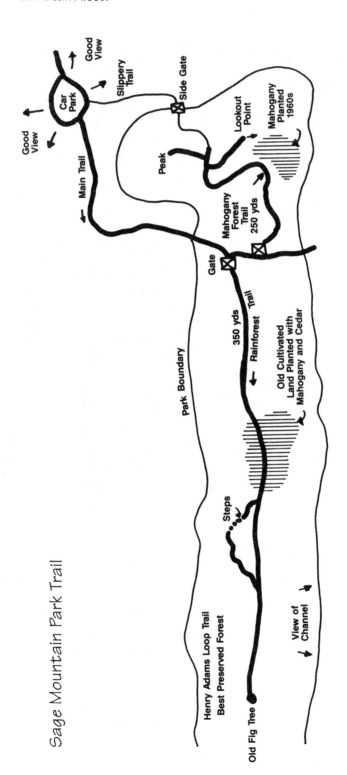

parking lot on the right and the magnificent view of Jost Van Dyke in the distance.

A single path leads to all three trails, which interconnect. The access trail is gravel-covered and at first skirts the edge of Sage Mountain. At 1,780 feet, it is the highest point in either the British or U.S. Virgin Islands. The park area was donated to the British Virgin Island government in the 1960s by Laurence Rockefeller. A concerted effort has been made to reforest the area.

At the outset, don't concentrate entirely on the panoramic view of Jost Van Dyke. Bovine droppings lumped among the gravel call for vigilance.

That hazard is left behind at the swinging wooden gate leading into the longest path, the Rain Forest Trail, and the short side excursion, the Henry Adams Loop Trail. The gate is kept latched (but not locked) to keep the poop off the loop. It's ten-fifteen minutes from the parking lot to this first gate.

 1. Rain Forest Trail

Time: 20 minutes, one way. **Length:** .75 mile. **Difficulty:** 1.

The entire trail is graveled and easy to walk. It alternates between thick, lush foliage and open spaces where the trees are stunted. Signs identify the wide variety of native trees in this area where some re-planting has been done. Most notable of all the rain forest trees is the white cedar, the national tree of the British Virgin Islands. The trail is thick with mountain guava, which is quite colorful when in bloom. Rose apple and redwood myrtle, Spanish oak and West Indian mahogany border the route. Big elephant ear plants are prolific. One of the more unusual trees is called the "stinking fish."

Two small unmarked paths lead to a toilet facility off to the right, and there's also a marked side-path that leads up to a look-out/rain shelter, its purpose dependent on this rain forest living up to its name.

After this shelter the trail descends and the forest grows quite thick. This is the place where you may hear birds. Mountain dove, Caribbean martin, pearl-eyed thresher and American kestrel live in the forest but it's not easy to spot them.

The trail officially ends at a large fig tree, although a pathway continues to the right. The brush thickens quickly and several logs across the path hint that you've run out of trail and that it's time to turn back.

2. Henry Adams Loop Trail

Time: 10-15 minutes. **Length:** several hundred yards. **Difficulty:** 2-3 as it is a steep hike to the top and could be slippery.

This short, marked trail leads off from the main Rain Forest Trail about mid-way.

The loop trail displays the best-preserved part of the forest. The massive bulletwood tree grows here, reaching a height of 100 feet and a girth of four feet. Bromeliads and ferns grow in profusion. This loop returns to the main Rain Forest Trail a few yards from where it cuts off.

3. The Mahogany Forest Trail

Time: 30 minutes from the entry gate back to the parking lot. **Difficulty:** 2, steady climbing much of the way.

When you return to the main gate after hiking the Rain Forest Trail, turn right to the clearly visible Mahogany Forest Trail sign. The trail begins behind another cow-blocking gate. The path does not contain tree/plant identification signs. It is not graveled, so it's slick during heavy rain. Red-arrowed signs prevent wrong turns.

This trail leads to the highest point in any of the Virgin Islands, so it's steady climbing for the first ten minutes. Enjoy the former plantation grounds where mahogany and white cedar were planted in the 1960s. In many sections, the ground is dense with a layer of ferns, though the forest alternates between thick and sparse growth. A marked side trail off to the right leads to a viewing point at 1,710 feet.

Returning to the main path, take the exit sign to the right, which leads to a barbed-wire fence and gate. On the other side, turn left and proceed down the rocky trail to the parking lot. This path, which can be slippery when wet, goes across open land and past a cluster of tree ferns, something unusual in the British Virgin Islands.

 Virgin Gorda

This very mountainous island—called the "fat virgin" by Columbus because of the bulge in her middle—is far less developed than Tortola. Reach it by ferry from Road Town, going over early in the morning and returning the same afternoon. The ferry docks near the Virgin Gorda Yacht

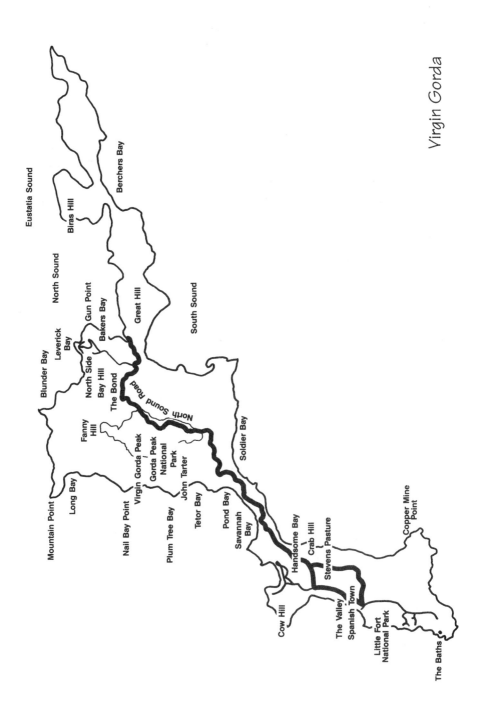

Virgin Gorda

Harbour in Spanish Town, also called The Valley. The easiest way to get around Virgin Gorda is by taxi. The drivers will either wait while you climb or come back at an appointed time. The drivers at Mahogany Car Rental are very tolerant of hikers and their quirks.

 4. Cow Hill

Time: 30 minutes, one way. **Difficulty:** 2, steady but not especially difficult climbing all the way to the top.

This triangular-shaped mountain with the rounded top is just to the left of the ferry dock, the most prominent feature on the horizon.

The marked trail up Cow Hill begins at the parking lot of the Little Dix Bay Resort. This is usually an open, hot hike, so it's best done early in the morning or late in the afternoon. In the dry season, the cactus scrub and dry woodland on the hillside can look almost dead. On a clear day, it's spectacular, with a good view of all the nearby islands.

5. Gorda Peak National Park

Time: one-way to the summit: 20 minutes the main trail, 35 minutes the longer route from the grassy carpark. **Length:** 800 yards, short trail; about double for the second. **Difficulty:** 2.

Located off North Sound Road, about four miles from the ferry dock. Two connecting trails lead to the summit of the fat virgin's belly at 1,359 feet.

Technically, everything above the 1,000-foot level is national park on Virgin Gorda. The park was established in 1974 to protect both the tropical forest and the watershed.

The main trail to the summit is prominently marked with a sign on the left side of the road. Stone steps begin the hike but quickly give way to dirt, rocks and tree roots. Be alert: the summit trail makes a sharp right just a few yards from the road, splitting from another pathway that goes straight ahead. Red paint on the stones and trees blaze the correct trail.

It's a leisurely fifteen-minute walk through the grove of small cedars before reaching the level clearing with three picnic tables and a portable potty. It's another eight to ten minutes to the large wooden observation tower, painted gray to blend in with the granite boulders at the summit. The trees obstruct the view toward Great Hill and Grassy Ground. You can actually see better from the North Sound Road.

Returning to the picnic area, a clearly defined but unmarked trail begins a twenty-five minute walk to a grassy carpark, a better alternative than retracing your steps. The trail ascends for the first few minutes, reaching a large, red, lichen-covered granite boulder worthy of close inspection. In fact, the huge stones along this particular route are the most interesting sights. They tend to be lichen- or moss-covered or have fig tree roots wrapped around them from the trees growing high above.

In Reverse: Begin from the car park and then return to the road via the main trail. The only area of overlap is from the picnic area to the observation tower.

 6. Copper Mine Point

Time: from 10-30 minutes. **Difficulty:** 1-2, depending on route.

Two miles from the Yacht Harbour are the stone ruins of a copper mining operation, first worked by the Carib Indians. They mined extracted copper for trade: copper was alloyed with gold to make the gold more durable.

The Spanish came by way of Puerto Rico after 1528 to mine for gold here, but found only copper. The mine was unused until the 1850s, when tin miners from Cornwall, England, worked the mine. A 160-foot-deep shaft runs under the ruins, which are fenced to keep visitors at a safe distance.

Below the copper mine, the Atlantic waves make a powerful display as they crash onto the point, surge high, then wash back down the gray-colored promontory. You can climb down the hill for a closer look, or simply take telephoto pictures from the top.

7. The Baths National Park

Time: 8 minutes, one way. **Length:** 300 yards from the road. **Difficulty:** 1.

This boulder-strewn beach is the most famous landmark in the British Virgins. The Baths take their name from the massive round granite boulders that form caves, pools and grottoes. There is nothing else like this huge boulder pile anywhere in the Caribbean or in this hemisphere. It was formed during the creation of the islands 100 million years ago, when volcanoes thrust from the seabed. It's been an up-and-down existence for the islands ever since. Today, all we see are peaks of a drowned mountain range which were once connected by land to Puerto Rico and the nearby

U.S. Virgin Islands. They became isolated after the last Ice Age when melting glaciers raised the sea level another 200-400 feet.

Geologists say the granite boulders are the product of molten rock that seeped up into the existing volcanic rock but never reached the surface. Instead, the molten rock cooled slowly, forming a hard crystalline rock layer. Eventually, the softer volcanic covering eroded, exposing the granite blocks. Weathering rounded the gigantic stones into the huge pebbles we see today.

A narrow passageway leads to the heart of The Baths, a stone-canopied pool almost perpetually shaded, which rises and falls with the tide. Careful climbing will take you to the top of The Baths. A small restaurant sells burgers and drinks, a perfect spot to hide from the extremely hot midday sun.

At times, The Baths are overrun with people because it is a popular playground for hikers and swimmers. Early in the morning—before the day sails from Tortola make anchor—is the least crowded time. That's also the best time for photography; in the afternoon, the best place to shoot is from a boat.

9. Devil's Bay National Park

Length: 600 yards from the road. **Time:** 15 minutes, one-way. **Difficulty:** 1.

The trail is to the left of the pathway leading to The Baths. It's a good idea to visit Devil's Bay, so you can get a cold drink later at The Baths' oceanside restaurant/bar.

This open, ever-descending trail leads to a secluded coral sand beach that sees far fewer people than its more famous neighbor, The Baths. The topography is also remarkably different. The open trail passes some of the same granite boulders, then goes through an enormous cactus garden. Organpipe cactus grow to twenty-two feet. Barrel cactus with flowering red tops, and jumping cactus (so-called because the ground stems break off into segments carried off by people and animals) are everywhere. Ground doves, crested hummingbirds and sparrow hawks (locally called killi-killi) may also be seen, along with small harmless ground snakes, geckos and lizards.

8. Sint Maarten/ Saint Martin

St. Maarten Saying:
Their money melted like butter against the sun.

Translation:
Visit the duty free shops in Philipsburg and find out.

Talk about an island with a split personality, this is it. Sint Maarten (the Dutch side) shares this tiny spit of land with Saint Martin (the French side) in what is the world's smallest territory divided between two sovereign states. Located 144 miles east of Puerto Rico, Sint Maarten occupies about seventeen-square miles, Saint Martin a hoggish twenty.

One reason the two groups are able to live together so harmoniously is that they ignore each other as much as possible. A road connecting the two sides was finally built in the 20th century.

Sint Maarten is a favorite cruise ship stop because of the extensive duty free shopping in Philipsburg and the excellent beaches in both Sint Maarten and Saint Martin. The French town of Marigot also offers shopping but on a less frenzied scale. The cruise ship shoppers usually stay on the Dutch side, so the French and Italian boutiques in Marigot tend to be far less crowded.

Except for its beaches, this island is not particularly scenic. With a maximum elevation of only 1,500 feet, the vegetation leans more toward scrubby than luxuriant; apart from the beautiful beaches, the scenic attractions here are man-made, not natural. A cruise ship stop of one day is just right for the length of time serious walkers would want to stay.

To the Indians, the island was known as Sualouiga, "land of salt," and indeed it was the salt pans that attracted the first serious European settlers. Because the island had no permanent water supply, the Arawaks and Caribs were left pretty much alone for the next 140 years except for occasional Spanish raids for slaves to work the gold mines. The French and

Dutch began making plans for occupation around 1630, but the Spanish forcefully returned and built a fort at Great Bay.

In 1644, Peter Stuyvesant of the Dutch West India Company attacked. The Dutch were victorious, although Stuyvesant lost a leg to a cannonball. It hardly put him out of commission, since he later went to North America and became the Governor of New York, then New Amsterdam. Four years later, the Dutch and French settlers signed a treaty of eternal peace.

Dutch Sint Maarten prospered growing tobacco, cotton and sugar until emancipation. Then it went into a steady and swift decline until the 1960s when tourists began taking advantage of its many fine beaches and superb climate. Today, tourism is the all-important, all-consuming pastime for Sint Maarten. The 20,000 residents of the Dutch side cater to 500,000 visitors annually, making it one of the Caribbean's busiest islands.

Saint Martin and Marigot still have their French feel, most obvious not at the nude beaches but in the incredible array of fine restaurants. This is the first (and so far, the only) place I ever dined on ostrich, which was delicious; I'll try it again at the next chance.

Travel Tips

Area: Overall, 37 square miles: 20 are French, 17 Dutch.

Language: Dutch and French in their respective domains; English is widely spoken.

Population: Over 30,000, most on the Dutch side.

Time Zone: Atlantic Standard Time, one hour ahead of Eastern Standard Time.

Rainy Season: This is a fairly arid place, with rainfall of only 45 inches a year. Rain falls mostly between September and December.

Getting There: Sint Maarten's Queen Juliana airport is one of the Caribbean's most accessible, with major airlines flying in from North America and Europe. American Airlines' Puerto Rico hub is nearby, so passengers traveling through San Juan frequently arrive from New York, Miami, Orlando, Raleigh-Durham, Los Angeles and Dallas/Ft. Worth. KLM and Lufthansa fly weekly, Air France from Paris three times a week. Getting here from other Caribbean islands is not difficult because of the many inter-island airlines that stop here. Cruise ships make Sint Maarten a regular stop.

Getting Around: Taxis are plentiful. Rental cars are reasonable and in good supply except during the peak season; arrange one when you book your hotel. International and foreign drivers' licenses are accepted. All driving is on the right side.

Where to Stay: Every type of resort imaginable, including gambling

Sint Maarten

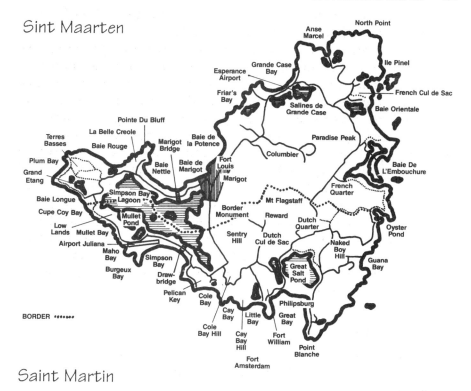

Saint Martin

casinos, thrive on the Dutch side. Small hotels and guesthouses are also available, although some will not accept young children or credit cards. The French side has far fewer rooms for visitors though the number is increasing. Nudists prefer the French connection. Camping is not available.

Taxes & Tips: Sint Maarten has a 5% room tax; a 15% service charge is common for both sides. When dining anywhere in Saint Martin, look for "Service Compris" on your bill; that means the tip has already been included.

Documents: U.S. and Canadian citizens need only birth certificates. All others need passports and visas. Cruise ship passengers or those in transit for a stay of less than twenty-four hours need some form of ID but not necessarily a passport. Air travelers need an onward ticket. Saint Martin entry requirements come into play if you decide to take the twenty-minute ferry ride to neighboring Anguilla; the ferry boats depart and return to Marigot. U.S. and Canadian citizens need some sort of picture ID and birth certificate; a passport is required of everyone else. There are no formalities for traveling between Sint Maarten and Saint Martin. The border is unmanned, designated only by signs or markers. After a few days, you tend to forget you're crossing from one country to another.

Currency: The guilder and the French franc are the official currencies, but dollars are accepted everywhere. You need never change; in fact, you'll probably get a poor rate for the franc if you do. Banks are open from 8:30 a.m. to 3 p.m. Monday through Thursday and from 4 p.m. to 5 p.m. on Friday.

Electrical Current: It differs on the Dutch and French sides: 110 on the Dutch, 220 on the French.

Safety/Health Warnings: Beaches are not secure places. Leave nothing valuable in your car, and leave nothing valuable on your beach blanket when you go for a swim. It might not be there when you get back. This is a very hot island; drink plenty of water, juice and other non-alcoholic liquids.

Hiking/Walking Services: None.

Snakes and Other Venomous Creatures: None.

For More Information: For Sint Maarten: In the US, Sint Maarten Tourist Office, 275 Seventh Ave., 19th Floor, New York, NY 10001; tel. 212/989-0000; fax 212/627-1152. In Canada, 243 Ellerslie Ave., Willowdale, Toronto, Canada M2N 1Y5; tel. 416/223-3501; fax 416/223-6887.

For Saint Martin, contact the French Government Tourist Board (See Guadeloupe or Martinique for complete details).

1. Philipsburg

Time: 1 hour walking tour, far longer if you shop. **Difficulty:** 1.

The capital of Sint Maarten, second only to St. Thomas in its duty free volume, is an unusually easy walk. It is situated on a narrow strip of land between the ocean and a shallow lake. There's room enough for two streets: Front and Back Streets. You can walk the length of the town in a half hour if you don't tarry. Front Street has the major duty free shops, and is a shopping/hotel/restaurant arcade. Back Street is more suited to Chinese restaurants and low-cost clothes.

Stores are open 8 a.m. to noon and 2 p.m. to 6 p.m. Prices should be checked carefully to make sure you're getting a good deal; some items cost the same back home. Shoppers have complained of several devious practices: merchandise being switched when it is wrapped, and being charged a sales tax when everything is not only duty free but without any purchase or luxury tax. Sad to say, but success may be ruining Sint Maarten. Let the Buyer Beware.

Philipsburg's most famous site is historic Watley Square, which faces

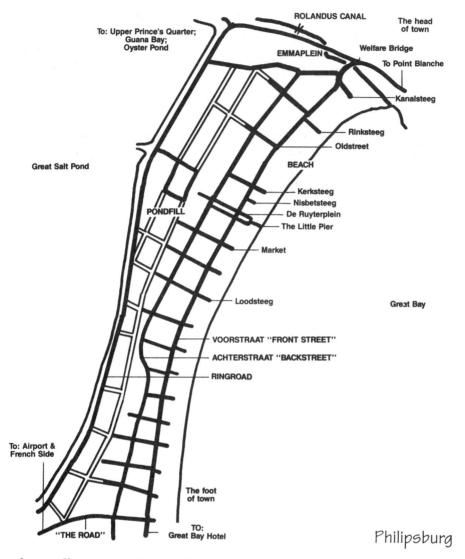

ROLANDUS CANAL

The head of town

To: Upper Prince's Quarter; Guana Bay; Oyster Pond

EMMAPLEIN

Welfare Bridge

To Point Blanche

Kanalsteeg

Rinksteeg

Oldstreet

Great Salt Pond

BEACH

Kerksteeg

Nisbetsteeg

PONDFILL

De Ruyterplein

The Little Pier

Market

Loodsteeg

Great Bay

VOORSTRAAT "FRONT STREET"

ACHTERSTRAAT "BACKSTREET"

RINGROAD

To: Airport & French Side

The foot of town

"THE ROAD"

TO: Great Bay Hotel

Philipsburg

the small pier near the middle of town. The old wooden courthouse and post office there date from 1793.

The Old Street Mall is a new shopping complex where all the buildings feature traditional Dutch architecture. Although the buildings are replicas, this is one of the most picturesque spots in Philipsburg.

If you stop in one of the bars, you may want to sample the Guavaberry Liqueur which has been made in local homes for over 200 years. Made from rum and guavaberries which ripen just before Christmas, it has a fruity/bitter/sweet/woody taste that is distinctive.

Sint Maarten also has a carnival at the end of April which is worth

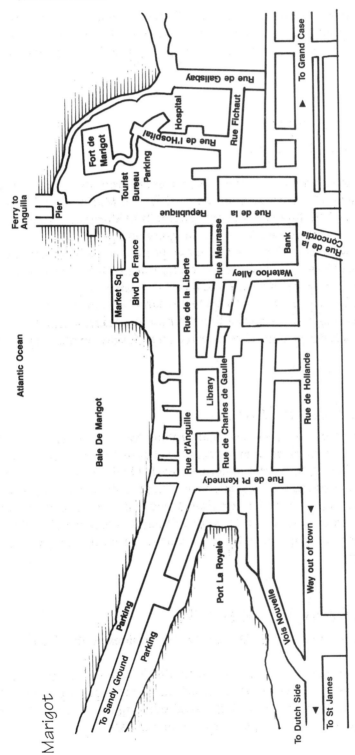

Marigot

seeing. It has all the revelry and competitions of a major carnival but on a more manageable scale. The costume parade is at a civilized hour, too: about 2 p.m.. This is a terrific photo opportunity in gorgeous natural sunlight.

2. Marigot

Time: 1-2 hours. **Difficulty:** 1.

Capital of the French side, this was a sleepy little town compared to Philipsburg until the opening of the Port Royale Marina and Shopping Center. This 1980s development brought malls to Marigot. The city began sprucing itself up, so the town looks brighter and prettier.

Shopping and eating are the main pastimes. Since everything is imported and based on the French franc, full meals can be expensive. However, you can always retreat to a cafe or pastry shop.

A small but lively fruit and vegetable market is held at the waterfront on Saturday. The people do not like their picture taken without permission. Overlooking the city is Fort Marigot, which you can reach by hiking uphill.

3. Beach Walks

Because the island has so many beautiful beaches, it's possible to make walks of a mile or more beside the surf. One of the most striking is Cupecoy Bay to Long Beach, the island's prettiest beach. On this trek of over a mile, you'll pass sandstone cliff formations, which provide interesting photography. Rouge Beach extends for almost two miles, ending at the coral formations at Pointe du Bluff. Mile-long Orient Beach is the official nude beach though sunning "au naturel" is sanctioned almost everywhere on Saint Martin.

4. Paradise Peak Hike

Time: 50 minutes each way. **Difficulty:** 2-3 considering the climb.

Just outside the town of St. Louis on Saint Martin, follow the sign and turn inland to Paradise Peak, which at 1,500 feet is the highest point on the island. This track can be driven but if you're feeling cramped and feel the need for a good uphill walk, this is your best chance.

Unusual rock formations are a distinctive feature on the Cupecoy Bay beach walk.

Begin the walk at the gate with two large urns on the right. As the highest point, this region receives the most rainfall (forty-five inches annually), so the vegetation is lusher here than anywhere else on the island. At the top you'll have to share the view with a radio tower, but ignore it and savor the excellent overlook of Philipsburg.

# 9. Antigua

Old Caribbean Saying:
Where horse is tied, is there he eats grass.

Translation:
Make the best of wherever you find yourself.

Long a favorite cruise ship stop, Antigua is the largest of the British Leeward Islands, claiming 365 beaches, one for every day of the year. Antigua (pronounced An-TEE-ga) does have many beautiful beaches, but take that "365" claim with more than a grain of sand.

From a walker's point of view, Antigua has some of the Caribbean's most historical strolls as well as some of the flattest.

Compared to so many of the other lively, pastel-colored port towns, St. John's is not visually appealing. It needs a new coat of paint to cover many of the old, drab exteriors. However, a few sections such as Redcliffe Quay have already been renovated to attract shoppers, so someone recognizes the potential of St. John's.

The contrast between old and new reveals Antigua as a relatively poor island, as are most of the former English possessions whose prosperity was once dependent on sugar cane. Today, tourism, offshore banking, and agriculture—mostly cotton, vegetables, fruit, and cattle—provide most of its income. Antigua's poverty is most obvious in the countryside, where luxury tourist villas sit alongside small shacks.

St. John's is primarily a shopping port, requiring only an hour or two at the most to explore. Those with limited time would do best to explore the countryside, since the most interesting sites are outside the city. A taxi ride will be considerably less frustrating than renting your own car. Signs are almost non-existent in the countryside, so venturing forth (even with a map) is an expedition into uncharted territory. You will eventually find everything you set out to look for; Antigua is only 108 square miles.

Antigua was settled as far back as 2,400 B.C. by the little-known

Ciboney (stone people). The rocky limestone island has no exotic, forested areas and the highest elevation is only 1,330 feet. Antigua is considered an ideal island by those who like typical beachfront resort vacations but, from the hiker/walker's point of view, it is worth only a day or two, at most. This is regrettable, since the people are among the friendliest and most civil in the West Indies. Remember: they do expect to be spoken to first.

Travel Tips

Area: Located 250 miles southeast of Puerto Rico, Antigua is 108 square miles. Neighboring Barbuda, virtually deserted, is 62 square miles.

Language: English is the official language but Creole is also spoken.

Population: 80,000, with about 30,000 residing around St. John's.

Time Zone: Atlantic Standard Time, one hour ahead of Eastern Standard Time.

Rainy Season: The island only receives forty-five inches of rainfall annually; this is a hot, dry place in summer. Showers are most frequent September through November.

Getting There: Antigua is an important Caribbean hub. Every major airline serving the islands stops here. A few carriers even fly directly from Europe. Antigua is such an important airport that it's possible to fly from here to twenty-four other island destinations and South America. Carriers include American, BWIA, LIAT, Air Canada, British Airways (direct from Gatwick) and Lufthansa (direct from Frankfurt).

Getting Around: Taxis are not metered; therefore all fares should be settled in advance. Make sure fares are being quoted in Eastern Caribbean Dollars. Taxis are easily identified by the "H" on their license plates. Government-approved taxi rates are usually listed in tourist booklets, which are available at the airport and hotels. Auto rentals are easily available as long as you pay that absurd US $12 for a local, temporary driving license. Look out for potholes and the narrow country roads. Many streets in St. John's are one-way, so observe signs and the traffic flow. Fuel is expensive—more than US $2 per gallon. Avoid driving around after dark because conditions can be dangerous.

Where to Stay: Although the landscape may not be as spectacular as other islands, Antigua has some of the Caribbean's best beaches and resorts, which is the reason why so many airlines fly here. Antigua can be very expensive. You'll find resorts as exclusive and as pricey as Jumby Bay (about US $1,000 a day in-season) and the St. James' Club (which caters to international celebrities). Closest major hotels to St. John's are the Ramada Renaissance Royal Antiguan, three miles out, and the Barrymore Beach Club on Runaway Bay, two miles out. Some properties close in September and October.

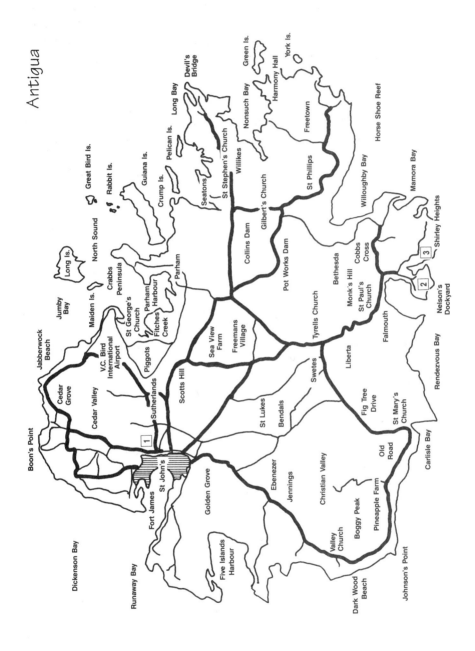

Antigua

Camping: Illegal and the ban is strictly enforced. Despite the degree of local poverty, this island likes to project an upscale image, and campers don't fill the bill. Furthermore, officials have been known to refuse entry to travelers who don't look like they have sufficient funds to cover their stay.

Taxes & Tips: A 7% government hotel tax and a 10% service charge. Taxi drivers expect 10% and porters EC $1 per bag.

Documents: A valid on-going/return ticket is a must. American, Canadian and British citizens need proof of citizenship. Everyone else needs passports and visas. South Africans are not permitted entry; not that many ever came here anyway.

Shopping: Shopping is available in hotel boutiques or the shops located in Redcliffe Quay or Heritage Quay. Some stores give locals a 10% discount but then compensate for this kindness by overcharging you. Almost everything closes Sundays.

Currency: The Eastern Caribbean dollar, worth about US $2.68. U.S. dollars are good anywhere. Most prices are quoted in EC. Banks are open 8 a.m. to 1 p.m. Monday through Thursday, from 8 a.m. to noon and 3 p.m. to 5 p.m. on Friday.

Electrical Current: 220 volts in most places, though 110 is provided in some hotels. Transformers are usually available.

Safety/Health Warnings: Not dangerous but highly annoying are the tiny insects called "no-see-ums," a nuisance on the beaches around sunrise and sunset. Carry repellent.

Hiking/Walking Services: None.

Snakes and Other Venomous Creatures: None.

For More Information: In the U.S., Antigua and Barbuda Dept. of Tourism, 610 Fifth Avenue, Suite 311, New York, NY 10020; 212/541-4117. In Canada, 60 St. Clair Avenue East, Suite 205, Toronto, Ontario M4T IN5; 416/961-3085. In the UK, Antigua House, 15 Thayer Street, London W1M 5LD; 071/486-7073/5. Fax 071/486-9970.

1. Walking Tour of St. John's

Time: 1-2 hours. **Difficulty:** 1.

Unless you stop to shop, you should cover St. John's easily in an hour. Frankly, there isn't much to see except the boutiques. St. John's started out as one of many towns built haphazardly on virtually every sheltered harbor, large or small, on Antigua. Eventually, six towns were recognized as official trading centers (places where goods could be sold legally) in an attempt to discourage smuggling and to better organize military protection.

St. John's became preeminent as far back as 1681 but it has suffered greatly. Two major fires (1769 and 1861) and two major earthquakes (1690 and 1843) destroyed the earliest structures, all made of wood. Yet much of the existing town is quite old by Caribbean standards, with a large number of buildings dating back to the 1840s. Not always well maintained, they give parts of the city a slightly ramshackle appearance.

Until the 1980s, one of those rundown sections was Redcliffe Quay, where old wooden "barracoons" once held slaves awaiting auction or shipment to other islands. Like Nelson's Dockyard, Redcliffe Quay has been restored, turned into one of Antigua's best shopping districts.

A description of St. John's published in 1844 says the main area along "a well made broad-street being inhabited principally by Scotchmen is known by the appropriate name 'Scotch Row'...You may, in truth, buy anything and everything in these 'Scotch Shops,' from three farthings' worth of tape to the most costly articles. Dresses of all kinds; ribbons, laces, flowers and bonnets; coats, vests, pantaloons, umbrellas and shoes...The streets of the capital all have their proper appellations, although no painted board announces such a fact to the traveler." Apparently the tradition of not supplying street signs to direct travelers is a long and honored one!

Today, a Saturday morning in the lively fruit and vegetable market on aptly-named Market Street is considered a hot ticket.

1) Court House/Museum of Antigua and Barbuda: Originally built as the courthouse in 1747, this stone building suffered considerably during the earthquakes of 1843 and 1974. During its heyday, it hosted bazaars, charity sales and official dinners. The restored building now houses the island's main museum and archives. The exhibits of pre-Columbian and colonial artifacts are well worth a look.

2) Heritage/Redcliffe Quays: Built in 1988 as a lure for cruise ship visitors, Heritage Quay is a very modern duty-free complex which lacks the charm and color of nearby Redcliffe Quay, where brightly painted wooden buildings make it a preferred shopping area. However, Heritage Quay does boast a casino with big-screen TV.

3) Anglican Cathedral of St. John the Divine: Usually referred to simply as St. John's Cathedral, this huge building dominates the town. Its baroque spires can be clearly seen from the waterfront. The original cathedral was a wooden one built in 1683. It was replaced in 1722 by a newer and bigger church, which was in turn destroyed in the great earthquake of 1843. Reconstruction began in 1845; the building was consecrated in 1848. The interior is encased in wood to protect it from both

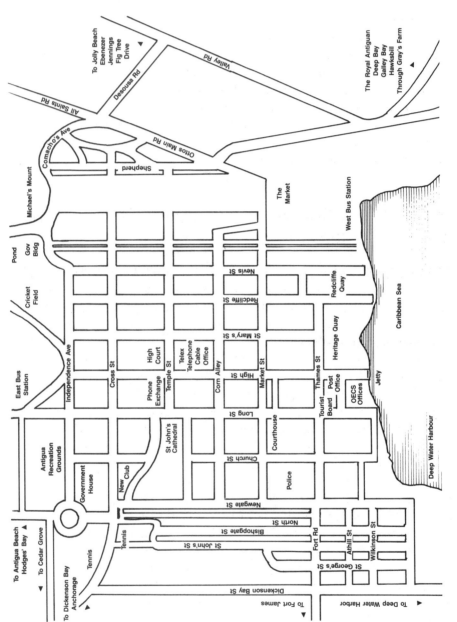

St. John's

earthquake and hurricane damage, one reason it survived the earthquake of 1974.

4) Police Station: Not that you'd want to tour the facilities, but the Church Street side has a decorative fence made of bayonets and old flintlocks.

5) Government House: the residence of The Governor General is not open to the public. It was originally two houses standing side by side with a street between them. The original buildings are of wood in 17th-century colonial-style, but extensions have been added in concrete.

6) Fort James: Used for defending the harbor entrance, it was originally built in 1675, though most of the buildings seen today date from 1749. Ten cannons, each weighing 212 tons, are still in the fort. The cannons required twelve men each to fire.

2. English Harbour/Nelson's Dockyard
Time: 1-2 hours. **Difficulty:** 1.

Nelson's Dockyard is a small nautical version of Colonial Williamsburg, Virginia. You will pay a very modest admission fee to enter this restored 18th-century garrison. The Dockyard was established by England's Royal Navy at English Harbour to protect ships with cargoes of sugar, once as valuable as gold or silver.

The garrison's namesake, Horatio Nelson, arrived in 1784 at age 26. Legend has it he gained command of Antigua after his predecessor put out his own eye while chasing a cockroach with a fork. No reports are given of how much grog was consumed during the cockroach chase.

Initially, this site was known simply as The Dockyard; Nelson was dead 150 years before it adopted his name, something he might have found amusing since he and Antigua didn't suit each other very well.

Nelson was extremely unpopular with both the locals and English merchants of Antigua because he insisted on enforcing the Navigation Act, which opened English Harbour only to English ships. Before Nelson's arrival, ships from the newly independent U.S. had been carrying on a lively trade in Antigua with the well-bribed approval of on-site officials.

English Harbour was important for its excellent anchorage: ships could ride out hurricanes there and repairs could be made under strong military protection. Damaged ships from other islands often had to travel all the way to the American colonies to be repaired because of the constant danger from marauding French and Spanish. Except for the sugar trade, little has changed in the makeup of Nelson's Dockyard since it went into use in the 1720s.

The Dockyard was shut down in 1889 and reopened in 1961 as a historical monument and as a well-equipped center for cruising yachtsmen. The main social center is the Admiral's Inn. Like most of The Dockyard's buildings, the Inn is built of local stone and brick imported for ballast. Its fourteen small rooms are furnished as they would have been a century ago, but it is the outdoor patio that attracts most of the attention as the area's favorite watering hole.

What once was The Dockyard's old copper and lumber store is now a restaurant and inn, imaginatively called The Copper and Lumber Store Hotel. It, too, has just fourteen rooms. I found both the Dockyard's inns to be quite interesting from a historical perspective, and the people running them were more than willing to let me wander the premises freely.

The building that Nelson lived in has been turned into The Dockyard Museum, containing charts, furniture and nautical memorabilia from the 18th and 19th centuries.

From The Dockyard, it's an easy walk to Fort Berkeley, situated on a thin spit of land overlooking the narrow entrance to English Harbour. Fort Berkeley defended the harbor with cannons, a stout chain and a timber boom which could be drawn across the channel during sieges.

3. Sundays at Shirley Heights

Time: 1 hour at the site, 2 or 3 more if you climb from and return to the base of the hill. **Difficulty:** 3 for the long walk.

Overlooking English Harbour is another restored garrison called Shirley Heights, where residents and visitors alike congregate on Sundays for the liveliest party in Antigua. This installation was named after General Sir Thomas Shirley, a former governor. One of the main buildings, known as the Block House, was put up as a stronghold in 1787 in case of a siege.

Shirley Heights commands a strategic and spectacular view of English Harbour. The impressive fortification was built to provide added security to The Dockyard, but on Sunday afternoons it is the site of the island's biggest cookout and steel band concert. It's not necessary to sample the barbecue to be welcome here; many people come to enjoy the music.

If you are really in the mood for a strenuous walk, park your vehicle at Clarence House and hike to Shirley Heights. After your climb to the ridge of hills overlooking English Harbour, you'll understand why the fortification was never in much danger of being taken.

Overlooking English Harbor from Shirley Heights.

 Barbuda

This tiny island, just sixty-two square miles, lies thirty miles north of Antigua. Daily flights on LIAT are the easiest connections, although an overnight boat charter is also available. Eight-mile-long Coca Beach is a spectacular strip of sand that so far has seen little development. It won't stay that way for long. The beach is gorgeous, the water clear. This is what Grand Cayman and other over-developed beachfronts must have looked like before the construction cranes arrived. Though there is no shade against the hot sun, the beach seems to stretch on forever. If you're a true beachcomber, get here quickly, before it changes.

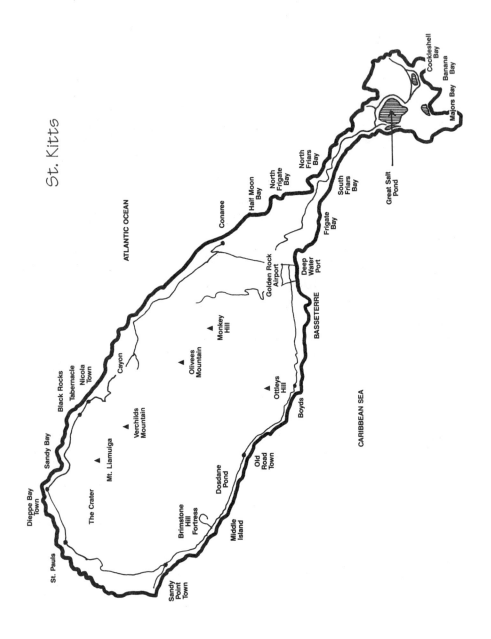

St. Kitts

ATLANTIC OCEAN

CARIBBEAN SEA

BASSETERRE

Cockleshell
Bay

Banana
Bay

Majors Bay

Great Salt
Pond

North
Friars
Bay

South
Friars
Bay

Frigate
Bay

North
Frigate
Bay

Half Moon
Bay

Conaree

Deep
Water
Port

Golden Rock
Airport

Monkey
Hill

Olivees
Mountain

Ottleys
Hill

Boyds

Cayon

Nicola
Town

Tabernacle

Black Rocks

Sandy Bay

Dieppe Bay
Town

St. Pauls

The Crater

Mt. Liamuiga

Verchilds
Mountain

Dosdane
Pond

Brimstone
Hill
Fortress

Middle
Island

Old
Road
Town

Sandy
Point
Town

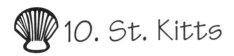# 10. St. Kitts

Old West Indian Proverb:
It is not for want of tongue that cows don't talk.

St. Kitts was officially known as St. Christopher, named by Columbus for his patron saint. However, everyone called the place St. Kitts for short, so in 1988 the island officially changed its name to St. Kitts to get in step with modern usage.

The tiny island was extremely important in establishing British domination throughout the rest of the Caribbean. St. Kitts was the first English settlement in the Eastern Caribbean (1623), and it was from here that settlers went to Antigua, Tortola, Montserrat and Nevis.

The capital city name of Basseterre (pronounced "bass-terr" with the first and last "e" silent) reflects the long struggle between the English and French over ownership. The French also used St. Kitts to launch colonists to Guadeloupe, Martinique, St. Martin and St. Barts. Since St. Kitts was the staging area for settlement of so many other islands by both the British and French, it is known as the "Mother Colony of the Caribbean."

The British did not gain full control of St. Kitts until 1783 as a provision of the Treaty of Versailles. Still, the French and British lived at peace for sixty years in the 1600s. One of their first cooperative projects was to wipe out the Carib Indians, who initially befriended the sixteen British colonists who landed in 1623. Very soon the French established a colony too, and it wasn't long before the Caribs were unhappy with the growing number of foreigners in the neighborhood. The Caribs decided to mount an offensive campaign, calling in Indians from adjacent islands to help.

The British and French caught wind of the plot and struck first. Although the Caribs were routed from St. Kitts, they did manage to leave behind one of the most intriguing sites on the island: a spot filled with petroglyphs that few tourists ever see.

For hikers, St. Kitts is a walking paradise. About 36% of the island (roughly 16,000 acres) is protected rain forest. It's been safeguarded since colonial times to retain the vital watershed.

The toughest walk of all is up the volcano, Mt. Liamuiga, (pronounced Lie-a-mee-ga) which is 3,792 feet high. This hike is not recommended without a guide as the path is very unstable near the top.

The large fields of sugar cane attest to how productive St. Kitts's soil is. Many of the great houses remain, used for private residences and tourist hotels.

Travel Tips

Area: 65 square miles.

Language: English

Population: 35,000, living mostly around the Basseterre area.

Time Zone: Atlantic Standard Time, one hour ahead of Eastern Standard Time.

Rainy Season: June through October, but some locals say the weather pattern seems to be changing and that visiting from May through early August is best.

Getting There: American Eagle services St. Kitts's Golden Rock Airport twice daily from San Juan. Other airlines serving St. Kitts include Continental, BWIA and LIAT. From the UK, the easiest route is to fly directly into Antigua from London. Otherwise, fly into one of American Airlines major cities such as New York, Orlando or Miami and continue on to St. Kitts.

Getting Around: To rent a car, you must purchase a local driver's license, US $12, at the police station. I would recommend a guided tour the first day. Ask to see the petroglyphs.

Where to Stay: The Ocean Terrace Inn, usually referred to as the OTI, overlooks the Basseterre harbor with fifty-three air-conditioned rooms and a comfortable, family-run feel. An older hotel, OTI is headquarters for Greg's Safaris which takes visitors on walks through the rain forest, on plantation tours and hikes up the 3,000-foot volcano.

The nearby Fort Thomas Hotel is much larger, covering eight acres, and caters to tour groups. Its balconies offer an excellent view into the interior.

The Bird Rock Inn sits on a bluff on the opposite side of the harbor. The only one of the three hotels situated on the water, guests of the Bird Rock Inn can swim and snorkel right in front of their rooms.

Camping: No campgrounds. Check with a hiking operator to see what they may be able to provide.

Taxes & Tips: There is a government room tax of 7% and most hotels add a service charge of 10%. Tipping is 10%.

Documents: A birth certificate and a photo ID will suffice for U.S. citizens. All others need passports.

Dress Code: Beach attire is not considered appropriate for walking around Basseterre, in shops or restaurants or on island tours.

Currency: The Eastern Caribbean dollar is the standard. US $1 equals about EC $2.65. Prices are quoted in EC $, but always check first. Banks are open 8 a.m. to 1 p.m. and sometimes from 3 p.m. to 5 p.m. on Friday. Shopping hours are 8 a.m. to noon, 1 p.m. to 4 p.m..

Electrical Current: A former British colony, the current typically is 230 volts/60 cycles, though some hotels have 110v.

Hiking/Walking Services: Greg's Safaris, c/o the OTI, P.O. Box 65, Basseterre, St. Kitts, WI; 809/465-4121/4122. Greg Pereira and his staff offer a full-day volcano tour, a five-hour rain forest tour and a six-hour plantation tour. Greg's Plantation Tour includes lunch at a private, 250-year old cut stone great house surrounded by exotic gardens. Also offering hikes is Kriss Tours at New Street, Basseterre, St. Kitts, WI; 809/465-4042.

Snakes and Other Venomous Creatures: None.

For More Information: Contact the Tourist Office at 414 E. 75th St., New York, NY 10021; 212/535-1234 or fax 212/879-4789. In Canada, it's 11 Yorkville Ave., Suite 508, Toronto M4W IL3; 416/921-7717 or 924-0345 or fax 416/921-7997. In the UK, c/o The High Commission of the Eastern Caribbean States, 10 Kensington Court, London W8 5DL; 071/376-0881 or fax 071/937-3611.

1. Walking Tour of Basseterre

Time: 1-2 hours. **Difficulty:** 1.

An hour's easy walk will show you the highlights of Basseterre, the capital of St. Kitts. Basseterre is ideal for exploring on foot since everything is laid out in square blocks.

Basseterre has been the British capital of St. Kitts since 1727, though it was part of the French sector when the two nations held the island jointly. The name Basseterre refers to low land, which most of the commercial district certainly is.

1)-2) The Pier Area: Includes three different piers, including separate ones for cruise ships and the "Caribe Queen," the island ferry that runs

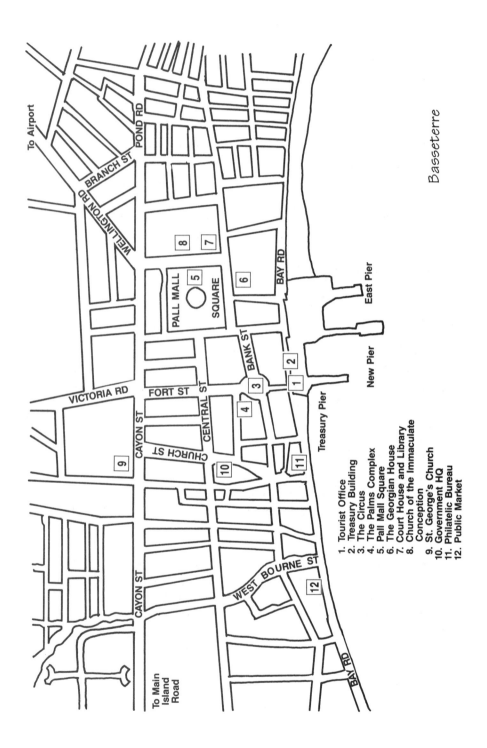

Basseterre

1. Tourist Office
2. Treasury Building
3. The Circus
4. The Palms Complex
5. Pall Mall Square
6. The Georgian House
7. Court House and Library
8. Church of the Immaculate
   Conception
9. St. George's Church
10. Government HQ
11. Philatelic Bureau
12. Public Market

between St. Kitts and Charlestown, capital of Nevis. Friday and Saturday are particularly good times to be at the pier, when the colorful produce and vegetable market is in session. Ask before taking photos of individuals and don't be surprised if they say no or want you to buy something first in trade.

Note the colorful red and yellow wooden fishing boats to the right of the pier with their nets drying in the sun; they make great photos.

A major new waterfront shopping arcade opened in 1991, expected to be *the* shopping row on St. Kitts, with duty-free shops representing all the major retailers. One of the most architecturally interesting structures here is the old Treasury Building with its big rotunda.

3)-4) The Circus: This name reflects the English influence. In British lingo, a circus is not a good time under a big canvas tent but a circular space at the intersection of several streets, as in London's Picadilly Circus. This small roundabout is lined with good shopping, particularly at The Palms Arcade. Dominating The Circus is a large green grandfather-style clock, a memorial to Thomas Berkeley, a former president of the Legislative Assembly.

5) Independence Square: Originally known as Pall Mall Square, it was built in 1790 for slave auctions and council meetings. Nothing remains of its bleak origins. Instead, a large fountain decorates the center and the perimeters are bordered by old stone buildings and neat, aged, wooden structures painted in white and colorful pastels, all excellent examples of British Colonial architecture.

6) The Georgian House: Bordering Independence Square, this restored brick home is now a gourmet restaurant.

7) Court House and Library: directly opposite Independence (Pall Mall) square and adjacent to the Catholic church.

8) Church of the Immaculate Conception: This open, airy church is a reminder that during the French period, Catholicism was the predominant religion.

9) St. George's Church: A large brownstone church located on an interesting and fiery religious battle site. Originally, the French built the church "Notre Dame" here in 1670, which the British burned down in 1706. The British rebuilt four year's later, naming their new Anglican structure after the patron saint of England. However, a fire in 1763, an earthquake in 1843, a hurricane, then another fire in 1867 resulted in St. George's being destroyed and rebuilt three more times. What you see standing is the result of the last restoration, in 1869.

2. Carib Petroglyphs

Time: 1 hour roundtrip to the canyon from the main road. **Difficulty:** 2-3.

Go west on the Main Road, which circles the perimeter of St. Kitts. The scenery initially features bright green fields of sugar cane. St. Kitts has many abandoned windmills once used to help process the sugar, and you'll probably want to stop to take photos of quite a few.

When you arrive at Bloody Point, you'll be in the area of one of the best petroglyph collections anywhere in the Caribbean, yet few tourists ever see the rock drawings. There are no markers or signs to indicate where the drawings are located.

The greatest difficulty is finding the starting point at Bloody Point, located on the island's main circular highway. Approaching Bloody Point, look on the right for a dirt road going uphill; this road is located almost directly opposite a large mahogany tree. Many locals know of the spot and can point it out. Walk up the road five to ten minutes to a bridge. Don't make the mistake of crossing the bridge; instead, look for a footpath near the right corner that leads down to the river.

This path criss-crosses the river several times, and in places you will have to scramble up and around boulders in midstream but you shouldn't get your feet wet unless the river is high. Be sure to wear non-skid shoes for the rock hopping. About fifteen minutes from the bridge—remember, you are going into the interior of the island all this time, not toward the coast—you will reach a narrow canyon about ten feet wide and eighty feet high.

Carib drawings will be all around you on the canyon walls, beginning five to seven feet up the cliffside. Some are difficult to discern because the rubbings are faded; others are unmistakable due to the way they've been outlined in red.

Most of what you see are human faces—the eyes, nose and mouth but no other parts of the body. However, you can make out other forms, too, including a bat, an owl and a three-cornered hat, the kind the first settlers wore. It is a remarkable sight and well worth the effort required to visit here.

Many petroglyphs will be in the shade. To photograph them, use either fill-flash or come prepared with high speed film. You could spend considerable time here, depending on how much you get caught up in the somber mood of the canyon. It is easy to let your imagination roam freely when you realize this is where the Caribs made their final stand on St. Kitts in 1626, three years after the first Europeans arrived.

It was here in this canyon of petroglyphs that over 1,000 Caribs were trapped and slaughtered by the combined British and French forces. The

Carib Petroglyphs on St. Kitts are some of the Caribbean's most easily accessible.

riverbed you're standing in literally ran red with Carib blood. The stream you walked up is Stone Fort River, and the spot where the Carib village once existed is known as Bloody Point.

A much more accessible petroglyph is just off the road leading to Romney Manor at Old Road Town, site of the first permanent English settlement in the West Indies and the original capital of St. Kitts. On a boulder on the left side of the road are two large figures outlined in white.

Continue to Romney Manor, home of Carabelle Batik, famed for its fashion items made by the 2,500-year old Indonesian process of batik printing. Wall hangings and clothing displayed at Romney Manor project vibrant bright blue, yellow and red designs, so at least window shop. Romney Manor itself is surrounded by six acres of gardens which you are welcome to explore. The huge tree in the front yard is a 350-year old Saman tree, sometimes called a raintree. If you wish, you may park near the petroglyph and walk to Romney Manor.

 3. Brimstone Hill Fortress

Time: 1 hour to explore the fort. Another 3-4 hours to ascend and descend the mountain by foot. **Difficulty:** 1 inside the fort; 2-3 for the climb up to it.

Continuing the island tour, the perimeter road leads to the great Brimstone Hill Fortress, one of the great fortresses of the Western hemisphere and the most important historical site on St. Kitts. The thirty-eight acre fortress had its first cannon hauled to the top of the steep cliff in 1690; by 1736 there were at least forty-nine cannon in place. Slave laborers needed almost 100 years to complete the massive seven to twelve-foot thick walls. Despite its impressive fortifications, the fort was captured by the French in 1782, who had to give it back along with the rest of St. Kitts— just a year later under the Treaty of Versailles. More soldiers died of yellow fever than from fighting during the fort's long history.

Severely damaged in the hurricane of 1843, the fort was never fully rebuilt and was finally abandoned in 1851. Since 1965 it has been a national park. Today, fully restored, Brimstone Hill Fortress affords one of the best island walks and offers excellent views of six neighboring islands.

Perhaps the most interesting feature is the architectural arrangement of the interior courtyard which can be reached only by crossing a moat. The courtyard floor slopes toward a center drain: the drain creates a 13,000-gallon cistern with all excess water directed through a privy area. In effect, the drain helped create a huge flush toilet, the ingenious intentions of Brimstone Hill's designers who took excellent advantage of the cloud and rain that often obscure the fortress.

4. Black Rocks

Time: 15-20 minutes. **Difficulty:** 1 on top of the cliff; 2-3 to descend and ascend the shoreline.

A dramatic reminder of the island's volcanic past is Black Rocks at the village of Belle Vue on the Atlantic coast. In all of its millions of years, Mt. Liamuiga has produced only one lava flow, and this is it. The continual pounding of the waves against the black lava cliffs created this cluster of oddly shaped boulders.

5. Southern Peninsula Hike

Time: 2-1/2 hours each way. **Length:** 5 miles each way. **Difficulty:** 2-3; take water.

Until a new highway was completed in 1990, the only way to reach the narrow southern tip of St. Kitts was by boat or by walking. This stark, desert-like terrain is very different from the lush forests of the north. To hike the southern peninsula, begin at Frigate Bay, once a favorite dueling ground but now a popular golf course. The pathway is obvious and should present no problem.

The main reason for taking this walk is the spectacular views of the Atlantic pounding against the coastline and the possibility of seeing monkeys, wild donkeys and deer. On early summer mornings it's also possible to find a sea turtle still in the process of laying her eggs.

The vegetation increases the farther south you go. Wear a bathing suit, because you will pass some beautiful empty beaches. Also bring something to drink because this open walk can be quite hot, and the only place to buy a drink is a small restaurant at the southernmost tip. The salt ponds near the end of the peninsula were the main salt source for many Kittians and Nevisians. In your wanderings, you may also pass the ruins of an old windmill tower. Who was crazy enough to try and live on this end of the island?

Mountain Hikes

6. The Volcano, Mt. Liamuiga

Time: 5 hours to the rim and back. **Length:** about 1-3/4 miles each way. **Difficulty:** 3-4.

This is St. Kitts's toughest hike, requiring a minimum of a half day to reach the crater lip at 2,700 feet, as high as you can hike on the trail since Hurricane Hugo. The volcano is almost inactive, although it rumbles on occasion and belches sulfur. Once easily spoken of as Mt. Misery, Mt. Liamuiga's new name is the Carib term for "fertile isle." It's pronounced "Liar-mweagre," most easily said if one has been drinking Carib beer.

Because of its circular route, the volcano hike takes you half-way around the island. Hikes usually begin at the 1,500-foot level where the road ends in Belmont Estates. In the rain forest where the trees tower 100 feet high, this is mostly virgin growth without any introduced species, such as bamboo. You'll find gummier and mastic trees, pigeon berry and lots and many varieties of ferns (over 120 species).

At the start, you'll have to go beneath and over three trees felled by 1989's Hurricane Hugo. Then it's a steady two-and-a-half hour moderate climb. The first half of the hike, along a ridge, is gentle. The second half is much steeper, and you have to make several ascents. Yet, at its worst the grade is little more than a forty-five-degree angle. You'll find plenty of roots to grab and pull yourself up with in the difficult stretches.

At about 2,500 feet, you enter the cloud forest and encounter vegetation that spends most of its life covered in white mist: mostly dwarf trees covered with orchids and mosses. A land of perpetual moisture, the trail here can be very slippery. However, it's over 1,000 feet higher to the summit, though you stop at the crater lip at 2,700-feet. At the peak of 3,792 feet, the growth is tropical alpine meadow.

At one time it was possible to descend to the crater floor but Hurricane Hugo destroyed most of the trees that were essential handholds to keep from falling down the steep slope. Hugo's winds, with gusts clocked at over 200 mph, swirled into the crater and eliminated the trees on one side—the side the descent trail happens to be on, which makes it relatively unsafe for climbing. Trees inside the crater on the opposite wall are still in prime condition, but no trail yet exists to come down that side.

 7. The Mansion Source Trail

Time: 2 hours. Length: 1-1/2 to 2 miles. **Difficulty:** 2.

This is a private trail, not accessible to the public. It is available only through Greg's Safaris; 809/465-4121.

This often slippery path is an excellent and easy introduction to the St. Kitts rain forest. Located eight miles from Basseterre, the walk goes along Verchild's Mountain, which has a fresh water pond on top. Before Hugo destroyed the trail, the source trail was a rugged 3-1/2 hour hike each way to reach the lake. Since Hugo, hikes are conducted through lower stretches of the secondary rain forest, starting from an altitude of 1,400-feet.

The perimeter of the rain forest is very lush, and growing such diverse crops as mango, dasheen, yams, peppers, christopheen, bananas and mountain cabbage palm.

In the rain forest live troops of African green monkeys (vervets) brought in by the French centuries ago. These creatures, which grow to eighteen pounds and gorge on fruit and leaves, cause so much damage to the farm crops, the government offers a bounty of approx. $10 EC for every body brought in. Researchers interested in live specimens pay up to $100 EC. Estimates of the St. Kitts monkey population run from 10,000-40,000.

Rain forest vegetation receives from 80 to 150 inches of rain annually, while the coastal regions where sugar cane is grown receive far less, only about fifty-five inches. Ferns, gum trees, philodendrons, elephant ears and clumps of bamboo (which can grow three inches per day). The climb is moderate but may be slippery and muddy in parts.

# 8. Monkey Hill

Time: 1/2-hour to the top. **Difficulty:** 1-2, a relatively easy walk popular with locals and tourists.

Located just west of Basseterre, this area gained its name from the vervet monkeys often spotted here. The path climbing the hill, 1,319-feet high, goes past the ruins of "The Glen," a former great house. From the top you have excellent views of fertile Basseterre Valley and the Caribbean coast. However, the best place for a close-up look at monkeys is at the primate research station at Estridge Estate open to the public on Sundays.

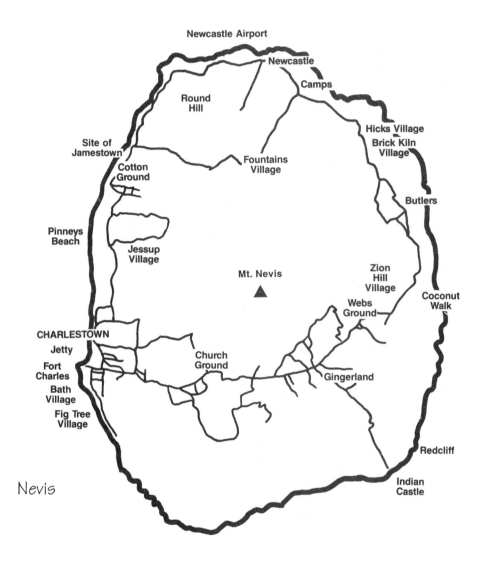

Nevis

 11. Nevis

Old Caribbean Proverb:
Canoes without good bottom can't go to sea.

Translation:
It's foolish to do something you're not properly prepared for.

Nevis is decades behind the rest of the Caribbean, a rare gemstone in a sea of costume jewelry. Only thirty-six square miles in size, Nevis (pronounced Nee-vis) didn't seriously become interested in tourism until around 1980, so most of its natural environment remains undeveloped.

The island's hallmark is brooding Nevis Peak, a lush green, square-shaped volcanic mountain emerging from the water in an almost perfect cone. Its summit at 3,232 feet is usually obscured by a sombrero of ever-present clouds. Seen from the water, Nevis Peak's white puffy shroud has a very primeval aspect, the kind of place where you wouldn't be too surprised to find a living species of dinosaur or even King Kong, himself.

The clouds that cover the Nevis Peak rain forest are typically so dense that from a distance they could be mistaken for snow. In fact, such a spectacle prompted Columbus in 1493 to christen the landfall "Nuestra Senora de las Nieves," Our Lady of the Snows.

That Nevis can appear moody, even threatening, from a distance is more than just a fanciful impression. Nevis has experienced several memorable earthquakes, including one as recently as 1950. That one was insignificant compared to the earthquake and tidal wave which destroyed the capital, Jamestown, in 1660.

Although it covers a tiny area, Nevis is unusually well-endowed with several spectacular beaches. The best is Pinney's Beach, the archetypal tropical beach; a wide ribbon of smooth, soft sand skirted by a thick coconut palm forest. Pinney's is considered one of the Caribbean's most beautiful beaches thanks to its combination of soft powdery sand, tall swaying palms and the striking view of mountainous St. Kitts sprawling on the horizon two miles distant.

Human habitation of the island goes back at least 4,000 years. Among the artifacts uncovered here are finely-made stone implements, flint cutting tools made from non-native materials, and beautifully colored pottery unearthed from burial mounds. The Caribs, the last Native Americans to "own" Nevis, called it "Oualie"—Land of Beautiful Waters.

Nevis has a long and rich history and is inhabited by people with strong ties to the land. Legendary names like Alexander Hamilton and Admiral Lord Horatio Nelson (who married a local Nevisian) pop up as naturally in conversation as the usually idyllic weather.

Nevis first drew public attention in 1607, when Captain John Smith visited on his way to establish the first permanent English colony in North America. Jamestown turned out to be a swampy, mosquito-ridden site; so miserable a place that twenty years later, Smith still fondly remembered his short but enjoyable six-day layover in Nevis.

Nevis was colonized by the British in 1628. Until the 1640s, ginger, indigo, cotton and provision crops for ships were the staple crops of Nevis. The introduction of sugar cane changed the island from a diverse agricultural base to a system of great sugar plantations in the 16th and 17th centuries. Many great houses were built (some now converted to inns) and the aristocratic planter class lived in splendid style. By 1778, the warm mineral springs of Nevis had made the island famous all over Europe, where it was called the Spa of the Caribbean.

Travel Tips

Area: 36 square miles.

Language: English

Population: about 9,000, concentrated around Charlestown.

Time Zone: Atlantic Standard Time, one hour ahead of Eastern Standard Time.

Rainy Season: September is the rainy month, although showers can occur any time of the year in the highlands.

Getting There: Shortly after the opening of the Four Seasons luxury resort, Nevis was added to the Puerto Rico-based American Eagle system, which makes Nevis quite easy to reach. St. Kitts still has the only runway for large jets, so the American Eagles are commuter-sized planes. LIAT also has twice-daily flights from St. Kitts. Ferry service from St. Kitts aboard the 150-passenger "M.V. Caribe Queen" is also possible, but the boat runs only in early morning and late afternoon. Further, it does not run on Thursdays (maintenance day) or Sundays.

Getting Around: Since Nevis is all of thirty-six square miles in size, it is possible to make the grand tour in a single (long) day. Skeete's Car Rental and Budget are the two main rental car choices. A local driver's license is $12. The one disadvantage in driving yourself around Nevis is that many of the mountain roads consist of two narrow ribbons of concrete. Capacity: one car at a time. It's easy to stray from the straight and narrow, and scrape the undercarriage as you veer onto the low shoulders. Fortunately, this type of damage is not readily apparent when a car is returned.

Where to Stay: In keeping with the upscale tone of the island, you won't find any designated camping facilities, although there is a field near the base of Mount Nevis, where climbers can overnight when accompanied by a local guide.

In contrast to the luxurious Four Seasons, the modest Oualie Beach Hotel bungalows are one of the island's better values. Rates are $80 for a single and $100 for a double in summer, increasing by $15 in winter. The unpretentious restaurant serves excellent local seafood dishes.

A short distance away is the Mount Nevis Hotel, which has a wonderful view of St. Kitts across the channel. In Charlestown itself is the Pinney's Beach Hotel. Also air-conditioned, summer rates are $50 per day for a single, $60 for a double. A room with breakfast and dinner included is only $70 for a single, $100 for a double. Winter rates are almost 50% higher for a double, $20 more for a single.

Keep in mind that it's warmer and more humid at the beach hotels. The mountain retreats, though cooler, get more rain.

Camping: No campgrounds. Generally not permitted unless you are off in the bush with a local guide. No rentals available.

Taxes & Tips: A 5% tax on rental cars. Hotels add a 10% service charge. Tip 10-15% in restaurants and 10% for taxis.

Documents: Everyone needs a passport except U.S. citizens, who need either a voter's registration card or birth certificate and a photo ID, such as a driver's license.

Currency: Based on the Eastern Caribbean dollar, with the rate of exchange pegged at EC $2.65-2.70 for each US $1. American currency is accepted everywhere. Not all hotels take credit cards but—and this tells you how genteel the island's traditional clientele has been—many will take personal checks. Banks are open 8 a.m. to 1 p.m. daily, 3 p.m. to 5 p.m. Friday. The St. Kitts & Nevis National Bank is open Saturday 8:30 a.m. to 11 a.m.

Electrical Current: Nevis is part of the new Caribbean and so uses standard 110 volts/60 cycles, same as the U.S. Any hotels still on 220 usually have transformers available.

Hiking/Walking Services: Sylvester Pemberton; 809/469-3841, or by writing c/o the Nevis Tourist Board, Main St., Charlestown, Nevis, West Indies; Spencer Howell (tel. 5-389) and Ira Dore (tel. 5-528), also of Charlestown, can also be contacted through the Nevis Tourist Board, whose direct number is 809/469-5521, ext. 2049/2037.

For More Information: Contact the St. Kitts-Nevis Tourist Board at 414 E. 75th St., New York, NY 10021; 212/535-1234. In Canada, 11 Yorkville Ave., Suite 508, Toronto M4W 1L3; 416/921-7717. In the UK, c/o the High Commission for Eastern Caribbean States, 10 Kensington Court, London W8 5DL; 071/376-0881.

1. Walking Tour of Charlestown

Time: 2 hours. **Difficulty:** 1.

Charlestown was founded around 1660 by eighty planters from neighboring St. Kitts, who came over to make their fortunes in tobacco. Unfortunately, Nevis's soil was far more rocky than St. Kitts's, so plans to create a major tobacco export center never materialized. The town itself, however, is one of the best-preserved old-port cities in the Caribbean.

Charlestown is a small place, ideal for a leisurely two-hour walkabout. You'll soon appreciate how Nevis' aristocratic past still influences the islanders: Nevisians retain a genuine, friendly civility. Nevis is a good place to walk, but be aware that some people don't like cameras. Ask permission before taking anyone's picture. Generally, you'll find the description of poet Don Hecox generally accurate: "There are no strangers, only those friends you have not yet met."

1) The combined Alexander Hamilton House Birthplace and Museum of Nevis History: marks the birthplace of this illegitimate son of a Scotsman and a Creole. Emigrating to America, Hamilton became a famed American statesman, serving as the first Secretary of the Treasury under George Washington. He was killed in a duel with his political rival, Aaron Burr. His likeness is immortalized today on the US $10 bill.

The original Georgian-style home was built in 1680, but destroyed by an earthquake during the 1840s. Now rebuilt, the first floor of the stone-block building contains Hamilton memorabilia, historical documents and photos of Nevis, and antique furniture. The Nevis House of Assembly meets on the second floor. A short distance from Charlestown is the Hamilton Estate, one of the last remaining sugar factories on Nevis, with all its production machinery still intact.

2) St. Paul's Anglican Church: Although the church was built as recently as 1830, grave markers in the sanctuary floor and cemetery date

Alexander Hamilton, America's first Secretary of the Treasury under George Washington, was born on Nevis. This museum at his birthplace honors him.

back to 1702. John Huggins, founder of the great Bath House hotel, was buried here in 1821. St. Paul's is stylistically similar to other English parish churches; a mix of gothic and classic elements. It is still an active place of worship.

3) **The Rookery Nook:** Built between 1850-1860 as a livery stable, The Rookery Nook has been a popular local tavern since 1940.

4) **Treasury Building (Customs House):** These government offices are typical of the Caribbean buildings of the early 19th century. Built in 1837, these ministry offices are on the site of a much older structure; pipes and pipestems dating back to 1650 have been found in the rear garden.

5) **Wesleyan Holiness Manse:** This is one of the oldest stone structures standing in Charlestown, dating to 1812. The second floor is considered the oldest wooden structure in Charleston, dating at least to 1802. Now privately occupied and used for church business, it was built by the Huggins family, founders of the great Bath Hotel (site #12).

6) **Charlestown Methodist Church:** Built in 1844, this is considered the most significant and most ornate structure of old Charlestown. A government-sponsored junior school uses the building's lower section. Amazingly, the yard and trees are little changed from the scene depicted in an 1802 print sometimes sold in the Hamilton Museum. This may sound backwards, but the ground floor is actually a much later addition, built in

Charlestown

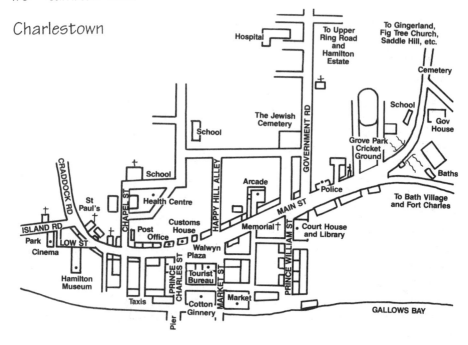

1886. It was not uncommon in those days to lift the older, wooden structure and build a more modern block structure under it. Considering the problem of wood rot in the tropics, the procedure makes a lot of sense.

7) St. Paul's Anglican Rectory: This is a typical cottage-style home of the 1870s, with a large entry and central living room. Now a private residence, it was the Government House of Nevis until 1890.

8) Jewish Cemetery: Although the Jewish community of Nevis is small, Jews were among the earliest pioneers. At one time Sephardic Jews from Brazil made up about 25% of the island's population. The cemetery, with tombstones in Hebrew, English and Portuguese, contains graves dating from 1679 to 1768, with most burials taking place before 1710. Normally the cemetery is closed to the public, but you may be able to obtain entry through advance inquiry at the Tourist Office.

9) Nevis Courthouse & Library: Built in 1825, the two-story stone structure you see today is a restoration, following the disastrous fire that swept Charlestown in 1873. The first floor has always contained the law court, in which the death sentence was passed for at least one pirate and where Horatio Nelson is said to have been sued over a matter of 40,000 pounds. The public library now occupies the second floor. Thanks to its unique truss construction, it's considered one of the coolest places in town. The clock tower, dating from 1909-10, keeps accurate time.

10) Tourist Board Office: Office of the very helpful Elmeader Prentiss, this is your best place for specific island information/directions.

11) Police Station: Not that you'll do anything wrong, but you will need to purchase a temporary driver's permit here if you rent a car. Appearing at the police station in person is a real hassle and waste of time. Perhaps this process will soon be conducted through the rental car companies themselves, as on other islands requiring special permits. No driving test is administered before granting the permit. At US $12, this is a more than nominal tourist tax. In the meantime, experience Caribbean bureaucracy in its most unnecessary form.

12) Bath Hotel: What an incredible place this must have been during its heyday. Its last guest checked out in the late 19th century; since then, the government has shored up parts of it as a tourist attraction, and the Spring House with its five hot thermal baths has been reopened. It costs only fifty cents for a plunge into the steamy, 108-degree waters, a pittance compared to what it once cost upper-crust Brits. Designed to house only fifty guests, The Bath Hotel was the ultimate getaway spa of its time and helped make Nevis' reputation as the "Queen of the Caribees" in the 18th century. John Huggins built the Bath Hotel in 1778 at an expense of 40,000 pounds. A novelty in its time, the Bath was reputedly the first hotel built outside of Scotland.

13) Government House: A relative newcomer to Charlestown, Government House was built in 1909. Closed to the public except by appointment, it is the residence of the deputy governor-general of St. Kitts-Nevis.

14) Fort Charles: This is more of a ruin than a monument. Originally called Pigeon Point, the fort was built on the site before the 1690s. Additions/renovations continued until 1783-90. As many as twenty-three cannons at a time faced the waterfront. If your time is limited, Fort Charles is a better place to read about than to actually visit.

15) Williams Grocery: This is more than a good place for a drink or snack, its a good example of functional Caribbean architecture. The bottom floor is used for commerce, the upper for residence. The steeply pitched roof serves two purposes: the high- ceilinged rooms underneath stay cool, and the larger roof surface provides a larger drainfield for rainwater, which is stored in a cistern.

16) Cotton Ginnery: Yes, indeed, one of the last true cotton gins still in use anywhere. It's open during the cotton picking season, but not to the public.

17) The Pier: This is where you catch the ferry to St. Kitts.

18) H.F. Henville Hardware Building: Another good example of a Nevis commercial building from the 1840s.

2. Circular Island Hike

Time: 1 full day. **Difficulty:** 3-4 because of distance and the long walk in the open.

There is much to see around the rest of the island, most of it near the coastline. Many people prefer to drive the twenty-mile main road encircling Nevis, but a roundabout walk is possible in a single day if you desire a good stretch of the legs. It's also a good way to get in shape if you plan to tackle Nevis Peak, one of the Caribbean's toughest hikes.

Nevis's main road passes through the flatland of Charlestown, but it also runs through hilly regions in the southwest, where you'll find most of the historical sites.

St. John's Anglican Church at Fig Tree, an ancient stone building featuring a bell tower, proudly displays the faded marriage certificate that reads "Horatio Nelson, Esq., to Frances Nisbet, widow, on March 11, 1787." The Duke of Clarence, who became King William IV, stood up for Nelson.

The Nelson Museum is nearby at Morning Star Plantation, where his books, pictures and letters are on display. Admission is free.

The poorly-marked Nelson's Spring is where Nelson took on fresh water for his ships. It must have once been an impressive outflow of water, but it's reduced today to a small reflecting pond. It is considered historically important as the site where Nelson supposedly met Fanny Nisbet, his future wife.

Indian Castle Estate is a long detour to the south, down Hanley's Road to a government farm raising cattle and experimental crops. This was once a busy place, with ships loading sugar and its by-products for export to the U.S., Canada and England.

New River Plantation was the last sugar plantation on Nevis to go bust, surviving until the 1940s. It was built in the 17th century and "modernized" by converting to steam in the late 1800s. Government-owned and open to the public, you can still see the ruins of the Great House and the big water cistern.

The Eden Brown Estate, built around 1740, is the island's haunted ruin. In 1822, it was occupied by Miss Julia Higgins, who was preparing to marry a gentleman named Maynard. On their wedding day, he and his best man had a falling out, and the two killed each other in a duel. One story says the distraught bride became a recluse and the mansion was closed down. Another version says that following the duel, she screamed until she died. Locals will tell you that whenever they're near the property, they feel the presence of someone...they're not sure if it is Miss Higgins or Mr. Maynard...but it's definitely...someone. The government owns the property, this is one haunted house that doesn't welcome overnight guests. Just day walkers.

The **Nisbet Plantation beach** is only a quarter of a mile long, but until Hurricane Hugo thinned out its palms, it was one of the most photographed ribbons of sand in the Caribbean. It's still worth a visit, if only to enjoy one of the fabulous burgers in the beach restaurant. The Nisbet Plantation is, of course, where Nelson's bride once lived. The Great House is an excellent restaurant, with an 18th-century ambiance, thanks to its fine dining room and mahogany bar.

The **Cades Bay Soufriere** is one of several active areas to remind you that Mount Nevis is not dead, only sleeping. Look for a burned-out gully or follow the unmistakable sulfur smell to its source. Steam sometimes shoots from the vents and the rocks are warm. This soufriere opened in 1951.

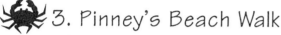

3. Pinney's Beach Walk
Time: 1-1/2 hours each way. **Length:** 4 miles. **Difficulty:** 1.

Many islands boast of excellent beaches, but little-known Pinney's Beach definitely ranks among the best in the Caribbean. The beach begins at the comfortably old-fashioned Pinney's Beach Hotel, on the edge of Charlestown, and ends at Oualie Beach. It is, for the most part, an undeveloped, narrow strip of sand flanked by a thick forest of magnificent, towering palms. The beach sand takes its tawny color from quartz.

Pinney's was hard hit by Hurricane Hugo, as the stumps of many downed palms reveal. However, new palms sprouting through the sand promise the beach will one day regain its full glory.

Fifteen minutes down the beach is the big, new, 196-room Four Seasons Hotel, the beginning of a mass tourist market that will propel Nevis into the 21st century and forever change Pinney's Beach. Development was inevitable; fortunately, a resort of the Four Seasons's caliber is in keeping with the island's long-established character. You'll still find several fishing shacks with their colorful wooden boats just beyond the Four Seasons property.

4. Saddle Hill and Nelson's Lookout
Time: 1 hour, round trip. **Length:** about 1 mile. **Difficulty:** 2.

Saddle Hill contains a small fort where Horatio Nelson, in charge of the

British fleet for this part of the Caribbean, supposedly spent his free time looking for approaching enemy ships. The site is now marked by a radio tower and all the major artifacts have been removed. The hike is on an open dirt road, and the view of Nevis, Redonda, Montserrat, St. Kitts and Saba is a fine one.

5. The Mountain Hikes

Mount Nevis would seem to offer the opportunity for numerous hikes, but only two trails are used regularly.

The Source
Time: 3 hours, round trip. **Length:** about 4 miles. **Difficulty:** 3-4.

The most popular hike on Nevis goes up a well-maintained trail to a small stream, the main water source for Nevis. The pathway passes through semi-tropical to tropical rain forest. At several points you will pass a centuries-old pipeline which brings water down from the stream to Stonyhill Reservoir, official starting point of the hike.

This is an easy trail to follow because the path has been used for centuries and is maintained by the government. The hike is more rewarding with a guide to explain the scenery. The path is three to four feet wide in most places, up to six or seven feet across in others. Most of the area is unpopulated, although Nevisians apparently lived in the region until the 1950s and '60s. My guide, Sylvester Pemberton, explained that one reason people have abandoned farming in the area is the continuing monkey menace.

How and why vervet (green) monkeys ever got to Nevis is open to speculation. Evidently, they were brought in for pets by the French. These are not tiny creatures, but can grow to a height of three feet, their tails almost twice as long as their bodies. Traveling in packs of up to forty, they can take a big bite out of local agriculture, which is why little farming is done in the high mountains today.

You may be surprised to hear the continual pounding of the ocean surf a good distance away. It is a pleasant sound that fades away about halfway up.

You'll pass by lemon trees, mangoes (ripe from April to August) and patches of what is known as "dung cane." Not to be confused with the sugar cane it resembles, dung cane can make your mouth swell up, a remarkably nasty side effect prized by plantation managers out to control pilfering.

The fruit trees eventually give way to rubber trees, figs, palms and

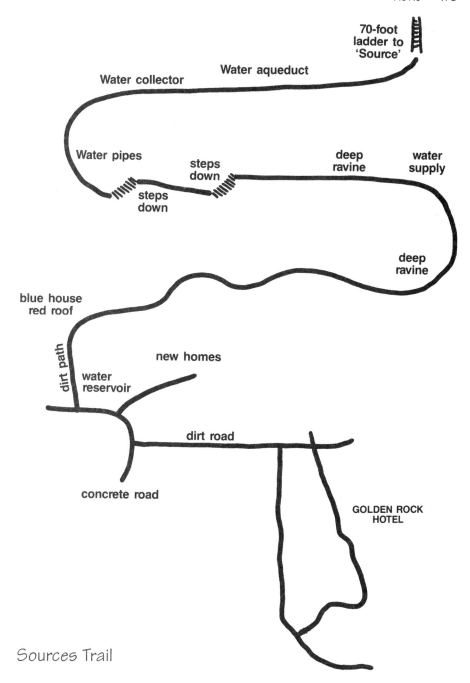

Sources Trail

ferns. About half way you'll reach a concrete water tank. Look for the massive rubber tree with a base like a giant cypress; it's a nice stop for a rest or a sheltered picnic, should it be raining.

From the water tank, the trail starts downhill. A deep ravine varying between 100 to 200 feet deep borders the right side. Locally, ravines like these are known as "ghauts" (pronounced guts). You'll come to two sets of steps (fifteen at the first, thirty-two at the second) just before the path curves to form a half-circle around a valley, actually part of a ghaut. After a fairly steep climb of about fifteen minutes, you'll reach a water collector on the left. At some points you'll have to duck under the water pipe. Keep going until you reach the seventy-foot-high ladder leading to The Source itself. You're welcome to make the climb and see where your drinking water comes from.

Climb to Nevis Peak Summit

Time: 4 hours, round trip. **Length:** 2 miles each way. **Difficulty:** 5.

As difficult as the climb is, the hardest part may be coming down...trying to avoid descending all at once. Referred to locally as "The Trail," this is one of the Caribbean's tougher hikes. Climb to the 3,500-foot-high crater rim of Mount Nevis' dormant volcano. You can have a spectacular view, if the clouds are absent—but they rarely are. Therefore, this is a climb to be made for the sake of the climb itself, not for what you'll see once you reach the top.

A guide definitely is required for "The Trail." The new starting point, near Zetland Plantation, is difficult to find; the old has been fenced off by a property owner desiring greater privacy.

The first fifteen minutes are some of steepest and slipperiest walking of all, as you stumble through big clumps of grass; if you find this too unpleasant, turn back. It gets worse later. After a few hundred feet, you join the old Trail, which is narrow but not nearly as difficult. As the forest closes in, you'll see lots of ferns, almond trees and an occasional mango. The smell is moist and earthy, a distinctive tropical smell. Only a few hundred feet more and the pathway opens to a breeze and a good view of Mount Nevis looming over you. Fifteen minutes from the outset, you arrive at a small plateau with a pond on the left. It is possible to camp in this field overnight, when accompanied by a local guide.

Continuing, the trail is once more enclosed by the forest and gets steadily steeper. After about a mile, you can make progress only by scrambling and holding onto trees and roots. It's extremely tough when the ground is wet because of the moss and the mud; guide Sylvester Pemberton claims the terrain is at a precipitous sixty to seventy degrees, so this is almost mountain climbing. The summit is often obscured by a halo of clouds, so sight-seeing may be limited.

# 12. Guadeloupe

The Caribs called Guadeloupe "Karukera," island of beautiful waters, and considering the hot water springs and tall tumbling falls, it was aptly named. Columbus, who never showed much poetic inspiration, gave Karukera another of his mundane saintly names: this one after the monastery of Santa Maria de Guadeloupe in Extremadura, Spain. The Spanish never settled here and the French, who arrived in 1635 with their sugar plantations and slave labor, never bothered to change the name.

Conditions on Guadeloupe were too unsettled for the island to prosper on the same scale as some of other parts of the French West Indies. Four chartered companies tried in vain to colonize the island, which was finally turned over to the French crown, to become a dependency of Martinique.

The British coveted the island so obviously that a threatened Louis XV bribed them away with Canada, through the Treaty of Paris in 1763. In 1789, the French Revolution's message of human equality sparked revolts on Guadeloupe; some plantation owners were guillotined, others fled. Slavery was abolished, but reintroduced in 1802.

The English controlled the island from 1810 to 1816. Following the abolition of slavery in 1848, the plantations went into decline because of the lack of cheap labor. Even indentured workers brought in from India could not take up the slack.

Sugar, rum and molasses are still important exports, but bananas now surpass them. Unemployment is high, averaging more than 20%.

The two sections of Guadeloupe, Grand-Terre and Basse-Terre, are separated by the Salee River. Guadeloupe is often described as an island

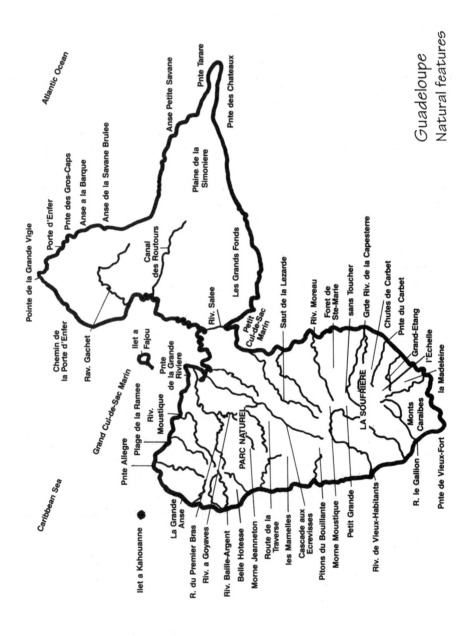

Guadeloupe
Natural features

shaped like a pair of butterfly wings. Grand-Terre and Basse-Terre couldn't be more different.

Grand-Terre, the flatter part of the island with several sandy coasts, is home to the capital city of Pointe-a-Pitre and the industrial base, as well as the majority of the resorts.

Basse-Terre, on the other hand, is a land of tall forested mountains, with a huge, smoldering volcano that caused a massive evacuation from this part of the island in 1976. A walk up the steam-vented sides of this restless volcano, La Soufriere, is one of the Caribbean's best hikes.

Basse-Terre is also home to the 74,100-acre Parc Naturel, which is not only one of the Caribbean's most visually lush parks, but one that is unique in that it has no gates, no admission fees and no opening and closing hours.

In all, about 40% of Basse-Terre is a tropical forest of gommier and mahogany trees, climbing vines and orchids. On the warmer coastal levels, bananas, sugar cane, coffee and vanilla plants account for most of the land usage.

Travel Tips

Area: 687 square miles total area.

Language: French and Creole; English is spoken in some tourist areas.

Population: About 150,000 in the Basse-Terre region; 190,000 on Grand-Terre.

Time Zone: Atlantic Standard Time, one hour ahead of Eastern Standard Time.

Rainy Season: July to November are the wettest months, with most of the rain falling between September and November. January to April is the official dry season.

Getting There: American Eagle from San Juan has good connecting flights from the States. Air Canada flies directly from Montreal. Inter-island service is available on LIAT, Air Guadeloupe and Winair, if you're hopping over from a neighboring island. Air France also flies direct from Paris, with other flights by way of Miami and San Juan. The airport is on the Grand Terre side at Point-a-Pitre, which is only a few minutes' drive from Basse-Terre.

Getting Around: The Raizet airport has the best stock of rental cars on the island, including international agencies such as Avis and Hertz. There is no need to purchase a temporary local driver's license. Driving is on the right.

Where to Stay: The Tourist Board has an office at the Raizet Airport; they can be very helpful in locating hotels, inns or campgrounds. Most of the major resorts are on Grand-Terre, not close to prime areas for hiking and exploring.

The Relais Creoles are small (from six to forty rooms) private hotels located in the countryside, usually with their own excellent Creole restaurants. These small hotels are represented in the U.S. by International Tours and Resorts, 4 Park Avenue, New York, NY 10016; 212/545-8469 or toll-free 800/223-9815.

Another alternative are the rooms and kitchenettes called Gites, which are popular with many budget-minded French travelers. A list of these are available from the tourist offices in Basse-Terre or Grand-Terre, or through the Syndicat d'Initative de Deshaies; tel. 28 49 70. The syndicat charges a 5% commission/rental fee.

Camping: Not only can you camp, you can arrange overnight treks of four to five days along the trails of the Parc Naturel with one of the forest service personnel. Their English isn't always the best, but the guides try their hardest to explain the amazing variety of terrain you pass through. Campsites are available (as are small bungalows) at Sable d'Or near Deshaies in Basse-Terre; tel. 28 44 60; Camping Traversee near Mahaut on Basse-Terre; and the Guadeloupe Hotel at Saint-Francois, also offering complete camping facilities. Or check with the local park service office or police about other sites that might look interesting to you.

Taxes & Tips: Checks will often come marked "Service Compris," in which case no tip is necessary. Otherwise 10-15% is standard.

Documents: American and Canadian citizens staying less than ten days do not need a passport, only some sort of identification and an ongoing ticket. All others need passports; residents of some countries need visas.

Currency: The French franc is the coin of the realm. Banks and exchange houses have the best exchange rates, although they may also charge a 1% commission and a 4% filing fee. Money exchange is handled only in the morning. Bank hours are 8 a.m. to noon and 2 p.m.-4 p.m. Monday through Friday.

Electrical Current: 220 volts/60 cycles.

Hiking/Walking Services: Contact the Organisation des Guides de Montagne le la Caraibe, Maison Forestiere, 97120 Matouba; tel. 590 80 05 79. They are familiar with all the best hikes inside the national park. Through them, you may arrange day hikes or treks of a week or more. My very helpful guide was Berry Gerard. Having him describe the terrain and vegetation on the Soufriere climb made all the difference between knowing and guessing about what we were seeing.

Snakes and Other Venomous Creatures: None.

For More Information: French West Indies Tourist Office, 610 Fifth Avenue, New York, NY 10020; 212/757-1125. In Canada, 1981 Avenue MacGill College, Suite 490, Montreal, PQH 3A 2W9; 288-4262 or 1 Dundas Street West, Suite 2405, Ontario NS 1-2-3; 593-6427. In the UK, 178 Picadilly, London; 071/491-7622.

Walking Tour of Pointe-a-Pitre

The real beauty of Guadeloupe is in the countryside, as the big-city, congested streets of Pointe-a-Pitre quickly demonstrate. Finding a parking place anywhere in Pointe-a-Pitre is a challenge unless you're there early in the morning, and even then you may have to walk a good distance to the center of town.

If this seems out of character for the Caribbean, then so is the stifled feeling created by the intense traffic. The city is so crowded compared to the open spaces of Basse-Terre's countryside that it feels almost claustrophobic.

So why visit Pointe-a-Pitre? For its historic and shopping qualities, which are considerable.

1) Place de la Victoire: Named in honor of Victor Hugue's victory over the British in 1794, this shady park is where Hugue put the guillotine to work, lopping off the heads of selected landowners. The streets surrounding the park contain the oldest buildings, though few of the truly old colonial structures survived the earthquake of 1845.

2) Marketplace: A daily event where island women in colorful costumes sell and haggle over the breadfruit, tomatoes, bananas and other assorted items. You can also buy hats and local spices; in fact, some of the sellers can be quite insistent about it.

3) Shopping: The main streets are Noizieres, Frebault and Schoelcher. In addition, a brand-new shopping arcade has just opened near the waterfront, targeted specifically at cruise ship passengers and other visitors.

4) Musee St. John Perse: Few outsiders know that a Guadeloupan won the 1960 Nobel Prize for Literature. The museum contains the complete poetry collection, personal effects, documents and photographs of St. John, poet and diplomat. Open Monday through Saturday, 9 a.m. to 12:30 p.m. and 2p.m. to 6p.m..

5) Musee Schoelcher: This museum commemorates the life of Victor Schoelcher, who helped abolish slavery in the French West Indies. The ornate building alone is worth seeing, even if you don't go inside. Open weekdays, 9 a.m. to noon and 2:30 p.m. to 5:30 p.m..

Pointe-A-Pitre

The Parc Naturel
Route de la Traversee

This road effectively divides Basse-Terre into northern and southern halves. Although the best hiking trails are farther south, this scenic roadway (about sixteen miles) borders the Parc Naturel, providing an excellent introduction to the plants and wildlife of Guadeloupe.

Route de la Traversee offers several very interesting stops and climbs you can do easily on your own without the services of a guide.

Starting at the village of Vernou (where the small hotel Auberage de la Distillerie is located), walk three miles to the carpark near the Cascade aux Ecrevisse. It's a short walk to where the picturesque waterfall plummets into the Corossol River. Feel free to swim, but beware of the very slippery rocks.

The Parc Tropical de Bras-David is two miles farther on. Its small network of hiking trails takes about an hour to explore if you walk slowly and take time to investigate the plant life. A small forest house has displays (in French) explaining much of the area ecology. Picnic tables make this a good place for a lengthy, restful stop.

Go another two and one half miles and you will reach Guadeloupe's version of Twin Peaks, called Les Mamelles, meaning "breasts." Mamelle de Petit-Bourg reaches 2,350 feet while Mamelle de Pigeon peaks out at 2,500 feet. Hiking trails here vary from easy to challenging. A lookout at almost 2,000 feet up Mamelle de Pigeon is spectacular, as is the scenery in the valley running between the twin peaks.

The stone steps to the Zoological Park and Botanical Gardens require almost no effort, and there you may view turtles, iguanas and cockatoos. Titi the Raccoon is the mascot of the Parc Naturel. These animals, however, are relatively rare in the wild, so this will be one of your few chances to see one close-up. The park is open daily 9a.m. to 5p.m.; admission fee.

La Soufriere

It's not often that you can walk the slopes of an active volcano, look into its sulfur spewing craters and experience the heat still radiating from deep in the earth. The region of La Soufriere is typically hidden in cloud and mist, which emphasizes the primordial atmosphere. Come prepared for drizzle, rain and brisk winds on the summit. Should the day be clear, be prepared for a lot of company on the trail, including entire classes of school children. Most of the trails depart from or near the parking lot of Savane des Mulets, which translates as savannah of mules.

Many different trails branch off from the main trail (Hike 1) circling La Soufriere, including Hikes 2, 3 and 4. Plan ahead of time how much walking you intend to do so you can join the trails accordingly and provision properly. Take a flashlight in case you end up on the trail longer than you anticipate. There is so much to distract your attention that it's easy to lose track of time.

1. Circuit of La Soufriere

Time: 1-1/2 hours for the circle walk around the volcano; 2-1/2 hours to include a visit to the summit. **Difficulty:** 3. Depart from Savane des Mulets, altitude 1142m.

This trail goes around the volcano, ascending on the west via the Chemin de Dames (Road of the Ladies), blazed in yellow. For the descent, the trail passes by Col de l'Echelle (Ladder Hill), an impressive area littered with boulders from the 1976 eruptions.

An information board (if you read French) gives the history of this volcano, which is a relatively young one. During the last thousand years, la Soufriere has shown considerable activity, marking the Basse-Terre region with lava lahars (flows) and heavy storm clouds. The longest major eruption was in 1976. Others occurred in 1797 and 1560.

The hiking trail begins with a few hairpin turns, then conforms to the gentle slope of the mountain. The path is interrupted by two flows and along the trail is a thick bed of dried sludge, which destroyed the vegetation on this part of the cone in 1976.

Approaching the west and northwest slopes, you'll border a zone which did not suffer the destructive effects of the last eruption; where the flora is intact. As you reach l'Eboulement (the landslide) Faujas after less than a half-hour of walking, you'll see peat-mosses, lichens and mountain pineapples hanging on the fault.

The panoramic view is exceptional: the southwest of Basse-Terre, the Caribbean Sea, and closer summits like Nez Casse ("Broken Nose") and Carmichael. Looking toward la Soufriere, the volcano shows its teeth—an amalgam of precariously balanced rocks.

A few minutes later you will arrive at the north-south Great Fault, also called the "North Crevice." Its sheer walls sixty meters high are barren of vegetation.

Here the trail divides. To the right is the summit hike, a round-trip of about an hour (described in Hike 2). If you're going to make the climb, now is the time to do it. Refer to Hike 2 now and begin.

The left path continues circling the volcano. About 100 meters beyond, after some hairpin turns, the trail joins a swampy plateau called the Great Savane, and a bit farther on you arrive at a second crossroads. If you continue straight ahead to the north, you'll reach Matouba by the Carmichael Trail (this is the starting point for Hike 3).

Near this path, about 100 meters from the crossroads, are the Collardeau Fumeroles; these ten vents are periodically used for gas samples.

At the crossroads, bear to the right toward Ladder Hill. Vegetation is sparse, mostly gray or orange lichens and mountain pineapples which, from 800 meters to the summit, decorate la Soufriere with big, red-spiked flowers.

If you're fortunate enough to have clear weather, you'll see the Northeast Fault above and to the right. Beyond the fault is Sanner Trail, a more strenuous path to reach the dome. Moving lower and to your left, the fumeroles of Carbet manifest themselves, through a strong odor of sulfur.

About twenty minutes after leaving the crossroads to the Matouba and Carmichael trails, you'll enter a craggy stone landscape. At the edge of this is yet another marked crossroads. The left trail joins the Chutes de Carbet Trail. However, for the volcano circuit, stay right and follow the trail blazed in blue which leads down to Ladder Hill.

This region was one of the places most affected by the 1976 eruption: it is here that on July 8th the most important explosion occurred, which reopened and reactivated the large southern fault that crosses the entire flank of the volcano.

The view is beautiful over the Windward Coast, the Capesterre region and Grande-Terre; when visibility is good you can even see the island of Marie-Galante.

At Ladder Hill you'll pass an enormous rock fractured into two pieces. On the left are the fumeroles of Ladder Hill: sulfurous vapors of 96°C escape from a hole where you can spot a sizable deposit of sulfur crystals. Still to the left and a little higher is the geophysical shelter, severely damaged by the last 1976 eruptions.

Leave Ladder Hill and descend across the debris. The trail, still marked with blue blazes, goes along the Matylis Ravine, which in 1976 was site of the main flows. While descending, you can observe to the right, on la Soufriere's southeast flank, the so-called "mouths of explosion," which hurled out the surrounding rocks now covered with a thick coating of lichens.

Zig-zag ahead for ten more minutes to reach the Citerne volcano, which is used as a TV relay. Bear to the right and within five minutes you should be back at Savane a Mulets, your departure point.

2. Summit of La Soufriere

Time: 2-1/2 hours. **Difficulty:** 3-4. Blazed trail, but can be very slippery. Depart and arrive at Savane a Mulets. For access, use Trail 1.

Arriving at the Great Fault on the north face, go right along the trail. It's a short climb—only ten minutes to the summit. Proceed with extreme caution and watch your steps carefully.

Don't expect to find a single immense crater, as you may have imagined. La Soufriere possesses clustered, numerous eruptive mouths called pits or craters, which are arranged in a string along the fracture zones.

Once on the plateau, you'll follow the length of the Great Fault, likely to be hazed over by escaping sulfur vapor. Your route, marked with green posts, highlights the most obvious formations. Feel free to leave the official trail to explore on your own. Now is when a guide would be most useful.

At the end of the Great Fault, take the rocky trail to the right, which climbs past a small concrete shelter and leads to la Decouverte, at 1467 meters, the highest point of la Soufriere. When the weather permits, the view is exceptional.

Continue south until you are above Dupuy Pit on your left. Then skirt the fracture of the Faujas Landslide and bear to the right. About a hundred meters, after la Decouverte is a trail bearing to the right to reach Piton Saussure or Piton du Nord at 1464 meters. The view of the leeward coast is grand.

Returning to the primary trail, you'll enter a vast lunar landscape, the result of an intense downpour of stone and sludge projectiles in the 1976 eruption: even the hardest rock formations were softened, rounded by this hellish brown sheet. Vegetation totally disappeared and is only now slowly coming back.

At your feet will be a pool established after the last eruption, not far from the former "Devil's Pool," which disappeared at the same time. Before you, bordering the cone to the southwest, is the piton (peak) of the South or Piton Dolomieu. That ascent is extremely dangerous and ill-advised.

Follow the green trail to la Porte de l'Enfer (Hell's Gate) on your left. To some, this rock resembles a tall silhouette of the devil. Others call it "la guenon" ("she-monkey" or "ugly woman").

Beyond is another vast basin of earth and stones. Before 1976 it was so rich in plants it was called l'Herminier Garden, named after a doctor and man of science living in Guadeloupe in the last century. The once-beautiful garden is now a wasteland.

Some ten meters after Hell's Gate is a natural bridge crossing the great north-south fault you followed at the beginning of the ascent. On your left, Dupuy Pit is filled with water and sludge from the last eruption. On your right is Tarissan Pit, so deep no one is certain what's at the bottom. On some days, Tarissan Pit will bathe you in sulfur fumes.

After the natural bridge, turn right and follow the looping trail to the south. On your left is Piton Napoleon, with many fumeroles. The side of this peak is also covered with a thick coat of sludge.

After climbing a little hill and bearing to the left, you'll approach the south crater at the extreme edge of the plateau. This cauldron, bubbling with thick vapors, may be invisible in foggy weather, but the odor is unmistakable and you're bound to feel its radiating heat.

Descending toward the southeast along the edge of the cone, you'll have an excellent view over Ladder Hill (Col de l'Echelle) 200 meters below, and over la Citerne, the volcano with the well-known classic cone.

For the return, you can either retrace your steps to reach the fork near the natural bridge, or reach the same destination by continuing toward the north, keeping Napoleon Crater on your right.

At the fork, keep the Tarissan and Dupuy Pits on your left and continue in a northerly direction along the Great Fault. On the right you will notice a little lake of dried mud surrounded by pathetic shrubs burned by the gas. A little farther, still on the right, vegetation is mostly mountain pineapples. You'll also find the Sanner Trail, which tumbles down toward the springs of Carbet. Continue retracing your ascent to rejoin the trail near the North Fault.

3. Carmichael Trail

Time: 3-1/2 hours to walk down, 4-1/2 hours to make the return hike.
Difficulty: 3 down, 4 to ascend.

Depart from la Savane a Mulets, altitude 1142 meters. This trail descends to the parking lot of the Forestry House at Matouba, at an altitude of 660 meters. It is marked in both directions. Be sure to take water.

If you join The Carmichael Trail while making the volcano circuit, (Hike 1) you'll already have completed an hour of walking. The Carmichael Trail is well marked. The vegetation on this great marshy plateau (the Great Savane) is primarily mountain mangroves, whose leaves resemble those of rubber plants. You'll spot a few mountain palms and mountain aralie.

On the left, ten meters away, are isolated fumeroles called Colardeau Fumeroles. A little farther, on the right, is a little-used path to Ladder Hill (Col de L'Echelle).

About forty minutes from the crossroads, the trail, which can be very muddy during the rainy season, takes you to the summit of Mt. Carmichael, a height of 1414 meters. After the summit, the trail descends, bends toward the west and reaches Morne du Col at 1281 meters. From both summits, the view in good weather is magnificent.

After a bend toward the southwest, the trail leads to a landslide overlooking a valley with a large cabin, the dilapidated shelter of the Montagnards, a mountain climbing club.

Go around the landslide and descend the straight ridge on the right which divides the sloping basins of the River Class to the right and the Red River to the left. At the hill, bear to the left toward the south. (The path straight ahead climbs the slopes of the Grande Decouverte and joins the Victor Hugo Trail.)

The trail descends rapidly, then reaches a flat and wet portion, where it splits in two again. To the left is a Montagnards' shelter. Continue on the main trail and descend in a southwesterly direction. The trail is wide, the vegetation grows thicker to become typical tropical forest. Numerous raspberry bushes line the trail's edge.

About twenty minutes after the last crossroads, the Carmichael Trail joins the Victor Hugo Trail. Thirty minutes later, you'll pass another fork. Continue ahead, ignoring the marked trail on your left that leads to the Hot Baths of Matouba, and return to Savane a Mulets by the Delgres Trail.

From this last crossroads it will take you less than thirty minutes to find the cultivated fields of Frezias and the reforested parcels planted with laurel trees. Next is the Forestry House of Matouba, your destination.

 4. Col de l'Echelle (Ladder Hill)

Time: 2 hours. **Difficulty:** 3. Trail is not blazed, and not especially difficult.

This hike acquaints you with the vegetation of high-altitude savannahs and provides beautiful panoramas of the Leeward Coast, the southern part of the island and the southern slope of the cone of la Soufriere. Depart and return to Savane a Mulets.

After fifteen minutes you'll see the branch trail to ascend l'Echelle from the south; first, you climb the Matylis Ravine, then go past the fumeroles of Morne Mitan and the electric line on the left which feeds part of the geophysical system that monitors the volcano.

Numerous switchbacks get you to the summit of l'Echelle in thirty to forty minutes. During the climb, you'll have a good look at la Citerne (Cistern) volcano with its circular crater partially filled with water. The low altitude vegetation here is often filled with blooms in October and November: fuchsias with garnet "bells," the yellow flowers of mountain daisies, gracious and delicate orchids with their sweet perfume, mountain pineapples with their red or yellow flowers and the lycopods which resemble tiny Christmas trees.

At 1397 meters, in front of you and quite near, is la Soufriere. Notice the different "mouths" of explosion from 1976.

You can then begin the rather delicate descent, toward l'Echelle, in a northwesterly direction; the trail passes beside a large rock, the "Devil's Footstool," and arrives at the hill of Morne Mitan where you find an electric post. Bear to the right toward the north, in the direction of the geophysical shelter, which you see below. The flanks of l'Echelle and Morne Mitan are covered with peat-mosses of different colors, scattered with flowers, and stones projected by la Soufriere.

At Col de l'Echelle, turn left between the fractured rock and the fumarole, then follow the blue trail into the mass of debris above the Ravine Matylis. You'll soon arrive at the road. Turn to the right; Savane a Mulets is about 400 meters away.

From l'Echelle you can also make the circuit of the volcano using Hike 1 in reverse.

5. La Citerne (Cistern)

Time: 1 hour, round trip. **Difficulty:** 2-3. Trail not marked but simple. Depart and arrive at Savane a Mulets.

La Citerne is an ancient volcano, perhaps merely dormant, whose crater, 200 meters wide and fifty meters deep, is occupied by the Camille Flammarion Lake.

From Savane a Mulets, walk out by the road leading to la Citerne, marked by the antenna of the television relay (which you may not see if the clouds are too low). After passing the impressive debris of Col de l'Echelle, the odor of sulfur is everywhere. Note the scattered fumeroles with yellowish surfaces (sulfur crystals).

Soon after the first fumeroles, on the right you'll see others scattered on the denuded and whitish slope of Morne Mitan. The fleshless trunks and tree branches bear witness again to the damage done in 1976, the result of asphyxiating vapors.

After Morne Mitan, on the left of the road is the trail climbing the southern flank of l'Echelle, described in Hike 4.

The Cistern Trail now takes a sharp turn to the right and arrives at the hill which separates l'Echelle and la Citerne. Ignore the left trail: it's only about 1000 meters long, a failed attempt to link this section with the parking area at the Falls of Carbet, farther to the west.

To this point you've been sheltered from the breeze. Now, the wind may feel as piercing as a harpoon, but you'll experience the true meaning of windward and leeward coasts.

Arriving at la Citerne, you'll find the classicly-shaped crater is dense with vegetation. You can quickly circle the outer rim. Following the trail, you will reach a television relay, the first relay transmitter erected on Guadeloupe. Near the relay is a trail to the left that's barely visible. It descends by way of the Plateau de la Grande Chasse to rejoin the Etang de l'As de Pique (Pond of the Ace of Spades). It is not maintained, and the trail is difficult to follow.

In the east, along the Plateau de la Grande Chasse, you should be able to spot Grand Etang (Big Pond), then the Windward Coast with Capesterre and its vast banana plantation. Farther in the distance is the island of Marie-Galante; to the northeast is Grande-Terre.

Looking toward the south, Madeleine tops out at 971 meters at Piton l'Herminier, and to its right is Morne Gros Fougas with its almost perfectly circular crater; at your feet are the banana warehouses of Moscou. With good visibility you can see Dominica.

On the summit of la Citerne, the vegetation is essentially mountain pineapple, upland lilies, mountain thyme, mosses and orchids. About 250 meters after the TV relay, a trail goes off to the left and leads to Galion Falls, the river whose upper valley you now overlook.

Now that you've circled la Citerne, rejoin the blazed trail for the fifteen minute trip back to Savane a Mulets.

 6. Karukera Trail

Time: 2 hours, each way. **Difficulty:** 3-4. Not marked. Advisable to take water.

Depart from Savane a Mulets. Descend to the Carbet Falls picnic area at 600 meters. The first part of this hike is the same as the last section of several trails: La Soufriere Circle, First Carbet Waterfall, and Col de l'Echelle. Always use caution during foggy weather, notably around Col de l'Echelle.

From Savane a Mulets, take the la Citerne route for 300 meters, bearing to the left a little before Matylis Ravine. A trail marked with blue dots leads to l'Echelle. At the hill, the trail bears to the right and follows orange blazes, first across cropped vegetation, then on rocky soil, between two ravines flowing out of the Carbet. After scaling the ravine on the right, the trail is dominated by a vertical wall. In the flat portion which follows is the departure point of the Karukera Trail.

Begin this rather steep ascent by the first path to the left—the other trails are cul-de-sacs. It takes about forty minutes. In the next thirty minutes, you'll cross three small ravines in thick mangrove forest where the humidity oozes, climb for several meters holding onto mangrove roots, and finally arrive at a clearing where the panorama is superb.

From the plateau, the trail veers immediately to the left, toward the east. Descending, you'll hear a dull roar grow louder: it's the second Carbet waterfall, which you'll soon see off to your left. About ten minutes later, you'll reach the picnic area of the waterfalls by a an old forest road passing among white gum trees, characterized by a slender, light gray trunk and a high, dense tuft.

7. Pas Du Roy and Galion Waterfall Trails

Time: 1-1/2 hours to the falls. It takes twenty minutes to get to Pas du Roy (Way of the King). **Difficulty:** 2-3. Marked only at the trailhead, this is an easy trail. Depart and return to the Bains Jaunes (Yellow Baths) parking area.

At the Bains Jaunes parking area, near the abandoned refuge, a stele marks the entrance to the Pas du Roy Trail, opened in 1887 by the Colonials. Until the recent opening of the path going off to the left, this trail was the only access to the volcano. At the beginning, you'll go along the basin of the Bains Jaunes, dry except in the rainy season.

About 300 meters from the start is a fork to the right leading to Galion Falls, goal of your walk. To the left, you can continue the Pas du Roy which ends at the tar road, then either go back down to the Bains Jaunes (Yellow Baths) parking area or to the parking area for Savane a Mulets.

Le Pas Du Roy

For about ten minutes the rocky trail has steps. In a dramatic turn to the left, a break in the greenery permits you to see the mountain mass of l'Echelle and below, at the bottom of the Galion Valley, an entire mountainside that was carried away in the 1976 slide.

Several minutes later, the trail continues climbing and comes out onto a little cleared plateau for a panoramic view of Belvedere. To descend, choose the short walk to Savane a Mulets or retrace your steps to Bains Jaunes.

Galion Falls

At the crossroads, continue to the right. The wide trail descends in a gentle slope across relatively low and sparse growth, mainly mountain mangroves, tree ferns and marble wood. The marble wood here is stunted due to the altitude. In dense forests at lower levels, marble wood can reach twenty meters in height.

After fifteen minutes, the view on your right opens to reveal Basse-Terre and its surroundings. To the southeast, surrounded by the banana warehouses of Moscou, is Morne Gros Fougas, a classic volcano form. If weather permits, you'll also see la Madeleine, whose summit, at Piton l'Herminier, reaches 971 meters.

The trail then plunges into a ravine and, after a few zigzags, runs beside the Galion River. It should have taken you about thirty-five minutes to come this far. Access to the falls is either by the trail going straight ahead or by climbing back up the riverbed to reach the foot of the forty-meter falls.

On the left bank, another trail will lead you across a maze of enormous rocks to the cascade of the Ty, just before it meets the Galion.

Retrace your steps to your departure point, a trip of forty-five minutes.

8. Vauchelet Cascade

Time: 45 minutes roundtrip. **Difficulty:** 2. This trail is marked only at the beginning.

This cascade, located about 500 meters northeast of Saint-Claude, was formed by a rupture in the bank of the Riviere Noire. Depart and return to the Saint-Claude police station across from the prefect's residence.

After parking near the police station, stay on the concrete road which ends at a house. Go around the house by walking to the left, below a small wall. The trail, narrow at the beginning and sometimes overgrown with tall grass, becomes wide and shaded.

The walk takes about twenty minutes, giving you time to notice several interesting plants: the chestnut, with large leaves and fat prickly burrs; and also the Resolute Tree (Chimarrhis cymosa), with its clusters of white flowers. Its yellowish-orange wood—very hard and insect-resistant—is used in construction.

Along the path's edge, you'll also see sang dragon (or swamp bloodwood, a large tree with enormous buttress roots and blood-red latex in the sap) heliconias, cannon wood, numerous tree ferns and the rose apple, whose fruits are delicious and fragrant.

The trail, now overlooking the river, bends to the right, then descends and becomes narrower, bringing you opposite the tumbling waters of the Riviere Noire. The cascade has at least a twenty meter drop. Halfway down, the water hits rock, fanning out into an elegant spray. Cross the bridge (flanked on the right bank by an enormous chestnut tree) to reach the cascade and its basin. To the left and a little before the pool are the remains of a shelter built by the Montagnards.

9. The Heights of Papaye

Time: 2 hours; Bains Chauds (Hot Baths), 1-1/2 hours, round trip. **Difficulty:** 2-3. A blazed trail, rather easy. Depart from the Clinique des Eaux-Vives of Papaye. Arrive at the Forest House of Matouba, altitude 667 meters.

At the foot of the northern slope of Nez Casse are 90°C sulfur springs. Their therapeutic properties are used by the Clinique des Eaux-Vives on the Papaye Plateau above Matouba. This "Clinic of Living Waters" draws the wealthiest people of Guadeloupe. It is also the starting point for your hike. Park in the lot.

The first 200-300 meters go along the road in a northeasterly direction, then climb past vegetable gardens and fields of grazing cattle. After crossing a muddy section, the trail becomes wide and more pleasant; this intermediate slope is rather gentle because you are following roughly the curves of the northwest side of Nez Casse.

About 1500 meters after leaving the fields, the trail curves to the left to reach the Chaude Ravine, a green opening composed of giant trees, tree ferns, heliconias and raspberries.

The trail leads you 300 meters farther to a fork. The path to the right will take you to the hot baths. It meanders for about twenty minutes through trees which are shorter the higher you climb. Eventually they become a stunted forest of mangroves and marble wood, a growth pattern that precedes the high-altitude savannahs.

After visiting the hot baths, you can either return to your departure point by taking the path described above, or continuing the trail for another hour to the ranger station of Matouba. From there, you can get back to the Plateau Papaye parking area by following the road going through Matouba village, with its pretty wooden houses and colorful gardens.

 10. The Matouba Waterfall

Time: 45 minutes. **Difficulty:** 2. A blazed and easy trail. The small Matouba Waterfall is not well known. Depart and arrive at the Josephine Residence in Matouba.

To reach the Josephine Residence, drive the Matouba Road from Saint-Claude. After the bridges crossing the Riviere Noire and the Ravine des Ecrevisses (Crayfish), get off National Route 3 by turning to the left at the curve not far from a stele erected in memory of Delgres (former head of the Basse-Terre district).

After 250 meters, first going in a straight line and then curving right, the road makes an abrupt turnoff to your right: a sign visible at the last minute indicates your destination. You'll drive through a vast banana plantation, then encounter a straight road bordered by red mahoganies, Gabon tulip trees with big orange flowers, American palms, and—finally—the Josephine Residence. Only the foundations of the main house and a few outbuildings remain. Park near the oak tree: a rare species for Guadeloupe.

Take a right past the banana seasoning shed and follow the rocky path until it curves to the left. Follow the sign to an alley bordered by sang dragon.

After a beautiful view of Soufriere and the Plateau Papaye, you'll head into the forest, and in five minutes more you'll reach the bed of the Saint-Louis River, and the Matouba Waterfall: a small cascade which spurts out of a volcanic gully into a deep basin.

Warning: What appears to be a refreshing paradise in the tropical heat may be dangerous to swimmers. Locals say a whirlpool at the foot of the falls has already caused some accidents.

11. The Third Carbet Waterfall

Time: 1-1/2 hours, round trip to visit the third waterfall; 2-1/2 hours to both visit the third waterfall and reach the Carbet Falls picnic area. **Difficulty:** 2-3. A blazed trail: provisioning is a good idea. Depart from Routhiers in the town of Capesterre-Belle-Eau, altitude 380 meters. Arrive at Routhiers.

The Truly Strenuous Path: Climbing up the Carbet, you also have the option to visit the first and second waterfalls using Hikes 12 and 13, and to visit la Soufriere. All this is a pretty strenuous route (Difficulty: 4-5) of about six hours.

Park trails can be rugged, but they are usually easy to follow.

To reach the departure point, drive to Capesterre. At the entrance to the city coming from the Basse-terre side, leave RN1 and turn left onto D3 toward Routhiers. D3 passes in front of the Marquisat factory; at the first crossroads turn right; at the second, after a long straightaway, take the left. Then 100 meters farther, turn right again. You are in Routhiers. The road turns into a macadam road going through a mahogany forest mingled with banana plantings. The road stops at our departure point three kilometers farther.

Park at the end of the road. Take the wide path (which can be muddy) across the edge of a sparse forest of mahogany, giant philodendrons, and tree ferns.

After twenty minutes, cross an enclosed ravine by angling to the left. Several minutes later you'll encounter a marked crossroads: to the right are the first and second waterfalls, Hikes 12 and 13; opposite is the third, which you are going to visit.

Reaching the river will take about ten minutes. Take special precautions while descending an uneven area about fifty meters long, which has been ravaged by landslides. Halfway down you'll see the waterfall: continuing the descent into the river bed shouldn't pose any difficulty.

Returning to the crossroads, you can either take the thirty-minute trek back to your vehicle or, by going left, continue your hike toward the first or second falls. The second falls are closer; about one and a half hours away.

If you decide to proceed, the trail goes along the Carbet River for about fifteen minutes, then crosses its tributary, the Dauriac. Some five minutes later, the trail crosses another tributary, then continues along a small ridge.

Afterwards, you'll cross a relatively flat zone where the forest is essentially gum trees and chestnuts, and an occasional yellow mangrove with its famous aerial roots.

Fifteen minutes after crossing the Dauriac River, you'll arrive at the edge of the Carbet and the foot of a very steep climb. During the first 600 meters of walking, you will ascend 170 meters. The trail follows the line of the largest slope, then descends and climbs again; forty minutes later, you're at another marked crossroads. To the right, the trail continues toward the first Carbet waterfall, one and a half hours away, then moves on to la Soufriere.

To the left, a ten minute walk brings you to yet another marked crossroads. From this point, you can be back at the picnic and parking area within fifteen minutes by turning left and following the zigzag trail after the bridge. Or, you can reach the second—and most spectacular—Carbet waterfall in even less time by taking the right fork.

On this hike you'll see about twenty species of lianas, vines which are large enough even for Tarzan to swing on, one of the most impressive aspects of this tropical forest.

12. First Carbet Waterfall

Time: 4 hours, one way. **Difficulty:** 4-5. A blazed trail, take water and snacks. Depart from the waterfall picnic area. Arrive at Savane a Mulets, altitude 1142m.

To reach the first waterfall, start from the Carbet Falls picnic area. At the end of Habituee Road, a break in the brush lets you see the first two Carbet falls. The farthest away is the highest: it plummets more than 125 meters in two stages. Its summit is 1005 meters. The other waterfall, actually closer, measures around 110 meters. Hike 13 will take you to it.

Immediately on your left is the zigzag track which goes around the flanks of l'Echelle. After going into the forest for 200 meters, another maintained trail leads to the left: the Karukera Trail, which leads directly to l'Echelle (the descent described in Hike 6).

Following the trail to the first falls, you'll snake downwards toward the river. Along the way you'll spot the white gum, a very tall tree easily identified by its straight, slender trunk. It is the source of an amber-colored resin. The trunk of this tree, hollow and wide, was once used to build long, narrow unstable boats, called gommiers. Gum-tree boats are no longer used in Guadeloupe, but can frequently be seen on neighboring islands.

You'll cross the Carbet by a footbridge. Several meters farther is your first crossroads; the left path leads to the second waterfall (described in Hike 13). Instead, follow the trail which climbs regularly in a westerly direction, through a luxuriantly forested hillside. About a kilometer beyond the crossroads, veer to the left and walk the steep incline into the Longueteau Ravine, tributary of the Carbet. Crossing to the other side, on the spur formed by the two valleys, is another fork. The right trail continues toward la Soufriere.

Stay left and in fifteen minutes you will reach the Carbet River bed and the first waterfall. There are two successive falls here: the first, from a height of 115 meters, falls onto a little platform, then becomes a second, ten-meter fall.

Returning to the crossroads, you have the option to walk toward l'Echelle, where the waterfall originates, and eventually come out at Savane a Mulets. Most people simply retrace their steps.

13. The Second Carbet Waterfall

Time: 1 hour, round trip. **Difficulty:** 2-3. Trail marked and simple. Depart from and return to the waterfall picnic area.

The very spectacular second Carbet Waterfall is the most frequently visited. Leave your vehicle at the Carbet falls picnic area. From there you can see the first two waterfalls: your goal—the second—is nearest.

Follow the signs to the second Karukera Trail (described in Hike 6).

From this first crossroads, the trail makes a rapid descent toward the river bed. You will notice some interesting trees: resolute wood, with large, light-green leaves; white gum, the resin of which is used for lighting fires; and sturdy chestnuts. The latter are the most abundant species in this dense forest and are frequently decked with impressive, elongated, aerial roots.

Ten minutes later you'll cross the Carbet River on a footbridge that was rebuilt in 1978, after the original was carried away by a gigantic volcanic flow five meters tall. This flow, courtesy of l'Echelle, also severely damaged the site of the second waterfall. A few meters past the footbridge is a crossroads: to the right is the access to the first and third falls; straight ahead is your trail.

Two hundred meters farther, bear to the right via the maintained trail that soon takes you to the river, which you now cross again. You can't help but see the impressive waterfall in front of you now. To get closer, the trail on the right bank continues to a rocky terrace where you can delicately make your way to the foot of the waterfall. The rocks here are always wet and you soon will be, too.

14. The Grand Etang Circle

Time: 1 hour, round trip. **Difficulty:** 2-3. The trail is marked.

When hiking the Soufriere range you'll see several bodies of water in the southeast which maps designate as "etangs" (pools or ponds). In fact, a Guadeloupean etang is a pool of sweet water comparable to a mountain lake. They form when depressions in the ground are enclosed by volcanic gullies which retain water.

This is how a former volcanic flow came to rest on Morne Boudoute to create the 748m Etang As de Pique (Ace of Spades Pool). Its overflow runs to the east and feeds, 350 meters below, Grand Etang.

Two other nearby ponds, Roche and Madere, are wedged between the southern flank of Morne Boudoute and the Madeleine range. Often dry, they may look like vast grassy expanses, a rare sight in a dense forest.

The circle of Grand Etang not only permits you to see the lake from different perspectives, it is also noteworthy for its plants and the many crayfish that live in its waters. The trail head is located at the Grand Etang parking area on the extension of State Road 4, about two kilometers west of the Grande Chasse Residence.

Park, and take the concrete road to the edge of the pond (about 300 meters), where a sign will direct you to begin the circle to the right. The wide trail ventures into a dense forest characterized by tall trees with powerful aerial roots, and by many epiphytes.

On the first part of the hike, the pond is scarcely visible. However, you will see great clumps of bamboo, which make an eerie creaking when the wind blows the reeds together. Abundant around the pond, bamboo was introduced from Asia two centuries ago on sites like this one, then transplanted just about everywhere in Guadeloupe.

After ten minutes, you'll reach a marked fork in the trail. The path to the right allows you to get back to Moscou and the Gourbeyre.

Continuing straight ahead, the lake appears on the left, its edges overgrown with aquatic plants. As you progress, a rustling sound becomes clearer: the stream feeding Etang As de Pique, whose divided bed you cross in three stages. Soon after, it rises several meters above the level of the pond.

Little by little, through scattered vegetation, you begin to discover Grand Etang and the grasses and mosses circling it.

You may see a thrush or a kingfisher at the lake edge. Grand Etang once had a reputation as a birdwatcher's paradise but the area has been overhunted.

At the southeast corner of the pond, you'll discover an enormous isolated rock in the water, decorated with plants and shrubs. Next, the trail passes above the subterranean overflow of the pond, which is audible.

The Caraibes Mountains

The extreme southern end of Basse-Terre is formed by a well-defined mountain range geologically separate from the rest of the island chain. The Caraibes arise from another, older and more western fracture, extending from Saint- Rose to Vieux-Fort and passing by Piton de Bouillante.

The departure point for hikes in the Caraibes Mountains is Champfleury, in the town of Gourbeyre, situated one kilometer south of Dos d'Ane on National Route 1. From there, after an hour's walk on a common section, two separate hikes are possible.

The first, Hike 16, leads to the west to rejoin the Marina de Riviere Sens south of the city of Basse-Terre.

The second, described in Hike 17, goes in a southerly direction, to the heights of Vieux-Fort.

15. The Champfleury/Coldu Gros Acajou Trail (Common Portion)

At the end of the Champfleury Road, leave your vehicle and take the path which extends from it to the south. Still paved for a good distance, the trail has concrete sections on the steepest slopes. The trail is sometimes blazed with white arrows and red dots. After the first fifteen minutes, it begins to rise steadily across a diffuse landscape and wastelands scattered with cannon wood. Turning around, you will have a beautiful view of the Dole banana plantations and Trois-Rivieres, overlooked in the north by the la Soufriere mountains.

At the paved platform, the trail bears to the right. As the slope becomes steeper, it gives way to a narrow path bordered by ferns and heliconias. A bit farther, you'll be in the forest, where you will recognize clumps of bamboo. After an hour you'll reach Grand Acajou Hill. This is where Hikes 15 and 16 separate. It is possible to do the Champfleury/Marina de Riviere

Sens/Vieux Fort/Champfleury loop, but it will take you eight or nine hours of walking. That is most suited for seasoned hikers.

16. Gros Acajou Hill to Marina de Riviere Sens

Time: 4 hours, one way. **Difficulty:** 3-4. The trail is marked in part; take water.

By taking the trail to the right, you will continue your ascent along a ridge line in the midst of a rain forest, ending on the coast.

Twenty minutes from the start, a sign will invite you to make a circle around the cleared summit of Morne Cadet, from which you can enjoy a beautiful view of Basse-Terre. This circle trail, leading off to the right, takes about twenty minutes to complete. On this side trail, you may surprise a partridge, or you may hear its call, seeming to well up from the mountainside itself.

Back on the main trail, you reach very quickly—in just 200 meters—the highest point of the Caraibes, Morne Vent Souffle. At 686 meters, it affords an exceptional 360-degree panorama almost defying description.

You quickly descend Morne Vent Souffle, first by a ridge leading to the south, then fifteen minutes later, by a second ridge to the right. Several meters lower on the trail, a break in the undergrowth allows you to see the Vieux-Fort lighthouse on the left.

On the right, the trail leaves the ridge to steeply descend in zigzags. It next veers to the left and meets another ridge which will take you to the two summits of Morne Grand Voute. After scaling a small section (there are handholds here, but rain can make them slippery) a trail on the right allows you to reach the first and nearest summit, 542m; 200 meters farther, the trail passes over the second summit, which peaks at 556 meters.

On the slopes of le Vent Souffle, you'll note the changes in the vegetation which surrounds you: the strange "tails" hanging from the branches, the dryer plant carpet, the diminished size of the trees. You'll see more and more rare epiphytes. You are in an intermediate stage between rain forest and dry forest, called mesophilic forest.

On the slopes of le Vent Souffle, and to a lesser degree on the slopes of Gros Acajou, this mesophile is well conserved and striking. Lower down, it has been largely stripped to create banana plantations, market gardens, cocoa and coffee plantations. Here is where the majority of forestry planting is done, especially the large-leafed mahogany.

From the second summit of Morne Grand Voute, the trail turns swiftly to the northwest. It ends at the Marina de Sens Riviere, which you can reach in ninety minutes. The descent, long and steep, traverses increasingly dryer vegetation. Two-thirds of the way down, on the western flank of Morne Griselle, the trail comes out suddenly onto a wide service road which you'll take to the right, in the general direction of the climb.

You'll then see the quarries of the Riviere Sens, where pozzolana, a material used in construction, is dug. Amateur volcanologists can see these quarries by taking the route along the sea which leads to Vieux-Fort. They are magnificent geological cuts.

After thirty minutes on the trail, you'll reach a parking area for factory equipment, on the level of the Marina and the shore. From the marina, go to Vieux-Fort by the seaside trail, leaving it a little before the crossroads access to the lighthouse and Anse Dupuy. To the left is another trail leading to the departure sign for the Vieux-Fort/Champfleury hike. Remember, this loop requires eight or nine hours of walking.

17. Gros Acajou to Vieux-Fort

Time: 2 hours, one-way from Gros Acajou. **Difficulty:** 4-5. Blazed in part; take water.

The first part of this the trail is common to Hike 16, described above. At Gros Acajou Hill you bear to the left to arrive at Vieux-Fort.

After fifteen minutes in this forest setting of bamboo and heliconias, the trail offers a view of the distant islands, the Saints. At your feet is the eastern flank of the range which you are about to cross, overlooked by two summits which jut into the sky. In front of you and slightly to the right is 573 meters Bout Morne, and below and to the left, Morne la Voute with its 404 meters peak. To the rear and on your right is the highest summit of the Caraibes Mountains, Morne Vent Souffle (686 meters).

Now that you've enjoyed the view, it's time to pay for it—your next fifteen minutes is dedicated to the perilous descent of a very steep slope, first by switchbacks, then across rocks of a small, dried-up ravine, to reach the Ravine Dejeuner (Lunch Ravine). Along the trail, swamp bloodwoods will accompany you practically to the end of the hike.

Then, after a brief climb, the trail divides into two branches which rejoin 250 meters ahead. The left pathway goes near a hut and looks out over the Ravine Grand Fond, wider and even more cultivated than the preceding ones. Its bottom is punctuated by numerous royal palms.

A little later, you'll reach the rocks of the Ravine Grand Fond, shaded by the mango trees and coconut palms growing there. Do not take the trail to the left, which descends on the perpendicular. Instead, bear to the right to climb the flanks of Morne la Voute. In only twenty minutes you'll arrive at the high point which permits you to appreciate the route you've been taking for the past hour, from Gros Acajou Hill.

A little farther, bypass the trail on the left which goes toward Beausoleil. Take the one on the right, marked in places with marks of red paint. It cuts through a dry forest, or xerophile, characteristic of the southern zones of the island. It lasts until the end of the trail.

A second trail goes off the left toward the coast, about 600m farther, but don't take it. Rather, follow the trail which climbs slightly and turns to the right.

You'll cross another ravine on the left soon after entering a cultivated section. Two hundred meters more of descent through woods, and you'll rejoin the road which leads to Vieux-Fort. To the right it crosses a small bridge and leads to the road to Basse-Terre; to the left, it goes back to town.

The hike back to your starting point at Champfleury, including the common trail, is about three hours.

18. Archeological Park at Trois-Rivieres
Time: 1 hour. **Difficulty: 1**

Easily found on any map showing Basse-Terre's south coast, the park contains petroglyphs dating from 300-400 A.D. The walk passes through a garden/boardwalk setting that passes some huge boulders with presumably Arawak (but perhaps Carib) petroglyphs. Some drawings are quite worn and faded; a brochure provided after you pay a modest admission fee locates and deciphers some of the sites and also explains the island foliage. The most important carving is the head of a chief who may be buried inside the cave marked by the drawing. This is a very pleasant walk requiring little exertion compared to most walking on Guadeloupe. It's a nice place to relax after your Soufriere climb.

13. Dominica

Old Caribbean Proverb:
When bull is old, you need tie him only with plantain thrash.

Translation:
Too often humiliation comes with old age.

If you make only one hike in the Caribbean, make it in Dominica (pronounced Dom-i-NEE-ca). The demanding, roller-coaster assault into the island's interior will take you to sites as wondrous as their names: The Valley of Desolation and the Boiling Lake.

Dominica, located between the two French islands of Martinique and Guadeloupe, is a ruggedly beautiful island. When Columbus was asked to describe Dominica to his fellow Europeans, the explorer simply crumpled up a piece of paper and placed it on a table. Supposedly he explained to his audience, "This represents Dominica, a small island with jagged peaks rising sharply out of the sea."

Early planters scalped many Caribbean islands of their vegetation and replaced the forests and flowers with fields of lucrative sugar cane. Dominica is the exception: its towering mountains, thick rainforests, cascading waterfalls and criss-crossing rivers were too tough to conquer. Dominica is probably the least spoiled island in the Caribbean. It has an estimated 365 different water sources (rivers, streams, etc.) and until recently was referred to as the "Water Island." It now likes to tout itself, and quite rightly so, as the "Nature Island of the Caribbean."

Approximately two-thirds of the island is natural vegetation, due to the inaccessibility of the interior. From 1962-67 a foreign logging company took its best whack at the undisturbed rain forest, but gave up because of the rugged terrain and wet, inhospitable climate.

The failed logging operation was enough to alert islanders to the need for protective measures and in 1975, Dominica established its Morne Trois Pitons National Park in the southern part of the island. Two years later it

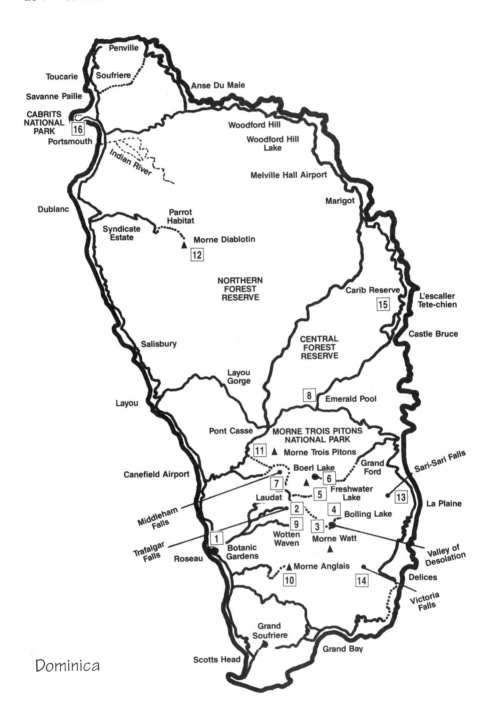

Dominica

added the 22,000-acre Northern Forest Reserve, with its fine examples of primary and secondary rain forest, montane forest and elfin woodland—the entire gamut of the tropical forest spectrum. The Cabrits National Park on the north-west point of the island was added to the park system in 1986.

Dominica is home to the last of the fierce Carib Indians, whose dreams of expansion and domination of the region were checked by the better-organized expansionists from Spain and England. Three thousand descendants of the once-mighty Caribs now live in the Carib Reserve on the northeast coast. However, the last true Carib-speaking Indian died many years ago. Today's Caribs are farmers who grow bananas, although they still practice their traditional basketry and canoe-building skills.

Dominica received its name because Columbus happened to be sailing by on a Sunday in 1493; the island just as easily could have been named Thursday or Friday. Columbus was obviously not feeling inspired that day. The Caribs had called it Waitukubuli, meaning "tall is her body."

The English and French fought over Dominica, deciding in 1748 that it would be better if no one owned it, and the island was left to its original owners, the Caribs. An innovative concept, but not honored for very long. In 1763 the English received ownership of Dominica through the Treaty of Paris. In 1795, the French evidently had a change of heart, because they tried to take the island back by force. Conflict between the English and French continued until 1805: the French finally were bought off with a ransom of 8,000 English pounds after they burned down the main city of Roseau.

Dominica remained a British Colony until 1967. In 1978, it became the fully independent Commonwealth of Dominica. The strong French influence still survives through many of the place and family names and the Creole which is widely spoken.

Travel Tips

Area: 29 miles long and 16 miles wide, covering an area of 305 square miles.

Language: English and Creole.

Population: About 82,000, most of them concentrated around the main city of Roseau.

Time Zone: Atlantic Standard Time, one hour ahead of Eastern Standard Time.

Getting There: Tiny Dominica is not on the air routes of any of the major carriers but LIAT, the inter-island airline of the Caribbean. Also serving Dominica are Air Guadeloupe, Air BVI and Air Caribe. There are two airports, Melville Hall and Canefield. Canefield is out in the middle of nowhere and a lengthy cab drive to the Roseau area, where most of the hotels are located. Opt for Melville Hall flights.

Getting Around: Rental cars are readily available. Taxi fares are set by the government and posted. Traveling the roads on your own is normally not difficult; however, there are few road signs, so a good map is essential. It is necessary to buy a local driving permit. Driving is technically on the left, although the locals seem to prefer driving fast and straight down the middle of the road. Traveling off the roads without a local guide is almost impossible. Minibuses run from point to point but their schedules aren't synchronized enough to use them to explore the island in a single day.

Where to Stay: The Fort Young Hotel in Roseau is the largest facility on the island, and the food and service are good. Most of the other places to overnight in Roseau are guesthouses of varying quality. Just outside the city are Reigate Hall atop King's Hill, where service is very slow; and the Anchorage, located on the Caribbean itself, where the rooms are large. The furnishings are slightly outdated, but the food is good and the service reliable.

Camping: Not permitted in the national parks and generally not allowed anywhere.

Taxes & Tips: A standard 10% service charge, plus a 5% government tax at hotels and a 3% government sales tax.

Documents: U.S. and Canadian citizens need only proof of citizenship; passports are required of everyone else. All arrivals are expected to have an on-going or return ticket.

Currency: The Eastern Caribbean Dollar. Banks are open 8 a.m. to 1 p.m. Monday through Friday and 3 p.m. to 5 p.m. on Friday.

Electrical Current: 220/240 volts/50 cycles.

Safety/Health Warnings: Regrettably, the walk around Freshwater Lake is attracting muggers and thieves who break into rental cars to steal valuables. Never visit this area alone, although you will be fine with several other people.

Hiking/Walking Services: Dominica has two well-organized and efficient tour operators. Ken's Hinterland Tours & Taxi Service offers all of the major hikes as well as scenic coastal drives. The guides are very knowledgeable locals. Contact Ken's Hinterland Tours, Box 447, Roseau, Commonwealth of Dominica, East Caribbean; or call 809/44-84850 during office hours, 809/44-83517 after 5 p.m.; fax 809/44-88486.

Henry Shillingford works out of the Anchorage Hotel and does an excellent job of leading hikes into the Valley of Desolation and the Boiling Lake. Henry, a Rastafarian, is an interesting person to talk with about local life. He can be contacted at 809/44-82638; fax 809/44-85680

The well-organized guide services charge about US $80 per person to reach the Valley of Desolation and the Boiling Lake. You can cut costs by taking a chance and picking your own guide in the village of Laudat near the beginning of the trailhead. Many locals claim to be able to guide, and some do a good job for far less money. However, you probably won't get any references or other credentials. In this case, your adventure begins as soon as you start looking for a guide. You may always contact the tourist office to see if they can recommend a guide.

Snakes and Other Venomous Creatures: The native boa (called the clouded-face boa) grows up to six feet long. It eats rodents and is harmless to humans.

For More Information: In North America, the Caribbean Tourism Association, 20 E. 46th St., New York, NY 10017; 212/682-0435. In the UK, the Dominica Tourist Office, 1 Collingham Gardens, Earls Court, London SW5 OHW; 071-373-8751; fax 071-373-8743. The most complete information is on-island at the Dominica Tourist Board, Box 73, Roseau, Commonwealth of Dominica (always include this formal title or your mail could go to the Dominican Republic), W.I.; 809/448-2186/2351. Mail is incredibly slow.

1. Botanic Gardens

These were reputed to be some of the most beautiful grounds in the Caribbean until 1979's Hurricane David did considerable damage. Situated below the Morne Bruce Hill, the forty acre tract is the largest semi-open space in the capital city of Roseau; it served as a popular cricket ground in the 1960s and '70s.

Although just sixty-eight feet above sea level, the gardens receive more than eighty-five inches of rain annually, making them an ideal site for growing a wide variety of tropical plants. Originally a sugar cane field, the ornamental planting began in 1890 with a fountain, iron gates, ponds and 500 species of exotic and indigenous shrubs and trees.

One interesting site displays the remains of a large bus crushed beneath a massive bacbab tree, an ever-present reminder of Hurricane David's devastation. The Forestry and Wildlife Division here offers *A Guide to Selected Trees and Shrubs* to help visitors identify the plants.

2. Trafalgar Falls

Time: A 15 minute walk from the parking lot to an observation platform near the base of the falls, it's another 10 to 15 minute scramble over the slick boulders to the reach the pool at the base, where you can swim. **Difficulty:** 1-2. Because of the easy access, this is a popular outing for cruise ship passengers.

Trafalgar Falls is one of the most visited sites in Dominica.

Trafalgar is actually the site of two 180-foot falls which converge in rocky pools. An unusual feature are the hot water springs which come out at the base. Anyone not in good physical shape is advised to stay at the platform because the boulders are large and slippery. A guide is a good idea for locating the easiest route to the hot water springs.

Morne Trois Pitons National Park

Located in the south central part of Dominica, this 17,000-acre park of primordial rainforest contains most of the truly spectacular hikes. You won't see any large mammals, but Dominica does boast a wide range of insects, birds, crustaceans and a few reptiles. There are four species of snakes, all non-poisonous.

A characteristic here, as on most islands, is the absence of bird calls in heavy forested areas at upper elevations. Although fifty-four species of birds nest on the island, the only one you're likely to hear on a steep climb is the Siffleur Montagne, a mountain bird heard only in Dominica and whose song has a striking clarity and sweetness. Dominica is also home for two endangered parrots, the Sisserou (Amazona imperialis) and the Jacquot (Amazona arausiaca). You're much more likely to see the Antillean Crested Hummingbird and the Purple Throated Hummingbird.

At sunset or when it rains, the little (two centimeter) tree frogs known as the Gounouge are responsible for the chorus of piping sounds. A remarkable example of adaptation to its environment, these are born as perfect frogs without an aquatic, tadpole stage. They don't have the luxury of a prolonged adolescence in still, safe water: because the rivers are so swift, the streams contain little food and the water flow is highly seasonal. To survive, the Gounouge must be born "standing up and talking back."

The Crapaud, or Mountain Chicken, is a bulky, solid frog hunted for food and occasionally offered on hotel menus during its season. Mountain chickens, which grow up to twenty centimeters, have been seriously depleted through over-hunting. They are considered a great delicacy.

 ## 3.-4. The Valley of Desolation & Boiling Lake

Time: 7 to 8 hours depending on weather. Always start early, by 8 a.m., to allow enough daylight. **Length:** 6 miles. The trail begins near the village of Laudat. **Difficulty:** 5. All gear should be kept in a backpack so your hands are free to scramble up and down the mountain. Take food and water.

Because this hike is so awesome, I am taking the liberty to describe it in more detail than any other hike in the book. As the Caribbean's best hike, it deserves such recognition...and respect. Guide Henry Shillingford likes to describe the hike in three different phases. The first hour is deceptively easy, starting with a moderate twenty-five-minute ascent, then some ups and downs until you reach the Breakfast River. The river was named by travelers crossing the island, who would stop here for their morning meal break. Phase II is a forty-five-minute walk up the side of Morne Nichols, a steep and sometimes very slippery climb. Phase III is the descent into the Valley of Desolation, which takes only five to ten minutes to cross, then another thirty minutes to the Boiling Lake.

I find the walk to Breakfast River a fairly easy one. Morne Nichols, however, is a deceptive trickster. In many places it seems as if you're about to reach the summit, but it always turns out to be just another bend in the path. There are always many, many more yards to climb.

About half-way up Morne Nichols we are enveloped in cloud and the valley on our left is completely covered in mist. The scene is like an Oriental painting showing a shadow world with only the outlines of trees and shrubs depicted in different shades of gray. Actually, we're passing through montane forest and one of the best stands of Wezinye Montany, the only native conifer of Dominica. Nearer the top we enter the fantastically-shaped elfin woodland, trees stunted by strong winds whose branches and trunks are nearly encased in mosses and lichens.

When we finally reach the 3,000-foot summit of Morne Nichols, Henry turns and asks if it has "gotten hellish yet." This is the half-way point, and while the mountain climb has been strenuous and constant, it isn't as bad as I expected. He smiles; I try very hard to decipher that smile. Is the worst behind us, or yet to come?

It is extremely windy at the top of Morne Nichols. The gusts literally are strong enough to push you off balance, precisely what happened several years earlier to a woman crossing a narrow path at the top—she either mis-stepped or the wind shoved her off the mountain. The fall killed her, the trail's one known fatality. I find this amazing. I'd have expected more heart attacks.

A long series of steps lead down from the summit, but they are placed so far apart it is impossible to simply walk down them. They are actually terraces, and were placed to keep the trail from washing away, not to aid hikers. That's why they're set so far apart. We pass a shelter near the summit. It starts raining five minutes later.

Now comes the hard part: a slow, very tricky descent into the Valley of Desolation on a slippery mountain-goat trail of rock and mud. It's very easy to mis-step here. Chivalry emerges for the first time as the men help the women (their shorter legs are the problem) reach some of the small stepping stones that jut out of the mountain. In some places it's easier to slide down on your rear or turn and step down, like descending a ladder.

This takes a half hour of tedious work. Descending, we get our first evidence of volcanic activity. We can see steam rising around a bend in a distant valley: at last, the Valley of Desolation.

First we have to work our way down a small waterflow, too small to be called a stream or creek. The rocks are a rusty red and the water is cold. We inch our way down a steep mini-waterfall next to a rock wall. At least it's a chance to wash off some of the mud.

Up until this point, we have followed an obvious path. Now, entering the Valley of Desolation, the path disappears. The valley floor is bare of vegetation, craggy and uneven. The earth is coated in minerals, colors of red, silver and black. Some rocks are also covered with yellow sulfur crystal. Brightly colored hot springs are scattered over the valley floor, their blue, white, black and orange colors the results of minerals deposited by the water.

The Valley of Desolation, located on the flanks of Morne Watt, stretches about a quarter-mile across: at the edge we can see several big steam vents, hear water bubbling and spot a few mud pots here and there. A small stream contains water that is oil-black in color, spilling over the rocks to create a white foam, an incredible contrast. The water here is quite warm.

We follow Henry closely. The main danger here is stepping through a thin crust of earth hiding a hot fumarole.

When first discovered in 1870, the region was thickly forested. Now only a dense mat of mosses and lichens grow, interspersed with yellow- and white-flowered "thyme sauvage" and grasses able to survive the harsh sulfur fumes. It is these fumes which are credited with wiping out the forest.

A volcanic eruption of ash in 1880, originating either from the Boiling Lake or this valley may have been responsible for the increase in the size of the fumarole area. Scientists predict the Valley of Desolation will remain an active fumarole region for decades to come.

Surprisingly, wildlife does exist: lizards, stoneflies, mayflies, ants, and of course the planet's hardiest survivor, the ubiquitous, indestructible cockroach.

At the far end is a huge steam vent that Henry invites us "to come stand in for your complexion." After crossing the valley diagonally through the middle, we are back in thick forest, where we walk for another twenty minutes before coming out at a stream where the rocks are coated white with sulfur. Henry draws an arrow for those lagging behind taking photos. Someone else draws a petroglyph of a smiling face on one of the stones; we all avoid stepping on the rock to keep from defacing the finger painting.

More climbing, as we cut diagonally across another valley, then start scrambling over large boulders. This is some of the hardest climbing of all. We all want to stop and rest—to eat and recharge. Not the slightest sign of the Boiling Lake. How much longer can this go on? Can we go on? And why did I assume the Valley of Desolation would be above the Boiling Lake, not below it?

We turn a corner and there it is: a big bowl of white milk virtually obscured by the thick steam. We wait for the winds to shift and push enough of it away to catch a momentary glimpse of the part that bubbles and churns, a relatively small surface area of only twenty to thirty yards. Ironically, Boiling Lake is Dominica's smallest lake.

The Boiling Lake is believed to be a flooded fumarole, a crack through which gases escape from the molten lava below. The natural basin of the lake collects the rainfall from the surrounding hills, which then seeps through the porous lake bottom, where it is trapped and heated by the hot lava.

Tests conducted in 1875 found the water temperature at the lake edge to be between 180°-197° F; the water temperature at the center, where the lake actually boils, could not be measured. The depth was recorded at more than 195 feet.

The Boiling Lake changes over time. After 1875, the water level decreased and a geyser developed at the center which spewed water and mud sixty feet. A photograph from 1895 shows a dry Boiling Lake, with a prominent pumice cone from the geyser in the middle.

Today, no one knows how deep the lake is. The cauldron sides are a mixture of pumice, clay and small stones. The water is usually described as a grayish-blue, but I still think it looks more like milk.

However, the water color is not a topic of conversation in my hiking group. We are too busy eating fresh pineapple and sandwiches, resting, and (with a good deal of dread) thinking about the walk out. We're all pretty tired.

Going back is worse than coming in. As we reach the mountain and descend rear-first, it begins to rain again. The mountain turns into a mass of slick clay; but even worse are the giant steps that lead back to the summit of Morne Nichols. Coming down was a snap compared to the climb up them. Scaling this stone ladder really stretches the leg muscles.

In one hour, we are back at the summit. Thank God! We rest briefly, wondering what the other side of the mountain will be like, now that it's rained. The answer is obvious: slick, slippery and muddy. Anyone who managed to stay clean until now quickly undergoes radical changes. So does our attitudes. Where we had walked diligently around any muddy spots on the way in, we are now so tired and the ground was so sloppy it

Boiling Lake and
Valley of Desolation

doesn't make any difference anymore. We are muddy, and getting muddier.

One hiker abandons the path and tries walking the narrow ridge above it to see if she can make better time that way. She slips, and instead of falling to her left and plummeting down the mountain she ends up straddling the ridge. She catches her breath and rejoins us in the trench-like trail.

We wash off when we get to Breakfast River. Some water bottles we left here earlier to chill are quickly drained.

The first phase, so easy when the hike began, now looks strange and unfamiliar. How many days ago was it that we passed this way?

We take a look at another amazing Dominican phenomenon, the Titou Gorge, which we'd ignored earlier in our anticipation. The sides of this narrow, very deep gorge undulate, indicating it was not cut by the river which now washes through it. Instead, as the molten lava that formed it was cooling, it split and pulled apart, like a drying mud puddle splits and cracks.

It was three days before my legs stopped hurting and I was able to assimilate everything I had seen and heard. Everyone on the hike reported a similar condition. Some local guides make the walk two or three times a week in season.

Would I ever do it again? You bet.

5. Freshwater Lake

Time: 2 hours roundtrip. **Difficulty:** 1. **Warning:** Robberies and hassles are being reported in increasing numbers in this area. Don't come here with fewer than three other people. Only singles and couples have been bothered.

Located two miles northeast of the village of Laudat, this is the largest of Dominica's five freshwater crater lakes. More importantly, several hiking trails into other parts of the Morne Trois Pitons National Park start from here. Floating on the lake are rafts of purple-flowered water hyacinth, a weed which clogs the waterways in many parts of southeastern North America.

The spring-fed lake is being used as part of a hydro-power project, providing electricity island-wide. The lake has been dammed and the water level raised twenty feet. A snaking trail of creosote-treated wooden pipes transports water from the lake to the power station at Laudat, a sight as lovely as an appendix scar.

Situated at 2,500 feet, Freshwater Lake is surrounded by montane forest, characterized by its short, thin trees and open canopy. High winds and shallow soil prevent the type of thick growth characteristic of the rain forest.

The montane forest is full of epiphytes, plants which use others for their physical support. They are so thick in some places it's almost impossible to see the trees on which they grow: a great place to view delicate, almost transparent ferns, large-leafed anthuriums and large, showy bromeliads.

At the highest level is the elfin woodland, called dwarf forest on other islands. The dominant species here is the gnarled kaklen, whose spreading branches and roots make parts of the forest impenetrable. Note how small and leathery the leaves are, and how from a distance the forest looks like a well-trimmed hedge.

The ridge east of the Freshwater Lake, actually a rim of an old volcano, offers a splendid panoramic view, one of Dominica's best. Morne Micotrine to the west is a young volcanic cone separating Freshwater from Boeri Lake, which also formed on the same crater floor. You'll also spot many peaks and ridges created by volcanic eruptions.

To the east is evidence of more modern changes, the villages of Grand Fond and Rosalie, with the Atlantic Ocean as the backdrop. There is an historic trail linking Freshwater Lake with Grand Fond that took about two and a half hours, but it is overgrown at this writing. Plans are being made to mark the trail as a self-guided hike hugging the side of the mountain. Before roads linked the small agricultural community of Grand Fond with the rest of the island, judges, even doctors and magistrates would ride this trail on horseback, since it was the only access to the village.

6. Boeri Lake

Time: 45 minutes one-way. **Length:** 1-1/4 miles. **Difficulty:** 2. **Warning:** during the dry season, the huge boulders surrounding the shoreline of Boeri Lake will be exposed, and are a real temptation to go rock hopping. These boulders are extremely slippery—always—and are renowned as ankle-twisters and leg-breakers. Admire them from a distance.

One of the two freshwater lakes in the Morne Trois Pitons National Park, it is reached by a hiking trail from Freshwater Lake. The walk to Boeri Lake takes you past hot and cold-water springs gushing from the side of Morne Macaque, past clear streams and through both montane and elfin forest. There are some abandoned gardens which the local wildlife has claimed as their own vegetable market.

Boeri Lake, one of Dominica's largest, is located at 2,800 feet in altitude, in the crater of an old volcano. Almost circular, with a surface area of only four acres, Boeri may be as much as 117 feet deep. It is fed by rainwater and runoff, which accounts for its dramatic variations. It may fall as much as twenty-five feet during a dry spell. The lake is at its highest level between October and December.

The montane forest here is dominated by cabbage palms, Maho kochon and Gombo moutayn, a relative of the hibiscus. Ferns, including tree ferns, are luxuriant along parts of the trail. The red and yellow heliconia, with lobster-claw-shaped flowers, add a considerable amount of color. The elfin forest, as all other forests on Dominica, is an open canopy, with tree stems and branches dripping with mats of mosses and liverworts.

The small tree lizards (zandoli) take on a different color pattern than those found at lower altitudes. This is another good place to hear the song of the mountain whistler, view migratory waterfowl and look for the Siwik, or river crab, which lives in the boulders along the shoreline.

The walk up the ridge to Boeri Lake offers some excellent panoramic views of Grand Fond and Morne Jaune to the east, though utility lines and poles are quite evident. To the south is Freshwater Lake, with its floating vegetation. Morne Nichols is also quite visible.

7. Middleham Trails

Time: the trail which begins at the village of Sylvania and ends at Providence takes about 2-1/4 hours. Going from Cochrane to Providence, about 1-3/4 hours, is more interesting because it passes a set of waterfalls and a collapsed lava tube still emitting hot air. **Difficulty (both):** 2 to 3, depending on the slipperiness.

These trails in the northwest portion of the national park wind through a 950-acre tract of primary rainforest that is perhaps the most beautiful and best preserved on all Dominica. The land was donated by a U.S. citizen, John D. Archbold, to the Dominican government through the Nature Conservancy. There are two major sets of trails plus one offshoot.

Starting at Sylvania, the trail passes the crumbling foundations of a former coffee plantation. Reclaimed by the trees, this is considered second-ary, not primary rainforest, which you'll see on the rest of the walk.

Starting from Cochrane, the trail passes through areas under active cultivation and several estates before entering the true rainforest. This trail is quite interesting in that it also passes the Tou Santi (Stinking Hole), a collapsed lava tube that emits hot air and houses many species of bats as well as an occasional snake. Farther on, you will pass a rain shelter, then a fork in the trail. The branch to the right dead-ends at Middleham Falls,

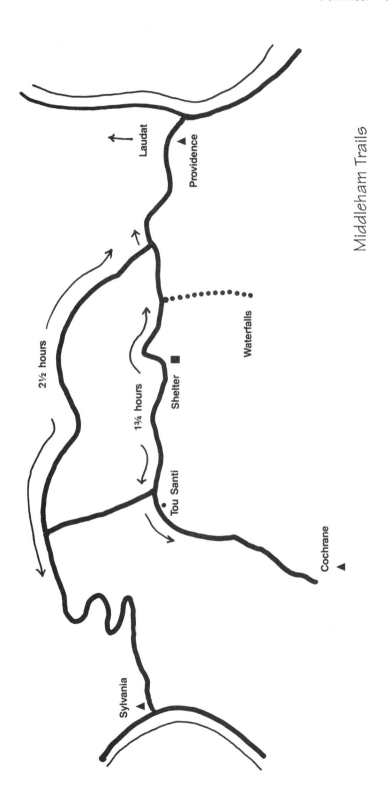

Middleham Trails

Laudat

Providence

2½ hours

1¾ hours

Waterfalls

Shelter

Tou Santi

Cochrane

Sylvania

some of the island's tallest. On the Cochrane route, you'll have to cross a half-dozen small streams, making this a moderately difficult hike in the rainy season.

A chief characteristic of the rainforest is the comparatively open forest floor. Because only about 10% of the sunlight is able to penetrate the thick forest canopy, hardly anything is able to grow on the ground, which makes for easy walking.

This rainforest is dominated by two species—Gonmye (Dacryodes excelsa) and Chatannye (Sloanea spp.) trees—yet there is also incredible diversity in some places. As many as sixty different species of trees have been recorded in one ten-acre plot. In wet areas where the drainage is poor, one of the most common species is the Mang blan (Symphonia globulifera) with its elaborate system of prop roots providing support on the thin soil.

 8. Emerald Pool

Time: 30 minutes. **Difficulty:** 1-2, some climbing. This is a favorite stop on the way to visit the Carib Indian Reservation.

Emerald Pool is actually a waterfall-fed pool which appears bright green in the tree-filtered sunlight. Reached by a half-mile loop trail, the Emerald Pool is by far the most accessible spot in the entire Morne Trois Pitons National Park. However, it is a bit of a drive to reach from Roseau, being located three-and-one-half miles northeast of Pont Casse on the road to Castle Bruce.

The forest here technically falls into what is known as a transition zone, not true rainforest or montane forest. The majority of plants are young trees—not shrubs—which create a massively thick canopy, with many vines growing upwards from ground level; others, established in the tree tops, send down their roots. Epiphytes are especially fond of the filtered sunlight, and the trees are covered with them.

Both the agouti, a guinea-pig-like rodent, and the nocturnal manicou, a small opossum, live here, but you are far more likely to see and hear birds, particularly hummingbirds, and hear the song of the mountain warbler.

It's possible to swim in Emerald Pool; in fact, on a hot day you'll probably want to. The rock behind the cascade has been eroded, leaving plenty of room for you to stand behind or in the waterfall. Be careful: the rocks are slippery.

The small loop trail provides two lookout points. The first offers a view of the wild stretches of windward coast at St. David's Bay and Castle Bruce. The second views the upper part of Belle Fille Valley, with Morne Laurent to the left. Both illustrate just how heavily forested and natural Dominica remains.

Part of the trail past the second viewpoint is paved for a short distance. This is part of the old trace used as a main road by the Carib Indians until as late as the 1960s.

If you happen to be here near twilight, enjoy the chorus of tree frogs and crickets. Bats, too, will appear at that time to dine, helping to control the island's insect population.

 9. Wotten Waven

Time: 15 minutes one-way. **Difficulty:** 1.

Wotton Waven is the name of the village a short walk away from the boiling mud pots that dramatize Dominica's volcanic history. The major mud pot here is notable for its constant noise and wave action. Its steam has a definite sulfuric smell. A sign in Wotten Waven tells you where to park and where to start the hike. An easy spot to find.

10. Morne Anglais

Time: about 1-1/2 hours each way. **Difficulty:** 3-4 depending on conditions.

Morne Anglais rises to 3,683 feet. Drive to the town of Giraudel, the start of this established park trail, known for a good view of the surrounding countryside and the south coast. The walk to the summit takes you through both an orchid-filled montane forest and an almost perennially cloud-covered elfin woodland which receives as much as 300 inches of rain annually.

11. Morne Diablotin

Time: 3-1/2 hour walk from the bottom to the top. **Difficulty:** to the summit, a 3-4. Steep, Some potentially tricky scrambling at the end.

Located in the Northern Forest Reserve, at 4,747 feet, this is Dominica's highest peak. You'll have spectacular views as you climb from rainforest through montane forest into elfin woodland. A constant ascent, you may have to scramble over and under trees in some areas.

Making the walk more than worthwhile is taking the short side trail to the Parrot Lookout, where you may be fortunate enough to see Dominica's two endangered species of parrot, the Imperial Parrot, largest Amazon parrot in the world, and the Red-necked parrot. Best times for parrot watching are sunrise and sunset, which may prove impractical to work into your hike. For faster access to the parrots, you can drive all the way to the end of the secondary road and then walk only twenty to twenty-five minutes to the Parrot Lookout.

Beyond the side trail to the parrots, the trail continues for another forty-five minutes through some of the best primary rainforest.

 12. Carib Reserve

Time: 2 hours to drive through the reserve, stop and see the sights. **Difficulty:** 1.

This 3,700-acre reserve on the northeast coast has a population of less than one person per acre. The Caribs practice agriculture, and fish from dugout canoes using hand-lines, as their ancestors did. No historical pageant, museum, or any sort of tourist attraction has been established, although several good stands offer Carib-made artifacts, including hand-woven baskets and carved turtles. In addition to trading with and observing how Caribs of today look and live, there are two short stops of interest.

One is called the trail of the snake staircase. It is actually a hardened lava flow jutting into the sea, the surface of each step in the flow patterned with a circle or mark, like a snakeskin. This natural formation is important in Carib history, although explanations differ.

One legend has it that a snake once came ashore to grab a virgin. Another version says that the Caribs used to follow the staircase up to its head in the mountains to obtain special powers. Considering the way the waves crash against and wash over the formation, it is unlikely that anyone ever set foot on the stone snake except on the calmest of days.

In 1991, a brand-new Catholic church was opened, an A-frame "mouina" called St. Marie of the Caribs. Its altar is of special note: a genuine canoe, like the ones which brought the Caribs from the Orinoco region about 1,000 years ago. Those original canoes were much larger, according to legend, able to hold as many as fifty occupants. Murals on the church walls inside and out depict Carib history. Plans are to convert the old Church of the Immaculate Conception at Salybia into a museum.

13. Cabrits National Park

Time: 2 hours. **Difficulty:** 1-2.

Established in 1986, this region is about to undergo rapid modernization. A major cruise ship terminal and a huge new luxury resort are planned, all around Portsmouth, the island's second most important town. Cabrits Park is 1,313 acres, but much of it (1,053 acres) consists of marine area. That includes coral reefs, two sandy beaches, sunken 17th-century shipwrecks and a coastal cave.

Two forested hillsides contain the scattered buildings of the Fort Shirley complex, on which restoration began in 1982. Clearly marked paths meander the hillsides past the Commander's Quarters, Douglas Battery and other sites. Only the main buildings have been cleared; ficus roots still hold most of the buildings hostage, although a small museum has been built in the remains of a powder magazine.

The highest point on the Cabrits headland is only 600 feet, so the trails are not difficult, though inclines in some spots may be steep for short stretches. Besides providing scenic coastal vistas, the walks offer a chance to see some wildlife, primarily lizards and hummingbirds. The plant life is particularly interesting. Highly recommended is the booklet *Cabrits Plants and Their Uses* available from the Forestry Division office at the Botanical Gardens in Roseau.

Martinique

 14. Martinique

Martinique is a lovely island with some very scenic trails. However, Martinique is a little island with a big ego. In too many places you encounter this attitude: if you don't speak French, you don't belong here. Even residents who speak English will regularly refuse to speak to you or acknowledge you if you cannot speak French. For an island with an economy partially based on tourism, this is a strange attitude to adopt. This is a culture where rudeness is considered an art form.

The reason for this remarkable behavior is that Martinique is more European than Caribbean. Martiniquans are French citizens and Martinique is officially part of France. In terms of its economic development, its telephone and road systems, Martinique is certainly on par with Europe. France has invested a lot of money in Martinique, and it shows. Martinique does not have the strained economic circumstances and poverty which face many Caribbean islands which were unfortunate enough to be former members of the British Empire. By comparison, Britain only took from its possessions and never returned much at all. The people on Martinique have every right to be proud of their prosperous circumstances.

France contributes 70% of its gross national product. Without French support, there would be no welfare or social services. Even so, Martinique's unemployment rate is among the Caribbean's highest, at about 25%. The majority of those who do work are in service jobs, connected to tourism.

If you speak French, you will probably have a very different experience.

Columbus named the island "Martinica" in honor of St. Martin. He said it was "the best, richest, sweetest country in the whole world." When he said it, the French had yet to arrive.

The Caribs, who had killed off all the Arawaks called the island "Madinina," or island of flowers. Because of constant battles with the Caribs, Spain gave Martinique up in favor of richer pickings elsewhere. The French planters and accompanying African slaves arrived in 1635. The Caribs wanted nothing to do with any settlers, fighting bitterly until 1660, when it was agreed by treaty the Caribs would live only on the Atlantic side. The treaty didn't mean much, and soon all the Indians were annihilated.

The English took Martinique in 1762, but traded it back to France in exchange for Tobago, St. Vincent, the Grenadines, Senegal and a sizable chunk of property called Canada. Martinique was far richer than these territories combined, because of its sugar plantations.

The French revolution's message of "liberty, equality and fraternity" was heard in Martinique, but disregarded as applying to the slaves. Anxious plantation owners, not wanting to experience the slave revolts occurring elsewhere, asked the British to return and keep the peace, which they did from 1794-1802. The French abolished slavery in 1848.

Martinique has a very active volcano, which completely destroyed the former capital city of St-Pierre in 1902. The city of Fort-de-France, built around Fort St. Louis in the 17th century, was named the new capitol. Located away from Mount Pelee and its destructive force, Fort-de-France is home to most of the island's population. The rubble of St-Pierre is one of the island's main tourist attractions. Mount Pelee, quiet since 1902, is the site of the many popular hiking trails.

Travel Tips

Area: 425 square miles; fifty miles long and twenty-two mile wide.

Population: 361,000, of which 177,000 live in Fort-de-France.

Language: French and Creole. Relatively few people, even in many hotels, speak English. You will be viewed as uneducated if you do not speak French.

Time Zone: Atlantic Standard Time, one hour ahead of Eastern Standard Time.

Rainy Season: Considerably more rain falls here than on many other islands because of the high mountainous terrain. The wettest period is from June to November; rain can be heavy and sudden. Always be prepared.

Getting There: American Airlines flies here, with connections through San Juan. Air Canada flies from Montreal and Canada. LIAT and Air

Martinique fly in from neighboring islands. The major carrier is Air France, flying from Bordeaux, Lyons, Marseilles, Nantes, Paris and other cities. Most of the people who fly here are French. However, most of the visitors from cruise ships are North Americans.

Getting Around: Rental cars are available at the airport, though you want to avoid driving in the congested downtown of Fort-de-France, where parking is legal only if you have a season pass. It is easier to take a bus or cab. Mopeds and bicycles are also easily available. Buses and taxis are options for getting out into the countryside. Guided bus tours are popular because of the cruise ships. The roads are incredibly well-marked and well-maintained for the Caribbean.

Where to Stay: Prices are high, equal to what you would pay in Europe. The best values are the family-run "auberges" in the more remote and scenic northern parts of the island, where you'll also find the best hiking. One of the most convenient is Auberge de la Montagne Pelee, located at the foot of the volcano at Morne Rouge. It offers eight rooms and several bungalows with hot water, a real necessity at this high, cool altitude. Reservations should be made well before arrival: tel. 52 32 09. Another good bargain are the "gites," furnished apartments and bunga-lows specifically designed for vacationers. Contact the national tourist board or the Association Martiniquinise pour le Tourisme en Espace Rural, Relais des Gites de France, Maison du Tourisme Vert, 9 Bd de General-de-Gaulle, BP 1122, 97248 Fort-de-France Cedex; tel. 73 67 92. There is a Club Med on Martinique, at the opposite end from the moun-tains. I found even the locals employed by Club Med were hostile, a very atypical situation in this hotel chain noted for friendliness.

Camping: Martinique is one of the relatively few islands where this activity is popular. Closest to Fort-de-France is the Courbaril Campsite at Anse a l'Ane with kitchenettes and bungalows; tel. 68 32 30. Located adjacent is Le Nid Tropical campsite, which rents tents, though you're welcome to bring your own. On the southern coast, Camping Municipal at Ste-Anne has shady sites on the island's best beach.

Taxes & Tips: A 5% government tax and a 10% service charge may both be added to your hotel room. Porters expect 1F per bag. It's not necessary to tip cab drivers.

Documents: This is Europe, remember. Passports, s'il-vous-plait? Visa are required of some nationalities, but not U.S. or Canadian citizens.

Currency: Since this is part of France, the local currency is the French franc. Many stores give a 20% discount on goods purchased with a credit card or traveler's checks. If you attempt to exchange your traveler's checks for francs, you will pay a 5% commission at the bank or exchange houses, then pay full price for any items you purchase.

Electrical Current: 220 volts/60 cycles.

Water Contamination Warning: The beautiful rivers naturally entice the weary walker to swim. Be very careful. Many rivers in Martinique are infested with parasites, especially the well-known bilharzia, which causes very serious problems. This is due to the insufficient sanitation control devices in rural areas. Do not swim in the lower sections of any of the rivers. Although the danger is less in the wooded highlands, don't even think about drinking the water. Carry all of your own provisions and everything will be fine. Don't let open wounds come in contact with any of the streams.

Hiking/Walking Services: An excellent city walking tour is offered from the Savanne in Fort-de-France by an outfit called Azimut. The walks last about an hour and a half, and the friendly, multi-lingual guides show you many aspects of Fort-de-France you would probably miss on your own. One of their stops is at a small cafe for a glass of cane juice; talk about sugar overload!

Hiking should be arranged through the national park office, Parc Naturel Regional, 9 Boulevard General-de-Gaulle; tel. 73 19 30. These tours are well organized and visit most of the popular sites. Most people speak French, which is no problem since you have a competent guide to get you where you need to go. If you speak French and want a private tour, you can usually arrange for a guide to climb Mount Pelee at Morne Rouge.

Beware the hiking company geared toward the American market, called Cariballad. It is not recommended.

Snakes and Other Venomous Creatures: The deadly fer-de-lance is native to Martinique. However, since it likes the warm coasts and you'll probably be spending most of your time in the cooler mountains, not to worry.

For More Information: French West Indies Tourist Board, 610 Fifth Avenue, New York, NY 10020; 212/757-1125. In Canada, 1981 Ave. MacGill College, Suite 490, Montreal PQH 3A 2W9; 288-4264. In the UK, 178 Picadilly, London; 071/491-7622.

1. Walking Tour of Fort-de-France

Time: 1-1/2 to 2 hours. **Difficulty:** 1 for walking; 5 for dealing with the locals.

You'll get the most out of this tour if you can arrange for a walking tour at the Savanne from the friendly, earnest guides of Azimut. However, since the city is laid out in a grid, it is quite easy to find your way around on your own.

1) Fort St-Louis: Built in the 17th century, it is still used as a military base and not open to the public. A real shame, since this would be one of the touring highlights of Fort-de-France or any city. It is said that the low ceiling arches inside were intended to disrupt the advances of invading British, who were taller than the average Frenchman.

2) La Savanne: A beautiful park and one of the best places to buy the local handicrafts. Beware: the local vendors can be extremely abrasive. Pay attention to the palms, tamarinds and other tropical trees or an impromptu soccer match. Or to the two historic statues. The one statue most visitors will relate to immediately is the white Carrara marble statue of Empress Josephine, born on the island in 1763, later the wife of Napoleon Bonaparte. The other memorial is of Pierre Belain d'Esnambuc, who established the first French settlement on Martinique.

3) Bibliotheque Schoelcher: This impressive building was constructed in Paris in 1889 for the Paris Exposition by the architect of the Eiffel Tower, Henri Pick. The building, described as Byzantine-Egyptian-Romanesque, was disassembled in 1890 and shipped here to house the extensive book collection of Victor Schoelcher, who was responsible for abolishing slavery in the French West Indies. Across the street from La Savanne, it still functions as a library and is open to the public. The interior is a must-see. The outside architecture is one of the highlights of Fort-de-France, best photographed in the morning.

4) Musee Departementale de Martinique: Pottery, beads and other items that belonged to the Arawaks and Caribs, including a partial skeleton excavated in 1972. There are exhibits illustrating colonial costumes, slave life and planter's furnishings. Open weekdays 8 a.m. to noon and 3-5 p.m.; Saturday, 8 a.m. to noon. Located at #9 Rue de la Liberte.

5) St-Louis Cathedral: The steeple of this baroque church, also the design work of Henri Pick, towers over the city skyline. Stained glass depicts the life of St. Louis. A number of Martinique's former governors are buried here.

6) Parc Floral et Culturel: A shady park with two exhibits, one featuring the geology of the island, the other, the magnificent vegetation. Fruit and vegetable markets near the Parc are open from 5 a.m. until sunset. You can also purchase flowers, coconut water and exotic candies. The fish market is near the Madame River.

7) Shopping: Rue Lamartine and Rue Isambert have most of the jewelry shops, crystal, china and silverware. Clothing is sold at the two galleries or malls on Victor Hugo. Remember to ask for the customary 20% discount for using credit cards and traveler's checks.

Fort-de-France

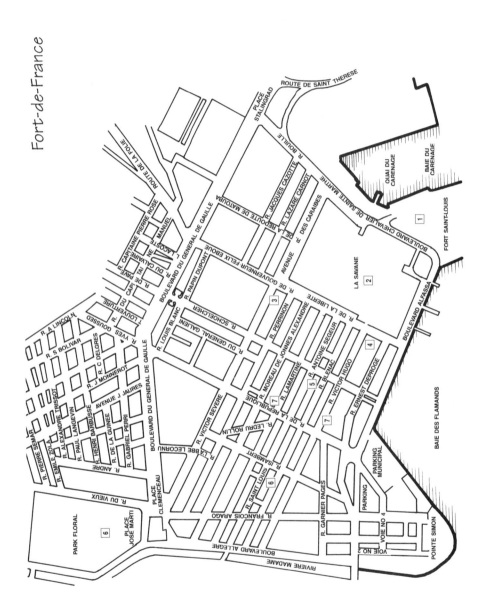

🦀 2. St-Pierre Ruins Walk

Time: 1 hour. **Difficulty:** 1.

Called the "Petit Paris" of the West Indies, St-Pierre was once the economic, cultural and political capital of Martinique. Of the estimated 26,000-30,000 population, only one inhabitant survived the explosion of Mount Pelee in 1902. In three minutes, maybe less, a cloud of ash erupted from the volcano and covered the city, calcifying the occupants and destroying the buildings. St-Pierre was quickly transformed from the Petit Paris to the Petit Pompeii. The lone survivor was a man thrown in prison overnight for drunkenness; he was protected by the thick walls of his cell. Everyone else died at 8 a.m., May 8, 1902. Once released, the prisoner, whose named is variously reported as Cylbaris or Syparis, spent several years traveling in the sideshow of the Barnum & Bailey Circus.

Not to be missed is the Volcanological Museum, open daily 9 a.m. to 12:30 p.m. and 3 p.m. to 5 p.m. It contains many heat-deformed and charred objects, photographs of the disaster and distorted clocks stopped at 8 a.m. The ruins, which cover two terraces, and the museum take about one-and-one-half hours to explore thoroughly. The new village of St-Pierre is growing up around the old city.

Martinique Trails — South Atlantic

🦀 3. The Macabou/Salines Circuit Beach Walks

Time: The Macabou to Cul-de-Sac Ferre takes 2 hours; add 3 more hours to join Cap Chevalier; another 1-1/2 hours to arrive at Anse Trabaud, and another 1-1/2 hours to arrive at Salines Beach. **Difficulty:** 2-3. Open sun the entire time. Avoid venturing into the mangroves, where the mud is often deep. Bring water and food.

This route skirts one of the most beautiful coastlines in Martinique. If you're not inclined to walk for ten hours even with swimming breaks from time to time, you can choose any of the four sections. All are accessible by car.

Grande-Anse du Macabou is the starting point for the hike. Leave N1 approximately five kilometers after the town of Vauclin, and take the road marked "Ranch Macabou." Past the gate of the ranch, follow the concrete road leading to Pointe la Voute, which separates Petite and Grande-Anse Macabou.

To get to Cul-de-Sac Ferre, you must take Fonds-Gens-Libres Road, one kilometer after leaving the town of Marin going toward Sainte-Anne. At Fonds-Gens-Libres, take the Cap Marin Road on the right. The path entrance is marked.

For Cap Chevalier, take the Marin-Sainte-Anne Road, fork to the left at Poirier to the sign "Piton Creve-Coeur." Take a right at the next crossroads and follow to the sea.

L'Anse Trabaud is one kilometer before the town of Sainte-Anne, in a wide curve to the right; take the stone road of "Baie des Anglais" to the left to reach the beach.

Salines Beach is reached by the indicated road from Sainte-Anne. Allow one and a half hours driving time to reach this trail from Fort-de-France.

Section 1: Macabou to Cul-de-Sac Ferre
Time: 2 hours

Beginning at Pointe la Voute, descend toward Grande Anse du Macabou by a narrow path found at the south of the Pointe. Grande Macabou Beach, bordered with coconut palms, extends to Pointe Marie-Catherine, which takes about thirty minutes. Notice the contrast between the point, where nothing can grow in the wind, and the lush growth along the beach, mainly coconut palm and sea grape.

From the top of Marie-Catherine Pointe, go back down to Anse Grosse-Roche, whose name comes from the huge rocks on the beach to the south. (The rocks, themselves, are obscured by vegetation.)

Arriving at Point Macrem, you'll discover Four a Chaux Beach and Baleine Beach. Here you can see the edges of the coral reef, defined by plumes of spray from breaking waves. Behind these beaches is an undergrowth of sea grapes and manchineel trees.

After two hours you'll arrive at the magnificent Cul-de-Sac Ferre, an almost enclosed bay bordered by mangroves and gently sloping hills covered with pale green vegetation.

Sections 2 and 3: Cul-de-Sac Ferre to Cap Chevalier and Cap Chevalier-Trabaud

Time: 1-1/2 hours each

After passing Trou Cadia and Pointe la Rose, which enclose Cul-de-Sac Ferre with impressive, sea-carved cliffs, follow the beach of Grande Anse du Cap Ferre to the cape proper. From there, you can take in the entire coastline, from Pointe Macre to Chevalier Island.

Walk along Anse la Balle and its beautiful stand of coconut palms. Past Pointe des Ebichets (where you may see frigate birds in flight), you'll walk along the shore of Anse Noire, divided by a small cliff. On Anse Esprit or Anse au Bois you may see several long, narrow fishing boats made of gum trees.

The next section of Cap Chevalier is a popular spot where a number of locals have vacation homes. The path turns inland in order to avoid both the private homes and the mangroves bordering the coast.

You'll rejoin the water at Baie des Anglais, which has some of Martinique's most beautiful mangroves. (Opposite the bay is the summit of Pointe Jaham. It would take about one and one-half hours to reach because of the deep mangrove forest growing well inland.) Remain on the beach, and when you're in sight of "les Anglais des Grottes," you'll need to cross a small bridge to the west bank. In the rainy season, this can be tricky.

Next, you'll pass beneath Baie des Anglais and the western flank of Morne a Vache before descending to Anse Trabaud, one of Martinique's most beautiful beaches.

Section 4: Anse Trabaud to Grande Anse des Salines

Time: 1-1/2 hours.

Walking the length of Anse Trabaud, you'll enter the Savane des Petrifications, a former petrified forest. Unfortunately, almost all the fossilized wood has been removed. Next is a very dry savannah, bordered by dramatic cliffs perpetually beaten by the waves of the Canal of Sainte-Lucie, where sea birds nest.

After Pointe d'Enfer, Anse Baham and Anse de l'Ecluse, you'll see the "Devil's Table" and the little island of Cabrits, the southernmost point of the island. A lighthouse and weather station occupy the summit.

Walk along l'Etang des Salines to the south and reach Pointe des Salines, where you'll find one of the most popular tourist spots on the island: Salines Beach, planted with coconut palms, sea grapes, manchineels, and pear trees, recognizable by their pale pink flowers.

4. Le Piton de Creve-Coeur
Time: 1 hour. **Difficulty:** 2-3.

Peaking at 200 meters, the Piton de Creve-Coeur overlooks the entire peninsula of Sainte-Anne and offers a remarkable panorama. Its volcanic formation has two heads in profile, a notable landmark for the southern part of the island.

From Le Marin take D9 toward Sainte-Anne. About two and one half km outside of town, take a left toward Cap Cabaret/Cap Chevalier. At the first fork, 1,000 meters farther, take the road to the right. After two kilometers the paved road will veer off to the left, and you will go straight ahead onto a wide dirt road. After about 1500 meters, the road will turn left to arrive at the foot of the peak, a vast grassy expanse with ruins of an old sugar factory. Leave your vehicle in the shade of a calabash tree.

After visiting the sugar mill ruins, now taken over by magnificent gum trees, you'll locate the summit trail to the right of the parking area, behind a hedge. The path goes around the peak from the north. First, you see the ruins of the old house. Above the house, a shelter maintained by the ONF (Office Nationale des Forets) permits a last rest before the ascent. The slope now becomes steeper, but steps to a ramp have been installed to help you up.

At 185 meters, you arrive at a flat area which offers a superb view of the southern part of the peninsula. Climbing to 200 meters and standing among the agave plants, you'll enjoy an even better 360-degree panorama.

The same road takes you back to your point of departure.

5. Morne Larcher Trail
Time: 2-1/2 hours, one way. **Difficulty:** 3. Constant sun and continual slope upward.

This walk will show you the entire southern coast of Martinique from the top of Morne Larcher (Larcher Hill) 400 meters high.

The trail ends are reached either by the Diamond (le Diamant) in the Anse Caffard district, which goes along celebrated Diamond Beach; or by les Anses d'Arlet in the "Petite Anse" district. Plan on a forty-five minute drive from Fort-de-France.

Leaving from the l'Anse Caffard end, the marked trail enters a dry, thickly wooded area with interspersed goat or sheep pastures. The foliage becomes denser as you climb. The species most frequently encountered is a shrub recognizable with pale green and orange leaves and a peppery odor when its leaves are rubbed; India wood, a shrub or tree with shiny leaves (a basic spice in Antillian cuisine); pear trees; red gum trees; and cacti.

After an hour's walk you'll reach a small savannah, scattered with mango and guava trees. This is also the highest point on the trail. From this point you'll see Diamond Beach in the foreground and the succession of points and bays named Marigot, Pimentee, and Philippeaux, which make up the Diamond Coast of Sainte-Luce. You'll also see in the background the entrance to the Baie du Marin and the peninsula of Sainte-Anne. Facing south, you may be able to spot the contours of St. Lucia, some thirty kilometers away.

After crossing the savannah around the summit of Morne Larcher, go down onto Petite Anse. The greenery is more moist, with many large trees, lianas and epiphytes. After about thirty minutes' descent, you'll cross a relatively flat area. Another twenty minutes from here is the district of Petite Anse and its beach.

 6. Morne Champagne

Time: 45-60 minutes roundtrip. **Difficulty:** 1.

This is a short and pleasant walk to a splendid view. The beginning of this trail is at the southern extremity of Grand Anse d'Arlet Beach between two houses. Park along the road. After taking the path behind the last houses on the beach, follow a gently sloping path on the flank of Morne Champagne (Champagne Hill). Along this road you'll see blocks of black rock: these are landesite, a form of lava, carved by erosion.

In about ten minutes you'll arrive at a savannah surrounded in the north, east, and west by a fairly steep cliff. You are now standing in the crater of a volcano, Champagne Bluff, which has eroded in its several million years. This is a great view of Grande Anse, its beach and the crystal-clear water where many sailboats are moored.

The path then leads to a small house. Not far from here you'll see a small pond bordered by calabash trees and large pear trees. This tranquil site is ideal for a picnic. Your return is by the same route.

Hikes to the Pitons de Carbet Mountains

7. La Demarche Morne Rouge

Time: 3 hours each way. **Difficulty:** 3.

This is a fairly easy trail which leads to beautiful views of the harbor of Fort-de-France and Case-Pilote. The last section of the trail is forested.

The trail starts either at Schoelcher by taking the first road to the right after Fond-Lahaye Hill and following it to the Demarche district; or at Case-Pilote by taking the road on the right before the summit of Case-Pilote Hill and continuing to the TV relay at Grand Fond.

The first hour is done in the savannahs on the heights of Schoelcher, in fields of thyme, onion and other home-grown vegetables. You'll already be able to see a good part of the harbor of Fort-de-France while going over this wide ridge. Next, you'll enter the forest and reach the first slopes of Morne Bois d'Inde. At first, the forest is shaded by large-leafed manjack trees and sweet pea. Then, after passing through a more humid forest of breadfruit trees, an hour's walk takes you to the Concorde Plateau, with its groves of mahoganies.

A few minutes later, you arrive at the fork leading to Morne Chapeau Negre (Black Hat Hill) and the Pitons de Carbet. Take a left toward Piton Belly, still in the forest. Before reaching Morne Rose, an hour later, you'll go through young groves of Caribbean pines and mahoganies.

8. Absalon-Verrier

Time: 4 hours, one way. **Difficulty:** 3. The trail presents no notable difficulties for those in good physical condition. The climb up Morne Chapeau Negre is difficult in some places due to erosion.

This path allows you to discover Martinique's gorgeous forest and views of Fort-de-France and Lamentin. Several routes are possible. You may climb to Piton Lacroix, whose ascent is particularly difficult, or go back down toward Morne Rose by way of the Saint-Cyr Savannah.

Arrive at the trail head either: 1) at Absalon via RN3, Route de la Trace (Trail Route); take the fork to the left about ten kilometers after Fort-de-France and continue to the watering place. Or, 2) at Verrier by Bellefontaine, take a right at the entrance to the town and continue to the Chapeau Negre house. In either case you should have no parking problem.

Martinique, like Guadeluope, has a well-organized system of mountain trails particularly dense with ferns.

Departing Absalon, the trail begins with a steep incline under a canopy of white gum trees, riviera wood, cannon wood and mahogany.

In about twenty minutes you'll arrive at a crossroads. Take the left to descend toward the Duclos River, which is full of the tiny crustaceans found in Martinique's streams. This path will lead you across the Concorde

Plateau and the Saint-Cyr Savannah, and into two forests of mahogany planted by the Office of National Forests.

Next, begin climbing Morne Chapeau Negre, which peaks at 912 meters. The climb begins in a forest of breadfruit trees and cannon wood. After about one and one half hours, the flora becomes the stunted growth of high altitudes, mostly ferns and mosses, with some mountain mangroves and laurels. The last part of the climb goes up a narrow ridge where you can look out over part of the northern Caribbean coast, the harbor of Fort-de-France, the plain of Lamentin, and the forests of la Donis, Morne Bois d'Inde and Morne Rose. On clear days, you can see part of the Atlantic coast to the south of the Caravelle Peninsula.

From the summit, descend by the west into Bellefontaine, a one and one half hour walk. Or, you can take the difficult ascent of Piton Lacroix in order to return via Piton Dumauze. You should count on three more hours to return to Absalon if you take the Duclos trail.

If you decide to return to Verrier, it will take you about an hour to return to the Chapeau Negre house. This descent goes through forest.

9. The Absalon Circuit

Time: 3 hours, round trip. **Difficulty:** 2.

One of the rare forested trails less than twenty kilometers from Fort-de-France, this path offers an especially easy and relatively short circuit.

Shortly after Balata, coming from Fort-de-France, leave the Trail Road and descend the little road from Absalon to the parking lot.

The trail starts at the watering station at Absalon, at the little bridge going to the swimming pool below. The path climbs for twenty minutes along a rather steep slope to a another crossroads. To continue your circuit, follow the wooded ridge overlooking the Duclos River Valley.

After a pleasant forty-five minute walk in the ridgeline, descend for fifteen minutes, crossing two streams to reach the parallel trail on the right, leading back to within ten meters of the departure point.

10. The Pitons du Carbet Circuits

Time: 6 hours. **Difficulty:** 5. Take water. Near-constant exposure to the sun. When rain makes it slick, climbs are like ski slopes, the descents become toboggan runs. Further, at the base of the descent from Piton Lacroix, going toward Alma and Dumauze peaks, you'll need to cross a very narrow ridge (about twenty centimeters wide). There's no shame in scrambling across on all fours, or sliding across on your rear.

These are tough hikes, primarily of interest to those who want a physically challenging climb. However, the summits offer the most spectacular views in all of Martinique.

Reach the trail either from the south or north. The walk is easier if you opt for the north, but there's no reason to miss the other route, departing from the Colson Hospital to get to the Boucher Plateau. Plan on an hour's drive from Fort-de-France, taking RN3 to the starting point at Trail Road.

If you start from Boucher Plateau, you face the longest climb of the trail. In about an hour you'll ascend some 400 meters along a very steep slope. If it's slippery, look for the stakes hammered into the most critical spots to help you ascend. As the climb progresses, you'll have views of Piton Gele, overlooking the crossroad of Deux Choux, Morne Jacob, and the village of Morne-Rouge.

The flora now becomes more stunted. The great trees of the Boucher Plateau rain forest gradually give way to high-altitude shrubs like cabbage palms, orchids, mosses, ferns, and mountain pineapple (no edible fruit), all interspersed with small trees twisted into fantastic shapes by the wind.

The trail between the summit of Piton Boucher and the ridge of Morne Piquet slopes slightly and is scattered with many hollows. The scrub is denser when it's sheltered from the wind, but otherwise virtually identical to that of the higher slopes on Piton Boucher.

The crest of Morne Piquet is an hour and several spectacular views of the coastline away. You'll see the village of Morne Vert and the district of Verrier. Note the grove of the Swiss Canton and Mount Joly. You'll go left there and begin the one hour ascent of 1196 meters Piton Lacroix, end of your hike.

From the peak, the view extends to the south as far as Diamond Rock and even to the neighboring island of St. Lucia. You can make out the city and the roads of Fort-de-France, the Sacre Coeur of Balata, replica of Sacre Coeur de Montmartre, and the agricultural plain of Lamentin. Between February and June you might see a plume of smoke rising from one of the two remaining sugar mills. At the foot of the peak is the splendid, almost primeval forest of the Concorde Plateau and Saint-Cyr Savannah, dominated by white gum and breadfruit trees.

It will take about an hour to descend to the crossroad, joining the Trail Road, either by way of the Piton Dumauze and Colson Hospital or by way of Alma Peak and the village of Colson. **Note:** The descent from Lacroix Peak may be perilous—a muddy and slippery slope.

11. Hike from Morne-Vert to Fonds Saint-Denis

Time: 3 hours each way. **Difficulty:** 2-3, a steep part near Fonds Saint-Denis.

This rates right after Pitons du Carbet as one of the island's most interesting hikes. It's easy, too, one of those rare family walks in the forest.

Since this trail doesn't loop, you have a choice of trailheads: either from Fonds-Saint-Denis on D1, one kilometer past town going toward Deux Choux; or Fond Caplet to Morne-Vert, the easiest approach, on a pleasant and narrow road which leaves from the town's church. You get to this district by taking the first road to the left, then the first right after crossing a river. Drive up the valley and park at the last house.

From the easier Fond Caplet side, you'll climb for forty-five minutes along the hillside in the midst of savannahs and food crops. You'll come to the edge of a mahogany forest on the hill between Morne Modeste and Morne Piquet. The view of the valley at the foot of the amphitheater of Morne Piquet is splendid.

Through the forest is a clearing at the foot of a beautiful and impressive cascade, an immense rock surrounded by rain forest. You can refresh yourself in the stream—but don't drink the water—then follow it to the steep slope leading into the forest. It's wooded silence may be punctuated by the song of a mountain widgeon.

Leaving the forest, you arrive at a small plateau offering one of this walk's most beautiful views. Next, cross a young forest of Caribbean pines, to a second stream, just as nice as the first.

One more small climb and another forest (this section often filled with raspberries), then you begin the descent for Fonds-Saint-Denis, the last third of the hike.

During the last hour, the path twists first along a ridge of alternating savannahs and groves, then crosses a field of Chinese cabbage. The descent becomes steeper. You'll reach the bottom of the Carbet River Valley by going through some produce fields overlooking Fonds-Saint-Denis.

On the bridge, stop for a moment to admire the rapids. This is the end of your hike. It remains only to climb back up to the national highway of Deux Choux to Fonds-Saint-Denis.

 12. The Morne Cesaire Trail

Time: 2 hours, round trip. **Difficulty:** 3.

As interesting as it is pleasant, this short walk around the environs of Fort-de-France is noted for the arboretum at la Donis as well as the superb views from the trail's beginning at the summit of Morne Cesaire.

Drive to the nursery of the ONF on Trail Road, just after Balata, going to Morne Rouge. The trail departs from the la Donis arboretum, near the picnic shelter at the upper entrance. The path climbs rapidly in a series of hairpin turns to a large savannah planted with anthuriums and other crops.

All along this short, thirty minute climb, there is a botanical itinerary which names the many trees of Martinique's forests. In addition, the view over the Pitons de Carbet, which spread out behind the nursery's great royal palms, is particularly beautiful.

The trail enters an abandoned mahogany grove, and after another thirty minute walk you'll reach the summit of Morne Cesaire, a balcony several meters above the Fort-de-France, Balata in the Ravine-Vilaine and Riviere-l'Or.

13. The Trail of the Jesuits

Time: 3 hours. **Difficulty:** 3. One ford on the Lorrain River. This trail departs from Trail Road (RN3), 1 kilometer after the tunnel of Deux Choux, going toward Morne-Rouge. It arrives on the Deux Choux/Morne-Rouge road (D1) about 3 km from the crossroads at RN3.

The Trail of the Jesuits is one of the best-known walks on Martinique, and one of the most interesting in the National Forest. It offers the chance to visit one of the best primeval forests in Martinique, one with a reputation for being an "ecological trail" of superior quality.

The two trail entrances are indicated by signs. A small parking lot is at either end. Markings are clear. A picnic area with shelter is maintained about 200 meters from Trail Road.

From RN3, the first 300 meters of Jesuits' Trail snakes along a ridge overlooking Trail Road. You'll view magnificent tree ferns, a panoramic view of Mount Pelee at the plain of Champflore, and the beautiful mahogany forest of Proprete.

Then the descent toward the Lorrain River begins, plunging into this pristine rain forest of silence, moistness and beauty. You'll see many white gums, breadfruits, riviera-wood, and magnolias. All are draped with epiphytes, ferns, mosses, and lianas.

After an hour's walk you'll see the Lorrain River, principal attraction of this trail. This is, in fact, a nice recreation area in the midst of splendid overhanging bamboo branches. Ford the river and walk another hour up the other side of the Lorrain Valley to the Deux Choux/Gros-Morne Road. You'll have beautiful views over the mountains to Morne Jacob and the Carbet Peaks, some hundred meters from your arrival point. Once out on the state road, go to the lookout point maintained by the ONF. A little farther toward the Deux Choux crossroads, you'll be able to look over the magnificent forest you've just hiked, as well as the entire northern part of the island.

14. Morne Bellevue to Reculee Hike

Time: 4 hours, one way. **Difficulty:** 3-4. Constant ascents and descents. Leave from Morne Bellevue 100 meters before Trou-Matelots on D1. This goes from Gros-Morne to Deux Choux, the easiest and most spectacular route.

Almost a third of this trail, accessible to any skill level, surveys one of the island's most beautiful panoramas.

The first forty-five minutes, or about a third of the walk, crosses a magnificent rain forest of breadfruit and gum trees. Then, during the second third of the trail, you'll follow a succession of switchbacks along a ridge overlooking the entire Lorraine River Valley, topped by the cone of Morne Jacob. On the right are mahoganies planted by the ONF.

Leaving the forest, you'll have a splendid view over the hills above Sainte-Marie. The trail continues along the ridge for forty-five minutes. You will see the tiny island of Sainte-Marie, Morne-des-Esses and Caravelle. The trail ends by entering another mahogany forest, that of Reculee, a circuit which can also serve as a departure point.

15. Mount Pelee by way of l'Aileron

Time: 5 hours, round trip. **Difficulty:** 4-5.

A guide is advised for this particular trail, which is rarely explored, even during the dry season. It is a steep slope to descend into the Caldeira with possibly dangerous holes covered by moss. From the summit, the panorama covers all of Martinique and the neighboring islands.

16. From Grande Savane to the Second Shelter

Time: 4-1/2 hours, round trip. **Difficulty:** 4-5. Open sun, tricky walking over pumice. Numerous, moss-covered holes at the Caldeira.

This trail, on the driest side of Mount Pelee, is noted for beautiful lookout points. It provides an ascent to the Caldeira with less likelihood of rain.

On route D10, at the southern entrance to Precheur, is a sign for the well-maintained road to your departure point. Another sign indicates the entrance to the trail itself. You'll find enough parking for several vehicles.

During the first forty-five minutes, the trail is mostly a wide road, suitable for an all-terrain vehicle. The fertile earth produces abundant tomato plants, carrots, cabbage, and onions. Trees are scarce.

During the climb, you'll discover a magnificent view of le Precheur and the northern part of the island not obscured by Piton Marcel. After an hour, you'll walk along a ridge overlooking two deep gorges with remarkable tree ferns and a view of the entire Bay of Saint-Pierre. From this point on, you'll encounter the high-altitude vegetation of Mount Pelee.

The slope now turns steeper, and in thirty minutes you'll reach the crossroads to a shelter beside the Caldeira. It's possible to ascend Chinois beside the third shelter.

In terms of scenery, the Caldeira is the real attraction. During the next thirty minutes, the trail will overlook the picturesque crater of Mount Pelee, with its vegetation of moss, ferns, lycopods, and mountain pineapples. Note the presence of orchids and a few raspberry bushes. The shelter appears soon, on the plateau at the foot of a rocky spur surmounted by a cross. Plan on about 1-1/2 hours for the return.

17. Hot Springs

Time: 4-1/2 hours. **Difficulty:** 3-4. Open sun; take water.

Situated in the southwest foothills of Mount Pelee, this simple walk provides the only look at current volcanic activity. Because the lower part is regularly used by the army for target practice, the trail is closed to the public Tuesdays, Wednesdays, and Fridays.

Go by way of CD10 from Saint-Pierre, three kilometers from the town exit. The beginning of the trail is marked by a sign.

After passing the gate by the zigzag trench, the rocky path rises in a regular slope toward the flanks of Mount Pelee. The first part of the trail crosses a shrub-covered savannah, a dried-out forest. You will encounter several trees, including guava and crotons. After one and one half hours' walking in the direct sun, you will find yourself in line with Morne Penet or Morne Leonard, which rises 150 meters to the east of the trail.

The dry vegetation gives way to a dense forest of ferns and a few stunted shrubs. The trail almost disappears in places under this tufted cover. Be alert: you might see or hear a mongoose scampering away.

After another thirty minutes' walking, you reach the escarped bank of the Riviere Chaude (Hot River), which becomes the Claire River. Feel for yourself how warm the water is (about 40ºC). Next, go along the upper course of the river. Don't hesitate to walk the river bed itself. The water isn't cold and it's safer than venturing on the steep banks with their crumbly rocks. In fifteen minutes, you'll be at the hot springs themselves.

Green algae is common in this warm water. The yellow-ocher of the rocks is sulfur.

Your hike terminates at a cone of debris about twenty meters high. You will now find yourself at an altitude of 750 meters, some 600 meters from the summit of Pelee. If you have to attempt the summit, watch for cave-ins and landslides. A rope is indispensable. This last section should be scaled only by experienced mountain climbers (as opposed to enthusiastic hikers).

# 18. The Caravelle Point Trail

Time: 3 hours, round trip. **Difficulty:** 2-3.

This walk, twenty minutes from Fort-de-France, goes through a natural reserve of 517 hectares composed of both mangroves and dry forest.

Leave N1 before Trinite. Go through the village of Tartane and continue to Chateau Dubuc.

The trail departs from the 17th-century Chateau Dubuc, whose history is told in the little museum at the entrance. Follow the botanical path and turn to the right at station No. 15, in order to descend toward the mangroves of Tresor Bay. These mangroves shelter oysters and mangrove mussels, crabs, blue herons, salt-pan plovers, and yellow-footed sandpipers.

Next, go along the coastline, a succession of calm bays and jagged capes beaten by the waves. From the meteorological station, climb to the 149 meters-high lighthouse, built in 1861. From there, you can see Vauclin Mountain in the south, Mount Pelee in the north, and the Carbet Peaks in the west.

From the lighthouse, you'll enter a forest of large-leafed grape trees, up to forty centimeters in diameter; pear trees with mauve flowers, and red gum trees. The trail will take you back to your departure point.

19. Hikes in Maintained Forests

The ONF has developed several recreation areas with shelters, benches, and walking paths. While not true hikes, they are the easiest means to see the forests of Martinique.

Montravail (Saint-Luce Community)
Time: 1 hour. **Difficulty:** 1

Arrive here via D8, between Riviere-Salee and Sainte-Luce. Signs indicate the direction of Montravail. At the entrance to the forest, a concrete road leads to a maintained parking lot near a picnic area.

A network of trails diverge from the road toward the undergrowth. A woodland trail, 2.5 kilometer long, is for runners. A sign with a detailed map provides directional details.

La Vatable (Trois-Ilets Community)
Time: 1 hour. **Difficulty:** 1.

Arrive here by D7 leading to Riviere-Salee at Trois-Ilets. A sign indicates the entrance past the ruins of the former distillery. Follow the central dirt road to a pathway entering a forest of mahoganies, Caribbean pines, and many other species, leading to the sea. Picnic shelters are at the beginning of the trail and seaside, which provides a glorious view of the Bay of Fort-de-France and its islets. A loop allows a return along the sea.

La Phillipe "Pointe Tenos" (Community of Sainte-Marie)
Time: 1 hour. **Difficulty:** 1.

Go by N1 leading to Sainte-Marie in Marigot. One kilometer after Fond-Saint-Jacques, a sign to the right indicates the entrance.

A map outlines two itineraries. Two shelters are situated along the route, with a view of the Bay of Sainte-Marie. A trail leads to a cliff overlooking the usually rough sea. Groves of mahogany, pear trees and Caribbean pines provide cool shade. Going toward Marigot by N1, you'll spot on the right the Pain de Sucre (Sugar Loaf) of Anse Charpentier, accessible only by a hiking path.

Riviere Blanche (White River)/Saint Joseph/Coeur Bouliki
Time: 1 hour. **Difficulty:** 1.

Take N4 leading from Fort-de-France to Saint-Joseph; turn left at the level of the stadium, take the local road La Durand and go to White River. Signs mark the road leading to the parking lot and to Riviere-Blanche.

Two shelters near the river allow rest and relaxation. Well-maintained trails permit views of beautiful tree specimens, particularly mahoganies.

La Donis to Fort-de-France
Time: 1 hour. **Difficulty:** 1.

Go by N3, called Route de la Trace (Trail Road). A sign and giant royal palms indicate the place, 10 kilometers from Fort-de-France.

In addition to the nursery where the ONF raises trees and ornamental plants, a well-maintained trail leads to an arboretum where you can examine the exotic, introduced species, all labeled. At the end of this path, in clear weather, you can view the majestic Carbet Peaks.

 15. St. Lucia

Old Caribbean Proverb:
All skin— teeth and laugh.

Translation:
Deception is often disguised by a smile.

Tiny St. Lucia (LOO-sha) is shaped like a tear drop, twenty-four miles long from north to south and fourteen miles wide. It is part of a relatively young chain of volcanic islands created by lava and ash from ocean-floor volcanoes. It is twenty-one miles south of Martinique and twenty-six miles north of St. Vincent.

St. Lucia's volcanic origins are most conspicuous in its two great spires—Gros Piton and Petit Piton, which jut up a full half mile. They are among the Caribbean's most striking natural landmarks, formed by eruptions thirty to forty million years ago. Coated with thick tropical vegetation, these pyramid-shaped cones capture every sailor's gaze, rendering insignificant all other features along St. Lucia's southern coast, even coal-black sand beaches that rival Hawaii's.

St. Lucia is home to what islanders call their "drive-in volcano:" a small valley and ridge of several acres, containing pots of boiling water, steam vents and a coating of sulfur and other compounds. It's only a ten to fifteen-minute walk from the car park until you come face to face with the small smoking craters and bubbling sulfur pools.

Nearby are Diamond Falls and the Botanical Garden, which contain warm sulfur baths fed by underground springs from the volcano's sulfur pools. Here, the St. Lucians take an annual dip, reputed to take off ten years and ten pounds. Obviously, you have to be an islander to benefit from this miraculous transformation; it's never worked for me.

St. Lucia's mountainous countryside is often a bright kelly green and very similar to Dominica in that many of the plants and animals are of South or Central American origin. About 11% of St. Lucia is primarily

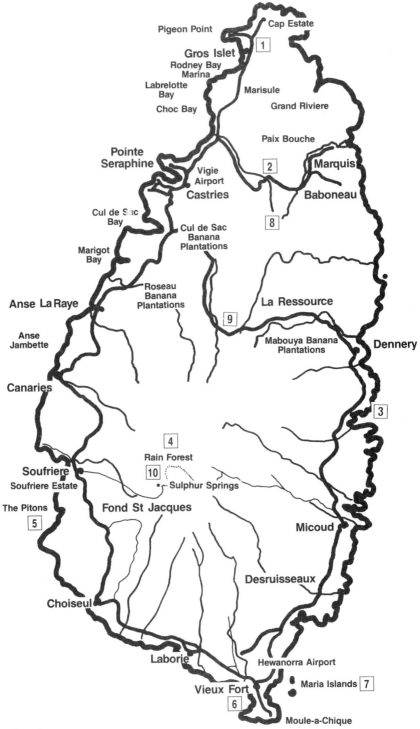

Pigeon Point
Cap Estate
1

Gros Islet
Rodney Bay
Marina
Labrelotte
Bay
Marisule
Choc Bay
Grand Riviere

Paix Bouche

Pointe
Seraphine
2
Marquis

Vigie
Airport
Castries
Baboneau

Cul de Sac
Bay
8

Cul de Sac
Banana
Plantations

Marigot
Bay

Roseau
Banana
Plantations
La Ressource

Anse La Raye
9

Anse
Jambette
Mabouya Banana
Plantations
Dennery

Canaries
3

4

Rain Forest
Soufriere
10
Sulphur Springs
Soufriere Estate

The Pitons
Fond St Jacques
Micoud
5

Desruisseaux

Choiseul

Laborie
Hewanorra Airport
Maria Islands
7
Vieux Fort
6
Moule-a-Chique

St. Lucia

rainforest. Ironically, most of the cutting was done in this century, not before. The remaining rainforest is now protected, to preserve the all-important watershed, as well as the wildlife.

St. Lucia is a land of many waterfalls, ridges and valleys, a true walker's dream. St. Lucians understand that they possess something very special, fragile and unique.

Although island legend says Columbus's discovered the island on St. Lucy's Day, December 13, 1502, it appears St. Lucia was discovered not by Columbus himself, but by his map maker. Columbus's logbook shows he never saw the island and wasn't anywhere in the area on St. Lucy's Day. A globe of 1520 shows the island already clearly named Santa Lucia.

The Caribs called it "Iouanaloa," land of the iguana, so these lizards must have been in great abundance when the Indians first arrived. The island was ignored by the Spanish. The first British settlement didn't take root until 1640. The French then decided they also wanted the island, and during the next 200 years of intermittent warfare, St. Lucia changed hands fourteen times, ending up British in 1814. In 1979, St. Lucia was granted independence.

The French may not own the island, but they certainly own the culture. English is the official language, but a Creole patois (virtually unintelligible to those who speak French) is the common tongue. Further, the city, landmark and inhabitants' names are mostly French. French cooking, with a strong Creole flair, predominates.

Although the main city of Castries is located in the north, St. Lucia's major sites (the drive-in volcano, Diamond Waterfalls and the Botanical Garden) are all south, near the town of Soufriere, a two-hour drive because of poor road conditions. For Castries-based visitors, the easiest and gentlest transportation is going by boat to Soufriere and getting a guide. The road system, though improving all the time, leaves much to be desired.

Travel Tips

Area: 238 square miles; 24 miles long, 14 miles wide.

Language: Officially, it's English but the locals favor a thick patois which is incomprehensible even to those who speak French.

Population: 121,000.

Time Zone: Atlantic Standard Time, one hour ahead of Eastern Standard Time.

Rainy Season: From the end of May through the rest of the year. January to April is the dry period.

Getting There: Travel to St. Lucia is easy. American Airlines funnels passengers through its San Juan hub to St. Lucia twice daily. American also offers a choice of airports in St. Lucia, an important consideration depending on your hotel's location. Those staying near Castries should use Vigie Airport located just outside the city. Unfortunately, larger planes and the earlier arrivals land at Hewanorra International Airport at the southern end a two-hour bumper-car ride away. BWIA, Air Canada and LIAT also serve St. Lucia.

Getting Around: The best way to explore the beautiful St. Lucian countryside is by taxi if you're on island for only a few days. Taxis are unmetered, so fares should be agreed upon beforehand. Prices fluctuate but a tour (depending on the distance covered) will range from US $50-$100. Rental cars are available, and are the only mode of transport that makes economic sense if you intend extensive exploring. Drivers must be twenty-five years old and possess a St. Lucian driver's license (EC $30 at the airport or at police headquarters at Gros Islet). Driving on the crater-pocked roads of St. Lucia is not unlike offroad driving over very bumpy terrain. Drive on the left.

Where to Stay: Anyone intending to hike daily will find Anse Chastanet, the most conveniently located hotel for the price. This 400-acre estate has been a leader in organizing walking and hiking tours for its guests with local, very knowledgeable guides. For information, call 800/328-5285.

Between Gros and Petit pitons, is the Dasheen, offering two- to three-bedroom villas in a truly incredible setting that was featured in the movie *Superman II*; tel. 47444.

Camping: Generally allowed on most beaches, but check first.

Taxes & Tips: Don't let these come as a shock. The government collects an 8% tax on hotel rooms. In addition, hotels add a 10% service charge to the bill. Combined, that's 18% tacked onto hotel charges.

Special Doings: Every Friday is fete or party night at Gros Islet, a fishing village just outside Castries. The Mardi Gras-like street party features crowds, blaring reggae, rum carts and coalpot barbecue cook stands.

Documents: Passport or picture ID with a notarized birth certificate for U.S. citizens. Also a return or ongoing ticket. Others need passports.

Currency: The Eastern Caribbean dollar or EC $, worth about EC $2.67 for each US $1. US $ can be spent anywhere but change is given in EC $. Banks are open weekdays 8 a.m. to 1 p.m., and from 3 p.m. to 5 p.m. on Friday.

Electrical Current: 220 volts/50 cycles.

Health/Safety Tips: Unfortunately, the rivers aren't very clean. Don't swim in them, much less drink from them. St. Lucia is one of the few islands with bilharzia (also called schistosomiasis) a parasite that generally occurs in slow-moving, snail-infested water. It can enter the body by being consumed or through open wounds.

A guide and/or group is recommended when touring remote areas. Crime being what it is these days—prevalent—a few tourists have been robbed while walking on their own. Don't be put off for a moment by this warning; just don't be a dumb tourist (wandering off on your own into strange territory) and you'll be fine. Apparently attacks on tourists are often drug-related.

Hiking/Walking Services: Hiking and walking are just now becoming popular in St. Lucia, and truly knowledgeable guides are scarce. That will change quickly and dramatically in this age of "ecotourism." Check with the very helpful tourist office reps at both airports and at Pointe Seraphine. The main number is 24094; also try 25978 at Pointe Seraphine. Walks are most frequently offered during the winter season when it's not as humid and more people are on the island.

The National Trust owns and administers Pigeon Island National Park and the Maria Islands Nature Reserve. The National Trust is becoming increasingly active in arranging and organizing hikes to study the plants in different parts of the islands, including walks up Gros Piton. They are also planning to make more parts of the island accessible for nature walks. For the latest information or guides for the Maria Islands Nature reserve, tel. 809/45-25005/31495; fax 809/45-32791.

The St. Lucia Naturalists' Society welcomes visitors to its monthly meetings at the Castries Public Library. Meetings are the first Wednesday of every month, starting at 6 p.m. The Society also conducts regular nature walks; check with the library for details.

Forestry Department guides can be arranged for rainforest walks at 809/45-23231.

Legacy Tours is a tour company which can help arrange a full day in the bush with a forest department guide: Box 665, Castries; tel. 20220.

In Soufriere, one of the most reliable and knowledgeable guides is Martial Simon, Bay Street, Soufriere, St. Lucia; tel. 47390. Or look for him at Servil's Boutique.

Snakes and Other Venomous Creatures: The fer-de-lance inhabits coastal areas.

For More Information: Contact the St. Lucia Tourist Board, 820 2nd Ave., 9th Floor, New York, New York 10017; 212/867-2950; fax 212/370-7867. In Canada, 151 Bloor Street West, Suite 425, Toronto, Ontario M5S 1S4; 416/ 961-5606; fax 416/961-4317. In the UK, 10 Kensington Court, London W8 5DL; 071/937-1969; fax 071/937-3611.

1. Castries Walking Tour

Time: 1 hour; **Difficulty:** 1.

Unquestionably, the true allure of St. Lucia is the beauty of its countryside, not its cities. Castries, St. Lucia's bustling capital city, has few buildings of interest, despite its 200-year history. The city was destroyed by fire in 1927 and again in 1948. That doesn't quite explain its stark, clapboard appearance, which I find very unattractive.

The few buildings of historical importance are near Columbus Square. The cathedral is much more colorful inside than out: the walls and ceilings are decorated with frescoes. The covered marketplace is busiest on Saturdays. Basketware is the best local handicraft.

Increasingly, cruise ships call at Castries Harbour so visitors can make day excursions into the countryside. To take advantage of this traffic, a complex of duty-free shops was built at Pointe Seraphine in the late 1980s. They are well-stocked with jewelry, crystal, perfumes and china. Bagshaw's, the noted producer of silk-screened and hand-printed designs sold only on St. Lucia, has a store at Pointe Seraphine as well as downtown Castries.

2. Pigeon Island National Park

Time: 2-3 hours to explore fully. **Difficulty:** 2-3.

This rugged national park is the most accessible and interesting walk in the Castries resort area. The walk from the park entrance to Fort Rodney at the end point of Pigeon Island takes about an hour.

Originally the French called the island "Le Gros Islet." The name lives on in the bay and its village. The Big Island, protecting the mouth of the bay, covers a forty-acre area. Its most noticeable natural features are the two peaks joined by a saddle ridge. Climbing the path on these peaks to Fort Rodney requires a little bit of stamina.

The American Revolution of 1776 changed the course of St. Lucia's history. When France declared its support for the colonies and went to war with England in 1778, the English promptly captured St. Lucia from the French and built a strong naval base there. The French attempts to harass the British fleet peaked by 1780, but never succeeded in re-taking the island. However, in October 1781, the most powerful hurricane ever recorded in the West Indies crippled the English fleet. Reinforcements arrived before the French or Spanish could take advantage of the chaos.

Out on the Island

You're apt to see a fair variety of animals as you walk through the amazingly varied terrain on St. Lucia. One of the most startling is the iguana, which grows up to six feet long and is bright green, with brown or black markings. The tail, about two-thirds of its total length, is a prized delicacy, which accounts for the iguana's relative scarcity.

More common are the three species of anoles, tree lizards called "zandoli" on St. Lucia. Anoles are interesting because of the males' elaborate display, which involves a lot of head bobbing and push-ups. A local myth says that anyone touching an anole will get white blotches on the skin where they touched it. Not true. The worst they can do is give you a slight nip.

The equally harmless gecko also has a bad reputation. The gecko is easily identifiable by its eyes, which are covered by a transparent membrane instead of eyelids. Geckos are also noted for jettisoning their tails, leaving them wriggling in the paws of a confounded enemy. The tails will grow back, but not as long as the originals.

Caribs called geckos "Mabouia," evil spirits. According to legend, these fast-retreating animals latch themselves so tightly to a person's skin that it requires a hot iron to kill the animal and remove it. The story is absurd. The myth apparently comes from the gecko's ability to cling to the smallest and smoothest object, even glass, gripping with the flap-like scales on the undersides of their toes.

The fer-de-lance (Bothrops caribbaeus Garman) is a pit viper of some importance (to avoid), so worth a few extra words. Any time a local talks about serpents, he's talking about the fer-de-lance. Although there are other snakes on the island, only the fer-de-lance is called a "serpent," with all the Old Testament evil this implies.

These heat-seeking snakes are either brownish-gray, yellowish or copper red. The belly is always a pale yellow. A zig-zag series of brown spots decorate the last two-thirds of its back. The head is broadly triangular. Although averaging only three to four feet in length, they can grow up to seven feet long. They are found mostly on the lower coastal areas, and rarely above 600 feet in elevation. Its normal range is from Roseau to Castries on the west coast of St. Lucia, from Marquis to Micoud on the east. They are particularly fond of piles of rock or coconut husks. They like to bask and sun in the afternoon outside their dens. The snakes are nocturnal, so it's possible to see them on the road near twilight after a heavy rain.

The boa constrictors (constrictor orophias) of St. Lucia grow from seven to ten feet long on their diet of rats and birds. Some St. Lucian farmers have even introduced them to their property to keep down the rodent population.

Undoubtedly the most colorful occupant is the St. Lucian parrot, the national bird, once hunted both for its meat and the international pet market. The blue-green parrots are most active in the morning and the evening. The birds mate for life, and the female lays only two eggs a year. They nest in the tops of tall gommier trees and travel in family groups of twos and threes. Known locally as the "jacquot," there may have been as many as a million living here when the first European colonists arrived. In 1990, there were only 400 birds; though this is more than double the 1980 census, so they are definitely making a comeback.

 3. Union Nature Trail

Time: 45 minutes. **Difficulty:** 1.

This trail, which includes a mini-zoo of St. Lucian wildlife, is north of Castries at Union, Forestry Department headquarters. Go past the Halcyon Beach Hotel and take the road going east to Babboneau.

The small zoo at the beginning of the trail offers guaranteed sightings of iguana, boa and agouti. Of even greater interest is the medicinal garden devoted to herbal cures ("bush medicine") used throughout the Caribbean. Islanders regularly used aloe and other, lesser-known plants until shampoos, medicines and other products were imported. There is now a renewed interest in the properties of bush medicines, which bodes well for everyone: for the locals because it is cheaper and for tourists because it ensures protection of the forests.

The self-guided nature trail takes forty-five minutes, an easy path used by young school children. A brochure explains the different kinds of trees and their uses: Caribbean pine used for cabinet making and the hearty gliricidia used for making fence posts. You also have the chance to see a variety of birds, including hummingbirds, thrashers, warblers and mockingbirds.

Although the official trail ends after a short distance, an old pathway to the mountain top still exists. With advance reservations through the Forestry Dept., you can extend the hike for a total of about two hours by climbing up the steep mountainside through more dry, secondary woodland.

North East Coast

A walk from Esperance Bay via the small village of Monchy will take you along the rugged Atlantic coast, where the waves can reach an incredible fifteen to twenty feet. At such times, this walk is not advised. You'll be kept cool by the trade winds that keep the salt-tolerant xerophytic vegetation trimmed low and scrubby. You'll see blowholes spouting huge plumes, as wave-induced jets of water explode upwards through grotesque flows of weathered lava. This is one of the only places to see St. Lucia's endangered barrel cactus, although it is common on other islands.

4. Frigate Islands Natural Reserve
Time: a half-day or more. **Difficulty:** 1-2.

These twin islands (huge lumps of rock, really), off the east coast of St. Lucia at Praslin Bay, are a new reserve operated by the National Trust. Here, you can take a leisurely walk through another striking display of xerophytic vegetation. Frigate birds are almost always soaring on the ocean thermals by the cliffs. Frigate birds are locally called "scisseau" (scissors) because of their distinctively forked tails. July is nesting time, the best month to see frigate birds, although they show up as early as May. Frigates prefer bushes low to the ground for building their nests.

The trail has been engineered across cliffs and up to an overlook opposite the Frigate Islands. You return via a strip of fringing mangrove, then pass through a dry ravine and past a small waterfall, which flows only during the rainy season. The ravine provides a shady canopy of tall bay trees and other dry forest species.

Birds that can be observed here are the Trembler (Cincloerthis ruficauda) and the St. Lucian Oriole (Icterus laudabilis). The Ramier (Columbia squamosa) sometimes nests in this area. If you're lucky, you may see a beautifully colored boa (Constrictor constrictor) sleeping on the ground.

Everyone visiting the preserve area should be accompanied by a guide, arranged either through the National Trust (25005/31495) or a tour operator. Since you don't actually walk on the Frigate Islands but look out over them from a distance, take binoculars or a good telephoto lens. The inflated red throat of a nesting frigate, like that displayed by many lizards, is a sight you'll long remember.

5. The Rainforest Hike
Time: 3-1/2 hours each way. **Length:** 7 miles. **Difficulty:** 3.

To enjoy the best hiking in the central mountains, you need advance permission from the Forestry Department, a requirement designed to limit hunting and tree cutting.

The rainforest has a protected interior zone of about 19,044 acres. A Rainforest Walk in the Edmund Forest Reserve and the Quilesse Forest Reserve regions extends between the villages of Mahaut and Fond St. Jacques. The west end of the trail near Fond St. Jacques offers the best view of the pitons, as well as the highest point on the island, Mt. Gimie (3,117 feet).

The Rainforest hike can be started from either the eastern or western ends. It's generally easier if you start from the eastern end near Mahaut because of the steep terrain on the western end. You need to arrange transportation in advance at the other end or make a return trip.

As this is the rainforest, expect to get wet. Rainfall here is 100-150 inches annually, not much compared to some islands, but a deluge compared to the drier northern end of St. Lucia (forty to fifty inches). It is often cloudy here, but if the weather clears, you'll enjoy some wonderful vistas.

6. The Pitons

Time: 3 hours if you go all the way to the top of Gros Piton. **Length:** 2,619 feet, straight up. **Difficulty:** 3-4 because the sides are sheer near the top. A guide is recommended because it is possible to become disoriented.

A climb of Gros Piton is definitely a worthwhile thing, although you'll probably appreciate the beauty of the piton more from a distance than when you're actually on it. The approach is most often made by boat from Soufriere; and it is impressive to see that mountain towering a half-mile above you, shooting straight up from the edge of the sea...a steep half-mile which is your route to the top. If you doubt your ability, admire Gros Piton from a distance through your camera lens.

You first come to a Brigand camp, named for the slaves Robespierre freed in the new Republic. The Brigands realized that when St. Lucia reverted back to English rule, their short-lived freedom would be ended. They banded together as "l'armee dans les bois" and instituted a reign of terror on the island.

Halfway to the top you'll notice significant changes in the vegetation. All four vegetation types, from dry coastal forest to elfin woodland or cloud forest, exist on Gros Piton, making it a wonderful natural laboratory. On top, you should be revived and exhilarated by the cool, damp atmosphere, as the clouds condense into droplets of water.

The natural hardwood forest at the top of Gros Piton is home to several species of rare birds, possibly including the Semper's Warbler. The warbler hasn't been seen since the 1970s, and may be extinct.

The Pitons greet hikers first thing every morning at the Anse Chastanet Resort.

Petit Piton: No one is supposed to climb Petit Piton, badly eroded from a 1987 fire. However, that doesn't necessarily stop the local guides from volunteering to take you up. It's your decision, but remember several people have fallen off, due to the unstable soil conditions.

7. The La Tourney Wildlife Refuge

Time: 1 hour or all day, depending on how much you wish to watch birds.
Difficulty: 1-2.

If birds interest you, a trip to La Tourney in the southern plains of Vieux-Fort will be very rewarding. This small marsh is incredibly rich in wildlife. It is well-stocked with a species of fish known locally as "Atkenson." These, the sedges and water lilies provide ideal habitat for waterfowl.

The best month for birdwatching is November, when migrating species from North America come to St. Lucia. Some birds give up commuting, and retire here permanently as in the case of the Little Blue Heron, the Green Heron, the Blue-Winged Teal and the Sora Rail.

Occasionally birders are rewarded by the arrival of a Great Blue Heron or the White Egret, as they alight quickly and assume the posture of a tree stump as camouflage. The Black Swift, Caribbean Coot and West Indian Tree Duck are some of the endangered species you might have the rare pleasure of spotting.

8. Maria Islands Nature Reserve

Time: about a half-day. **Difficulty:** 1-2.

Located well south, in the Vieux-Fort area, these offshore islands are tiny. Maria Major is twenty-five acres, while Maria Minor encompasses only four. As small as these landfalls are, they contain plants and wildlife that are colorful, diverse and not found anywhere else in the world.

The islands are about 3,000 feet from the St. Lucia shore, separated by a shallow bay that sometimes turns quite rough. Visitors board small boats at the Interpretation Center at Pointe Sables for the crossing.

What makes these islands unique is that they have not been as disturbed as St. Lucia by man and his imported exotics. Unfortunately, man-made fires have swept over the islands, and goats have been grazed on Maria Major. These animals are notorious for doing a lot of damage in a very short time. But, even with these intrusions, the Maria Islands still contain close to 120 different plant types. With a yearly rainfall of about forty inches, cactus and other desert species are quite common.

The kouwes (Dromicus ornatus) may be the rarest snake in the world. It is found only on Maria Major, with an estimated population of fewer than 100. The snake once lived on St. Lucia, as well, before the mongoose was introduced in the early 20th century. It was thought to be extinct until 1973, when a kouwes was found and identified on Maria Major. Ten years later a new species or subspecies of butterfly was also found.

Another endemic species found nowhere else in the world is the large ground lizard, zandoli te, which numbers about 1,000 on Maria Major and 50 to 100 on Maria Minor. They are most active in late morning and late afternoon. The males grow as much as fourteen inches long, with bright blue tails, yellow bellies and dark blue backs. Females and juveniles, almost identical, are smaller, brown with dark stripes but no bright colors. The zandoli te was discovered in 1958.

Other residents include geckos, terns, ground doves, Caribbean Martins and one of my favorites, the Red-billed Tropic Bird, with its gorgeous, long, white tail plumage. Sadly, pelicans and frigate birds were hunted heavily during colonial times. Their oil and grease was believed to have powerful healing properties, especially for gout. Brown pelicans have now almost disappeared.

Visitors on Maria Major follow a trail that leads to an observation point in the woodland area. The lizards will normally venture quite close if people are quiet.

Contact the National Trust to make a trip to the Maria Islands, which are closed to visitors from May 15 to July 1, during the peak nesting season: tel. 25005/31495 for the trip schedule. The interpretive center is located at Anse de Sables, near Vieux-Fort, the island's second-largest city.

Other scenic spots in the Vieux-Fort district include the Moule a Chique peninsula at the southernmost tip of the island, which provides a good view of all St. Lucia; on a clear day, you can see St. Vincent, twenty-one miles to the south. This is a dramatic spot because the peninsula is 800 feet high and extends for a mile offshore. You have to walk the last stretch to reach the lighthouse where the Caribbean and Atlantic meet, for the best panoramic views.

Also in the Vieux-Fort area are the Bellvue Historic Site, ruins of an 18th-century sugar mill, and Savannes Bay with its thick mangroves and diverse birdlife.

 ## 9. Piton Flore

Time: 4-5 hours. **Difficulty:** 2-3 depending on how slippery the conditions.

Before the hurricane damage of 1980 closed the main access, the Forestry Department used to run half-day trips to the top of the 1,871-foot peak. Although never officially reopened, people can walk the trail, which is muddy, steep and in general disrepair. However, as the mountain peak contains true rainforest and some excellent views, it is worth the effort.

Go to the village of Forestiere and follow the road to the end, where there is a forestry house on the left. Walk through the forest plantations for about three-quarters of a mile until you come to a block house, where you turn right onto a small path. This is the route to the summit. A guide is not necessary but still a good idea. You'll have some fine views of the Cul-de-Sac Valley.

10. Barre de l'Isle/Mt. La Combe

Time: 30-45 minutes. **Difficulty:** 1.

This is a short, loop trail of about a quarter mile in the Barre de l'Isle, a ridge down the center of the island which divides St. Lucia into its eastern and western halves. The hiking trail is marked on the south side of the road at the beginning, about mid-way between the two coasts. The loop leads to a picnic table and an excellent view of the interior highlands. Cul-de-Sac Valley is to the west; Mt. Parasol, Grand Bois Forest and the Caribbean are to the southwest.

A small cave near the summit looks down into the Mabouya Valley. Mabouya is an Amerindian name for calling up evil spirits, so this area has had a bad reputation for centuries. The tiny cave is said to be haunted. Many years ago a man was robbed and killed and his body dragged into the cave. His restless soul seeks revenge, so every full moon his ghost stalks the region, hoping to find a descendant of his killer so he can extract his own vengeance. As long as you have a guilt-free pedigree, the ghost will not harm you.

While we're telling ghost stories—and St. Lucia has many spirits said to roam the island after dark—I should warn you about La Jablesse, another one of those fatally attractive supernatural women. She is known for stealing men away from their wives and girlfriends, treating the hapless victims to a passionate experience and then stealing their souls. It's said that such a man is never seen again.

La Jablesse keeps a matinee schedule, and appears only during the day. She is incredibly beautiful, with long black hair flowing to her waist. She has one obvious flaw: a cow foot which she conceals under a long robe or tight, figure-enhancing jeans.

In rural areas, men were taught never to entertain any beautiful strange woman who might accost them. What a great story to raise young boys on to scare them from later straying as husbands and boyfriends! Talk about psychological warfare between the sexes.

So how do you tell if you're being accosted by La Jablesse or just a mortal woman of extraordinary beauty? La Jablesse is afraid of smoke; and dogs will scare her away.

11. Drive-In Volcano/Sulfur Springs

Time: 45-60 minutes. **Difficulty:** 1.

The sign near Soufriere advertising "the world's only drive-in volcano" marks the entrance to what is perhaps the most accessible sulfuric fields anywhere in the Caribbean. A kiosk at the entrance (small admission fee) will pair you up with a guide, whether you want one or not.

The presence of sulfur is often strong enough to discolor silver jewelry. Mineral deposits have left the earth colored with orange, green, yellow and purple streaks. The bubbling mud pots bordered by steam vents jetting as high as fifty feet are impressive. At one time it was possible to walk among this field in the remnant of a volcanic crater, but after a few hikers stepped through the earth's crust, a concerted attempt has been made to keep everyone on a path above the spot. You can get close enough to see everything clearly if you take binoculars and a telephoto lens. This is a hot, open place; far from what you would call beautiful, compared to the high surrounding vegetation, but endlessly fascinating. The walk is a very short one. You can see the active area from the car park.

12. Diamond Falls/Mineral Baths

Time: 1 hour. **Difficulty:** 1.

The baths were built by Louis XVI so his soldiers could take advantage of the strong curative mineral content of these waters. They were almost destroyed in the Brigand revolt during the French Revolution. They were reopened in 1976. Because they're out in the open, swimsuits are required. Underground pipes feed the baths, which are of differing temperatures, heated by an underground stream from the sulfur pools (above). An attendant on duty can explain the procedure to you.

Diamond Falls is also located here, as is a lush, well-landscaped garden. An admission fee is charged; this is one of the tourist hot spots.

13. Coastal Walks

Time: varies from 30 minutes to 3 hours, one way. **Difficulty:** 2-3.

As the least accessible coast of St. Lucia, the northeast region is also one of the most interesting. Four marine turtle species—leatherbacks, logger-heads, hawksbills and greens—come ashore to nest from February to October. You might be able to accompany a turtle watch with the Natural-ists Society in Castries. Care should be taken around rock and coconut husk piles since this is fer-de-lance territory.

Some of the better coastal walks in this and other areas are:

Esperance to Pt. Hardie, 6 miles

Ti Tance to Grand Anse, 3 miles

Anse la Guadeloupe, 2-1/2 miles

Mandele, 3 miles

Vierge Point, 1-1/2 miles

Anse Noir (Black Bay to Laborie), 1-1/2 miles

Choiseul to Anse l'Ivogrne, 3 miles

Brigand Tunnel Canelles, 1 mile

Several additional areas, particularly around Grande Anse, are under consideration for National Trust protection. St. Lucia, fortunately, is taking steps in the right direction to preserve its environment, while at the same time coping with the increased pressures brought about by growing tourism.

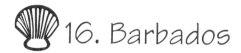# 16. Barbados

Old Caribbean Proverb:
Don't drink bush for other people's fever.

Translation:
Don't take on someone else's problems.

Situated 1,612 miles southeast of Miami and 575 miles south-east of Puerto Rico, Barbados is located in the region known as the deep Caribbean. Though this may be well off the beaten tourist path, approximately 360,000 visitors come by plane and even more by cruise ship each year. Canadians, especially, have a fondness for Barbados.

Barbados is the Caribbean's most densely populated island, so it understandably lacks the remote forest hikes of the more rugged, mountainous islands. Exploring is confined primarily to the Bridgetown area, to various historical structures scattered throughout the countryside, and the almost-deserted Atlantic coast. This is tenderfoot-grade walking, some of the Caribbean's easiest.

If you don't mind crowds, you can join the Barbados National Trust's weekly hikes, which cover the natural, historical and cultural aspects of the island.

The Portuguese were first to locate the island, calling it "Os Barbados" after the bearded fig trees growing on the beaches. However, the only impact the Portuguese had on the island was to leave behind some wild pigs, which thrived. Indians had been on Barbados for at least a thousand years, but they were gone—and only the pigs remained—when the English arrived to colonize in 1627.

One of the strangest early European visitors was Ferdinando Paleologus, who is buried in St. John's Church Yard. He claimed to be one of the last descendants of the Greek royal family, forced to flee Constantinople when the Turks invaded. He chose Barbados for his exile, though some say he was only a great impostor. In any case, the tale makes a good story and the "royal" grave is interesting to visit.

Barbados was one of the first Caribbean countries where sugar cane was introduced, brought by Jewish immigrants from Brazil in the early 1620s. Following its success here and in Martinique, sugar cane became the dominant crop of the Caribbean, a fact which has determined the social, environmental and economic climate even to this day.

Agriculturally, Barbados was far more blessed than many islands. Much of its limestone base had transformed into a rich, loamy soil. Even in recent years, as much as 80% of the land has been planted in sugar cane or sour grass, used as mulch and fodder for cattle.

Although tourism is now more important, sugar proved a solid bedrock for centuries. It was on the old Bajan sugar plantations that a whole new industry developed that would affect the rest of the Western world—the development of world-famous Barbados rum. The Spanish first distilled a spirit from the molasses residue left in the refining process, but considered the product so low-grade, it was fit for only slaves and Indians.

In Barbados, however, "Rumbullion" became a popular export appreciated throughout the hemisphere. Although rum technically may not have been invented in Barbados, the name clearly did originate here, and Barbados was the first country to export it.

Travel Tips

Area: 21 miles long and 14 miles wide, with almost 800 miles of hard-surface road.

Language: English; no other European culture ever gained a foothold here. The country has been referred to as "Little England."

Population: About 255,000 people, making it one of the most densely populated countries in the world.

Time Zone: Atlantic Standard Time, one hour ahead of Eastern Standard Time.

Rainy Season: Not very long, since Barbados boasts 3008 hours of sunshine annually. Temperatures vary between 75-85°, but winter nights with a brisk wind can be chilly.

Getting There: American Airlines offers frequent service, as does LIAT, BWIA, Air Canada and British Airways. Note that any tickets you purchase for trips originating in Barbados have an added 20% tax levied on them.

Getting Around: With 800 miles of paved road and a new highway from the airport, driving is the recommended way to see the island. Taxis

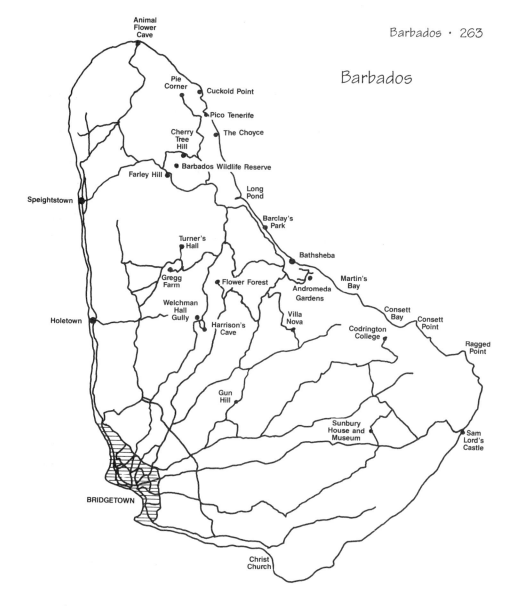

Barbados

can be expensive and drivers don't always go by the posted fares. Motor-cycles can be rented. A local driver's license (US $5 from one of the police stations) is necessary. Driving, of course, is on the left.

Where to Stay: Much of the Caribbean coast on the south and west sides is ringed with hotels, some of the Caribbean's best and most expensive. The rougher Atlantic side, generally too rough for safe swim-ming and diving, has a few hotels for those who want to be far away from the crowds. The Hilton, Grand Barbados and Cunard Paradise Beach are convenient to Bridgetown. Dumfries, a youth hostel, is also close to Bridgetown; 809/426-1449/4368. The tourist board can provide a list of guest houses, apartments and villas. Hotel rates can be as much as 50% less in summer.

Camping: Not permitted.

Taxes & Tips: A 5% government tax and 10% service tax are customary.

Documents: Barbados is considered one of the strictest countries for entry. A valid passport is required and some nationals need to arrange visas in advance. Neither a driver's license nor voter's registration card is acceptable. Technically, an ongoing ticket is also required for admittance. If in doubt about the length of your stay, over-estimate rather than under-estimate. If you decide to stay longer, you have to go to immigration for an extension and you could encounter problems when trying to re-enter the country at a later time.

Currency: Although everything is quoted in dollars and cents—it's in Bajan currency. One dollar US is worth $2 Bajan, so cut the posted prices by half to get the U.S. equivalent. Banks are open from 8 a.m. to 3 p.m. Monday through Thursday, and 8 a.m. to noon and 3 p.m. to 5 p.m. on Friday.

Electrical Current: 120 volts but 50 cycles instead of 60. Some hotels have transformers or 220 volt outlets.

Safety/Health Warnings: If you're out after dark, stay out of Nelson Street and the poorer areas of Bridgetown. In general, this is a very safe island.

Hiking/Walking Services: You're pretty much on your own unless you want to join one of the large weekend hikes sponsored by the National Trust. The times and places are posted in the local tourist brochures or call 809/42-62421 in Bridgetown.

Snakes and Other Venomous Creatures: None.

For More Information: Barbados Board of Tourism, 800 Second Ave., New York, NY 10017; toll-free 800/221-9831; fax 212/573-9850. In Canada, Suite 1508, Box 11, 20 Queen Street West, Toronto, Ontario M5H 3R3; 416/979-2137 or 800/268-9122. In the UK, 263 Tottenham Court Road, London, W1P 9AA; 071/636-9448/9; fax 637-1496.

 # Bridgetown on Foot

Time: 1-2 hours. **Difficulty:** 1.

Almost half the island population lives here. Bridgetown is a very easy place to walk around, taking a couple of hours at most to explore. This is a hot sun, so wear a good hat and sunblock.

1) Trafalgar Square: My biggest surprise in Bridgetown was finding a statue of Admiral Lord Nelson in a place called Trafalgar Square. I knew Barbados was "Little England," but this seemed a bit much. However, Bridgetown's Lord Nelson is not an imitation of London's. Native Bajans had a strong affection for Nelson. He visited Barbados, in command of the British fleet, just six months before his death at Trafalgar in 1805. The square was renamed Trafalgar and his statue erected in 1813, about thirty-six years ahead of England's more famous monument.

2) Dolphin Fountain/The Fountain Gardens: Bridgetown had piped-in water as early as 1861. A local newspaper suggested a proper fountain be erected in a central spot; the citizens donated money and the fountain, with its water-spewing dolphins, was installed in 1865. Work on the gardens surrounding the fountain didn't begin until 1882. Note the curious cannonball tree here.

3) Public Buildings: Barbados has the third-oldest parliamentary body in the English-speaking world, dating from 1639. The earliest building was built in 1640 but burned in the Bridgetown fire of 1668. For the next thirty years, the officials had to meet in people's homes and—quite frequently—public taverns. The west wing of this building was completed in 1871, the east in 1874. Both the Senate and House of Assembly meet here. Stained-glass windows in the east buildings depict many statesmen back to the time of Queen Victoria, including Oliver Cromwell.

4) Chamberlain Bridge: According to legend, the capital city of Bridgetown received its name from the Arawak Indian bridge the first settlers found spanning the inlet. Known simply as "The Bridge," it was changed later to Bridgetown. Today, the Chamberlain Bridge spans the inlet where the Indian bridge probably existed, at a spot known as The Careenage. The Careenage, a concentration of waterfront restaurants, colorful fishing boats and fishing charters, marks the place where the old sailing ships were tilted over (careened) so their bottoms could be scraped.

Note the colorful wooden boats in this area. These are the flying fish boats, for taking that most popular of local foods. Bajans eat flying fish the way Americans eat hamburgers.

5) The Independence Arch: Built in 1987 to mark the island's 21st year of independence.

6) St. Michael's Church: The present church was built in 1789 and became a cathedral in 1825. Its arched roof was at one time the widest in the world. Many famous Bajans are buried here.

7) Central Bank Building: At eleven stories, this is the tallest building on Barbados. It also contains a 500-seat modern concert hall. The entire structure cost $60 million.

8) The Synagogue & Montefiore Fountain: Claiming to be the oldest

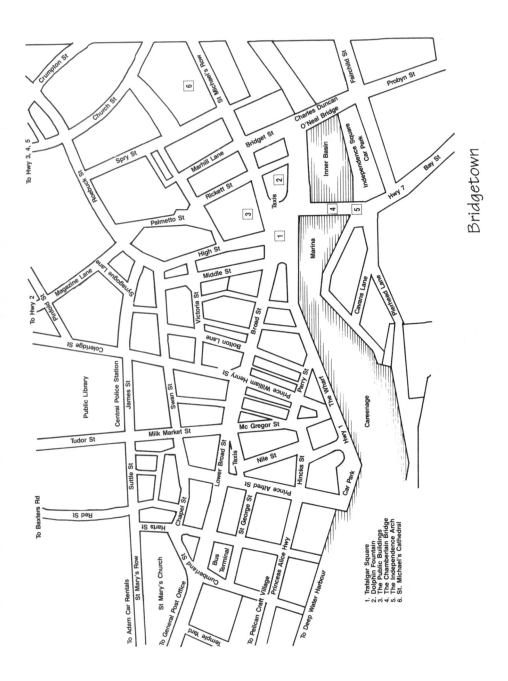

Bridgetown

1. Trafalgar Square
2. Dolphin Fountain
3. The Public Buildings
4. The Chamberlain Bridge
5. The Independence Arch
6. St. Michael's Cathedral

synagogue in the Western Hemisphere, the original building went up in 1654, came down in the hurricane of 1831 and was re-constructed in 1833. The adjoining Jewish Cemetery, still in use, has tombstones dating to the 1630s. The Jews who came to Barbados from Brazil in the 1620s introduced sugar cane to the Caribbean.

9) Pelican Village: Located near the Deep Water Harbour along Princess Alice Highway, this is the main arts and crafts center established by the government.

10) Queen's Park: Originally this was the residence of the person commanding the British troops in the West Indies. Before the days of Queen Victoria it was known as the King's House. The area is now undergoing renovation by the National Conservation Commission. A Baobab tree in the park with a sixty-one-and-a-half-foot circumference is the largest tree in Barbados. The tree, a native of Africa, is an estimated 1,000 years old. That seed had to float a long way in the ocean currents.

Out on the Island

 1. Farley Hill

Time: 30-45 minutes. **Difficulty:** 1.

Yet another opulent testament to the past glory of Bajan gentry is Farley Hill, once a beautiful mansion that was a regular stopover for visiting English royalty, including Prince George, later King George V. Farley Hill overlooks acres of cane fields; the grounds are well-forested and lushly landscaped. It is picturesque enough to be a movie set—and was—for *Island in the Sun*. Fire gutted the interior in 1965 and only the shell remains, but the site is still worth visiting for the panoramic view and a taste of the greatness that once existed. It is a protected park, with picnic tables set out under the trees near the abandoned great house.

2. Barbados Wildlife Reserve

Time: 1 hour. **Difficulty:** 1.

Located opposite Farley Hill, this small, three-acre sanctuary created in 1985 is to protect/control the green—or vervet—monkey imported from West Africa. This is the same pest found on St. Kitts and Nevis. Bounties were offered on these agricultural pests as early as 1680 because of the massive crop destruction they cause. They became a problem again during this century, and instead of reopening hunting of them, this wildlife reserve was created which manages the population through trapping and sale of the animals for use in medical research. "Green" monkeys are actually brownish-grey with green flecks. They are allowed to roam free in a sizable stand of mahogany trees. Other animals on exhibit include rabbits, caimans, agoutis and otters. A walk-in aviary is also featured.

3. St. Nicholas Abbey

Time: 45-60 minutes. **Difficulty:** 1.

The second-oldest building in the English-speaking world (the oldest is in Virginia), the surviving structure demonstrates that early sugar plantation owners lived as sumptuously as any English nobleman. Historically the most important home in all Barbados, built twenty-five years after the first settlement, the manor house is virtually in its original condition. That is partly due to its construction of durable coral stone. The main quarters are as sound today as when built sometime around 1650. One of the owners, a Sir John Yeamans, helped colonize South Carolina, becoming its third governor. Furnishings include antiques of European and Bajan origin.

4. Harrison's Cave

Time: 1-2 hours. **Difficulty:** 1.

This may not technically be a hike since it involves a tram ride underground before you can get out to look and photograph. However, it is one of the island's greatest natural spectacles. Harrison's Cave is a huge, natural, underground system charted as far back as 1760 but somehow lost until heavy rains opened an entrance a few years ago.

The government quickly recognized what a unique attraction this would make, so it built the Caribbean's first subterranean tram ride. This is a very organized excursion. After a slide presentation, you board a thirty-six passenger electric tram for an hour-long tour. Very effective use has been made of indirect lighting to magnify the eeriness and beauty of the caverns. Most memorable are the several cascading waterfalls and the great Rotunda Room, a 250-foot-long by 100-foot-high and wide chamber glistening with cream and white geologic formations. Tours are given every day on the hour, but since long lines can form, this is one place you do need advance reservations.

5. Welchman Hall Gully

Time: 1 hour. **Difficulty:** 1.

The Barbados National Trust owns this 3/4-mile-long natural gully. Part of a cave whose roof once collapsed, this humid gully is protected from high winds, allowing incredibly luxuriant plant life to grow out of the side walls. Its subterranean origin is revealed by a gigantic pillar more than four and one-half feet in diameter, reputedly the world's largest example of a stalactite and stalagmite coming together to form a single column. There are excellent views of the north end late and early in the day, which is a prime time to see lots of monkeys. There is an admission fee.

6. Turner's Hall Woods

Time: 1-2 hours. **Difficulty:** 1.

This fifty-acre farm contains a remnant of the lush tropical forest, including the indigenous Macaw Palm, that covered Barbados until the introduction of sugar cane in the 1600s. At least thirty-two species of trees have been identified, including Silk Cotton, Sandbox, Bulletwood, Trumpet Tree, Locust, Fustic and Cabbage Palm. The woods, with a fairly steep hiking trail of about a half-mile, are a popular place for walking and hiking, a showcase of Barbados at its most natural. The higher you walk, the thicker the vegetation. This is not a true rainforest, despite the multi-layered tree canopies and the presence of lianas and ferns. Only about sixty inches of rain falls here annually; a true rainforest receives 200 inches or more. The farm can be reached from above by the Gregg Farm-Turner's Hall Plantation Road, or near Haggats if coming in from below.

7. Atlantic Coast

Time: You can plan several hikes for this area: Ragged Point to Consett Point, 2 hours; Consett Bay to Martin's Bay, 2 hours; Martin's Bay to Bathsheba, 1-1/2 hours; and Bathsheba to The Choyce and Pico Tenerife, 4 hours. All times are one way. **Difficulty:** 1-3 depending on hike.

The Atlantic Coast, one of the best spots on Barbados to get away from the crowds, is reminiscent of the British isles.

As you'll soon discover, everything in Barbados is located according to its parish. Scotland District, with its stone fences and sloping green hillsides, does indeed recall the British Isles. It's a beautiful stretch for a walk, either on the beach or on the road. The beaches can be wide or narrow. One of the best places for walking is near Barclay's Park just north of the town of Bathsheba. Between Bathsheba, almost to Long Point, the road parallels the coast, one of the easiest places for walking. Yet, you'd be surprised how few tourists ever stop to enjoy this area. The giant boulders scattered along the coastline near Bathsheba are an awesome sight, especially on a rough day. Andromeda's Garden, a scenic overlook and tiny garden, is just beyond Bathsheba. Also of interest is the region around Pie Corner because of the artifacts left by the Indians; and I would love to learn how nearby Cuckold Point got its name.

 8. Gun Hill

Time: 30 minutes. **Difficulty:** 1.

This was a 17th-century signal station as well as garrison for soldiers. The ten-foot-tall, white limestone lion standing at Gun Hill commemorates British strength of centuries past. Its inscription translates, "He shall have dominion from sea to sea and from the rivers unto the end of the world." This commands a stunning view of the entire southern half of the island, best viewed in late afternoon. Soldiers were once sent here to convalesce.

9. Gardens & Great Houses

1) The Flower Forest in St. Joseph parish is a fifty-acre tropical garden on an old plantation. It offers many beautiful trees and shrubs and spectacular views. The plants are labeled for a self-guided walk. There is an admission fee.

2) Animal Flower Cave receives its name from the sea anemones that once lived here in great numbers, but which have now largely disappeared. Admission fee.

3) Codrington College, which opened in 1745, has become the oldest seminary in the Western Hemisphere. It has scenic grounds. No fee.

4) The Sunbury House and Museum have one of the island's finest collections of antique furniture, antique tools and vehicles. Admission fee.

5) Villa Nova is another superbly preserved "great house," this one from 1834. The tropical gardens are beautiful. Queen Elizabeth once visited here. One of the owners was a former British prime minister, the late Sir Anthony Eden, Earl of Avon.

10. Christ Church

Time: 30-45 minutes. **Difficulty:** 1.

As this is written, the Christ Church presently standing is the fifth parish church. All the others were destroyed by hurricane, flood and fire; not a tranquil place. The happenings at Christ Church in the 1800s are more than an eerie tale. Rather, they are true historical oddities yet to be fully explained. This is where the famous moving coffins of Barbados kept shifting around in the sealed Chase Vault.

The well-documented unsolved mystery is as follows: in 1812 the vault was opened for burial of Col. Thomas Chase. To everyone's amazement, the heavy lead coffins were found scattered about the vault. The same situation was observed twice in 1816 and once in 1817. At the next opening, in 1819, the Governor of Barbados was present when the vault was reopened. Once again the scattered coffins were put back in their proper place and the governor placed his royal seal in the vault as it was cemented closed. In 1820, the coffins were found again to be strewn about the vault. Practical joke? A true but unexplainable phenomenon? The matter was resolved when all the coffins were removed and buried separately in the churchyard, where they have happily stayed to this day. Obviously, the family that lives together doesn't always want to spend eternity together.

11. Sam Lord's Castle

Time: 30-60 minutes. **Difficulty:** 1.

Sam Lord's Castle is the administrative building for the huge Marriott resort of the same name, but the grounds and former residence are open to the public. Sam Lord was a Bajan planter, reputedly the local version of Blackbeard the pirate, though of a more refined nature. Instead of stalking and attacking merchant ships at sea, Sam Lord lured them onto the reefs near his home. He supposedly built his Castle in 1820 from the spoils taken off the wrecks. The castle looks more like a theme park exhibit than the real thing, but take a look at the furniture, paintings, plaster ceilings and beautiful mahogany columns inside. You will be convinced of Sam Lord's wealth, if not his good taste. The windy beach with its big stands of coconut palms is also worth a look.

17. Grenada

Old Grenadian Proverb:
If you have patience, you will see ant's belly.

Translation:
If you wait long enough, you will get what you want.

Grenada is one of the Caribbean's lushest landfalls, rich in rainforest, waterfalls and agriculture. It so reminded early Spanish sailors of the beloved green hillsides above their home port, they named it Granada. However, the French and British later corrupted the name to a different spelling and pronunciation. The Spanish city of Granada is called "Grah-NAH-dah," while the deep Caribbean island of Grenada is known as "Greh-NAY-dah."

Located 158 miles southwest of Barbados and 100 miles north of Venezuela, Grenada is only twelve miles wide and twenty-one miles long, yet its mountainous interior provides much scenic—and accessible—hiking. Grenada began protecting its natural resources well before the concept of "ecotourism" was invented, so the landscape is wonderfully unspoiled.

Grenada's highest mountains receive more than 160 inches of rain a year, creating a verdant forest with 450 species of flowering plants, 85 different types of trees and 150 kinds of birds.

Called "the spice basket of the Caribbean," Grenada produces twelve different spices, including cloves, nutmeg, ginger, cinnamon and mace. Sailors claim they can smell their sweet fragrance as much as twenty miles out at sea. Grenada's most important spice is nutmeg, supposedly introduced to the island in 1843 as a surprise addition to the rum punch at a local bash. Since then, no one in Grenada would consider drinking rum punch without it. Nutmeg is also used locally against colds and is even an

Grenada

ingredient in the Vicks VapoRub cold remedy. Grenada is the world's second-largest nutmeg producer, after Indonesia.

Grenada had been an independent country within the British Commonwealth since 1974. Grenada received world-wide publicity in October, 1983, when the U.S. invaded the country, an action the grateful Grenadians refer to as "The Intervention" because it brought them a democratic government. American troops were warmly welcomed when they came ashore, and Americans are still held in high regard by most locals. Of course, Reagan's $57.2 million commitment to stabilizing the Grenadian economy, which transformed the pitiful road and telephone systems into some of the Caribbean's best, didn't hurt.

Overall, Grenada rates as one of the friendliest Caribbean isles for visitors from all lands. The main port city of St. George's, a horseshoe-shaped harbor known as the Carenage, is very photogenic. Its Saturday morning market is lively and colorful, perhaps the best open-air market in all the Caribbean. The best place to photograph it is from a balcony, overlooking all the activity.

Travel Tips

Area: 21 miles long, 7 miles wide.

Language: English

Population: 115,000

Time Zone: Atlantic Standard Time, one hour ahead of Eastern Standard Time.

Rainy Season: The rainy season lasts from June through November. Although the sun is frequently out in coastal areas during this period, you can count on the mountains being socked in. Rain may last for several days at a time in summer.

Getting There: American Airlines flies into the Point Salines Airport. BWIA also serves Grenada through Antigua. British Airways flies to Grenada weekly from London, Heathrow via Antigua.

Getting Around: Cars rent for an average of US $40 per day. A local driving permit (US $12) is not required if you have an international driver's license. Driving is on the left. Taxis are plentiful and fares are set by the tourist board. A water shuttle runs regularly to Grand Anse Beach from the Nutmeg Restaurant in St. George's.

Where to Stay: Grenada's major hotels tend to emphasize personalized service, which means they are much smaller than the norm. The Ramada Inn, with 186 rooms, is the island's largest property. The next largest, Liberty Club, has fewer than fifty rooms. Most are located along Grand Anse Beach or in L'Anse aux Epines Bay. Away from the normal tourist route and costing 30% less than the normal US $150 per night are: the ten-room Mama's Lodge on Lagoon Road (809/440-1459), which is affiliated with the legendary Mama's Restaurant, still family owned and operated; and the eight room Tita's Guest House in St. George's where guests share bathrooms (809/444-2390). Villas can be arranged through Grenada Realtors Ltd. Box 124, St. George's (809/444-4255).

Camping: Available in the Grand Etang National Park in the cool tropical rain forest.

Taxes & Tips: Hotels have an 8% tax and a 10% service charge. Meals are subject to a 20% VAT.

Documents: A passport is necessary for all but U.S. citizens, who will need two documents, one with a photograph, proving citizenship.

Currency: The East Caribbean Dollar (EC$) is the local currency. The exchange rate for US $1 is about $2.67 for hard currency and $2.68 for traveler's checks. US currency is freely exchanged in stores but the exchange rate there is much less than at the banks, down to about $2.60. Banks are open 8 a.m. to noon or 8 a.m. to 2 p.m. Monday-Thursday and from 2:30 p.m to 5 p.m. on Friday.

Electrical Current: 220/50 cycles. A transformer is needed for all U.S. appliances.

Hiking/Walking Services: Grenada boasts the services of two of the Caribbean's best, Denis Henry of Henry's Tours (809/443-5313) and Telfor Bedeau (809/440-8163). I highly recommend either one. They approach hikes differently, so choose the style you're most comfortable with.

Telfor is one of the Caribbean's original hiking guides, in business since 1962. He explains his background and philosophy:

"I started with some youngsters—but we were all young at the time—not even thinking I would be hiking thirty years later. So far I have covered over 350 hikes and walked a total distance of over 6,000 miles. So these legs of mine have done a wonderful job and I don't know how long they will continue, but I plan to keep hiking as long as I am fit. I have hopes of getting younger folks (Grenadians) interested, so that instead of doing all sorts of nonsense and mischief, they will go hiking, learn about their country and make themselves better citizens."

Telfor Bedeau is based at his home in Soubise, about a mile south of Grenville, and at present all his organized hikes begin and return from his home base. The reason: Telfor doesn't have a car yet to transport people to other parts of the island. Should you have a car and engage Telfor for a day, the entire island is at your disposal. On the other hand, Denis Henry has a fourteen-passenger, air-conditioned van and makes many of the same hikes.

Both Telfor's and Henry's hikes are designed not just to walk but also examine closely the best parts of the countryside, including waterfalls, old buildings or plantations still under cultivation. Henry (who goes by his last name) advises that mosquitoes are a problem down low in the rainy season (July through September) when the insects "just want to be friendly, to rest for a while on your arm for a taste of sweet blood." Henry also says that in the dry season he can almost promise to take you "into the rainforest in your white sneakers but they stay clean enough that you can still play tennis afterwards."

Snakes and Other Venomous Creatures: None.

For More Information: Grenada Dept. of Tourism, 820 2nd Avenue, Suite 900-D, New York, NY 10017; 212/687-9554 or 800/927-9554. In Canada, the Grenada Tourist Office, Suite 820, 439 University Avenue, Toronto, Ontario M5G 1Y8; 416/595-1339. In the UK, Grenada High

Commission, 1 Collington Gardens, London SW5 0HW; 071/370-5164/5; fax 071/370-7040.

 Walking Tour of St. George's

Time: 2 hours. **Length:** 1 mile. **Difficulty:** 1 (2 up steep hills).

The harbor, easily accommodating cruise ships, was once an inland lake, and may be the crater of an extinct volcano. The town of St. George's is one of the Caribbean's most attractive. The old homes are painted delicate shades of yellow, beige and rose; their second stories flaunt ornate ironwork balconies.

St. George's is divided by the spine of a steep hill: the most picturesque is the harbor side, known as the Carenage, while the drab-looking Esplanade side fronts the Caribbean. However, the small mountain cutting through St. George's is quite steep, so this is not an easy walk. During the annual carnival, the floats have to be winched up and down the main roads because motorized vehicles have great difficulty hauling heavy loads up and down the dramatic inclines.

1) **"Bianca C" Statue:** Commemorates the gallantry of the Grenadian people in saving passengers aboard the 600-foot Italian luxury liner which caught fire in St. George's Harbour in 1961. Three crewmen were killed in the boiler explosion. The "Bianca C" now rests in 160 feet of water offshore, the largest Caribbean wreck accessible to scuba divers.

2) **Cannon and Cobblestones:** This is an excellent example of St. George's many cobblestone streets and illustrates a practical use for all the old cannons removed from Grenada's various forts. The cannon are used as bollards to tie up ships and to protect corners of masonry walls from cars and trucks.

3) **National Library:** A former brick warehouse is where the library has been located since 1892; the library itself was established in 1846.

4) **Warehouse Roofs:** Look closely at the red tiles on these 18th- and 19th-century stone and brick warehouses. They are fish-scale tiles originally brought in as ballast.

5) **Antilles Hotel:** One of St. George's oldest buildings, it has served as French barracks, a British prison, a hotel and a warehouse. Now the Grenadian National Museum, it houses a small collection of artifacts and old newspapers dramatizing the island's history and culture. Included are Arawak petroglyphs, the marble bathtub of Empress Josephine (who grew up on Martinique) and a rum still.

6) **Traffic Police Control Station:** Watch the policeman control traffic

St. George's

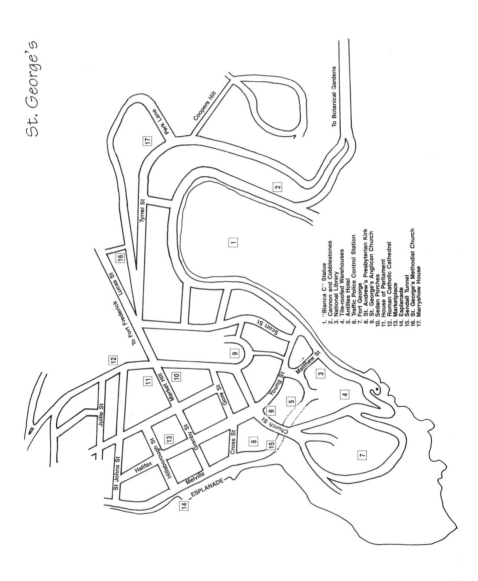

1. "Bianca C" Statue
2. Cannon and Cobblestones
3. National Library
4. Tile-roofed Warehouses
5. Antilles Hotel
6. Traffic Police Control Station
7. Fort George
8. St. Andrew's Presbyterian Kirk
9. St. George's Anglican Church
10. Sedan Porches
11. House of Parliament
12. Roman Catholic Cathedral
13. Marketplace
14. Esplanade
15. Sendall Tunnel
16. St. George's Methodist Church
17. Marryshow House

as he stands safely above the motorized vehicles in a special box. Considering the steep inclines, this is the only way drivers from all directions can see the traffic signals. Stoplights have yet to appear in Grenada.

7) Fort George: Built by the French in 1705 to overlook the harbor mouth, it is now the city's main police station. The imposing fort supposedly contains a system of underground tunnels once linked to other fortifications. A tour is difficult and can be made only through advance arrangement. This is where Maurice Bishop and his colleagues were killed in 1983, prompting U.S. intervention.

8) St. Andrew's Presbyterian Kirk: Better known as Scot's Kirk and located on Church Street, it was built in 1831 with assistance from the Freemasons.

9) St. George's Anglican Church: This beautiful stone and pink stucco building was completed in 1825. It contains many plaques commemorating British victims of Fedon's Rebellion, a slave uprising of 1765.

10) Sedan Porches: These porches are open at both ends so wealthy planters in sedan chairs could travel under the row of roofs and avoid the rain.

11) House of Parliament: Both the Senate and House of Representatives of Grenada meet here.

12) Roman Catholic Cathedral: The tower dates from 1818 and is the oldest part; the rest of the cathedral is much later, built in 1884 on the site of an 1804 church.

13) Marketplace: Site of the unbelievably colorful fruit and vegetable display on Saturdays, where women sell small bags of spice (cloves, cinnamon and nutmeg) to tourists as useful and fragrant reminders of Grenada. The spices sold are pretty much the same; it is the colorful packaging (cloth sack, straw box or reed box) that should determine who you buy from. Take time to shop and compare; the spice ladies won't go anywhere, I assure you.

14) Esplanade: The commercial waterfront area of St. George's, including the fish market, most active at the end of the day when the catch is brought in, or almost anytime on Saturday.

15) Sendall Tunnel: named after the governor when this technological wonder was completed in 1895. Still used today, the 340-foot-long tunnel is a shortcut through the hill to link the Carenage with the Esplanade. Not to be walked because of the heavy traffic.

16) St. George's Methodist Church: Built in 1820, it is the oldest original church building in St. George's.

17) Marryshow House: This fine creole building was the home of T.A. Marryshow, the Grenadian leader who attempted to turn the entire West Indies into one nation. Today, it is the local center for the University of the West Indies, headquartered in Trinidad.

St. George's Saturday morning market is one of the liveliest of any island.

Hiking Grand Etang National Park

Situated high in true tropical rain forest where the mountain peaks are frequently obscured by clouds, Grand Etang Park is a wonderful example to governments around the world. Grand Etang, headquarters for Grenada's National Park System, is supported by the British Development Division, the United Nations Development Program, The Organization of American States, the U.S. Peace Corps, the U.S. Agency for International Development and the government of Grenada. That's quite an impressive array of backers, and it makes one wish this sort of international cooperation was a commonplace practice, not something to point out as unusual.

Grenada's best hiking is in the Grand Etang National Park. Only eight miles from the center of St. George's, the park is more than 2,000 feet above sea level, high enough to cause decompression sickness (the bends) in anyone foolish enough to scuba dive, then go hiking the same day. Grand Etang ("large pond" in French) is named after a small lake there, actually an old volcanic crater.

The park vegetation is extremely diverse, including cloud forests, montane thickets, palm brakes, and elfin woodland, as well as rainforest. A modest interpretive center called the Park Centre has a receptionist and guide who, if contacted in advance, will personally escort you. Displays also feature the island's wildlife, forestry and natural history, including more than twenty different wood samples. Several small food stands located near the Park Centre sell cold drinks.

Most hiking trails are well-marked and require little assistance, although it's always more enjoyable to have a guide who can share the local folklore. With 160 inches of rain falling annually, the trails can be quite muddy and slick.

 ## 1. Morne LaBaye Trail

Time: 15 minutes. **Length:** Less than 1 mile. **Difficulty:** 1.

An interpretive trail with excellent examples of Grenada's rich foliage begins in back of the Park Centre. One of the first plants displayed is the endemic Grand Etang fern, found in this area of Grenada and nowhere else in the world. The fern has a distinctive spore pattern under the fronds. Unlike most other plants, ferns reproduce by spores instead of seeds. The mountain palms, whose fruit and fronds Grenadians use in many different ways, are also characteristic of this part of montane forest.

You'll observe an interesting symbiotic relationship between the slender bois canot tree (Cereropia) and the ants living in its hollow trunk.

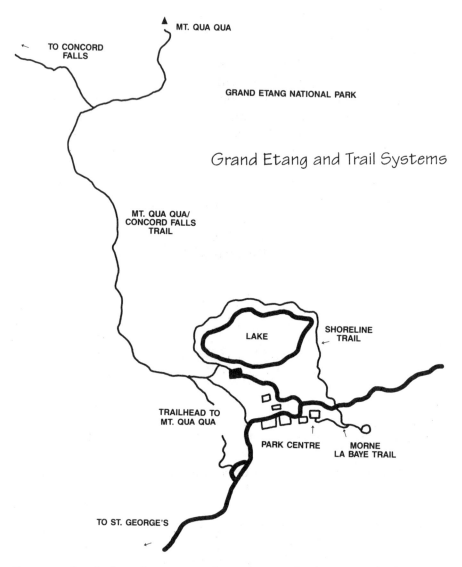

▲ MT. QUA QUA

TO CONCORD FALLS

GRAND ETANG NATIONAL PARK

Grand Etang and Trail Systems

MT. QUA QUA/ CONCORD FALLS TRAIL

LAKE

SHORELINE TRAIL

TRAILHEAD TO MT. QUA QUA

PARK CENTRE

MORNE LA BAYE TRAIL

TO ST. GEORGE'S

In return for shelter, the ants repel possums and other animals that try to climb the tree to graze on tender new shoots. What botanists call a pioneer species, bois canot is one of the first to reappear after severe hurricane winds destroy a forest.

Another pioneer species is the colorful heliconia (or balisier, pronounced "bah-lee-zyay"), a member of the banana family. You've probably seen the blooms, shaped like a long row of lobster claws, made into decorative bouquets in hotel rooms. These yellow, orange or red ornamentals have flower-like bracts that are almost scimitar-shaped.

You'll have to look skyward to see the tall marouba tree, with its spreading branches and small leaves. The marouba takes its nourishment from the sun above the high canopy, instead of from the forest soil. Locals say marouba bark can drug or stun fish, making them easy to catch.

Besides bamboo, the Morne LaBaye Trail contains lots of elephant grass, which resembles sugar cane, but is distinguished by its jointed stem. Elephant grass was originally planted decades ago to provide convenient refueling stops for horse and donkey-drawn wagons crossing the island. It is still used for fodder when meadows on the farms wither away in the dry season.

At the morne ("small hill" in French) itself is a small weather station which monitors the complex and frequently changing conditions of Grand Etang. At the River Turning Crater you'll find lingering evidence of Hurricane Janet's destruction in 1955: a stand of huge, dead gommier (gum) trees, now serving as display posts for countless air plants.

The gommier (Dacryodes excelsa) is the most common large tree of the rain forest. Its bark contains a gum that can be used to light fires. These gommier trees have no bark. Their trunks withstood the hurricane's 150-mph winds, but their branches and leaves were stripped away. Unable to photosynthesize (the process which turns sunlight into the sugar), they died.

2. Grand Etang Shoreline Trail

Time: 1-1/2 hours, round trip. **Length:** 2-3 miles. **Difficulty:** 2.

This relatively easy walk begins on the Morne LaBaye Trail and encircles the lake at the edge of the palm break.

Grand Etang, in the caldera of an extinct volcano, has five different sub-climatic plant communities. This is one of the Caribbean's few hikes as high as 2,000 feet: be more prepared for wind and cold than for hot sun.

Before reaching the lake, you'll cross a small pond. Look closely into this runoff from the lake, and you may be able to spot both crayfish and ling (a small-scale freshwater lobster).

Moving along the lake shore, you'll walk through a palm break dominated by fern trees and mountain palm (Euterpe palm). Above the palm break is a colorful forest of mahogany trees with orange, scarlet and yellow hibiscus growing on the trees. The mahogany was brought in from Jamaica after Hurricane Janet. Besides helping reforest Grenada, the timber has a remarkable blue/green grain that makes outstanding furniture and handicrafts; it's also used in fencing.

If you didn't see any Mona monkeys hanging out at the food stands near the Park Centre, you're almost certain to spot some around the lake. Most active at sunrise and sunset, as they swing through the forest canopy, Mona monkeys were brought from northern Africa during the early days of slavery. If you don't see them, listen for their deep "buff-buff" grunt as they call out to one another. Mona monkeys (and possums) like to hang out in the clusters of giant bamboo, which grow as high as sixty feet.

Incidentally, Grenadians don't anthropomorphize their animals (they did not grow up watching Bambi and Thumper or other cuddly Walt Disney characters) but make full use of their wildlife. So you'll not only see monkeys as pets, you sometimes will find monkey—and possum and armadillo—on the menu at Mama's and other restaurants in St. George's. The monkey and armadillo are tasty; pass on the possum.

Along the shoreline are cattle egrets, which migrated from Africa and first appeared in Grenada around 1950; hooded tanagers (iridescent plumage with a black cap) and little blue herons. The symbol of Grenada's national park system is the broadwinged hawk (brown and white with a banded tail), which likes to soar high over the water. The lake itself is slowly filling with reeds and may one day become a grassy marsh.

3. Mt. Qua Qua Trail

Time: 2-1/2 to 3 hours, round trip. **Length:** 3 miles. **Difficulty:** 3-4, depending on slipperiness.

The hike to Mt. Qua Qua passes through true rainforest which is apt to live up to its name suddenly, so bring a windbreaker for showers and the cool tradewinds. Take water and snacks for a break at the summit.

This is a challenging hike leading to the rocky summit of Mt. Qua Qua and its famous view of the northeast coast. At various points there are also some good panoramas of distant Grand Etang. This is an excellent hike for photography but keep your camera in a backpack or holster; you need both hands for scrambling up and grabbing tree roots.

The Mt. Qua Qua trailhead begins a few hundred feet from the Park Centre, off the paved road leading to St. George's. A sign on the right clearly marks the start.

You'll experience little gradient until you pass a junction sign leading to the Grand Etang trail on the right. From this point the trail keeps going up and down, sometimes quite steeply, and the red clay soil along the crater rim is icy-slick when wet. In some places, the slippery trail is only a few feet wide: dramatic dropoffs on either side demand caution. As troublesome as this wet clay may be, early settlers found it ideal for chinking their wood and bamboo dwellings.

As you start to climb, the plants and trees on the lake slope take on the characteristics of elfin woodland, forest that's been stunted and sculpted by the ever-constant tradewinds. In fact, on windward slopes throughout Grenada you'll see similar formations.

Interpretive "Q" signs mark several places. Q1 is a vantage point to appreciate how the foliage overlooking the lakes have been sculpted and stunted by constant high winds to form the fairy-like elfin woodland. Q2 is a large bui tree (Micropholis chrysophyuoides) blown over by Hurricane Janet; its huge roots make good shelter from the rain. Q3 identifies many mosses overhanging the trail. Forest workers use the moss, which is almost always damp, to wrap around newly grafted tree branches to speed healing.

Q4: This is razor grass, which you want to avoid. It's sharp enough to cut through light clothing. If you feel compelled to test its edge but want to avoid drawing blood, use a blade of it to shave some hair off the back of your arm. Q5 is a mountain almond (Bandizabocu) which has a distinctive mottled bark; it produces a large, inedible fruit in the fall.

Q6 is a bois gris or bagui tree, an excellent hardwood that becomes even stronger in water, making it a preferred material for docks and sea jetties. Q7 is a possible landslide area, so be careful near the edge. It offers a good view of Grand Anse beach and the southern end of the island. Many of the trees descending to the valley below (an important watershed region) are bois jab or tree ferns.

Proceeding, you'll see a clearing on the left: a fire break not worth following. Instead, keep bearing to the right, where purple orchids drape over the different bushes.

Q8 marks the boundary into true elfin forest, which looks like it's kept cut back and miniaturized by Japanese bonsai artists; yet it's all wind effect.

As long as you grab tree roots and trunks where necessary to combat the mud, you should have no real problem making it to the top of Mt. Qua Qua, 2,372 feet above sea level. Near the summit you won't even be walking on clay, but a thick mat of tree roots. You'll know when you've begun walking on air because your ground support will suddenly feel spongy, almost trampoline-like. The situation lasts for only a few yards; and quite memorable ones they are, too, since the real ground is a couple hundred feet below.

Even though the Mt. Qua Qua trail is marked clearly enough that no guide is necessary, I met several people who'd turned back, claiming the trail was too slippery and impassable.

Grenada's hiking can be extremely scenic. This is the trail to Mount Qua Qua with Grand Etang Lake in the background.

You know you've arrived at the summit when you reach a tall boulder on the right and you have a wonderful view of the eastern mountains, the windward coast and the new Point Salines airport.

Walk around the high boulder to a pathway between it and another large rock. Step to the edge and—after the hot, humid climb—greet what feels like all the winds of the world. Amazingly, it's only the full, unblunted force of the twenty-two mile-per-hour trades that blow constantly across the peak, the same northeast-north breezes that brought Columbus and the other early explorers across the Atlantic. If the breeze is too much (it will be around twelve degrees colder than at sea level), backtrack and shelter in the boulder's lee side. If you're up for some rock climbing, it's possible to scale the summit boulder for an even more elevated look around.

 4. Concord Falls
(including Fedon's Camp)

Time: 4-1/2 hours, one way, including 1 hour on the Mt. Qua Qua trail. There is no need to make the return to Grand Etang Park. **Length:** about

10 miles. **Difficulty:** 3-4, depending on how wet the conditions. A walking stick is advisable.

There are several ways to visit the falls, one easy (so easy you don't even have to get out of your vehicle), and one quite challenging. Since one of the reasons you're in Grenada is to walk, let's look at the more difficult option first. It involves taking the first hour of the Mt. Qua Qua trail, then branching off left, to the falls, for the climb down.

The Concord Falls Trail wanders under rainforest canopy, over hilltop vistas and across clear streams, putting you in the heart of the Grenada countryside, where you will see most of the eighty-five different species of trees.

The Concord Falls Trail has a limited number of interpretive markers. Branching off from the Mt. Qua Qua path and going down, C1 indicates numerous trees at the beginning of the descent, mostly handsome small-leafed santai (Slonea caribea). Despite its appearance, the wood is not durable and so not widely used. C2 marks the bois rouge tree (Guavea macrophylloides), known for its attractive red grain, popular in furniture making.

Grisly as it might sound, if you fall off the mountain you'll probably be shipped home in a relative of C3. The bois lait tree (Neoxythece pallida) is used primarily in making coffin boards, since the white timber is very tolerant of wetness. The tree produces tiny red blossoms in September.

Symbolically, opposite the coffin board marker and off to the right is a steep, thirty minute climb to Fedon's Camp, a site associated with some of Grenada's greatest blood-letting. Julien Fedon was a Grenadian hero, a mulatto planter who led the slave uprising of 1765. The flag motto of "Liberte, Egalite ou la Mort" was closely adhered to: it was death for almost everyone involved.

With supplies brought in from Guadeloupe, Fedon and the slaves overran Grenada, slaughtering many British settlers and suspected collaborators. Fedon had such control of Grenada he was able to take the British governor and fifty other hostages to his mountain stronghold, where he murdered them. The British spent a year retaking the island and capturing the revolt's ringleaders, who were executed or exiled to Honduras. Fedon himself was never taken, and is believed to have escaped—perhaps to Cuba—or drowned while attempting to reach Trinidad. Fedon's insurrection left Grenada in a shambles.

Fedon's former estate at Belvedere, from which he masterminded the revolt, is below the peak known as Fedon's Camp. The Fedon's Camp lookout has a superb view.

Continuing down the Concord Falls Trail, C4 designates the broad-leaf seegum plant used for cattle fodder. It must be good stuff, because locals warn against feeding too much of it, or the cattle may get "too fat to breed." C5 is the sturdy mauricif (Byrsonima martincensus) used to build scaffolding. The mauricif is typical of many rainforest trees that have buttress roots to hold the trees upright in the shallow soil. Frequent rainfall leaches the soil of nutrients, which is replenished only by decomposing leaves and animal bodies. Because of the poor soil, 80% of the nutrients in a rainforest are hoarded in the plants themselves, leaving only 20% in the soil; that's the exact opposite of a temperate forest, where the soil is typically thick and rich.

The tight-grained, hard fibers of the penny piece (C6) is burned to make cooking charcoal. It also provides a yellow, edible plum-like fruit in May and June. C7 is the maruba tree (Simarouba amara) which resists warping and splitting, making it highly prized for construction.

After passing the damarin tree at C8, descend the slope to the river carefully. The official trail terminates across the river on the right, but you'll have a choice of whether to travel another ten minutes on a very obvious pathway to either the lower or upper Concord Falls.

As lower Concord Falls is a very popular tourist attraction, especially with cruise ships visitors, you may find the gaggle of tourists annoying after the solitude of the mountains. I recommend postponing your re-entry into civilization; take the left trail to the more secluded upper falls for a plunge in the large natural pool. After five hours on the trail, you'll be ready for a dip. Most tourists who see Concord Falls merely drive to the lower waterfall, look and leave; only a few take the extra twenty minutes to walk to these upper falls.

At the lower falls you can buy drinks as well as paddle around in the basin. Walking this last leg, you'll pass through a nutmeg plantation. The nutmeg trees, always green, grow sixty feet tall. Their fruit looks like a small yellow apple, and is popular for making jams and preserves. When ripe, the fruit splits open and falls to the ground, revealing a brown shell covering the brown nut inside with a red wax netting over it. The red wax netting is the source of the spice called mace. The brown nut is processed into nutmeg. If you want to see how the whole process is carried out, visit the Grenada Nutmeg Cooperative Association in Gouyave.

Concord Falls is normally a crowded place, so you may be able to get a taxi back to your hotel. If not, walk downhill another thirty minutes to Concord Village and flag down a St. George's-bound minibus; they run until 5 p.m. Monday-Saturday.

Concord Falls The Hard Way: make the ascent up from Concord Falls, climbing to Grand Etang. That takes about six hours, a 4-5 difficulty level.

5. The Seven Sisters

Time: 1-3 hours each way, depending on guide. **Difficulty:** 2-3.

The Seven Sisters is a series of cascading waterfalls with deep pools, located a mile below the Grand Etang. They are far more remote than Concord Falls. Guides Telfor Bedeau and Denis Henry offer different approaches, though both will custom-tailor their hikes.

Telfor walks for several hours through small towns like Grenville, Lower Capital, and Birch Grove, before reaching the falls, a round trip that takes all day. Or he may spend more time in the forest by heading up the Villa Road onto Mount St. Thomas and La Digue, then go through Belviewland to Dry River, a route for the more sure-footed hiker, because there is no forest trail and you've got to make your way unassisted.

Denis Henry usually drives to the closest approach and then hikes forty-five to sixty minutes to the falls, taking a picnic lunch and making it a more leisurely outing. Since Henry begins walking closer to the Seven Sisters, he can also lead you from the base of the falls to the top, ending at the Park Centre. One approach is not necessarily better than the other; it depends on how much walking you care to do and how many different parts of Grenada you wish to see. In either case, you end up walking to the falls on a rugged road of stones that requires careful footing. At the falls are two large pools for swimming. From the bottom, the most you can see is two sets of waterfalls, known as St. Margaret's Falls.

6. Beach Hike

Time: about 8 hours. **Difficulty:** 3.

Telfor Bedeau's most popular easy hike is from home in Soubise to Carobet Beach.

In Telfor's own words:

"We leave Soubise at seven and we walk down southward to Marquis, a little village that's the straw capital of Grenada. They use the wild pine to make hats and bags and mats and so on. Close to Marquis itself we have one of the most spectacular waterfalls in Grenada, the Mt. Carmel Falls, what some people also call Shoto.

"From Marquis we enter another village which we call La Poterie, a little way inland from the main road. From La Poterie, we head into beautiful, isolated areas. At each beach we reach we take a dip, so we walk with our trunks on. Some of the hikers, while crossing the stream, might pretend to fall just to take a dip. Then we take another dip when we end in the bay before we climb over the other headland. At the end we sometimes roast breadfruit or have smoked herring or some type of thing. We bathe or relax or sometimes we play cricket on the beach. Around 2 or 3 o'clock in the evening we set out for home again. That's what we call a small hike."

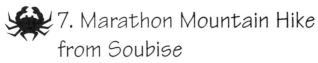

7. Marathon Mountain Hike from Soubise

Time: About 10-12 hours. **Length:** 30 miles, including six mountain peaks. **Difficulty:** 5.

This is the hike Telfor Bedeau recommends for "tough guys who like to walk." "There are several ways we can go. By the end, you will have walked thirty miles and over six mountain peaks. This is one for the real front-line hikers, the tested hikers."

8. Annandale Falls

Time: 30 minutes, round trip unless you picnic, swim, whatever. **Difficulty:** 1.

At the other extreme of the marathon mountain hike is this easy—though hilly—walk, to a mountain stream regularly visited by tourists and Grenadians alike. The stream falls fifty feet into a beautiful tropical pool surrounded by elephant ears and lianas. You're allowed to swim or picnic.

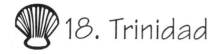 18. Trinidad

Trinidadian Saying:
Okra don't bear peas.

Translation:
Children inherit traits.

Trinidad, the southernmost of all Caribbean islands, has more different bird and animal species than any other island. Trinidad is an extension of the Venezuelan mainland, an annex of South America instead of part of the West Indies. Its Northern Range is actually an eastern spur of the Andes, all that remains of a sunken mountain range. Situated seven miles off the coast, Trinidad was joined to South America as recently as 10,000 years ago.

Trinidad boasts 108 different mammals (many of which are bats), compared to the handful found on most Caribbean islands. Ocelots, Capuchin and Howler monkeys and wild hogs are just a few of the animals Trinidadians refer to as "moving scenery."

Trinidad is butterfly heaven, with 620 different species. The variety of orchids—700 types—is unbelievably diverse. As for reptiles, Trinidad has fifty-five different kinds, twenty-five of amphibians. At least 2,300 species of flowering plants are known to exist.

Plants and animals thrive because Trinidad's terrain is so diverse. Roughly rectangular in shape and 50% forested, Trinidad is crossed by mountain ranges, savannahs, undulating plains and brackish and fresh water swamps. Elfin forest, montane rain forest and lowland rain forest, along with the fresh and salt water swamps, all contribute vital habitat.

Although Columbus discarded Trinidad's Indian name, Lere, meaning "land of the hummingbird," thousands of hummingbirds representing several dozen different species still remain. Like most of the 400 different avian species found on Trinidad (and Tobago), they are primarily

South American birds, not the typical West Indian varieties. The bird population here contrasts so greatly from that of the Northern Caribbean that it's not unusual for experienced birders to add as many as 120-150 new species to their "life list" on a single visit.

You'll need a calculator to keep an accurate bird count at the Asa Wright Nature Center, a haven for 200 avian species; that's half of Trinidad's total species in just this one spot. In addition, butterflies roam freely.

For sheer natural spectacle, the shaded, foliage-rich trails of Asa Wright deserve to be on anyone's list of the Caribbean's Top Ten walks. I rank it No. 2; an avid birder might place it No. 1. If you see no other spot on Trinidad, let it be Asa Wright.

Although you may never have visited Trinidad, you probably are already familiar with part of its culture. It is in Trinidad that calypso, limbo and steel bands originated; the unique, lively music and dancing that have come to characterize the islands. They all were born in Trinidad, not as gimmicks to attract tourists, but as enthusiastic expressions of everyday life.

Known locally as "Pan," steel band beating is an outgrowth of the religious drumming traditions of both Africa and India. Steel band competitions are equivalent to national football and soccer league championship clashes.

The steel bands at Carnival are unmatched anywhere else. They are enormous, with 300-500 players. Trinidad's Carnival is the Caribbean's largest and loudest celebration. Early French settlers would mark in masked processions from one house to another (thus the local name, "Mas,") a custom slaves adopted after emancipation in 1834.

Outsiders are invited to party during the annual celebration. In fact, to be authentic, you may buy your own Carnival costume at a Mas Camp. Trinidad is the birthplace of the Caribbean's most lively musical spirit.

Trinidad, long a melting pot of many ethnic groups, is accustomed to welcoming newcomers. It is home to more than forty different nationalities including East Indians, Chinese, Portuguese, Syrians, Jews and Latin Americans. No other Caribbean island has a population as diverse as these "Rainbow People."

Until the 1980s, Trinidad prospered far more than most islands. Where did the wealth come from? Right out of the ground, from the island's oil wells. The government owned 51% of all the local drilling operations, in addition to sole ownership of one of its own. As a result, much of the oil money remained right in the country, giving the island a standard of living that was the envy of many of its sister states. Unfortunately, when the price of oil decreased dramatically in the 1980s, so did the local economy. Today,

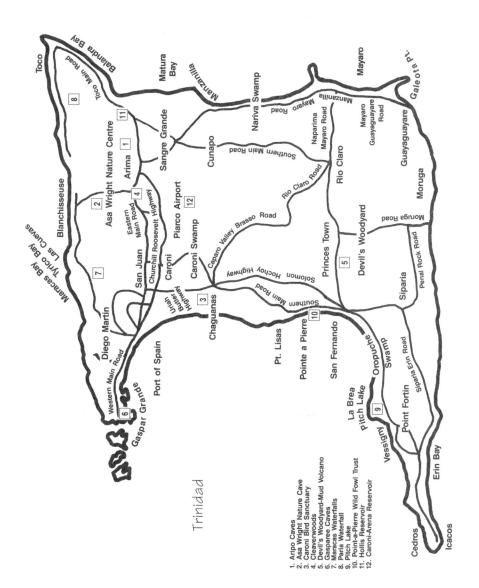

Trinidad

1. Aripo Caves
2. Asa Wright Nature Cave
3. Caroni Bird Sanctuary
4. Cleaverwoods
5. Devil's Woodyard-Mud Volcano
6. Gasparee Caves
7. Maracas Waterfalls
8. Paria Waterfall
9. Pitch Lake
10. Point-a-Pierre Wild Fowl Trust
11. Hollis Reservoir
12. Caroni-Arena Reservoir

tourism plays an increasingly important role.

Columbus discovered Trinidad in 1498 on his third voyage. Before embarking on that third journey, Columbus dedicated his expedition to the Holy Trinity and vowed to name the first landfall he spied "La Trinite."

The Spanish established their first outpost in Trinidad in 1532, and the English under Sir Walter Raleigh destroyed it in 1595. One of Raleigh's main interests was an unusual natural resource, the asphalt at Pitch Lake which provided excellent caulking for ships. Trinidad remained in Spanish hands until the British fleet came calling in 1797 and the local governor quickly surrendered the island.

In the 1800s, Trinidad was officially ceded to Britain, and in 1877 Tobago was turned over to Trinidad as a ward. In 1888, the British politically lumped together Trinidad and Tobago which never really had much in common before or since. The islands are now an independent republic within the British Commonwealth.

Exploring Trinidad's remarkable diversity, it will seem that no matter where you go, you're continually discovering something unique, colorful and exotic. Trinidad is the best place in the Caribbean to view wildlife, and lots of it (especially during Carnival).

Travel Tips

Area: Trinidad is roughly rectangular in shape, 37 miles wide and 50 miles long, a total of 1,864 square miles. It is only 7 miles off the coast of South America.

Language: English with some French and Spanish occasionally spoken.

Population: Approx. 1.2 million, one of the most heavily populated islands in the Caribbean.

Time Zone: Atlantic Standard Time, one hour ahead of Eastern Standard Time.

Rainy Season: June through December: showers can be torrential, real frog stranglers, but usually clear quickly. Both Trinidad and Tobago are south of the hurricane belt, but powerful storms still clobber the region periodically.

Getting There: Trinidad's Piarco Airport is the main entry for visitors to Trinidad or Tobago. U.S. visitors have a choice of American Airlines or BWIA. Canadians can take Air Canada or BWIA from Toronto. British Airways and BWIA fly from Europe. The airport is sixteen miles from Port of Spain, so allow plenty of time when leaving. An exit tax is required upon leaving: TT $50 and it must be paid in the local currency.

Getting Around: The official taxis have an "H" as the first letter on

Steel Band music originated in Trinidad when local musicians discovered they could "tune" the tops of oil drums after World War II.

their license plate. Negotiate ahead of time and know whether the price is in TT $ or US $. Other taxis that have the "P" registration of a private car on the license are known as pirate taxis. You may be able to negotiate a better rate with them; however, they may drive off with your luggage. In time you will discover route taxis with the "H" initial; these are far cheaper but drive only a specified route, like a bus. They stop and pickup wherever you wish along that route. The only way to tell a "regular" from a "route" taxi is ask the driver. Some taxis also charge 50% more after midnight.

Rental cars are available but difficult to come by for weekends because many locals, who cannot afford the exorbitant price of a car, lease on a long-term basis. Make sure the rental company accepts credit cards.

Being on your own will give you a chance to sample the incredibly diverse cuisine created by the mixtures of cultures. The Indian curries are particularly good, as are rotis, an East Indian version of a burrito with meat, potatoes and curry. You'll need to wash one down with large amounts of Carib, the favorite local beer which advertises "every bottle tastes different." Locals seem to think that a plus, not a problem with quality control.

A popular local drink is mauby, made from a tree bark soaked in sugar and spices. It tastes like sweet ginger beer. Angostura bitters originated on

Trinidad; a dash of it to any drink—cola or beer—dramatically changes and usually improves the taste. Be careful, as this stuff (full of unspecified secret ingredients) may be addictive; there are worse vices.

Where to Stay: To overnight in the heart of a bird-rich rain forest, contact the Asa Wright Lodge (Tel. 809/667-4655; fax 809/667-0493.) The Lodge can accommodate up to forty guests in its twenty twin-bedded rooms, each with private bath and hot and cold water. This is hardly roughing it. Meals are Trinidad-style, featuring fresh fruit, vegetables, bread and pastries, home-made jams and jellies.

Port of Spain has several large hotels, including the Hilton, the Normandie and the Bel Air Piarco at the airport. Guest houses are an excellent alternative. Monique's Guest House in Maravel (tel. 809/628-3334) is on the road to Maracas Bay; the people are very friendly, the food excellent, the rooms large. The Bed and Breakfast Association of Trinidad & Tobago, Diego Martin Post Office, Box 3231 (tel. 809/637-9329; fax 627-0856) also has an office in the Trinidad airport near immigration.

Camping: Not recommended on Trinidad for safety reasons.

Taxes & Tips: If a service charge hasn't already been added, 10% is the standard tip.

Documents: U.S. & Canadian citizens need a birth certificate and a current photo ID. Passports are required of anyone over sixteen years old. South African and Taiwanese passports are not valid for entry. Visas are required of some citizens. Entry permits are good for one month. If you plan to stay longer, ask for up to three months on arrival since extensions can be a time-consuming process. An ongoing, dated ticket (not open-ended) may also be required at immigration, plus proof you are able to support yourself during your stay. A specific address for your stay will also be requested.

Currency: The Trinidad and Tobago or TT dollar is worth about TT $5 = US $1. It has steadily been declining in value since 1985. Banks are open 9 a.m. to 1 p.m. Monday through Thursday and 9 a.m. to noon, 3 p.m. to 5 p.m. on Friday. US currency is readily accepted everywhere. All banks charge a fee for cashing traveler's checks.

Electrical Current: Either 110 or 220 volts, 60 cycles on both Trinidad & Tobago.

Safety/Health Warning: Stray from the marked trails and marijuana farmers with their trap guns could pose a problem, particularly in the Northern Range. Due to increased crime, Port of Spain, including the Queen's Park Savannah, is not considered safe to walk at night. In fact, be watchful and careful anywhere after dark.

Hiking/Walking Services: The Trinidad Field Naturalists Club, 1 Errol Park Rd, Port of Spain, has monthly field trips which tourists are welcome to join. These include visits to caves as well as long distance walks. Tel. 809/624-3321. Taxi drivers and other guides know the way to most of the places mentioned, though you should be able to find them on your own.

The Asa Wright Nature Center can arrange guides for field trips to the various birding hot spots on both Trinidad and Tobago. Contact the Lodge directly at 809/667-4655; fax 809/667-0493. Or Caligo Ventures, Inc., 387 Main St., Armonk, NY 10504-0021; toll free in the U.S. and Canada 800/426-7781; fax 914/273-6370.

Snakes and Other Venomous Creatures: Trinidad has forty-seven different snake species, of which only four are poisonous: the bushmaster, fer-de-lance and two species of coral snake. Exercise proper caution and snakes should be no more a problem here than elsewhere.

1. Port of Spain Walking Tour

Time: 2-3 hours. **Difficulty:** 1.

At first glance, your reaction to Port of Spain may be one of disappointment. The coastal waters are muddy thanks to the Orinoco River, and Port of Spain itself is a big, commercial port with high-rise skyscrapers, totally devoid of that charming tropical island look. You could be in Miami or San Juan.

Take heart: the real beauty of Trinidad is in its lush countryside and in its people. Still, there are a few parts of even industrialized Port of Spain that should pleasantly surprise you.

1) Woodford Square is named after governor Sir Ralph Woodford (in office from 1813-28) who was responsible for importing a landscape architect in 1820 to create the country's beautiful Botanic Gardens.

2) On the South side of the square is the **Anglican Cathedral of the Holy Trinity** noted for its hammer-beam roof decorated with many carvings. The church was consecrated in 1823.

3) Red House. Also across from Woodford Square Red House is painted just that color and very brightly, too. This is where the parliament meets. The huge building, built in 1907 on the site of its predecessor which was destroyed by fire in a 1903 riot over an increase in water rates. It has to be the most conspicuous building in the entire city because of its color and size. It was painted red to mark Queen Victoria's Diamond Jubilee in 1897. There was an opportunity to change the color when the new Red House was built, but by then people had kind of grown fond of the garish color.

4) Port of Spain's most picturesque section is north of the town center at the 200-acre **Queen's Park Savannah** situated in the foothills of the Northern Range. Once used to graze cattle, Trinidadians claim this is the world's largest roundabout; at two and one-half miles, they may be correct.

In the dry season (January to May), Queen's park Savannah boasts a striking display of flowering trees, including pink and yellow poui, purple and white petria and the brilliant "Shower of Gold." This big open field has cricket and soccer fields and a racecourse with stands.

5) Magnificent Seven: Flanking the entire western edge are old, elaborately decorated buildings known as the "Magnificent Seven." These are European styled mansions which represent some of the finest surviving European architecture in the Western Hemisphere. They do deserve the title magnificent, though some are becoming run down. All but one was built in 1904. They are best photographed in the early morning sun before the area becomes crowded. Do not walk here at night.

Going northwards along the Savannah, the first building is Queen's Royal College, a German renaissance design. Next is Hayes Court, residence of the Anglican bishop, built in 1910. Third is Ambar's House, built in the French Baroque style with marble imported from Italy.

Fourth is "Mille Fleurs" or Prada's House, a town house typical of the turn-of-the-century with impressive iron fretwork. Fifth is the Roman Catholic archbishop's home built in 1904. Next to it is the opulent Moorish-style mansion known as White Hall which formerly was the Prime Minister's office. It now contains several government departments.

The last of the "Magnificent Seven" is Killarney, a brick and turreted residence also called the Stollmeyer house after the family who built this miniature Rhine castle.

6) On the south side of the Savannah are two buildings of note, **Knowsley** also from 1904 and the **Queen's Park Hotel**, Art Deco architecture from 1895.

7) Zoo and Botanical Garden: North of the Savannah but still within walking distance are the Emperor Valley Zoo and the Botanical Garden. The zoo covers eight acres with a good representation of Trinidad's different mammals, reptiles and birds; it also contains a number of imported species. Ironically, the name comes from the Emperor Butterfly which was common to this valley before development.

Adjacent is the seventy-acre Botanical Gardens, which have the best single display of orchids on the island. The Botanical Garden displays its most colorful foliage between April and June when plants like the scarlet Isora, bougainvillea, oleander, jacaranda, and the pink poui are in flower. The gardens, with their meticulously designed walkways, were laid out in 1820. Besides local plants and shrubs, the Gardens have a good variety of

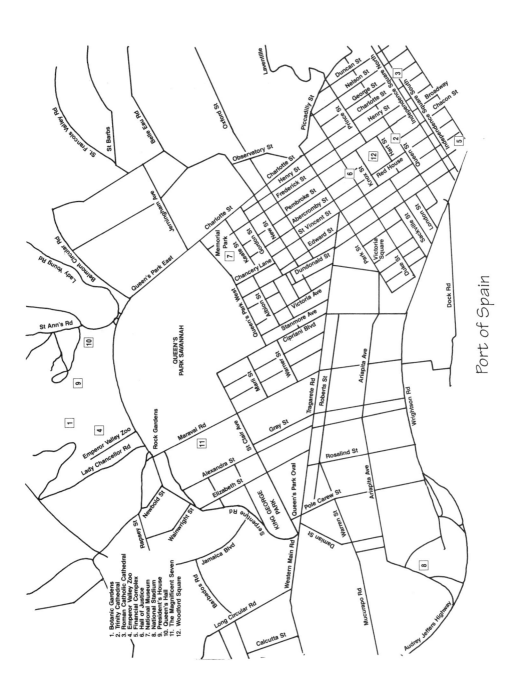

Port of Spain

1. Botanic Gardens
2. Trinity Cathedral
3. Roman Catholic Cathedral
4. Emperor Valley Zoo
5. Financial Complex
6. Hall of Justice
7. National Museum
8. National Stadium
9. President's House
10. Queen's Hall
11. The Magnificent Seven
12. Woodford Square

tropical and sub-tropical trees and shrubs from South America and southeast Asia. The former Governor's House, built on the grounds between 1873-75, is now the residence of Trinidad and Tobago's president.

Out on the Island

2. Asa Wright Nature Preserve

Time: at least a full day, preferably 2 or 3. **Difficulty: 1.**

The nature center, founded in 1967, is located in the Northern Range on Spring Hill Estate, a coffee-cocoa-citrus plantation partly reclaimed by secondary forest. The climate is tropical and humid, in mid-montane rainforest. A light sweater or jacket is often necessary in the evenings, not for dining but to ward off the cold. Temps vary from 65°F to a maximum of 86°F. Dress is informal at all times. Sneakers, cotton slacks, long-sleeved shirts and a hat are all recommended. Bring a light-weight rain coat and flashlight.

Summer seminars are offered in nature photography, entomology, ornithology, tropical ecology and drawing/painting. Vegetation is at its most striking in the dry season, January to May.

Nowhere else in the Caribbean compares to Asa Wright for observing such a huge diversity of bird, animal and plant life. A series of nine trails meanders through a good portion of the preserve, all intended to provide the best possible introduction to South American birding. Accommodations are limited to forty, so call ahead at least twenty-four to forty-eight hours to arrange for a guide, etc. However, you need never move out of a rocking chair to see scores of different birds: the main building has a huge front porch with numerous bird feeders just a few feet away.

Asa Wright has what is considered the world's most accessible colony of oilbirds (Steatornis caripensis), the only nocturnal fruit-eating bird on the planet. Normally limited to the South American continent, the oilbird measures eighteen inches in length with a wingspan of three to three-and-a-half feet. It has short legs, is rich brown in color with white spots, and has a large, hooked beak with conspicuous rictal bristles.

Oilbirds were given their name in 1799 by scientist Alexander von Humboldt who observed the Venezuelan Indians were taking the very fat young chicks from their nests and rendering them for cooking oil and oil for their torches. The young develop slowly, staying on the nest for up to 120 days. They are also incredibly fat: at seventy days they may be 50% heavier than an adult.

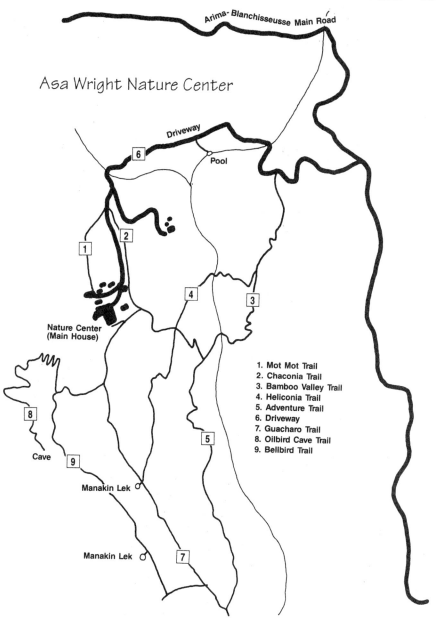

Asa Wright Nature Center

Arima- Blanchisseusse Main Road

Driveway

Pool

6

2

1

4

3

Nature Center
(Main House)

8

Cave

9

5

Manakin Lek

Manakin Lek

7

1. Mot Mot Trail
2. Chaconia Trail
3. Bamboo Valley Trail
4. Heliconia Trail
5. Adventure Trail
6. Driveway
7. Guacharo Trail
8. Oilbird Cave Trail
9. Bellbird Trail

When disturbed, the oilbirds scream, snarl and chuck, an incredibly weird and unforgettable sound from your worst nightmare. The Amerindians called oilbirds Guacharos, meaning "the ones that wail and mourn." Trinidadians refer to them as the Diablotin.

The life of an oilbird probably appears dull, unless you are one. They stay on their nests (with or without young) in dark caves during daylight. The nests, made mostly of regurgitated matter, are used year after year and eventually form into low cylindrical mounds. A clutch typically has two to four white oval eggs.

At dusk, oilbirds depart to dine on the fruit of palms, laurels, incenses and camphor, traveling as far as seventy miles to feed.

Oilbirds are similar to bats, not only in lifestyle, but in their ability to employ echo-location to find their way around obstacles in the dark. Oilbirds see quite well, too, and use sight whenever light is adequate.

3. Chaguaramas National Park

Time: 2 hours each way. **Length:** 6 miles each way. **Difficulty:** 3.

Everything from mountain climbing to snorkeling is available in this one park which encompasses the er.tire Chaguaramas Peninsula, at the west-ern-most point of Trinidad. This is one of the most arid areas in Trinidad, so be watchful of your liquid intake to prevent dehydration. This scrubby area was leased to the U.S. during World War II and some of the old buildings remain.

The hike up Mt. Catherine (1,768 feet) begins at Carenage Bay. The six-mile trail is impassable to vehicles, so this is a true walk. The track passes through dry scrub woodlands and eventually overlooks the Tucker Valley on the east. Chaguaramas is home to the red howler monkey, so keep a sharp eye for him at all times.

The Gasparee Caves with striking stalactites and stalagmites are located on Gaspar Grande island, one of five islands located off the Chaguaramas Peninsula. The cave entrance is a few hundred feet from the jetty which services this resort island. One underground section is known as the Cathedral because the formations are similar to the inside of a Gothic cathedral, complete with organ pipes and pulpit. Tour guides, restrooms and picnic facilities are available at this popular attraction.

Uphill from the caves are two guns surviving from World War II.

4. Blue Basin Waterfall

Time: only a 5-minute walk, but plan on swimming. **Difficulty:** 1.

From the town of Diego Martin it's a five-minute walk down a bridle path to Blue Basin Waterfalls, a popular tourist site long before nature centers. A tropical pool at the base of the waterfall was once hidden by the village of Blue Basin and used only by locals for bathing. A short hike and a relaxing swim. Do not leave anything of value in the car.

5. Maracas Bay Beach/Waterfall

Time: 2 hours for the waterfall hike. **Difficulty:** 2.

The drive through the forested Northern Range to Maracas Bay on the North Coast is one of Trinidad's most photogenic locations.

For decades, Maracas Bay Beach has been Trinidad's most popular swimming areas. The white sand borders the Atlantic, not nearly as scenic or as safe as the Caribbean. If you go swimming here, look for the red flags that mark off areas subject to undertow.

The 300-foot Maracas Falls, however, is not near the beach but in the mountains above the Maracas Valley. The site is accessible from St. Joseph, just six miles east of Port of Spain. Take the Maracas Royal Road and look for the marked road to the right leading to the waterfall trail. This secondary road goes for a mile before depositing you at the trailhead.

You have a choice of two trails. The shorter and easier walk (less than a mile) takes you to the base of the falls and the picnic recreation area. The other trail, a much tougher hike, and one for which a guide is recommended, requires some rock hopping and a climb up a slippery path to the top of the falls. You may swim here, too, in a stream pool upstream from the falls.

6. Mt. Tabor/St. Benedict Monastery

Time: 1-3 hours, depending on trail. **Difficulty:** 2-3.

At 1,800 feet, Mt. Tabor supplies some impressive views of Port of Spain on the west, El Tucuche to the north and the Caroni Plains to the south.

Hiking trails begin at the Mount St. Benedict monastery, which has a public guest house. The rates are a bargain at US $40 a day for lodging, breakfast and dinner. The monastery is reached through Tunapuna via the Eastern main Road with a turnoff at St. John's Road.

The guest house grounds, located at 800 feet elevation, are filled with birds at daybreak and twilight. Trails lead to the top of the peak and to various parts of the mountain. All tend to be steep but not too difficult to climb. Photography seminars are held here periodically.

7. Caurita Plantation

Time: 1-3 hours. **Difficulty:** 1-3.

Set 1,200 feet above sea level in the Northern Range, this 400-acre estate is another special nature center rich in tropical flora and fauna. Field trips are provided through the stream-lined mountainside, including special trips to Amerindian rock inscriptions found only in this area. The lodge has four double rooms with bath, two without. Contact Gordon Dalla Costa, 143 Edward St., Port of Spain.

8. Aripo Caves

Time: 5 hours each way. **Length:** 9 miles. **Difficulty:** 3.

Trinidad's highest peak is El Cerreo del Aripo (3,083 feet), a noteworthy climb of nine miles that will also take you to the Aripo Caves, Trinidad's largest cave system. These caves are home to oilbirds, which are often seen from the entrance. Four miles east of Arima, a steep road follows the Aripo River to Dandrade Trace, a distance of approximately ten miles. As you pass through Aripo village on the way, arrange a guide for the ascent trail, which is sometimes difficult to discern. The undulating path crosses streams, goes up and down limestone cliffs and through upper montane rain forest. All in all, it's an excellent variety.

9. Matura Beach/Fishing Pond

Time: variable depending on how well the turtles cooperate. **Difficulty:** 1 if you're well rested; 5+ if you need sleep.

Located on the east coast, these two sites are prime turtle-watching spots from mid-April to July when the world's largest marine turtles come ashore at night to deposit their eggs. These are the giant leatherbacks, which may weigh as much as 1,200 pounds. The carapace, often more than six feet in length, is distinguished by its longitudinally ridged shell which looks like leather stretched tight over a frame. The carapace is colored a dark bluish gray and spotted with white.

During the nesting season, leatherbacks come ashore at night to lay their eggs above the high water mark. After digging a hole three feet deep, the female deposits between seventy to one-hundred twenty billiard ball-sized eggs, which she then covers and conceals. The female returns to the sea, but her nesting is far from over. Leatherbacks may return as many as eight times in a season, at intervals of about ten days.

The nestlings hatch in sixty days and head straight for the sea. For many years it wasn't known where baby leatherbacks went but recent research shows many find their way to the Sargasso Sea.

Turtle eggs are protected by law, although they are occasionally poached. Asa Wright conducts turtle watching tours in season.

 10. Pointe a Pitre Wildfowl Trust

Time: Go early in the morning or the evening for optimum bird watching. **Difficulty:** 1.

This former Texaco Oil Company operation, the largest refinery on the island, was bought by the government in 1984. Volunteers have created a wildfowl preserve on the two lakes to breed endangered species of birds and reintroduce them to natural wildlife areas. Hundreds of different species nest here during a year, many visible from the forest trail and walkways around the lakes. Although considered a pest in North America, Moscovy Ducks were eaten to extinction on Trinidad and are part of the repopulation program, as are black-bellied, fulvous and white-faced whistling ducks. More exotic species include the blue and yellow macaw and the blue-headed parrots. Gallinules, herons, cormorants, flycatchers and tanagers are among the birds usually found here year-round.

An Environmental Learning Center with library, audio-visual room, a small museum of Amerindian artifacts and a souvenir shop is open daily from 10 a.m to 5 p.m. Birdwatchers will be admitted as early as 7 a.m. and may stay as late as 6 p.m. Since this is a volunteer operation, reservations must be made in advance: 809/637-5145/662-4040. A small admission fee includes a guide. Visitors are welcome to bring a picnic lunch.

11. Pitch Lake

Time: 1 hour. **Difficulty:** 1.

The Pitch Lake at La Brea (Spanish for "pitch") on the southwest coast is the largest deposit of asphalt in the world, measuring 135 feet deep and covering a surface area of eighty-nine acres. Like most parking lots—and that is what it looks like—you can actually walk on the goo but it is springy underfoot. Avoid air holes bubbling up from the pressure. You leave an imprint as you walk, and if you stand still, you'll start to sink. They say it takes one to two hours for someone to totally disappear, to become a preserved tar baby that may one day reappear. The lake is continually being stirred, so everything from prehistoric tree trunks to fast food garbage occasionally surfaces.

Official tours are no longer given around the lake, but many former guides are present to haggle over a tour. Set a fee in advance and make certain whether it's TT $ or US $. It's the history and lore of the lake that makes it fascinating more than the actual sight of it.

Sir Walter Raleigh is credited with discovering the lake in 1595 and found it to be excellent ship's caulking because it did not appear to melt in the sun. He was wrong. After carrying pitch back to England and asphalting Westminster Bridge for the opening of Parliament, the asphalt did melt and clogged the coach wheels and horses' hooves. Since then, it has worked more successfully covering streets not only in Port of Spain but Cairo, Singapore, Bombay and London.

12. Devil's Woodyard

Time: 30 minutes. **Difficulty:** 1.

Located at Princess Town, the Devil's Woodyard is an active mud volcano that emits warm, bubbling mud through surface cracks which form into cones as it cools. Some local Hindus hold this to be a sacred spot and worship here.

The Devil's Woodyard first erupted in 1852 and until the discovery of another mud volcano in 1964 at Moruga, it was thought to be the only one on the island. Since 1964, eighteen other mud volcanoes have been located, usually in places where oil is produced.

13. Trinity Hills Wildlife Sanctuary

Time: 1 hour each way. **Length:** 2 miles. **Difficulty:** 2-3. Advance permission may be necessary from the Trinidad and Tobago Oil Co. (TRINTOC) at Pointe-a-Pierre.

This 16,000 acres in the Southern Range is reached by going west of Guayaguayare. Dating from 1934, it is one of the oldest preserves, giving sanctuary to monkeys, deer, opossums, bellbirds, parrots, toucans and pigeons. The mud volcano of Lagon Bouffe is also in this region.

The climb to the highest summit (1,010 feet) begins on a marked track off the main sanctuary road. The path is narrow and steep but provides some of the most scenic overviews of the Southern coast, which admittedly is not quite as spectacular as the Northern Range.

 # 14. Paria Falls

Time: 3-1/2 hours each way. **Difficulty:** 3. Take food and water.

The Paria River begins in the foothills of the Northern Range. This is a goodly little hike of several hours through the forest which eventually brings you to the clear, natural bathing pool of Paria Waterfall. Taking the Arima-Blanchisseuse Road, go east 6.4 km. to Brasso Seco and turn left onto the Paria Morne Blue Road. You'll have to leave your car and walk to the 4-3/4 mile post where there's a house on the left just after a bridge. The trail starts here, highly visible with no turnoffs. The trail winds north for the first one-and-a half hours until you cross a stream flowing east. Then, thirty-five minutes later, you'll arrive at the Jordan River, which you cross. After another hour, climb over the hill and you will arrive at a beach where you turn right, walk for two minutes to reach the wooden bridge crossing the Paria River. Walk another five minutes up the right bank to reach the waterfall.

Tobago

St. Giles or
Melville Island

Little
Tobago

Bird of
Paradise
Island

Goat
Island

Tyrells Bay

Charlotteville

Pedro
Point

North
Point

Man
of War
Bay

Corvo
Point

Prince's
Bay

Carapuse Bay

Richmond Island

Roxborough

Windward Rd

The
Brothers

Parlatuvier Rd

Goldsborough Bay

Bloody
Bay

TOBAGO FOREST
RESERVE

Pembrooke

Smith's Island

Parlatuvier
Bay

The Sisters

Englishmans Bay

Ester Field Rd

Mason Hall

Mt. St.
George

Hillsborough
Bay

Minister
Point

Castra Bay

Northside Rd

Fort George

Bacolet Point

SCARBOROUGH

King Peter's Bay

Vale Rd Arny

Plymouth Rd

Orange Hill Rd

Rocky
Bay

Culloden Bay

Grafton Rd

Buccoo
Bay Rd

Red Point

Fort James

Petit Trou

Courtland Point
Great Courtland Bay

Stone Haven
Bay

Bon Accord Rd

Columbus or
Kennedy's Point

Mount Irvine
or
Courtland Bay

Buccoo Bay

Canoe
Bay

Buccoo Reef

Pigeon Point

Sandy Bay
Store Bay

Crown Point

Sandy Point

Robinson
Crusoe's
Cave

 19. Tobago

Although joined politically to Trinidad, Tobago's geologic origins are still debated. Some scientists say only Trinidad was once a part of the South American mainland; others believe Tobago, located twenty-two miles off Trinidad's northeast tip, also broke from the continent, just considerably earlier: millions of years earlier.

Yet another theory claims Tobago was never part of South America at all. These scientists say that it explains why Tobago does not harbor any poisonous snakes. Further, the variety of bird species differs considerably for two landfalls so close together. Tobago has twenty bird species that do not live in Trinidad.

Tobago has endured second-rate status to oil-rich Trinidad. For example, electricity didn't arrive on Tobago until the 1950s. That's probably why Tobago retains a rare old-Caribbean feel and charm; slow living, friendly, genuine. You don't find the huge shopping malls or highrises that have sprouted on Trinidad.

Tobago has always been considered one of the backwaters of the world, the perfect place for castaways. Daniel Defoe's *Robinson Crusoe* was set on Tobago. Walt Disney built a tree house in a huge Saman tree near the town of Goldsborough for filming the movie. The tree house, left as a tourist attraction, was destroyed by a hurricane. The Saman tree, now covered with bromeliads, still stands.

Columbus discovered Tobago in 1498 and called it "Bellaforma," one of his more original names. Tobago was left alone until 1629, when the Swedes, British, French and Dutch all attempted settlements. Following the transplant of 100 families from Europe by the Duke of Courtland in

1654, Tobago became another island whose prosperity was based solely on sugar cane and cotton.

Today, Trinidad overshadows Tobago in every way. Trinidad's Asa Wright Nature Center—a wonderful place to view birds—enjoys an international reputation. Still I rate the bird preserve of Little Tobago an equally good if not a far more dramatic walk because of the uncharacteristically rugged scenery. In addition, the chance to get close to nesting birds is truly unusual.

Scarborough, the main city, has good botanical gardens worth exploring but, quite honestly, little else to recommend it.

Travel Tips

Area: Located 22 miles from Trinidad, Tobago covers just 116 square miles. The island is cigar-shaped, 26 miles long and 9 miles wide.

Language: English.

Population: 47,000.

Time Zone: Atlantic Standard Time, one hour ahead of Eastern Standard Time.

Getting There: BWIA, the national airline of Trinidad and Tobago, offers frequent shuttle service from Trinidad; at least twelve flights daily but weekends can be very crowded. LIAT also flies in from other islands. The airport runway has been extended so it can now accept direct international flights. Check other carriers, particularly American Airlines, for the latest schedule.

Getting Around: Rental cars are readily available. Driving is on the left. If you want a taxi tour to familiarize yourself with the island, friendly and knowledgeable Cecil Lyons is a long-time sightseeing specialist (it's even on his card.) He knows most of the good photo spots as well as most everyone on Tobago. His home phone is 639-2766; at the airport, 639-0509.

Where to Stay: Most of the tourist hotels are near the southern coast near the airport and the capital city of Scarborough. However, Little Tobago and the Main Ridge Reserve, the two main hiking areas, are at the opposite end. The Blue Waters Inn on Batteaux Bay, Speyside, is located directly opposite Little Tobago and tours depart here regularly. In addition, it is conveniently located near the Main Ridge hiking trails. Tel. 809/660-4341; fax 809/660-5195. The tourist board also has a list of guest houses.

Hiking/Walking Services: To fully appreciate Little Tobago, you need a guide. I recommend the group of forest service officers who offer individual and small group tours. Tel. 809/660-5529, the home phone number of forest service officer, William Trim, in Goldsborough. Trim is one of the best guides I had anywhere in the Caribbean because of the enthusiastic way he shares his knowledge about his beautiful homeland.

Snakes and Other Venomous Creatures: None.

Main Ridge Reserve Hiking Trails

The Main Ridge recreation center, located about six miles beyond of the village of Roxborough, argues that it is the oldest forest reserve in the Western Hemisphere. Dominica and St. Lucia also make similar claims. The Main Ridge covers two-thirds of the island, running like a spine on a northeast-southwest diagonal. Tobago's reserve was mandated by the French as far back as 1765 who perceived the importance of the forest as a major watershed.

Due to a technicality—the rampage of Mother Nature—Tobago definitely cannot claim to have the oldest protected plot of trees. Hurricane Flora destroyed most of her namesake in 1963. The lush, thick rain forest you see flourishing today is relatively young with few old trees; incredible testimony to the awesome, destructive force of hurricane winds.

One tree that survived Flora's fury is also one of the largest, a Fiddlewood with an enormous eighteen foot girth. The tree is hollow, so you can actually crawl inside it and stand erect. The Fiddlewood is only forty-five to fifty feet high; it's top was broken off.

The Main Ridge Reserve is totally user-friendly. On Sundays, many locals use the barbecue pits for cook-outs. Camping is not only permitted but encouraged. In fact, youngsters from all over the Caribbean come here on holidays and during summer. Weekdays, the park is practically deserted.

1. The Gilpin Trail

Time: between 2-3 hours. **Length:** 3.5 kilometers. **Difficulty:** 2-3 for the first 2.5 kilometers. From about 2.5 kilometers to 3.5 kilometers, the continual steep ascent rates a 3-4.

This is the park's main hike, named after an old road islanders used to walk to Bloody Bay. The true road eventually veers off after the first couple of miles; the remaining trail is newly cut and leads uphill to the main visitor center/picnic area. From the visitor center back to the starting point, the last leg is along open road.

The trailhead is at mile marker 1.25. The distance covered in the forest itself is about 3.2 kilometers (That is not a misprint: in Tobago, road distances are measured in miles, hiking distances in kilometers. There's talk of adopting a uniform system.)

Most people do not complete the full circuit but walk to the first or second waterfall, then retrace their steps. The roundtrip takes about an hour.

In addition to a sign, the trailhead is marked by a collection of a dozen or more walking sticks angling out of the ground like a patch of denuded forest. These sturdy sticks are provided, since the trail is often slippery. Naturally, it's requested you return your borrowed walking stick for other hikers. The foresters themselves often wear rubber boots on this hike; it's that muddy. Curiously, the mud here comes in enough different colors that mas players frequently visit the forest to get pigment for their carnival costumes.

Orange-winged Parrots, Red-rumped Woodpeckers, Cockey Crows and many different kinds of hummingbirds occupy the reserve. One of the rarest is the White-tailed Saberwing hummingbird, which one forester has seen only seven times in six years. He says that each occasion "was a privilege and honor."

Agouti, armadillo, possum and a several harmless snakes, including the counterfeit coral snake, live in the thick foliage. Cicadas call loudest, just before the rainy season begins and ends. Another signal that the rainy season is on the way is the yellow poui tree, which flowers just before the regular showers begin.

An underground stream also appears at the start of the Gilpin Trail. A tiny brook initially, after the first kilometer it's carved a gully over one hundred-feet deep. You must cross on a large, reinforced log.

The trail is described according to how people usually divide up the walk:

Trailhead to the first waterfall: This short 1.4 kilometer walk is the one most people make—then never venture further. You'll see at least thirty different species of ferns, including small tree ferns, and lots of bamboo.

Termites and ants furnish several unusual stopping points on this short segment. There are between eleven and thirteen different kinds of termites, and each species exudes a kind of repellent to keep away predators. The system works: some of the Little Tobago mounds are huge.

Even more impressive is the six-foot-tall nest of leaf-cutter ants at the base of a Tapana tree. The leaf cutters are the ones who carry small bits of green leaves in a wide line, so it sometimes seems the forest floor moves along like an escalator. A large ant trail on the right looks like it was created by a person sliding down the bank. According to folklore, these ants are handy if you to cut yourself: the theory is to use the ants to bind your wounds. You let them bite you, then pinch their bodies off and leave the heads there. Tough on the ants, though.

At 1.4 kilometer you will reach a small unnamed waterfall that is part the Gold-Silver River. The river gained its unusual name partly from the color of water, which has a shiny silvery color. However, the background material the water flows over is gold in color, created by oxides deposited by the river. Hence the name Gold-Silver River. It takes a little over an hour to walk to this point.

From the first to the second waterfall: At 1.7 kilometer on the trail, just fifteen minutes beyond the first waterfall, is a second and smaller waterfall. Until the Gold-Silver River, the trail is worn and muddy from frequent use. But since the heavy travel ends there, a layer of vegetation covers the path. The second waterfall, though small, is striking because of the water falling on the dark green ferns. The stream is so small here you can literally step across it.

From the second to third waterfall: at 2.5 kilometer is another small waterfall with a narrow stream that can be stepped across.

From the third waterfall to the interpretive center: the toughest part of the hike from 2.5 to 3.2 kilometer because of the occasionally steep grade. The first third is uphill. The middle section undulates up and down. The toughest climbing has been saved for last. Good physical condition and a walking stick are essential. This last section of trail, opened in 1986, contains the hollow Fiddlewood tree you can stand inside. You'll also see another small waterfall. The recreation center is at 3.5 kilometer, a trek of two-and-a-half to three hours from the outset.

 **2.-3. Spring/Blue Copper Trails**

Time: 1 hour. **Length:** 2 miles. **Difficulty:** 2.

Combined, these trails cover a distance of about two miles. The Spring Trail starts near a water pipe where the clean spring water comes gushing out. This is about four and one-half miles from the village of Roxborough on the way to the park recreation center. After about twenty minutes, the Spring Trail connects with the mile-long Blue Copper Trail, named after the very tough and hard wood known as Blue Copper. The Spring Trail may be the best bird walk in the entire reserve: common are Yellow-legged Thrush, hummingbirds, Rufus-tail Jackamot, Colored Trogans and more. Considerable nesting activity occurs along this trail, more than you'll probably see on the Gilpin Trail. The forest is not as thick because of some selective cutting.

4. Sevrette Trail

Time: 15 minutes. **Length:** .5 kkilometer **Difficulty:** 1.

This short .5 kilometer trail is designed primarily as an educational trail for visiting school children. Once completed, the trail will have a plot with interpretive/name signs for the different flora.

Elsewhere on Tobago

5. Argyle Falls

Time: 20 minutes. **Difficulty:** 1.

One of the easiest and most scenic spots on Tobago, it's about a ten minute walk to the falls from the main road. Because the four falls are at different levels, you can choose from several different pools to bathe in. The largest is at the bottom. This is cool spring water, so be prepared for the shock. A popular tourist attraction, you're charged a fee according to how high up you go. The higher, the prettier (naturally!).

6. Bay Walks

Time: up to 4 hours. **Difficulty:** 3.

This walk passes a series of three bays with a rugged hill climb at the end. Lowland sections can be quite hot; take water.

Begin at Batteaux Bay and follow the coastline to Belmont Bay, which has a lovely view even though most of the trees have been cut down and the beach has washed away. Starwood Bay, the real object of this walk, is between forty-five to sixty minutes from the outset. There is absolutely nothing to see except a grand beach. It's so isolated that it's often used for skinny dipping. The walk is quite easy for the first three-quarters, but the last section is a steep incline normally kept clear by the government.

Between Belmont and Starwood Bays is an unmarked trail that climbs rugged Flagstaff Hill. Unless you want to retrace your same steps, make the climb. Eventually you will come out on a road that is half asphalt and half stones. This will take you out to the main road, which goes to Speyside or Charlotteville. This circuit takes four hours.

7. Murcheson Trace

Time: 30 minutes. **Difficulty:** 2.

A sign on King's Bay Road points to the road leading to Murcheson Trace. Before reaching the house atop the hill, a trail to the right will bring you back down to King's Bay beach and its facilities. After you descend, you're only a couple of hundred feet from what was one of Tobago's prettiest waterfalls, its flow now greatly reduced because of the need to dam it to provide drinking water.

8. Rainbow Waterfall

Time: 1.5 hours each way. **Length:** 3 miles. **Difficulty:** 2-3.

This three-mile hike starts at Goldsborough and follows the riverbed to the waterfall. The ascent is gradual. The difficulty of the walk depends on how much water is flowing in the river. It takes about and hour-and-a-half to make the climb. The waterfall's name is based on the "rainbow people" phrase coined by Archbishop Desmond Tu Tu of South Africa when he visited the Caribbean. Trinidad and Tobago currently have adopted the slogan, "The Rainbow is Real." Although Trinidad has a very diverse heritage with a strong Indian influence, most Tobagonians are of African descent.

9. Hillsborough Dam

Time: 1-2 hours. **Length:** up to 5 miles. **Difficulty:** 2.

Located a few miles from Scarborough off the Windward Road headed toward Speyside is Mount St. George. The road that heads inland from there (identified on maps as the Mount St. George-Castara Road) can be used as a walking trail. Greebs, anhingas, herons and martins reside in the reservoir area, filled by stream runoff from the Main Ridge. Some locals claim alligators also live here. An old road beyond the damn climbs to the top of the Main Ridge. Depending on how far you care to walk, this can total as much as five miles. The views of Scarborough and Mount St. George are especially panoramic.

10. Fort King George

Time: 30-45 minutes. **Difficulty:** 1.

Historical sites don't play a major part in walking/hiking around Tobago, but this magnificently restored fort 400 feet above the capital city of Scarborough has beautifully kept walking paths and excellent panoramic views. Built in 1777, Fort King George consists of a lighthouse, powder magazine and officer's mess. One building has been converted into an art gallery. There are lots of cannon on display, and either these or their ancestors were put to good use. After a prolonged battle, the French took the fort, renamed it Fort Castries and occupied it from 1781-1793. Recaptured by the British, it changed hands in battle several more times, so it's amazing anything at all is left. It was abandoned in 1854.

Locals will tell you that Tobago changed hands politically thirty-one times in 200 years, making it one of the most oft-traded landfalls in the Caribbean. They're proud of having been so highly prized.

Little Tobago

Little Tobago, a 243-acre uninhabited island located one and one-half miles off the coast of Tobago proper, is one of the Caribbean's best hikes. In terms of both bird watching and sheer spectacle, the only thing I can compare it to is the Galapagos Islands off the coast of Ecuador, a much farther and considerably more costly trip. Little Tobago also is the easiest place in the Caribbean to view the sleek and majestic Red-Billed Tropic Birds in vast numbers.

Little Tobago hosts only about 2,000 people a year. Because so few visit, the government hasn't yet had to enact quota restrictions, even during the nesting season when sea birds are so plentiful you have to step around nests containing boisterous fledglings.

The main nesting season is from April to August. At least thirty-three species breed on Little Tobago, including frigate birds, laughing gulls, bridled and sooty terns and brown boobies. Year-round residents include Audubon's shearwaters.

Spring is excellent for hummingbirds, too, when the trees are flowering. Forestry officials say it's possible to see as many as thirty-four different hummingbird species, more than enough to tire the eyeballs of even the most avid birdwatcher.

Trails on Little Tobago can be quite slick and slippery immediately following a rain. It's recommended you wait at least two hours for the sun and wind do their work and let the ground dry out. Otherwise, some sections will be like a water slide. Tree roots criss-cross the path at many points, so the ride will be bumpy and unpleasant. However, because most of the trails are well inland; you don't have the danger of falling off the side of a mountain.

Little Tobago offers more than twenty different trails. Expect to spend three or four hours on this fascinating preserve to explore it unhurriedly and take pictures.

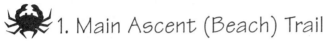 1. Main Ascent (Beach) Trail

Time: 10-15 minutes. **Difficulty:** 1-2.

The trail starts at the jetty/picnic shelter where most boats land. It climbs steadily to what will one day be an active interpretive center. The trail is well shaded much of the way with a canopy consisting mainly of sabal thatch palm.

Because of the poor nature of the soil, trail erosion is very much a problem on Little Tobago. Concrete steps were selectively placed on this main ascent trail to prevent runoff from sweeping away the path. Only the main trail has these occasional steps; the rest of the island is still in a natural state.

On this ascent, you'll pass bamboo water troughs which the Forest Service has to keep filled during the dry season. When cisterns on Little Tobago run dry, water is hauled in by boat from Tobago, an impressive indication of how dedicated the government is to maintaining Little Tobago as a permanent, year-round bird sanctuary.

The interpretive center at the top of the hill dates back to the early 1960s. Lack of funding has prevented its completion. At present it has both inside and outside toilets (the latter always work). Plans call for outfitting a kitchen and sleeping quarters for as many as twenty people. Ventilation at night could be an interesting problem since the building is currently sealed after dark to keep out bats.

A fruit garden of cashew, banana, guava and sour sop is cultivated near the house for the benefit of birds, not people.

2. Bird of Paradise I

Time: 20 minutes one-way. **Length:** .5 kilometer. **Difficulty:** 1-2. The trail ascends at the beginning, then winds around part of the cliff.

This is the first trail you encounter after leaving the interpretive center.

Located on the left about a hundred yards away, this connects with Bird of Paradise II.

After an initial moderate ascent, the trail follows the hillside, taking you along the route where the Bird of Paradise was most commonly seen. Good luck on spotting one here today; the sign is as much a tombstone as a trail marker. The last sighting of a Bird of Paradise in the wild on Little Tobago was November, 1981.

According to local accounts, forty-eight pairs of these colorful birds were introduced to the island in 1909 and another pair added in 1912. What happened to the birds is unclear. They apparently fell victim to predators and storms. Because of their limited ability to fly, it's believed they did not simply flap off to South America.

The Birds of Paradise may have flown the coop, but in this area you may see the Blue-crowned Motmot (also known as the King-of-the-Woods) which grows to eighteen inches and is noted for its racquet-shaped tail; the tiny yellow and black Bananaquit, mockingbirds and the Crested Oropendola, commonly called Yellowtails.

 3. Bird of Paradise II

Time: 30 minutes. **Length:** less than 2 kilometer. **Difficulty:** 2.

This trail is a continuation of Bird of Paradise I. It goes up a hill and then across the mountain.

 4. Yellowtail Trail

Time: 45-minutes roundtrip. **Length:** 1.3 kilometer. **Difficulty:** 2.

This entrance lies just beyond the entrance of Bird of Paradise I, and was named for the impressive number of the unique and distinctive yellowtail nests hanging from the trees.

Curiously, although Birds of Paradise disappeared years ago, some yellowtails apparently copied their call and adopted it as their own.

 5. Seabird View I

Time: 3-5 minutes. **Difficulty:** 1.

Located about a hundred meters from the interpretive center, this lookout

is an astonishing, surprising sight. You walk up on it without warning, unaware that before you stretches the windward side of the island, the rolling Atlantic and a cove of sheer cliffs peppered with birds. Most magnificent of all are the Red-billed Tropic Birds continually circling over the bay, a major fishing ground. Below you are some of the most turbulent waters in all Trinidad or Tobago, and the vista is an incredibly impressive one.

In the distance are the St. Giles Islands, a clump of rocks that are a thriving nesting area. Boat tours are available around St. Giles in good weather but landing at the preserve is prohibited.

If you feel active, you may take a branch trail down to the rocks to observe sea bird nests close-up. Noddy and sooty terns, laughing gulls and brown boobies all nest along this coastline. Tropic Birds, which build their nests at the cliff's edge, are said to do so because they have short legs and need an easy landing site. This branch trail takes five minutes going down; a tough ten minutes scrambling to get back up. It may be closed off at the peak nesting times.

6. Mockingbird Trail

Time: 10 minutes. **Length:** .4 kilometer. **Difficulty:** 2.

Named for one of the birds commonly found in this area, this trail borders West Indian cherry trees that were planted to attract and feed the birds. It passes an old building once used by naturalists studying here. The hill climbs steadily and moderately, then flattens out a little at the end. The brief walk leads to a crossroads (Hike #9).

7. Seabird View II

Time: 15 minutes. **Length:** .86 kilometer. **Difficulty:** 2. This may be muddy and requires a slight ascent.

This marked path veers off to the left just before you reach the ruins of the old naturalist house. Seabird II is another panoramic platform for observing major sea bird nesting colonies. The trail passes under a palm canopy and beside a fair amount of bamboo. If you hear something rustling through the ground cover, it may be a huge hermit crab. The crabs, which usually wear whelk shells, are very inquisitive and if you hold the shell long enough, the crab will come out.

The brown "cold snake" is sometimes found in this region; it feeds on

Seabird View II overlooks Alexander Bay. The rocks on the far shore contain many nesting seabirds. This finger of land is also the longest hike on Little Tobago.

the young nestlings of species that lay their eggs on the ground. Locals say the snake, which grows between eighteen and twenty-four inches, seems to love the smell of rank things, hence its name. Of course the rustling noise might also be a green iguana, sometimes seen on this trail.

If you notice a pronounced ammonia smell, you're not crazy; it's the pronounced presence of the bats that reside in this section.

The Seabird View II is not as dramatic as Seabird I, but it is still impressive. The coastline is fringed with cactus, especially prickly pear and Turk's Head. Boobies, terns and laughing gulls inhabit this area. Birds sometimes build their nests closer to this site than at Seabird I. However, the drop is so sheer it's not possible to see what's directly below you at the shoreline on Alexander Bay.

The opposite shore is a finger of land that leads to a light beacon. Thousands of birds lay their eggs here in nesting season. Except for the workers who service the beacon, few people make this ridge walk, a scorcher in dry season.

 8. George Ride Trail

Time: 10 minutes. **Difficulty:** 1.

This trail, named after one of the island's first custodians, leads from Sea Bird View II and passes through one of the oldest fruit gardens. You may spot evidence of cotton, since sea island cotton was grown here for several years. Feral fowl are also on the island, further evidence of earlier inhabitation.

 9. Campbell's Walk

Time: 45 minutes each way. **Length:** 2.4 kilometer. **Difficulty:** 3.

Branching left off the George Ride Trail, Campbell's Walk leads to the light beacon. First, you descend a rugged and bushy area before the access smoothes out. This is one of the longest and most rugged trails on the island.

Just after one-third way along Campbell's you'll encounter a difficult stretch with dense undergrowth. When it clears out, look for a rugged branch trail (about one hundred yards long) that leads down to the nesting tropic birds and laughing gulls. This is not an easy descent because of the thick undergrowth.

If you continue to the light beacon at the end of the point, you'll need to scramble a bit to actually reach the marker because of the rugged nature of the trail and the loose soil.

 10. Crossroads

Time: 5 minutes. **Difficulty:** 1.

Coming back from the light beacon on Campbell's Walk, turn left when you reconnect with the George Ride Trail. In a few minutes you will be at a major crossroads where George Ride intersects with three other trails: Mockingbird Trail (Hike #5), Ingram's Trail (Hike #11) and the WalJack Dam walk (Hike #10). At this point, you are only .5 kilometer from the second Seabird overlook and .4 kilometer from the beginning of the Mockingbird Trail. To return to the beach, take Mockingbird Trail which will take you back to the interpretive center.

11. Waljack Dam

Time: 7 minutes descent, 15 minutes ascent. **Length:** .5 kilometer. **Difficulty:** 2-3 depending on how slippery the conditions.

This is a water catchment area, a natural spring named after two naturalists, Wallace and Jack. Built in 1990, the dam is four to five feet high and about ten feet long. The all-season watering hole is an excellent bird attractor for white-tipped doves, yellowtails, pigeons, king-of-the-woods, Bananaquit, the Caribbean Martin and even hummingbirds. The dam, located near the coastline, is a dead-end walk.

12. Ingram's Walk

Time: 10 minutes. **Length:** .34 kilometer. **Difficulty:** 3.

This leads to the highest point on Little Tobago, regrettably not nearly as scenic as the Seabird overlooks. Only .34 kilometer long, Ingram's Walk takes about ten minutes because it is a steep climb.

13-14. Dinsmoor/Shearwater Trails

Time: 5 minute descent, 10-15 minute return ascent. **Length:** about 1 kilometer. **Difficulty:** 2-3.

At the end of Ingram's Walk, continue along the short seventy-yard Dinsmoor Trail, which connects with Shearwater. The whole purpose for having such short trails as Ingram's and Dinsmoor seems to honor naturalists who've worked here. These just as easily could have been a single trail.

Shearwater is one of the more rugged trails because it is not kept as clear as the others; shrubs and vines clog the trail, and it is steep in some parts. Shearwater leads to a seasonal Yellow Crown Night Heron nesting area.

 # 20. The Dutch ABCs: Aruba, Bonaire, Curaçao

Antillean Saying:
There are more days than weeks, so don't rush time.

You don't need a new vocabulary to learn the Dutch ABCs. Aruba, Bonaire and Curaçao spell perpetually warm, sunny weather, a myriad of activities and friendly people. That goes well in any language.

These picturesque Dutch lands off the coast of Venezuela are isles of perpetual summer, with almost never a cloud to mar the days. The rainy season lasts from September to November, when most of the precipitation (only twenty inches annually) falls. The excellent climate is only part of their allure; the islanders themselves account for the rest. They are people descended from the Dutch and intermixed with other European stock to create their own unique culture, including a special language called "papiamento," a blend of English, Spanish, Dutch and Portuguese. But not to worry: everyone speaks several languages, including English.

The ABCs escaped the often-brutal patterns of colonization seen elsewhere in the Caribbean. The dry climate did not favor the one crop that changed the face of the Caribbean—sugar cane. Land-hungry and labor-intensive, growing sugar cane required great tracts of land and a slave economy. The ABCs were one of the few islands where the natives were not slaughtered by European colonists. On Aruba and Bonaire, the Arawaks were not only left alone, but allowed to maintain contact with other Indians on the mainland. They were permitted to raise cattle, sheep, horses and goats. However, the Arawaks were forcibly removed from Curaçao to Hispaniola as slave labor.

Because the islands lacked gold, the Spaniards labeled them "useless islands," and never spent much time on them. The Dutch, looking for wood to build their ships, salt to preserve their foods and a military foothold in this hemisphere, took up forceful occupation in the ABCs between 1634-36. The Dutch invasion of Bonaire in 1636 is reported to have found only six Arawaks and a few cattle on the island.

The vividness of today's bright, white-washed buildings with colorful orange roofs is a remarkable contrast to the desert-like terrain of each island: large cactus and scrub are the ABCs only natural vegetation. According to legend, early explorers cut down all the trees for ship building, and goats have kept new forests from growing.

Goats were introduced by the Spaniards in the 16th century because they were an easily maintained source of protein on these barren islands, and by the 17th century Aruba was known as a "goat island." The hardy breed that evolved here causes real problems in dry years because the animals will graze on every green leaf they spot. About once every ten years conditions will be so dry that the goats will even devour the evergreen lignum vitae, which they normally overlook. Their feeding kills the saplings of this slow-growing tree.

The goats that roam free over the islands often appear to have no owners, but hit one with your car and you'll be amazed how quickly a grieving claimant will pop out of the cacti. Many locals would like to declare the goats a public nuisance and hunt them virtually to extinction, but the goats belong to someone, usually the poorer people. So, for the most part, they have to be tolerated. As the saying goes, "Every goat is still a vote!" meaning that politicians aren't as active as they might be in eliminating these harmful pests from the national parks and other protected areas.

Although Aruba, Bonaire and Curaçao are located within a few miles of one another, each has managed to develop its own distinctive characteristics. Although Aruba lacks a large national park, it does have a few marked trails and boasts one of the most famous natural bridges in the Caribbean. The national parks on Bonaire and Curaçao are both interesting, but the best is Bonaire's extensive Washington National Park, with its flamingo ponds. Bonaire also has some excellent caving that demands little more skill than turning on a flashlight.

The port city of Willemsted on Curaçao is one of the Caribbean's most picturesque, so don't miss it.

Travel Tips

Area: Aruba: 70.9 square miles, 19.6 miles long and 6 miles at the widest point. Bonaire: 122 square miles, 24 miles long and 3-7 miles wide. Curaçao: 180 square miles, 38 miles long and from 2 to almost 8 miles wide.

Language: Officially, it's Dutch but Papiamento, Spanish and English are widely spoken.

Population: Aruba, 67,000; Bonaire, 11,000; Curaçao, 140,000.

Time Zone: Atlantic Standard Time, one hour ahead of Eastern Standard Time.

Rainy Season: The islands receive less than thirty inches of rain annually. Most showers occur from September to November. They are usually short, quickly pushed away by the trade winds.

Getting There: Aruba and Curaçao are easy to reach, but Bonaire can be a challenge, depending on the day of the week you fly. The major gateways to the ABCs are Miami, Atlanta and New York. Venezuela's Aeropostal has direct flights to Aruba from Atlanta and Orlando, as stopovers on the way to Caracas. Continental and Air Aruba also supply daily service, and KLM flies from Europe several times weekly. The national carrier, ALM Antillean Airlines, provides the majority of flights to Curaçao and has the only direct air service to Bonaire. Unfortunately, ALM is notoriously inefficient.

For the best airline routing, as well as hotel packages, contact Maduro Travel, 1080 Port Blvd., Suite 100, Miami, FL 33132; 305/373-3341. Because of its volume business in the ABCs, Maduro can often arrange substantial discounts on some of the airlines.

Getting Around: Rental cars are available on all the islands and most of the major international companies (Avis, Budget) are represented. Cost is reasonable, around $200 per week for a small car. Driving is on the right.

Where to Stay: Aruba has many large resorts and hotels, with prices averaging US $125-US $174 a day.; however, the tourism authority has a list of guest houses and apartments as low as US $30 per day.

On Bonaire, if you're scuba diving as well as walking, try Captain Don's Habitat, one of Bonaire's best resorts. Captain Don Stewart started taking divers on tours in 1962, long before diving was available in much of the Caribbean. Stewart is one of Bonaire's greatest natural attractions. Most other Bonaire resorts are also dive-related. The tourist board here maintains a list of small guest houses.

Curaçao has a wide selection of hotels, resorts and guest houses which also are available from the tourist board.

Camping: It's possible—though not easy—to camp on all of the islands except Curaçao at Brakkeput, which adjoins Spanish Waters; Arrowakenweg 41A, P.O. Box 3291; tel 674428. The facility has showers, toilet facilities and tents available. Camping on some Curaçao beaches is possible but drinking water is a problem. The same is true for Bonaire, which has no designated camping areas whatsoever. On Aruba, you must obtain a permit from the police station to camp, and this involves a ten day waiting period, during which you must have a local address on the island. That, for all practical purposes, kills camping in Aruba.

Taxes & Tips: A 5% government tax and a 10-15% service charge are standard. Some hotels also charge an extra US $3-5 a day energy surcharge.

Documents: Americans and Canadians need valid proof of citizenship. All others need passports. A return or onward ticket and proof of sufficient funds may also be required.

Currency: Aruba has its own currency, called the Arubian florin. The Antillean guilder is not accepted and can only be exchanged at banks. Regardless of island, every American dollar is worth 1.77 florin (or guilder). Prices are often quoted in both currencies. Dollars are readily accepted everywhere and the Antilleans are usually scrupulously honest at working out the exchange rate. Bank hours vary on all islands but generally are open from 8:30 a.m. to noon and 1 p.m. to 4 p.m.

Electrical Current: This, too, is different on every island. On Aruba, it's the same as in the U.S., 110/60 cycles. On Bonaire, it is 127 volts/50 cycles, or 220 volts/50 cycles which causes problems for appliances that normally run on 60 cycles, such as hair dryers. Curaçao is also 50 cycles instead of 60. Borrow a transformer from your hotel.

Safety/Health Warnings: Because of the constant, cooling trade winds, many people do not realize how hot the sun is in the ABCs. These are among the southernmost islands in the Caribbean and precautions are necessary to avoid burning to the color of a robust rose wine. Dress appropriately and carry water on any long walks. The tap water on all three islands is some of the purest anywhere; because the islands are so dry, the drinking water is actually desalinated sea water.

Hiking/Walking Services: Check with the national park offices on each island for the latest information. To explore safe, dry caves, see the Barcadera description on Bonaire. There are no hiking/walking companies as such, though taxi drivers should be able to find all the spots mentioned.

Snakes and Other Venomous Creatures: You'll rarely find reference to rattlesnakes in the ABCs, but Aruba is home to a venomous rattlesnake, the Colebra (Crotalus durissus), though they are seldom seen. These snakes normally inhabit the most sparsely populated areas of Aruba between Jamanota, Fontein and San Nicolas. All other snakes are harmless. Locals believe that possession of a snake rattle is good luck, perhaps because they are so rare.

For More Information: Contact the Aruba Tourism Authority, 521 Fifth Ave., 12th Floor, New York, NY 10175; 212/246-3030; toll free 800/ TO ARUBA; OR fax, 212/557-1614. In Canada, 86 Bloor Street West, Suite 204, Toronto, Ontario, M5S 1M5; 416/975-1950.

The Bonaire Tourist Office, 275 7th Avenue, 19th Floor, New York, NY 10001; 212/242-7707. Curaçao Tourist Office, 400 Madison Avenue, Suite 311, New York, NY 10017; 212/751-8266.

 Aruba

Aruba is the westernmost island, situated just fifteen miles from the Venezuelan coast. Aruba is not technically part of the Netherlands Antilles group but is a separate entity within the Kingdom of the Netherlands. Aruba got tired of the central government in Curaçao controlling everything, particularly which airlines flew in. Breaking the monopoly of government-owned ALM Airlines, Aruba peacefully seceded and its tourism has been booming ever since.

Aruba is best known for two things: beautiful palm-lined beaches and shopping. The beaches are some of the cleanest and brightest in the Caribbean. They seem to stretch on forever, making them ideal for early morning and late evening walks.

While the beaches and shopping district of Oranjestad are the main hubs, you'll find a great deal more to see on the tiny island. Driving is easy because the roads are good, but navigating is hard because many are unmarked. You will have to consult the local road maps frequently. Or, you can take your bearings from the ever-present divi-divi trees. The divi-divis are all bent eternally in the direction of the easterly trades, which means they all point southwest.

You'll spot plenty of curious man-made objects as well: Ayo features Indian petroglyphs. Slightly more modern, but in a similar spirit are the ornate carvings of flowers and strange symbols bordering the doorways and windows of many old cottages. Formed in cement, these are hex signs, made to ward off evil spirits.

Across from the Concorde Hotel & Casino is The Old Mill, a full-sized windmill brought over from Holland. It's still in operation, not as an energy source but as a very popular and unusual restaurant. This is also near the Palm Beach area, a hot bed of windsurfing activity. With a sixteen mile-per-hour trade wind, this is a superior place to put in some board time or learn how to windsurf.

Gold mining was once an important industry on Aruba. It was one goldfield the Spanish managed to overlook. Gold was discovered in 1825, and more than 3,000,000 pounds were mined before operations were shut down when it was no longer economically feasible.

A huge oil refinery, at one time the world's largest, was built near San Nicolas. Tourism is now the number-one industry; however, Aruba lacks the developed hiking trails found on Bonaire and Curaçao. It's more a matter of locating the most interesting sites and then walking around.

Birdwatchers will want to obtain the color booklet entitled "Stinapa 26, Discover Aruba's Wildlife," available locally in bookstores or from the

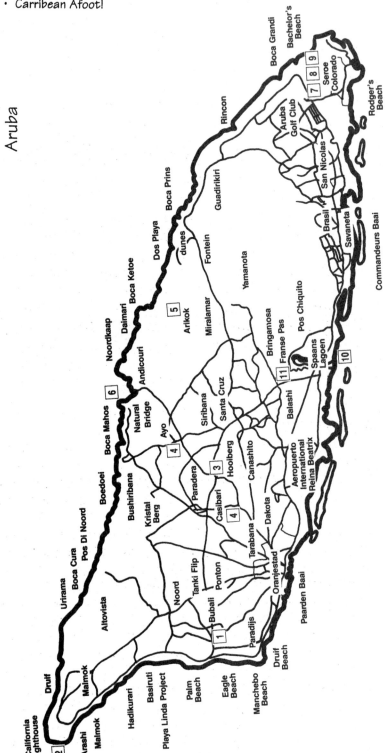

Aruba

Aruba Foundation for Nature and Parks, Seroe Colorado P.O. Box 706, Aruba, Netherlands Antilles.

1. Bubali Pond

Time: 30 minutes. **Difficulty:** 1.

Located near the beach, opposite the Concorde Hotel and south of the windmill restaurant, this pond is one of the best, as well as most accessible, for seeing birdlife on Aruba. Originally a salt pond, it is now kept wet year-round by serving as an overflow for the sewage plant. This is not as yucky as it might sound, because the nutrient-filled waters are rich in fish life, which in turn attracts a host of birds. This puts Aruba in the vanguard of an exciting new wetlands technology now being explored in many major U.S. cities.

Brown pelicans are particularly fond of this spot, and squadrons of them can sometimes be spotted flying in perfect formation, scooping the water's surface for dinner. Other birds common at this site are Black-crowned Night Herons (Nycticorax), the common egret (Egretta alba), little Green Herons (Butorides virescent) and the beautiful snowy egret (Egretta thula), sometimes called "the lady with the golden slippers" because of its yellow feet and black legs. As at most birding locations, best viewing is near dawn and dusk.

2. California Point/Lighthouse

Time: 1 hour. **Difficulty:** 1.

Located on a hill at the northern end of Aruba, the lighthouse is named for the 1891 wreck of the "California," located offshore in only fifteen to thirty feet of water. The shallowness of the water between here and Venezuela has led some scientists to theorize that Aruba was once part of the South American continent. However, most believe the ABCs were broken from a formation somewhere in the mid-Atlantic and simply drifted down the continental shelf towards South America.

California Point is an important nesting area for brown pelicans. The lighthouse is encircled with huge boulders that make the landscape almost moon-like. On the drive here you may be fortunate enough to spot Aruba's largest lizard, the iguana (Iguana iguana, Yuana) which grows as long as three feet. Totally vegetarian, with a special fondness for hibiscus blossoms, the iguanas are highly prized as a food delicacy.

3. The Haystack

Time: 45-60 minutes. **Difficulty:** 2.

This volcanic formation, officially called the Hooiberg, is located in the center of Aruba and can be seen from virtually anywhere on the island. The vegetation consists of yellow poui and the typical cacti. You may see the real divi-divi tree or Watapana (Caesalpina coriara), as opposed to other plants which are often mistaken for it. The true divi-divi has inconspicuous but fragrant blossoms and thick, curled pods rich in tannin. At one time the pods were exported to Germany for use in the leather industry. Use them to shine your shoes.

But wait until after you've climbed the several hundred steps that lead to the top of the Haystack, which peaks out at 541 feet. From the steps you can easily reach the summit; a maintained trail is planned for the future. On a clear day, you can see Venezuela, and view yellow orioles and several species of doves.

4. Casibari/Ayo

Time: 45 minutes to 1 hour, each. **Difficulty:** 1.

These two spots are littered with boulders that have been weathered into fanciful shapes by the trade winds. At Casibari, climb the rock steps to the top to survey the island or view the Haystack. The more developed of the two spots, Casibari has a souvenir and drink stand. It is ranked the second most popular tourist spot in Aruba.

Ayo, northeast of Hooiberg and usually less crowded, has been called the "Stonehenge of Aruba." No steps have been cut into the rocks, so you have to do all the scrambling yourself. A wall is planned to keep out the goats, who find Ayo a highly desirable hangout.

At dusk or dawn, if you're lucky, you may spot a burrowing owl or one of the rare mammals found here.

5. Arikok National Park

Time: 45 minutes to 1 hour. **Difficulty:** 1.

Located on a triangle of land between Boca Prins and San Fuego, the park has a few easy trails that are well laid out and easy to follow. Petroglyphs are evident on some of the rocks. As in all the ABCs, the sun and heat are overpowering, so take water. The park centerpiece is Mt. Arikok, which at 577 feet is the island's second-tallest peak. A small garden at the foot of the mountain (hill, really) displays most of the trees and shrubs common to Aruba.

6. The Natural Bridge

Time: 1 hour to explore thoroughly. **Difficulty:** 1.

Probably the most visited tourist site on Aruba, the Natural Bridge on the northeast coast is considered the Caribbean's finest. Viewed from the water, people walking across the rock span are the size of toy soldiers. Tours come by the bus load, particularly in the middle of the day. Later in the afternoon it is often quieter and the light is better for photography. A small cafe and souvenir stand are open throughout the day. A small sandy cove frames the pounding surf that hurls itself against the Natural Bridge. The bridge may not have been formed by this violent wave action, however. The bridge was formed inside-out, by rainwater coming from the land side to wash away weak spots of the coral rock. An interesting theory, but it doesn't rain that much here.

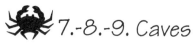

7.-8.-9. Caves

Time: 1 hour each. **Difficulty:** 1.

There are several sets of caves to choose from throughout the area known as the Seroe Colorado and north along the coast, all easy walking if you have a light and stay on the main path. Flashlights are often provided by guides or vendors at the cave mouths. Admission to the caves is free.

The Fontein Cave near Boca Prins is a large chamber with natural pillars at the entrance, that leads to a tunnel with Indian paintings. This, the largest of Aruba's caves, may undergo a massive facelift to make it more accessible to the public. Rumor has it that these Indian paintings may not be real, but were painted by a film company several years ago.

The Guadiriki Caves contain two large chambers lit by sunlight coming through an opening. The chambers are connected by a tunnel and require a light. Bats also live in this cave system, but none on the island are infected with rabies.

The Huliba Cave, also known as the Tunnel of Love, is a thirty-minute walk with a ten minute return to the entry point on the surface. The cave contains stalagmites and stalactites.

10. Spanish Lagoon

Time: 1 hour. **Difficulty:** 1.

A desalinization plant and the Aruba Nautical Club are at the mouth of this old pirate hangout. Go to the other end for some of the best birdwatching on Aruba: egrets, herons, frigates, and brown pelicans. This is where large green and yellow parakeets—about twice the size of those usually seen in pet stores—nest in the steep cliffs along the roadway. Sunset is the best time to see them. Three types of mangroves—red, black and button-wood—are represented. Repellent may be required when you're out of the wind.

11. Frenchman's Pass

Time: 1 hour. **Difficulty:** 1.

Situated south of Spanish Lagoon, Frenchman's Pass is a scenic walk/drive through a pass where the branches overhang the roadway. The road veering to the right leads to the Bushiribana gold mine ruins from 1898. The cement ruins are a favorite hangout for parakeets early in the day. Going east, you can walk/drive to the top of Mt. Jamanota, which at 617 feet is the highest point in Aruba. This area is being proposed for national park status.

Bonaire

Antillean Saying:
No matter how strange, ugly, evil or crazy someone is,
there will always be admirers.

Bonaire is considerably larger than Aruba, though it is far less developed. Although it also lacks Aruba's beaches and shopping opportunities, Bonaire more than compensates with its myriad of outdoor activities.

Bonaire has been described as a desert island surrounded by an oasis of coral reefs, some of the lushest and most colorful in all the Caribbean. Not surprisingly, most visitors are scuba divers from the U.S. You don't

Bonaire

need to be a scuba diver to explore Bonaire's underwater treasures. The snorkeling is excellent. You'll see bright orange sponges the size of boulders, convict-striped Sergeant Major fish that love to be hand-fed, and amazing black and white crinoids that look like sea lilies.

Island touring on Bonaire is divided into two distinct segments, south and north. Taking up almost all of Bonaire's southern tip is the solar salt works, where salt water is let into shallow flats called pans. Over a period of time, the water evaporates to leave salt crystals. The salt is scooped up by shovels and loaded into trucks, then washed and piled to dry before being shipped to the U.S. and elsewhere.

On Bonaire's northern end is Washington-Slagbaai National Park. Bonaire is home to a large population of flamingoes. Flamingoes, in fact, have traditionally outnumbered the people on Bonaire. The park is also home to many migratory birds and herds of free-roaming goats. You don't have to be in the park to encounter goats; they roam all over the island.

The Goto Meer, near the town of Rincon, is easily Bonaire's most scenic inland region. Here you can be sure of finding several hundred flamingoes strolling this inland lake. Many are usually close to the road, but they will start walking away as soon as you open the car door. This is a good place to watch the daily flight of flamingoes to Venezuela at sunset.

Lac Bay is a beautiful cove on Bonaire's east coast, a favorite picnic spot. The water is shallow with a sandy bottom, perfect for shelling or swimming. You'll also see many fishermen's huts lining the shore and large piles of empty conch shells that are free for the taking. Like many Caribbean islands, Bonaire is suffering a shortage of conch but is attempting to restock by growing its own.

 Kralendijk

Time: 1 hour. **Difficulty:** 1.

Pronounced "Crawl-in-dike" and meaning coral dike, Kralendijk is Bonaire's main city. Kralendijk is a relatively new city, situated on a natural harbor on the lee side with the additional protection of neighboring Klein Bonaire.

With about 1,700 residents, Kralendijk is still quite small, though it's been undergoing a massive facelift since the end of the 1980s in order to compete for more cruise ship business. The main street, Kaya Grandi, parallels the coastline and runs north-south. It takes about ten minutes to walk through the island's main business district.

Mirroring the yellow and orange structures of Aruba and Curaçao, Kralendijk offers a pleasant, safe walk, day or night. The more interesting stops are the Governor's House, built in 1837 and restored in 1973. Fort Oranje, designed to repel any invaders, was built shortly before the end of the 18th century. The waterfront, Roman-style fish market, usually selling more vegetables than seafood, dates from 1935. The center of town is the newly renovated and quite picturesque Wilhelmina Square. The small Protestant church in the middle of the square dates from 1857.

The prettiest time to walk Kralendijk is in the afternoon. As the sun sets in the west, the colorful buildings lining the harbor reflect the beautiful yellow glow. Watch for the rare and famous green flash, which—if it is going to appear—will happen immediately after sunset.

1. Solar Salt Pans

Time: 45 minutes to several hours, depending on how much territory you wish to explore. **Difficulty:** 1, but the sun can be a scorcher.

These are located so far south of Kralendijk, you should drive rather than attempt to walk to the salt pans.

Salt was valuable to the Dutch as a means of preserving herring, the sale of which provided an important livelihood. With salt, the herring could be preserved indefinitely; without, the fish would rot in a few days. The Dutch had obtained their salt from Spain until the Eighty Years' War between the Netherlands and Spain. These hostilities made them look elsewhere for salt. Venezuela and the Caribbean turned out to be the best sources.

Salt is always present in a dissolved form in sea water. The flat southern end of Bonaire was ideal for creating large flat pans in which the sea water could evaporate, leaving behind salt in its crystalline form. The salt was then scooped up and sent to the Netherlands.

This was labor-intensive work, however, requiring the importation of slaves. Salt pan work was considered some of the toughest—not only because of the work involved, but the constant glare from the crystals was hard on the eyes. After emancipation in 1863, solar salt production was no longer profitable and the pans were abandoned until this century. Using the latest in modern equipment, the Antilles International Salt Company resumed work in 1966 and it has continued ever since. Most of the salt is exported to the United States for industrial use, including water softening and sprinkling on snow-covered roads.

Approaching the solar salt works, the first thing you'll see are the crystallizers where the sea water is evaporating. During the process, which takes about a year, the water turns some shocking pink and purple colors. People who photograph the pans in this condition are often amazed at how much film they shot.

The salt crystals are scooped up by trucks, then slurried with brine and cascaded over grates to remove the impurities. The crystals are then loaded aboard ship by conveyer belt, and stored in the cargo holds.

The small huts—so small you have to stoop to enter—on the shoreline were once used to house slaves, who slept two by two in the tiny huts. However, they were not forced to spend the whole week at these huts. On Saturdays, they were given the opportunity to walk the seven hours to their homes in the village of Rincon in the northern hills; on Monday, they walked back.

The tall stone obelisks near some of the huts have no religious significance. Instead, the four stone markers were vital to ship captains for their bearings; much of the lee island is protected by shallow reef, and it would not be difficult to pile up a ship on shore. The obelisks were each painted a bright color for easy visibility at sea: red, white, blue and orange. An appropriately colored flag would be hoisted to let the approaching captain know which pan to approach. The orange obelisk has since been destroyed.

If you've a mind to, you can spend the night in one of these huts. Obviously, you need to supply your own bedding and any other comforts. If it turns out to be too uncomfortable, make sure you have transportation back to your hotel.

The Flamingoes

As if the salt pans themselves weren't interesting enough, the solar salt works are also one of the few nesting places in the world for the pink flamingo. The special sanctuary where the flamingoes lay their eggs in twelve to fifteen inch high conical nests is closed to the public and maintained by the salt company. Flamingoes are easily disturbed and there is always concern about frightening the birds off.

At one time, the number of flamingoes was estimated at only 1,500 on Bonaire; the population is now believed to be ten times that size.

The flamingoes only go to the sanctuary during egg-laying season. The rest of the year they can be seen close to the road in the crystallizers or other places around the salt pans, or in Washington Park on the north tip of the island. A good pair of binoculars is necessary to observe the shy birds, who will move away as soon as you leave your car and attempt to approach them. You are not allowed in the sanctuary itself.

Some Bonaire flamingo trivia: they were reported nesting on the island as early as 1681. Only three other places in the world have nesting colonies of pink flamingoes: the Bahamas, Mexico's Yucatan peninsula and the Galapagos Islands off Ecuador. Out of a world population of 60,000 flamingoes, 20,000 live in the southern Caribbean. Flamingoes make a high nasal honking sound like geese: "chogogo," also the Bonairean name for the birds.

New World flamingoes are technically known as red flamingoes; those of the Old World are the true "pink" flamingoes, though Bonaireans obviously don't care about this distinction because they paint everything pink after the birds. Flamingoes are born a fluffy gray; the carotene in their natural food supply of brine shrimp. algae, brine fly pupae, lagoon snails and tiny clams gives these birds their bright color. They live eight to nine years. When food is scarce on Bonaire, the flamingoes will fly two to three hours to feed in Venezuela.

The trick question is how do you tell male from female flamingoes, since they both have the same plumage? Well, during the mating season, the birds often walk in rows with their necks extended straight up. The birds with the longest necks are the males. I swear it's true! I can cite references!

 2. Barcadera Caves

Time: 1 hour. **Difficulty:** 1-2.

When taking the coastal road to Washington Park, you'll pass some excellent caves in the area known as Barcadera. Take the sharp turn uphill to the Caribbean Club hotel and bar; immediately on your right you'll see a stone pyramid which marks the entrance to the caves. Flashlights are essential.

The current owners of the Caribbean Club are incredibly friendly and a member of the family will sometimes take you on a free caving tour of about a half hour if you'll buy some drinks and snacks as a kind of trade-out. Better yet, negotiate for a full three-hour tour of the caves; the reasonable price may surprise you.

These caves are something that most visitors to Bonaire are unaware of, yet they are one of the island's best natural attractions. To contact the reasonably-priced, forty-room Caribbean Club, fax 599-7-7900; the telephone is 7901. Rooms are US $60 a day for a double. Three basic meals a day are an extra US $25, a bargain price for Bonaire, where food is expensive. The guide to ask for is Armyn van Dyke. He is rapidly becoming the caving expert on the island.

There are both wet and dry caves on the north and south ends of the island. Except for the Barcadera group, the best way to locate caves is to talk to locals.

3. Washington-Slagbaai National Park

Time: 5-8 hours. **Length:** two routes, 15 and 22 miles. **Difficulty:** 3-4 because of the distance and exposure to the sun. Start your walk when the park opens at 8 a.m. No overnight camping is permitted.

Actually a 13,500-acre game preserve primarily for birds, the park occupies most of the northwestern portion of Bonaire. Because it occupies both the rough Atlantic coast and the calm lee side, it has the most spectacular beach and cliff views on the island. Some viewpoints are breath-taking in their grandeur.

The park opens daily (except holidays) at 8 a.m. and closes at 5 p.m.; however, no one is admitted after 3:30 p.m. The reason visitors are not allowed in after 3:30 p.m. is the length of the two self-guided routes: the short route is fifteen miles, the long route is twenty-two miles. The roads are rough and though most tourists ignore the warning, some rental car companies state on their contracts that damage done on park roads is not covered by insurance. The best time for birdwatching is early in the morning.

The park was once a divi-divi, aloe, charcoal and goat plantation. It was sold to the government at the end of the 1960s by the last surviving member of the Herrera family, Boy Herrera, on the condition that the land remain in its natural state.

This area became the first preserve in the Netherlands Antilles. The name Washington goes back to the 1920s, when the Herrera family first purchased the property and named it "America." They later changed it to Washington.

It is possible to hike both routes in one day. Start early, bring plenty of water and snacks and wear a bathing suit so you can cool off occasionally at one of the beaches. Bring snorkeling equipment, too. As they say here, "Those who have not looked under the surface of the sea have seen only half of the island!"

Because of their length and the heat, a Difficulty Level of 3-4 is assigned both walks. If you bring your car, the drive might not rate much better. Make sure you have a spare tire, a jack and plenty of fuel or you may end up walking anyway. The trails overlap at the beginning and mid-way through. The difference is that the yellow trail follows the dramatic windward (eastern) coastline while the green cuts through the center of the park. Both routes join at a point just before Playa Funchi.

Please consult the accompanying map since the yellow route has a certain amount of backtrailing that will surprise you if you go on foot.

Yellow/Green Route Overlap

Y-G 1. Just about every type of plant common to Bonaire is found at this point, especially the large Kadushi cactus (Cereus repandus), which grows in jointed segments and whose thorns point in all directions. Kadushi may grow more than thirty feet and look almost tree-like.

The straight-standing and roseate-bristled Yatu cactus (Lemaireocereus) is the species used to construct most of the fences and other enclosures on Bonaire. Stick a cut-off piece of Yatu into the ground and it starts growing again; these living fences hardly ever need to be replaced and they certainly never need painting.

You'll also find prickly pear (Opuntia wentiana), mesquite (Prosopis

Although goats are terrible pests who destroy foliage and keep the Dutch ABCs desert-like, locals are not anxious to eliminate them. Goats have free run almost everywhere, and woe to the tourist who runs over one.

juliflora), divi-divis and the long-spined acacia. Note how many of the plants on Bonaire are protected from goats. The mesquite is an important source of charcoal and an increasingly-favored wood for grilling food.

Y-G 2. Salina Matijs: Salina Matijs is sometimes flooded long enough during the rainy season to attract waterfowl, and sandpipers and black-winged stilts are the most common birds when this area is wet. Divi-divi trees are also common here.

Yellow Route

Y-3. So many prickly pear grow at the beginning of the yellow route that even goats take the road. This stop is designed to illustrate the dramatic difference between the vegetation on the top of the hill ahead, which is exposed to salty trade winds. Vegetation exposed to constant winds, whether in the high mountains or along the shore, never grows as tall.

Y-4. Playa Chiquitu: Playa Chiquitu (meaning "Small Beach") may look appealing but it is too treacherous for swimming because of the strong undertow. As park officials like to point out, you are in the park at your own risk and if you decide to ignore the warnings, that's your problem. Liability insurance isn't well understood on Bonaire (lucky Bonaireans!). Of interest at Playa Chiquitu are the formation of sand

Washington Slagbaai National Park

dunes, made possible by the presence of creeping crab-grass (Sporobolus virginicus) whose extensive root system permits the sand to accumulate.

Y-5. Boca Chiquitu: Boca Chiquitu contains sharp-pointed limestone rocks that host lots of land snails (Bonaire has ten species). A huge boulder broken off the wall contains fossil corals and is home to plenty of scuttling crabs. The seaweed floating in the bay much of the time is Sargassum, found all along the windward coast.

Y-6. Ceru Grandi: Ceru Grandi is a rock outcropping which is a relic of the so-called higher and middle terraces, formed during past ice ages. The road itself is located on the lower terrace. The higher terrace is the oldest, formed about one million years ago, when the sea level was about 180 feet above today's level. The middle terrace is between 340,000-510,000 years old, limestone deposited during a period of rising sea level when the polar ice caps supposedly melted.

Y-7. Cara Corra: The road to Cara Corra ("Red Face" in papiamento) at Ceru Grandi is a bleak one, with only a few button mangroves surviving the constant wind and salt spray. Cara Corra is a boulder at the base of Ceru Grandi, whose holes and clefts are said to resemble an Indian face. To the left of the rock you can climb Ceru Grandi, though you'll need to scramble on all fours near the top. The top of the middle terrace has a few caves which were once mined for phosphate.

Y-8. Boca Cocolishi: Boca Cocolishi has many fossil shells on the top of its terrace. This bay is famous for its flat pulpit-like rising above the surfline. The bench consists of calcareous algae and worm shells which cover the limestone and make it resistant to the wave action. Erosion is actually less at such a protected spot. The bench creates a quiet pool partly surrounded by sand which is about three feet deep and calm, no matter how turbulent the waves.

Y-9. Pos Mangel: Pos Mangel, or "Sweet Well," is one of the few places in the park where fresh water is always available. As such, it is one of the best places on the island for birdwatching; creep up slowly in order not to scare them away. The bird species found here include the yellow-winged parakeet, the yellow warbler, ground dove, common bananaquits, tropical mockingbirds and many more. Other parakeets may be present, but they have a tough time surviving the droughts on Bonaire, which occur every five or six years. Besides facing starvation and drought the birds have to feed in the village fruit gardens, where the parakeets are often caught and caged for show.

Y-10. Boca Bartol: Boca Bartol is another prime birdwatching spot. Yellow-crowned night herons are almost always present halfway up the terrace or near the water. Snowy egrets, brown pelicans and cormorants are frequent visitors.

If you're up for what is considered some of Bonaire's finest snorkeling, stop at Playa Benge. The groove and spur coral formations are a little over twenty feet deep, and lots of fish are always present. Continuing, the hill on the right is known as Shishiribana and is 300 feet high. The yellow route now joins the green route at Playa Funchi.

Green Route

G-11. Rooi: Entering the park on the green route, the first stop is a rooi running parallel to the road for several hundred feet before crossing it. During rainy periods, roois contain running water, something hard to imagine during the dry season.

G-12. Ceru Kepton: Ceru Kepton provides an excellent view of the west coast. Straight ahead is the hill, Shishiribana, and to the left is the tallest hill on all Bonaire, Brandaris, at 800 feet high.

G-13. Subi Brandaris: Subi Brandaris is a by-road that ends at a parking lot where you can begin the one and one-half hour climb (Difficulty: 3) to the top of Brandaris, Bonaire's highest point. The hike starts with a footpath which soon gives way to a ridge. The ridge route is marked with yellow circles painted on the boulders. From the top you'll have an excellent view of the entire island, perhaps as far south as the salt pans. Mountains in Venezuela or Mount Christoffel, Curaçao's highest peak, may also be visible.

Close the fence gate that separates Slagbaai from Washington; Washington is loaded with marauding goats, while Slagbaai isn't; and everyone wants to keep it that way. Don't be responsible for devastating part of the island's fragile ecology.

G-14. Put Bronswinkel: Put Bronswinkel is another freshwater well that is superb for birdwatching. Move quietly. The trees may appear to be filled with many nests, but these are actually epiphytes (air plants). This is the place to see some of the island's rarest birds, but to do so you must sit quietly for a long period of time. If you're feeling too restless, pass up this spot out of consideration of the serious birders who will go from ecstatic to murderous if you noisily blunder into their sanctuary.

Yellow Green Route Overlap

Y-G 15. Playa Funchi: Playa Funchi is home to a subspecies of lizard found only on Bonaire, the harmless Cnemidophorus murinus ruthveni. They are quite tame at this spot, well acquainted with bread crumbs, and will eat out of your hand if you're quiet enough. Females and juveniles are brown, while the brightly colored male has a blue head and greenish-blue hind feet and tail-root.

Playa Funchi was the harbor for Washington plantation, as the pier remnants show. Today it is a very popular place for snorkeling, swimming and sunbathing. There is no current inside the bay, making this a safe place to swim.

Y-G 16. Road to Brasia: Near Brasia, the road crosses into Slagbaai with a goat grid over the road to keep the pests from following. The road goes along the coast. Early and late, it's possible to spot iguanas sunbathing near the cliff edge, where they can escape quickly by diving into the sea. Brasia is named for the dyewood or Brasil wood (Haematoxylon brasiletto) which yields a red dye when rasped. The oldest known map of the Caribbean, from 1513, designates Bonaire as the "island of the Brasil tree." These grooved trees were once an important export.

Y-G 17. Pos Nobo: Pos Nobo, or "New Well," has a drinking fountain for humans, and two shelving sides so there will always be water for the birds. It's possible to climb Brandaris from here, though the route is not marked.

Y-G 18. Boca Slagbaai: Boca Slagbaai is one of the finest snorkeling and swimming beaches on the island. Dive boats come all the way here from the Kralendijk area, as much as forty-five minutes away. Historically an important harbor, it got its name from the dutch word "Slagten," meaning slaughter. This is where the cattle on the northern part of the island were processed and turned into steaks for export. Salt was also exported from here for a time. Besides being one of the finest swimming spots, this is another excellent birdwatching site: snowy egrets and flamingoes are almost always in the salina here.

Y-G 19. Salt Pans: Salt pans with straight narrow dams are leftovers from the plantation days. In the dry season (February to September) you'll normally find a white crust.

Y-G 20. Cactus: Fasciations are an unusual cactus: all their points may grow at random instead of in a distinctive pattern.

Return to Yellow Route

Y-21. Ceru Sumpina: Beyond the Fasciations, the two routes divide again. Here the yellow section is known as the "panorama road" because of its excellent overviews of other parts of the island.

Ceru Sumpina, or Thorny Hill, offers good views of Slagbaai and Brandaris. You'll note that vegetation here is more dense than in Washington, due to the climbing plants, particularly milkweed.

Y-22. Ceru Chubatu: After a steep descent, the road climbs to Ceru Chubatu, or Billy Goat Hill, another area noted for its climbing plants. The inkberry (Randia aculeata) is the dominant species.

Y-23. Ceru Corra: Ceru Corra is a red rock called Jasper, made of quartz, though the red color suggests a high iron content. This is a typical ceru, a place where a rock formation is more resistant to erosion than the surrounding rock, so that it rises high above its surroundings.

Y-24. Salina: This salina offers good flamingo viewing most of the time. However, don't approach too closely or they will walk away. Use binoculars or a telephoto lens. The yellow route continues north through overgrown aloe fields and thorny woodland, joining the green route at #26.

G-25. Flamingo Island: This section of the green route leads to what is called Flamingo Island, a peninsula in salina Slagbaai where you may see flamingoes at the closest point yet. The square island in the middle of the salina always contains a few birds, some of which breed there. Slagbaai is an important feeding area for the flamingoes, who skim the water for brine shrimp or graze (dive) to a depth of about three feet for their forage.

G-26. Lignum Vitae: Lignum vitae are evergreen trees with a dark green top and smooth, white-spotted trunk. Because of their high resin content, lignum vitae are highly prized in shipbuilding, particularly for creating a water-tight seal around propeller shafts.

Yellow/Green Route Overlap

G-27. Juwa-pass: Juwa-pass on the left shows interesting examples of intrusions created when liquid rock (magma) fills in the spaces (fissures, holes, etc.) of older formations, then congeals. These hexagonal basaltic columns were formed on the bottom of the ocean, an estimated 70-100 million years ago. This is also an excellent overview area.

G-28. Parakeet Watch: After descending through the pass and climbing over undulating terrain, the road leads to an excellent parakeet watching tree called the Broadleaf Caper (Capparis hastata). Parakeets often build their nests inside these trees, which typically contain deep cavities.

G-29. Agave Cactus: After crossing another goat grid that leads back into Washington, the final stop is at an agave field, where yellow flowers begin blooming in April and attract many bananaquits and humming-birds. In days past, the Agave vivipara was sliced, roasted and eaten like a biscuit. Locally it is known as "kuki'indjan," or Indian biscuit.

 Curaçao

Antillean Saying:
I need to be paid for my services.
Just saying thank you is not enough.

Curaçao is not only the largest of the Dutch ABCs, it is the busiest of the islands. Of all Dutch ports, Curaçao's Willemstad Harbor was for decades second only to Rotterdam in importance, primarily because of the large oil complex developed here over the years.

Taking your first look at Willemstad, you may experience a case of deja-vu, and no wonder. It seems whenever magazines or advertisers want to depict the cheerful, Old-World architecture found in some Caribbean cities, they often choose Willemstad's striking yellow and orange waterfront. Understandably so, since these stores and homes, many dating back several hundred years, create a welcoming atmosphere that modern neon and plastic can never match.

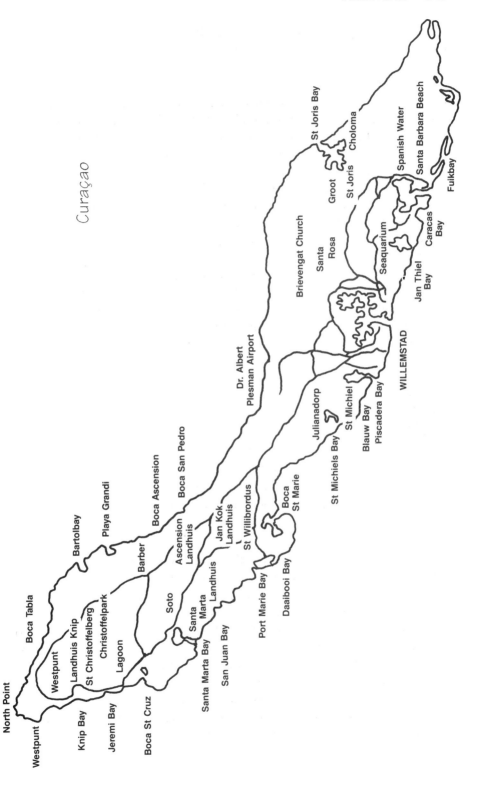

Curaçao

North Point

Westpunt

Knip Bay

Jeremi Bay

Boca St Cruz

Boca Tabla

Westpunt

Landhuis Knip

St Christoffelberg

Christoffelpark

Lagoon

Bartolbay

Playa Grandi

Barber

Soto

Santa Marta Bay

Santa Marta Landhuis

San Juan Bay

Boca Ascension

Ascension Landhuis

Jan Kok Landhuis

St Willibrordus

Port Marie Bay

Daaibooi Bay

Boca St Marie

Boca San Pedro

Dr. Albert Plesman Airport

Julianadorp

St Michiels Bay

St Michiel

Blauw Bay

Piscadera Bay

Brievengat Church

Santa Rosa

Groot

St Joris

St Joris Bay

Choloma

Seaquarium

Jan Thiel Bay

Caracas Bay

Spanish Water

Santa Barbara Beach

Fuikbay

WILLEMSTAD

However, Curaçao's Dutch influence could reduce you to the stilted pronunciation of the recently literate when it comes to the local tongue-twisting names: like Grebbelinieweg or Goeroeboeroeweg. When it comes to writing directions here, a single scrap of paper may not be enough; some of the street names have more than thirty letters.

Willemstad is divided into two separate entities by the main channel which makes this such a valuable port. A pontoon bridge known as "Queen Emma" conveys pedestrian traffic across to the other side of the channel. When Queen Emma is retracted to allow a ship to pass through (or when it's put out of commission because a tanker has collided with it), a ferry transports you across instead.

The two sides of Willemstad are known as Punda and Otrobanda. Punda, meaning "point" is on the east bank and is the older settlement, dating back to 1634. In Otrobanda, which means "the other side," development began in 1707. Punda is more visitor-oriented. Not only is this the section with most of the old restaurants and stores in storybook colors, it is one of the great shopping areas of the Caribbean. With offerings as varied and sophisticated as New York, London or Paris, it far surpasses even Aruba. Many visitors also find Punda's large floating market with Venezuelan produce equally intriguing. The boats come from the mainland regularly, so this is the freshest produce you can buy on the island, and it is quite safe to eat.

Curaçao's cosmopolitan population (more than seventy different nationalities) is best reflected in its tremendous choice of dining establishments. The local specialty is the rijsttafel (pronounced rice-tah-fel), an Indonesian smorgasbord containing from fifteen to forty different dishes including pork, shrimp, chicken, beef, vegetables and fish that are broiled, stewed or fried. Peanuts and a relish of chopped peppers can be added to spice things up even more.

Christoffel Park

Opened to the public in 1978, Christoffel Park consists of three former plantations: Savonet, Zorgvlied and Zevenbergen.

The park opens Monday through Saturday at 8 a.m. but admission to the mountain closes at 3 p.m., to the ocean side at 4 p.m. Sundays, the park is open from 6 a.m. to 3 p.m. Guided tours are possible; special walks at dawn and dusk occasionally offered, including an excursion to see the rare Curaçao deer. Call 640363 for full information.

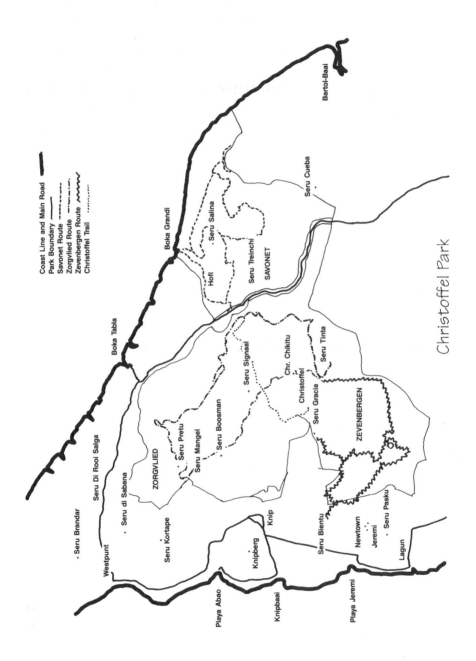

Christoffel Park

Coast Line and Main Road
Park Boundary
Savonet Route
Zorgvlied Route
Zevenbergen Route
Christoffel Trail

Bartol-Baai

Seru Cueba

Boka Grandi

Seru Salina

Seru Treinchi

Hofi

SAVONET

Boka Tabia

Seru Signaal

Seru Tinta

Chr. Chikitu

Christoffel

Seru Boosman

Seru Gracia

Seru Pretu

Seru Di Rool Salga

Seru Mangel

ZORGVLIED

ZEVENBERGEN

Seru di Sabana

Seru Brandar

Knip

Seru Pasku

Westpunt

Seru Kortape

Knipberg

Seru Blentu

Newtown

Jeremi

Lagun

Playa Abao

Knipbaai

Playa Jeremi

Savonet Plantation

The Arawaks farmed this territory rule until the Dutch took possession in 1636. At that point, the Indians left and it was necessary to attract farmers to work the soil. Savonet Plantation, one of Curaçao's largest, was established sometime before 1662. Dairy products, wool and cattle provided what one planter called a "moderate and relatively decent living" in this fairly harsh land.

Droughts, however, could kill as much as 50% of the livestock within a year or two. The year 1877 proved an unusually brutal one, first because of drought and then because of a wayward hurricane which killed off the sheep population so that it never recovered. By the end of the century, Savonet was known for its mule breeding.

Because of the lack of water, farming was limited strictly to drought-resistant plants such as millet, peanuts and beans. These foodstuffs were given short shrift on space, only about 10% of the plantation.

Savonet banked its agricultural future on importing Agave sisalana (hemp) used in the manufacture of rope. Coincidentally, all of the island's 25,000 coconut trees died that same year from scale insect attack, and since coconuts also yield fiber for rope-making, it looked like the agave plantations held excellent prospects. Like everything else, however, it was also doomed, because of the low profit. These agave plants are scattered throughout the park but are very difficult to differentiate from their more famous cousin, the century plant.

One of the most elaborate cultivation projects involved insects rather than plants. Cochineal, a crimson dye, brought a much better price than indigo, but came only from the female cochineal, a scale insect (Dactylopius coccus). In turn, this bug thrived only on the juices of the thornless nopal cactus (Nopalea cochenillifera).

A nopal cactus nursery was begun at Savonet in 1838 but did not do well until 1848. This limited success was never repeated. As soon as the fences protecting the cactus fell into disrepair, the cattle devoured the spineless succulents, completely wiping them out. Today, this cactus survives only in the island zoo and in private gardens.

1. Savonet Route

Time: 3 hours of walking. **Length:** almost 6 miles. **Difficulty:** 3 if you choose to walk in the open sun. Take drinks and snacks.

Blazed in a very obvious shade of blue, this route begins on the left just inside the park, starting at the Savonet country house. It is suggested that you walk/drive this route before walking any of the others, in order to become familiar with the park plant life. The route goes along the north coast and offers a look at caves with Indian drawings.

The medium-sized country house of Savonet, rebuilt after a surprise attack by the British in 1806, is considered typical 18th-century architecture. It is oriented east-west, surrounded by a parapet, and has no interior corridors.

The parking lot is shaded by the dreaded manchineel tree, whose sap is caustic. It is readily identified by its deadly, small green apple, known as the "apple of death." If you follow the path to the old orchard, you will also find mahogany trees, easily distinguished from the manchineel since its trunk is rugged, rather than smooth, and the fruits shaped more like pears than apples.

Continuing, you will pass mesquite (Prosopis juiliflora) and divi-divi trees, whose pods were in great demand for their high tannin content (60%). Savonet exported forty tons of pods annually in the late 1800s, by far the most important export crop for Curaçao, until chrome alum replaced tannin as a tanning agent near the turn of the century.

Large fields of prickly pear have been flourishing since the mid-1950s. Prickly pears were able to establish themselves quickly because the discs readily snap off, to be transported by animals or humans. The discs then fall to ground and take root. It's possible to use prickly pears for animal forage, but you have to eliminate the thorns.

Lignum vitae, which often has black tears of resin on its spotted trunk, was an important wood for shipbuilding. Because of the high resin content, the wood formed a water-tight seal around propeller shafts. An evergreen, its blue blossoms produce a heart-shaped orange fruit.

As the road turns right, you'll pass dyewood trees which, for a time, were an important export crop for Savonet. Rasping the wood produces a red color suitable for dyeing cloth. The trees are easy to distinguish because their trunks are unusually grooved.

At the crossroads, go straight. From here it is one-way traffic as the road steeply descends into a "rooi."

In the rooi and along the sides of the road near it is a plant with clearly visible hairs on its broad leaves and branches, which should not be touched. The shrub is called locally "bringamosa" ("fighting young lady") and the Latin name is Cnidoscolus urens (translates as "burning"). The stinging hairs have a substance which causes itching and scratching and, for very allergic people, a high fever. Also growing in the same area is a natural antidote for those unlucky enough to touch the fighting young lady, called Flaira (Jatrophya gossypifolia). It looks just like the fighting young lady but lacks the stinging hairs and has red flowers. If you rub juices of this plant on you, the itching usually fades.

As you emerge onto a plateau, you will see a sign that indicates a good view of the north coast. If you get out to walk here, beware the ground cactus. It's amazing the kinds of shoes those thorns are able to pierce. Boka Grandi is a rough, wave-swept beach on one side of the viewpoint; Savonet house and Christoffel Hill are on the other.

Look carefully among the melocaccti if they are in bloom. Whiptail lizards love dining on the pink flowers and fruits, as do several species of hummingbirds, including the Ruby-Topaz (Chrysolampis mosquitus) and Blue-tailed Emerald Hummingbird (Chlorostilbon mellisugus).

The road makes a steep descent onto a salt flat (or salina). Many salt-resistant trees grow on the sand barrier separating the salina from the sea. In the shallow, calm waters here you may see herons and American oyster catchers.

Look carefully at the limestone soil and you'll probably see ribbed, milky-white snail shells that look like old-fashioned wicker bee hives. These land snails, which need lime to build their shells, are endemic to these Dutch islands. The fact that no South American snail species are present gives added credence to the theory that the ABCs were never connected to South America.

Besides the divis, another tree that might attract your attention is the "mata piska" or fish killer (Jacquinia barbasco) which exudes a penetrating, sweet smell when in bloom. Resembling the lignum vitae but with a much rougher trunk, the white flowers become orange-red fruits. The fish killer tree gains its name this way: if you throw berries, leaves or bruised branches into still (non-flowing) water, you'll soon have fish floating on the surface. Fish have been caught this way for centuries by South American Indians. The toxin is not harmful to humans.

The road ends at a parking lot a short distance from Indian drawings and caves. On the walk, you'll pass a sheer rock face that houses a fair number of wasp nests. These wasps (Polistes versicolor) are not aggressive but should be left alone.

The reddish-colored Indian drawings, looking almost as if they had been done in crayon, are fenced to protect them from being defaced. Similar drawings have been found on the South American continent, and from the pottery shards here, it appears the makers originated in Venezuela. The Indians did not live in the caves but in oval houses made of wood and intertwined branches. Figures drawn in the caves, estimated between 500 and 2,000 years old, are considered abstract figures that probably had some religious significance. The figures are drawn in white and black as well as terra cotta.

The most interesting cave is the second one, but the bottleneck at the entrance requires that you scuttle inside on all fours. You'll need a light to go farther, but the cave soon opens so you can standing upright again. The cave extends for a distance of about 410 feet. Its floor is covered with grayish-brown guano from the four species of bats that reside here; no vampires within, all are harmless. If that description isn't unappetizing enough, consider that the guano may seem alive because of the millions of harmless mites (Antricola silvai) swarming through it.

Stomach under control, you'll soon take a sharp right to enter the white chamber whose walls are made of soft marl. Over thousands of years, drops of water have formed the stalactites and stalagmites. Another of your worst nightmares may suddenly appear in your light beam: a fearsome-looking cave spider which is harmless. Actually related to the whip scorpions but lacking their poison glands, the spider's first pair of long thin legs are used in mating.

Finally, you'll enter the well-lit sanctuary of the "cathedral" hall which has a small and a large ceiling window. Barn owls, with their heart-shaped face masks, are spotted here.

The return road offers fine coastal views with the opportunity to scale a couple of large boulders. Note that the traffic eventually goes from single lane back to two-way.

2. Zorgvlied Route

Time: 3-5 hours, depending on the route taken. **Length:** an option of 4.7 miles or 7-1/2 miles. **Difficulty:** 3-4 if you walk the entire route. Shade protection from the relentless sun and plenty of fluids are essential.

The green-blazed route explores the Zorgvlied plantation, which was merged with Savonet in 1830, making it one of the largest and most important on all Curaçao in the 1800s. The trail involves both driving and climbing, and ends atop Mount Christoffel.

Like Savonet, the Zorgvlied Route is a botanical, geological and historical tour. One of the first items of interest you pass is one of those exotic-import ideas that went badly astray not only here but on some other islands: the rubber vine. Cryptostegia grandiflora was brought from Madagascar during WWI to produce latex, which is made into rubber. The plant actually bleeds latex if you pinch it, so the concept was a good one—too good.

The rubber vine, with its whip-like runners, thrived in Curaçao and soon overgrew the local vegetation. Officially considered a pest, it is too difficult to eradicate because the roots must be dug up to prevent the plant from sprouting anew.

At the country house ruins you'll find a row of West Indian cherry trees (Malpighia punicifolia) that bear a marble-sized red fruit. The fruit is

A silhouette of Christoffel Park's two most common plants, the divi-divi tree and cactus.

extremely high in vitamin C: only three cherries supply the minimum daily requirement for an adult.

The Dutch name Zorgvlied means a place "where worry flees." The plantation was begun in 1716, but no one has worried about the country house since 1832, when this plantation merged with Savonet. Only the walls are still standing, though the porch is in decent shape.

The aloe plants on the slope in front of the porch are part of the plantation's export business. The sap was boiled down and the resulting resin sent to England and the U.S. for use in sunburn creams and laxatives. This is the miracle aloe being touted in health stores and beauty shops. It is less well known that in desperate times, the resin can substitute for hops in brewing beer. An all-around miracle, aloe contains healing properties for the inside and out.

After leaving the ruins, the road descends steeply to provide a good view of Mount Christoffel. If you go left at the T-intersection, it will take you to the foot of Christoffel, where you can begin the climb. Ahead of you is a once fertile valley were millet was grown. If you're tired of the scenic tour and ready to walk, turn left to Christoffel.

Going straight, the road descends into two more roois (overflow areas). If you're driving, right after this second rooi, shift into low gear to make it up the steep slope. Two Z-bends lead to a hilltop overlooking an area known as Rancho Grande. The geology of the hill covers an incredible time span. The lower terrace is an estimated 125,000 years old; low inland hills comprising the middle terrace are 510,000 years old. Rocks on these hills are an estimated 100 million years old, part of the Curaçao Lava Formation. The geology of the ABCs, obviously long and complicated, is well-explained in the park guide that is for sale at the entrance.

The trail goes along a ridge that is the most scenic part of the entire Zorgvlied Route. After a final steep descent, the route takes you to the foot of Mount Christoffel. Or, you can continue for about .3 miles to the top of a small hill where you can view small Christoffel. The real reason for visiting here is the opportunity to see the endangered white-tailed hawk (Bueto albicaudatus), with its distinctive "kee-weet, kee-weet" call. Sometimes hunted, though this is against the law, the large birds feed on lizards, insects, and the meat of freshly killed goats. In the mid-1980s, there were only five to ten breeding pairs on all of Curaçao.

 3. Zevenbergen Route

Time: 2-3 hours. **Length:** almost 7 miles. **Difficulty:** 3, due to the sun and occasional climbing.

Marked in yellow, this undulating road passes through the Curaçao Lava Formation. It offers several interesting side excursions, as well as the opportunity to climb Christoffel (yes, that's where all roads and trails eventually lead).

Begin by walking from the parking lot at the start of the yellow route to make a ten minute climb of Seru Tinta. Besides excellent panoramic views and the chance to study the island's geology, the real reason for the climb is Piedra di Monton—what looks like a large heap of stones deposited by several dump trucks.

These rocks represent the dreams of escape of slaves during the 18th and 19th centuries. The story handed down is this: salt is a crucial food item in the tropics. Without salt, you will soon lose your own body salts by sweating. Slaves apparently believed that if they didn't eat salt, they would be able to fly (probably because of the feeling of light-headedness symptomatic of salt deprivation). It was believed that every slave who had not eaten salt could place a stone at the foot of Mount Christoffel and sing a song to enable them to fly back to Africa. In the 20th century, the stones piles (Piedra di Monton) were appropriated to help maintain the park roads. Although it may be tempting, it is forbidden to collect anything, even stones, in the park.

Taking the main yellow route, climb about 190m for an excellent view of Santa Martha Bay to the south. In this spot are the only two species of orchids that occur on the island. The prettiest is the purple orchid, which blooms in July and August. White orchids peak in December and January but are present anytime there's sufficient rain.

A chain crosses the road that leads to Seru Gracia (975 feet), but it's only a fifteen minute walk to the summit. If you really wish to go exploring, you could follow the col between Seru Gracia and Seru Christoffel and climb Christoffel by this unmarked route. The roundtrip time is about ninety minutes.

Continuing along the main road, you'll come to the Seru Bientu trail, a ten minute path to the top of a hill whose name literally means "wind" (bientu). The climb is not steep but the wind can be strong enough to literally stop you in your tracks. The trail begins among dyewood trees and shrubby kamalia, although lichens and bare rock soon become characteristic on the right side. In the valley below is a manganese mine that closed in 1881.

At the summit, the leaves of the sabal palms are a soothing but dynamic sound in the ever-present wind. Another ten-minute walk on the trail will reward you with impressive views of the Knip and Lagun regions.

The final stop is the Zvenbergen mansion, an unusual two stories instead of the typical single level. The name Zevenbergen means "seven mountains," and you have a view of them all from here. Unfortunately, when this plantation was merged with the one at Knip in 1864, the new owner lived at the Knip site and the Zevenbergen Plantation buildings have been allowed to be leveled by wind and time.

4. Christoffel Trail/Climb

Time: 1 hour from the base to the top. **Difficulty:** 2-3. Christoffel is about 1,230 feet high.

Two routes lead to the summit of the park's namesake. Starting at the park visitor center, it's an easy thirty-minute walk to the parking center at the foot of Christoffel. From there, it's another hour to the top. Or you can take a shortcut by driving to the foot of the hill. Whatever the route, it's recommended you begin early because of the constant sun and heat. Furthermore, the pathway—blazed in red—is on the lee side of the hill, out of the wind, so you don't have the benefit of the trades to keep you cool.

If you start at the visitor center, you'll be using the main road, turning left at the T-intersection. The sign that marks the beginning of the footpath is on the right. The path follows a large rooi bordered by numerous rubber vines and manchineel trees. Gradually the rooi narrows and you'll see clear evidence of the strong torrents that have carved out the steep banks and moved large rocks down the trail toward the sea.

In the rooi, birdwatching may be quite good: sparrows, bananaquits and warblers. You're more likely to hear than see the shy St. Christoffel pigeon which lives in the tree-tops. Its easily identifiable call is "roo-coo-coo."

Moving along the footpath and to the left out of the rooi, the vegetation is still small-leafed and thorny. Gradually it will change to larger leaved, thornless species. The cactus also begin to thin out and are not as large as the ones found nearer sea level.

Instead of turning at this first left, you could continue up the rooi for another eighty meters and turn left at the next small rooi. This is more difficult climbing and will actually entail crawling over/under a few fallen trees.

On either route, the trail starts to climb now. Keep a lookout for the green juvenile iguanas and the camouflaged adults. As on Aruba, these are widely hunted for their meat. You may also spot whiptail lizards (Cnemidophorus murinus murinus); when the males run at full speed, they raise their tails and the front part of their bodies, looking like dinosaurs on the move. You're likely to see light brown lizards with a gray lateral stripe (Anolis lineatus) on tree trunks or twigs.

Curaçao has two snake species you may encounter, the meadow snake and the minute silver snake, neither of which are poisonous. Only one frog inhabits the island, the dori (Pleurodema brachyops), with distinctive red patches on its hindquarters. It was accidentally introduced into Curaçao in sand imported from Aruba for building a wharf in Willemstad in 1910.

Curaçao is the only Caribbean island where deer were present before Columbus. This white-tailed deer (Odocoileus virginianus curassavicus) isn't much larger than a goat. The antlers and its way of moving identify the quickly retreating creature as the white tail, the shyest animal on all Curaçao.

Gradually the transition to a more humid micro-climate becomes evident, with beard moss and other lichens and a definite predominance of large-leafed, thornless trees. A couple of ferns are evident in the rocks off to the left.

Like the rest of the ABCs, the vegetation on Curaçao is short and stubby.

Now it may seem as if you're on a totally different island; the flat terrain of Curaçao grows steeper and steeper until you reach an open place on the slope which may be slippery if it has rained. You'll encounter a grove of twenty "Clusia rosea," a sub-tropical tree that on Curaçao grows only on Christoffel.

It's necessary to scramble the rest of the way to the top, where the blessed trades will soon cool you off. The views from here, the top of Curaçao, are exceptionally panoramic. On clear days, you can spot Aruba to the west, Bonaire and the distant mountain ranges of Venezuela to the east. Sit, relax and enjoy the view.

Colophon

The text of this book was set in a digital version of Palatino, a typeface created by noted type designer Hermann Zapf in 1950 for the Stempel Foundry. The design is Zapf's modern interpretation of 16th-century calligraphy. The chapter headings and subheads in the book were set in Tekton, a digital typeface created for Adobe by David Siegel. Tekton is based on the hand lettering of Frank Ching, a Seattle-based architect and author of several books on design and drawing. The book was designed and composed by Frank Logue of Carolina Graphics Group in Rome, Georgia.

The maps were created by Lee Elliot, and all of the photographs in the book are by the author. *Caribbean Afoot's* cover illustration is by Leslie Cummins.

Printed and bound by Vaughan Printing in Nashville, Tennessee.